IN SEARCH OF STONES

M. Scott Peck, M.D.

IN SEARCH
OF STONES

A Pilgrimage of Faith, Reason, and Discovery

COMPASS PRESS

BOSTON ✳ OXFORD ✳ MELBOURNE

Published in Large Print by arrangement with Hyperion in the United States and Canada.

Compass Press Large Print Book Series; an imprint of Wheeler Publishing, Inc., USA, ISIS Publishing Ltd, Great Britain and Bolinda Press, Australia

Set in 16 pt. Plantin.

Library of Congress Cataloging-in-Publication Data

Peck, M. Scott (Morgan Scott), 1936–
    In search of stones : a pilgrimage of faith, reason, and discovery
/ M. Scott Peck.
        p.   cm.—(Compass Press large print book series)
    Originally published; New York ; Hyperion, c1995.
    Includes bibliographical references.
    ISBN 1-56895-270-8
    1. Peck, M. Scott (Morgan Scott), 1936– . 2. Religious biography—
United States.   3. Megalithic monuments—Great Britain.
4. Great Britain—Description and travel.   5. Large type books.
I. Title.   II. Series
[BL73.P43A3   1995b]
150'.92—dc20
[B]   95-36055
                                                                      CIP

L.T.E.
150.92
P367

First published in Great Britain 1995
by Simon & Schuster, Ltd.

Published in Large Print in Great Britain 1996 by ISIS Publishing Ltd,
7 Centremead, Osney Mead, Oxford OX2 OES, England
by arrangement with Simon & Schuster, Ltd.

Published in large print in Australia by Australian Large Print Audio and
Video Pty Ltd., 17 Mohr Street, Tullamarine, Victoria, 3043, Australia

The moral right of the author has been asserted

National Library of Australia Cataloging in Publication Data
Peck, M. Scott (Morgan Scott), 1936–
In search of stones
ISBN 1 86340 613 1 (ALPAV Pty Ltd)
I. Title
248.4

British Library Cataloguing in Publication Data
Peck, M. Scott
In Search of Stones—New ed.—(Compass Press Series)
I. Title   II. Series
248.092
ISBN 0-7531-5401-3 (ISIS Publishing Ltd.)

To our children and our ancestors

Make for Me an altar of earth and sacrifice on it your burnt offerings and your sacrifices of well-being, your sheep and your oxen; in every place where I cause My name to be mentioned I will come to you and bless you. And if you make for Me an altar of stones, do not build it of hewn stones; for by wielding your tool upon them you have profaned them.

—Exodus 20:24–25

CONTENTS

ACKNOWLEDGMENTS

As with my other books, two groupings of people have made this one possible. Their brief mention here is regretfully pallid in relation to the size of their contribution.

One is my personal "support system." I could name dozens, but four individuals need to be singled out for particular thanks: Valerie Duffy, who keeps the home fires burning; Susan Poitras, our office manager and computer whiz, who turns yellow pages handwritten on bumpy airplane rides into polished manuscripts; Gail Puterbaugh, my program director, who gets me to wherever I have to go and does so much more; and Lily Peck, their general manager and mine.

The other grouping is that of literary professionals. Jonathan Dolger, my agent, discerned this work's uniqueness from its inception and has championed it throughout. Christopher Peck, its illustrator, has helped it come alive. Brian DeFiore is not only its associate publisher but has been its acquisition editor, broad-brush editor, and line editor as well. Thank you.

One major segment of this professional grouping seldom receives the thanks it deserves. I have long been grateful for booksellers, and am glad for this opportunity to acknowledge you.

And to apologize. as an "evangelist of integration," I have inadvertently placed you in a dilemma: It has been most unclear where you should feature my works. Do they belong in the psychology section or the religion section? The self-help section or the New Age section? On Occasion, the fiction, murder mystery, or children's sections?

This work, the most integrated of all, can only serve to augment the confusion. As well as the others, you now have four new additional possibilities: travel, history, archaeology, and autobiography. Good Luck!

—*M. Scott Peck*
NEW PRESTON, CONNECTICUT

CHAPTER 1

REASON
Sunday May 31

It is 9:15 on Sunday morning, the thirty-first of May in the year of our Lord, 1992. Lily and I are sitting in the middle of Paddington Station in the city of London, waiting to board the ten o'clock train for Cardiff, Wales. In comparison to the rest of London, which had been swept quite clean, the station is remarkably littered. Why? Propelled by curiosity, we look more closely. It is, we observe, because of a total lack of waste receptacles provided on the premises. But why such a lack? To this slightly deeper question we have no answer. We also have no doubt that if we took the time and trouble to do the research required, we could discover one. There is a reason for everything.

Or so we think.

This is going to be an account of many things: history, archaeology, philosophy, and religion, among others. Most specifically it is an account of a wonderful three-week journey upon which Lily, my wife, and I are embarking. More than anything, however, it is perhaps an account of me. Not an accounting, thank God, just an account. It

1

is probably the closest thing to an autobiography that I will ever write.

But it is not autobiography. I am too clever for that, and possibly too humble. Millions of autobiographies have been written. A few thousand of them have been published. A few hundred have been commercially successful in their time. Only a handful have survived for long outside of historical archives. Autobiography might be looked upon as the most difficult of arts—virtually impossible—and this is not an attempt to beat the odds.

It is not just that the autobiographer is too close to his subject, I suspect, but also that he is prone to suffer from the delusion that he understands the subject: himself. One would think a psychiatrist, above all, could understand himself. Not so. The longer I stayed in practice the more I gradually became aware that I was largely operating in the dark not only in relation to my patients but also in relation to myself.

One weekend afternoon of the autumn that I was ten, while my parents were away playing golf, a friend and I gathered together a collection of wrenches. At my instigation we carried them out to a hayrake that a farmer had left in a field in back of our house. Methodically we proceeded to take that large machine apart into over a hundred component pieces and then scatter those pieces across a dozen acres. Why this wanton destructiveness? I could say that perhaps I wanted to impress my friend. I could imagine that I was somehow angry at my parents and the authority of the adult world. But those would only be guesses. All I can remember is that it somehow seemed like great fun at the time. Of course I could simply say, "Boys will be boys," which explains absolutely nothing. The fact is I do not understand my ten-year-old vandalism. Nor do I understand why today, almost fifty years later, in response to some petty frustration or in response to nothing at all that I can account for, I will suddenly experience a wave of rage so intense I would dearly desire to destroy *something*—if only I knew what it was.

Some might think such matters unimportant (although not the poor farmer who owned the hayrake). Let's take something of seemingly greater consequence in my life. The dominating event of my existence for over a decade has been the fact that I happened to write a uniquely successful book about spiritual growth that has led hundreds of thousands to envision me as some kind of a guru. I can give a pretty good account of the complex of reasons for the popularity of that book. What I cannot account for is why I wrote it in the first place. Why Scott Peck and not someone else? Was its genesis programmed in my genes or in the stars? I do not know the answers. While I shall delve into the subject more deeply, it will basically remain a mystery.

So, since we human beings are not particularly reasonable creatures, this will not be an autobiography in the ordinary sense. Indeed, although not a novel, it will be much more a mystery story. One focus will be the mystery of me. But that focus will be interwoven with the mystery of Lily and our marriage, the mystery of this particular

3

journey, the mystery of God, and, perhaps above all, the mystery of our not so reasonable human race.

Roughly three hundred years ago, Western civilization emerged into what is frequently called the Age of Reason. As far as I know, we are still in it. What this means is that the educated people of this civilization and age have come to believe that there is, if you just dig deeply enough, a rational explanation for all that happens. Thus the Universe can be explained by the Big Bang and the messiness of Paddington Station by its absence of trash containers.

Into the Age of Reason we (of Western civilization) emerged out of the Age of Faith. Faith in what? In many things unproved and perhaps forever unprovable, some more essential than others. Most central was faith in a single God who not only created the Universe but ultimately did so for the specific sustenance of human beings whom He loved so much that in the form of His only begotten son, Jesus Christ, He came down to live and die as one of us, thereby laying upon us an obligation to live our lives in constant worship of Him and adoration of Jesus. A quaint notion, but one that eight hundred years ago governed every aspect of the life of every citizen of England within two hundred miles of Paddington Station (which then, like the railroads, was not yet extant).

Today, it is hard for us to imagine that twelfth-century life. It was so orderly, so ritualized. Now, our waking hours are divided into meaningless,

4

mathematical minutes. Then, they were separated according to prescribed periods of worship: nones, matins, diurnum, vespers, compline. Today, our year has four sun-determined seasons; theirs had a hundred different feast days to honor saints who had exemplified the teachings of Jesus. They named their streets and villages after those saints. We name ours Lemontree Lane, Rollercoaster Road, and Jacksonville. And while we watch television in the evening, they, for fun, flocked together to build cathedrals to the glory of God.

I am romanticizing. They also died like flies. And they didn't have railroads.

One age does not turn into another overnight. Between the Age of Faith and the Age of Reason there lay at least three hundred years of confusion. An old Age does not die easily. Today, firmly ensconced in the Age of Reason, we look back upon its pioneers—men like Galileo—with admiration and respect. For the Inquisition that persecuted him, we have only disrespect and find it hard to imagine how the authorities of the church could have been so narrow-minded, stupid, and downright cruel. Yet were we able to look through the eyes of those authorities at the dawning of the Age of Reason, we would not only have seen a crumbling of faith, we would also have been filled with terror at the impending disintegration of civilization and loss of all that gave meaning and coherency to life. Perhaps the greatest sins of religion are not those of faith per se but of faith threatened.

Just as we still tend to think in terms of feet

and miles and acres, of ounces and pounds and tons, so a few vestiges of the Age of Faith persist at the end of the twentieth century—including the concept of the twentieth century itself. So it is A.D. 1992 that Lily and I are sitting in Paddington Station—A.D. meaning anno Domini, which is Latin for Year of the Lord, the Lord being Jesus Christ, who we assume to have been born on December 25, one thousand, nine hundred, ninety-two years previously. Actually, in this Age of Reason, we recognize this to be an assumption of convenience, a likely inaccurate holdover from earlier times. For all we know Jesus was born in 3 or 4 B.C. or A.D. 3 or 4, and we are virtually certain that he was not born on December 25. There is considerable evidence that that date was cooked up some five hundred years later by monks attempting to Christianize east Europeans. December 25 roughly coincided with their pagan celebration of the winter solstice, and the monks cleverly decided a substitute holiday would be preferable to none at all. Perhaps in the twenty-first century we will evolve to some sort of universal "metric system" of dating, acceptable to Jews, Christians, and Muslims alike, with regularly, more rationally spaced bank holidays but no more true holy days.

Whatever . . . the fact of the matter is that my primary identity is that of a scientist, and I am very much a child of the Age of Reason. What, then, are the reasons that Lily and I, thirty-two years married and late into middle age, are sitting at 9:15 A.M., May 31, 1992, in the middle of Paddington Station?

One answer is that I am spastic about missing the boat (or in this case, train). Our travel agent had suggested we would have plenty of time if we left our hotel by 9:30. That seemed to me to be calling the connection perilously close, so we left at 8:45, thereby giving us an hour to inspect the litter.

This is typical of me. Because I am a man of so little faith, I spend most of my life running scared. Will I get to the airport on time? Will there be a flat tire on the way? Will I get on the wrong plane? I have flown thousands of times now and have never once gotten on the wrong plane, yet I am convinced there is a high likelihood I will do so at the very next airport from which I depart. And if and when I finally reach my destination, will there be a bathroom there?

Obviously, being a man of science and reason does not itself relieve one of anxiety in this life. Indeed, it enables me to think up more and more reasons for fear. But this is not to say that religious faith is the cure for anxiety either. It is not that simple. Although Lily is titularly less religious than I and also very much a child of the Age of reason, she does not suffer my style of spasticity. She adjusts remarkably well to mine, but left to her own devices she would properly have departed the hotel a half an hour later. What other cause for my anxiety might there be then?

Ah, as a psychiatrist, here I could have a field day. For the moment, however, I shall restrict myself to a single vignette. Just as there are some like me who compulsively get themselves to airports and train stations early lest they have to bear the anxiety of being late, so there are others who actually take delight in playing it close. My father was one of them. Throughout the gas-rationing years of World War II, when I was age five to nine, we would travel by train on Fridays from New York City to our country home a hundred miles north. The train was the 4:02. My mother, older brother, and I would arrive in Grand Central Station around 3:30. At 3:45 the gates would open, and we would rush in with the crowd to get ourselves the best seats, including one that we saved for my father. By five minutes to four my mother would be saying, "I wonder where your father is?" By four she was frantic. At 4:02 on the dot there would be a great hiss of steam and the conductor would call out, "Allllll aboard!" Gates clanged shut. The train lurched and began to move forward. At that precise moment, panic stricken, through the window we'd see my father, briefcase in hand, dash along the platform and leap aboard just in the nick of time. It was invariable.

My father did like to play certain things close. In retrospect I have a suspicion that on many of those Friday afternoons he hid for some minutes behind one of the platform pillars waiting for that dramatic final second, because he also liked to give us a good scare. He succeeded.

There are other reasons I can give—and some I will as the occasion arises—for my fearfulness and obsessive-compulsive tendencies. It is a great principle in psychiatry that "all symptoms are overdetermined." This means that they have more than one cause. Among her other problems, an early patient of mine, Clarissa, had a bizarre and obviously psychosomatic dermatitis of just one hand. After four months of psychotherapy we discovered a juicy Freudian explanation for this unusual symptom. I can remember rushing home that evening to tell Lily, "I've cured Clarissa, I've cured Clarissa!" But I hadn't at all. Her dermatitis persisted. Four months later we uncovered a second reason for it. It remained unchanged. A few more months went by and a third reason emerged. Then a fourth. When a fifth reason was clarified after a year and a half of therapy, Clarissa's hand then—and only then— became as good as new.

I want to scream this from the rooftops: "All symptoms are overdetermined." Except that I want to expand it way beyond psychiatry. I want to expand it to almost everything. I want to translate it, "Anything of any significance is overdetermined. Everything worth thinking about has more than one cause." Repeat after me: "For any single thing of importance, there are multiple reasons." Again, "For any single thing of importance, there are multiple reasons."

My shrillness in this matter is provoked by a problem with the Age of Reason. Because we assume there is a reason for everything, we go looking for *it* when we should be looking for *them*. Recently, speaking of the riots in Los Angeles following the jury's decision that the police who beat Rodney King were not guilty of a crime, a highly educated, intelligent, and successful, white stockbroker told me with assurance that the reason for the riots was "the decline in family values." He deduced this from his observation that virtually all the rioters were young black males. "If they'd been married and working to support their families, they'd been married and working to support their families, they wouldn't have had time to riot," he explained.

I practically exploded. I told him how for two hundred years under slavery we didn't *allow* most blacks to marry or have legal families. We made their family values illegal. I gave him several cultural historical reasons why, on the average, black women are better educated and more employable than black men. I reminded him that the economic recession in California at the time was worse than that of any other state. I spoke of the decline of *government* values in the United States. I talked about the oppression of prejudice and the psychology of despair. "The 'decline' of family values may have been one of the reasons for the riots," I concluded, "but only one of many, of a whole complex of reasons."

Looking for a single reason for this man's strange stupidity, it would be tempting to simply write him off as a bigot. But I travel widely, and wherever I go I find the mass of well-educated people offering or seeking simpleminded explanations for complicated phenomena ranging from riots, homosexuality, and abortion to poverty, illness, evil, and war. I propose that insofar as it suggests a single reason for everything, the Age of Reason actually promotes intellectual bigotry, and that in this Age such bigotry is the norm. I do not propose that we attempt to turn back the clock and revert to the Age of Faith. I question, however, much of our supposed "rationality." I believe it would often be considerably healthier for us to dare to live without a reason for many things than with reasons that are simplistic. Either the Age of Reason has a long way to go or else we need to evolve into some yet more sensible Age.

Meanwhile, we're still in the Age of Reason and still in Paddington Station. I've explained a little bit about why Lily and I are there so early. But what is the complex of reasons for us being there at all? Why is it May 31? And why are we headed for Wales?

Our nephew, David, was married the day before to a young Englishwoman, Cordelia, in the ancient London church of Bow Bells. It was an event planned many months in advance. Fortunately for us, we had the money not only to attend the wedding but to also afford to use the event as an excuse for a larger vacation. We had flown from the United States to London on May 25 in time for all the extensive prenuptial celebrations. The day after the wedding, the rest of our extended family flew back to America, but Lily and I embarked on a three-week trip to Wales, Scotland, and the Lake District of England. This is the tale of that trip.

But why did we decide to go to these places? Why not France or Ireland or the rest of England? There are reasons, of course,. Neither Lily nor I speak even passable French. Both of us had been very busy for a long time. We wanted this to be a restful vacation and had no desire to face the stress of negotiating a foreign language. So

France was out. Twelve years ago we'd spent ten days each traveling through Ireland and southern England. In addition, I'd been to southern England three times in my premarital youth. But neither of us had ever been to Wales or Scotland. The Lake District would be on the way from one to the other, and it was the only renownedly beautiful part of England we hadn't seen. So Wales, the Lake District, and Scotland it was. The reasons seem straightforward enough, do they not?

Actually, there were more reasons as well. They will gradually emerge as this account proceeds. Some of them we were well aware of at the time. Others we were not. Indeed, perhaps the most important reasons of all were those we weren't aware of in the least. It is possible, in other words, that at the most profound level, in taking this trip we didn't really understand what we were doing.

At five minutes to ten it was announced that the train to Cardiff was ready for boarding—barely enough time to scramble on with our seven bags. As our train began to emerge from the London suburbs into the countryside, Lily looked up from her science fiction novel to comment, "I hope we'll get to see some stones on this trip."

"Me, too," I replied.

It was not an extensive dialogue. After thirty-two years of marriage—of shared experiences and accumulated knowledge of each other's tastes—much can sometimes be said in a few words. A stranger, overhearing our words, might well have wondered at Lily's hope and exclaimed, "Of course you'll see stones. Aren't there stones everywhere?"

Lily would then have had to reply, "I mean prehistoric stones."

The stranger might have looked just as perplexed. "Aren't all stones prehistoric?"

Again Lily would have had to explain, "Yes, all stones are prehistoric, but I'm speaking about large ones that prehistoric people placed in certain arrangements like circles."

But she didn't have to explain all that to me. During our 1980 trip together we had visited Stonehenge in the pouring rain. Lily had been enchanted. I was not, but only because I had seen it back in 1950 with my parents, when I was just fourteen, before the site had been roped off or bordered by concession stands—and on a dry day.

I also knew that by "this trip" Lily didn't mean our train ride. On trains, as on planes and buses, Lily nods off like a heroin addict when she isn't alert enough for her science fiction or crossword puzzles. So she meant she hoped we'd see some stones at some point during our whole three-week journey.

As did I. But I also hoped I might see some on our little train ride as well. Unlike Lily, I don't much like to read in moving vehicles. I do write in them, but at this point I was on a determined vacation. As far as sleeping is concerned, I can't even doze unless I'm in a bed. I had also had an experience Lily hadn't. At the age of twenty-one, during another one of my previous youthful trips to England, I was on a train to visit some friends and by pure chance got to see a long row of standing stones in a field outside the fast-moving window. I wished I could have somehow stopped the train and gotten out to hug them. The sight had haunted me ever since. It had stayed so vividly in my memory I'd even wondered whether it might not have been a dream.

So for most of the three-hour ride from London to the Severn Tunnel I stared out the window looking for another such wonder. I saw not a stone or anything of much note except several of the many nuclear power stations that dot the English countryside.

The Severn Tunnel runs under the Severn River separating southwestern England from southeastern Wales. For much of its length the river is more of a bay, and the tunnel is very long. No sooner were we out of it than our engine broke down. The train did not move for the next two hours. It struck us as ironic that right outside our stalled train window was a huge sign, the bottom of which in bold letters said, WELCOME TO WALES. The irony seemed greater and greater the longer we sat there.

Above this English welcome on the sign there was painted a large and ornate, thorny, bright red dragon or griffin. This, we correctly assumed, was the national symbol of Wales. And above the dragon, in equally large letters as the English, was written, CROESO I GYMRU. This, we assumed, also correctly, was a Welsh translation of "Welcome to Wales." We further assumed that this use of Welsh was a quaint way of offering tourists a touch of local color.

14

That assumption couldn't have been further off the mark. The reality, we slowly came to learn, was that the English "Welcome to Wales" was the gracious condescension to the tourists. And that the "Croeso i Gymru" at the top of the sign was a profound statement saying, "We are Welsh, not English. Welcome to our country, but don't for one moment think we're English."

Why? Why the necessity of that statement? What's the reason for it? In this Age of Reason we customarily turn for such answers to history.

First, a definition of history. There is geological history. With a certain amount of accuracy—plus or minus a thousand years here or a hundred thousand there—we can trace the changes of the British land mass back through the ice ages, through when it was connected to France and there was no English Channel, not only to a time when it was uninhabited by human beings but even to times before human beings ever existed. There is also fossil history by which we can guess at the evolution of flora and fauna in the British Isles. My primary concern, however, is with human history.

I mentioned Lily's and my hope that on this trip we might see some stones erected by prehistoric people. What do we mean by "prehistoric people"? We mean people about whom we know so little that we cannot give any coherent account of their history. We do not know the names of their leaders; we don't know the names of their tribes; we don't have any name for them at all. We don't know anything about their language, their religion, their stories, or their myths, and we don't know how they got there in the first place. But of the fact that they were there, we have no doubt. They very much left their mark. Or marks. Indeed, it is their marks that, more than anything, will turn this account into something of a mystery story. To put that mystery in perspective, however, we need take at least a passing glance at the later history that we do know—and to understand why the Welsh were so definitive about informing us that they are not English.

The human history of Britain then, as opposed to its prehistory, begins with the Celts.

Who were the Celts?

They were a somewhat racially diverse (both light- and dark-haired) people who originated roughly 1,000 B. C. in the area of Switzerland speaking a related group of Indo-European dialects called Celtic. In other words, they had a language we can identify and a name derived from that language. How and why they originated there we do not know. That's prehistory.

Shortly the Celts exploded in all directions throughout Europe. One of their many tribes, the Parisi, for instance, founded the city of Paris. By 500 B. C. other tribes had conquered the prehistoric peoples of what is now northwestern France, Ireland, and Great Britain.

Why this explosive growth and success in conquest? The phenomenon was undoubtedly *overdetermined*. Although their language was not yet written, the Celts had a rich oral tradition and culture.

They loved to tell stories (Beowulf is such a tale well known to us today). Their art and jewelry, using multiple and often elegant geometric designs, was far more complex and developed than that of prehistoric peoples. They were fierce warriors renowned for their bravery. Perhaps most important of all, they had discovered the secret of making iron. For approximately a thousand years the prehistoric people of Great Britain knew how to create bronze, but iron made for vastly superior tools (plows and wheels, for instance) and weapons. The years 1500 to 500 B.C. are sometimes referred to as the Bronze Age. With the coming of the Celts, Britain entered the Iron Age.

This is not intended to be a history book, much less a text. I am a consumer of historical scholarship, not a creator of it. In my consumption I've been guided by a mentor, Idries Shah, a modern-day Muslim mystic who taught (and I paraphrase) "It is not enough simply to study. First one must determine what to study and what not to study; when to study and when not to study; and who to study under and who not to study with."

So I am not enamored of history for the pure sake of it. Only occasionally, when it offers reasons that give some semblance of meaning, will I dip into it. For instance, I have defined prehistory because that *will* be a major theme. I made reference to the probability that there was once no English Channel, since it helps explain how prehistoric people likely got to the British Isles in the first place—they walked. I spoke of

17

the Celts, who sailed over, because we will be traveling through Celtic lands. And I mentioned bronze and iron, because they will eventually come to have a certain relevance in this account.

History itself may be reasonable or unreasonable. In my sophomore year of college I took a course in modern European history under a professor with the intriguing name of Pardon Tillinghast. I liked the man. I hated his course. Although obviously a potentially eloquent, well-spoken person, his lectures were nothing more than rapid-fire recitations of disconnected facts and dates. Obediently, I studied hard, which meant mere memorization and an A grade on the midterm. But by the time the final exam rolled around I'd had it. Consequently, instead of answering the questions on the exam, I used the hour to fill up three "blue books" with an elaborate critique of the way he taught his course. I praised his intelligence and articulateness, but only to point out that he could have done it better, that in my opinion he owed us students much more. I told him I thought it his job to make history come alive, to make it meaningful by connecting the facts into patterns that explained the why of things, that gave reasons for matters of importance, reasons that made such matters relevant and significant. At this task, I concluded, he had utterly failed.

Pardon Tillinghast quite properly gave me an F on that exam. With my midterm grade I ended up with a C minus for the course. As a result, however, he also asked me to his home for dinner with his family. He was, I believe, a better father than a professor, and I learned more of significance on that evening than I had from his whole course.

The story is perhaps prophetic. It means more than that I was simply in the grips of an adolescent rebellion at the time. For to this day, almost forty years later, I remain a rebel of sorts, a rebel with a cause, and that cause is meaning.

In the service of that cause some of the history of the relationship between the Celts and the Romans must be noted.

Since the prehistoric peoples had been thoroughly assimilated by the Celts over the course of six hundred years, when the Roman legions invaded Britain in A.D. 43 they were seeking to conquer a Celtic people they called Britons. In the relatively flat and fertile land of the south and east they succeeded. In the more mountainous land to the west and north, despite repeated attempts over several centuries, they failed. Historically, the reason for the difference has always been assumed to be purely geographical. But as a champion of overdetermination—of multiple reasons—I wonder if there might have been a little more to it than that. My just married nephew once referred to the English as "the Vichy Celts," alluding to how the Vichy French, under Marshal Petain, collaborated with the Germans during World War II. Perhaps the flatland Celts were easy collaborators because amid their fertile surroundings over the years they'd somehow gone "soft." Who knows?

Whatever, in A.D. 410, their empire collapsing all about, the Romans pulled out, leaving

Romanized people in an area that gradually (as a result of subsequent forays by the Angles from northeastern Europe) came to be called Angleland and later England. These Romanized people had become the English. The un-Romanized people of Wales and Scotland, however, remained thoroughbred Celts who, to this day, retain a national and cultural identity that is in a number of ways quite distinct from that of the English. Many of them also retain the Celtic language and are bilingual.

Linguistically, at the time of the Roman Conquest the Celts of the area were divided into two branches speaking different dialects: Gaelic (or Goidelic) and Brythonic. The Celtic spoken by the Scots and the Irish (whom the Romans never attempted to conquer) is Gaelic. That spoken by the Welsh and Bretons of Brittany is Brythonic. The Brythonic word for Wales is Gymry and the Welsh are the Cymry.

So we have a somewhat rational explanation— a reason—for the "Croeso i Gymru" over the red dragon outside the window of our stalled train. This is why, as a child of the Age of Reason, I love *good* history: It offers reasons. We do not know the "whys" of prehistory, such as why the Celts got started in the first place. But knowing the divergent histories of the Celtic tribes in the British Isles explains much about why, even though they now have the same monarch, the Welsh and Scots in many respects dislike the English, and why the English in return tend to dislike the Welsh and Scots. And something about why the Irish of southern Ireland unequivocally hated the English and got rid of the English "yoke" entirely.

Such understanding can make us more civil. Imagine how Welsh or Scottish people might feel when they are in America and are referred to as English! It is a mistake I hope I will not make again.

It would be wrong, however, to think that history can answer all questions or totally explain such things as the enmity between the Celtic peoples of Ireland, Scotland, and Wales and those less Celtic Britons, the English. Such would be the sin of historical determinism to which certain Marxists and others have fallen prey. Might we not have a *choice* as to how we respond to history? And might there by some things in this modern day and age for which we *can't* discover a reason?

In any case, the officials eventually discovered that whatever had caused the engine of our train to stall, it was, for the foreseeable future, irreparable. A new engine was called for and arrived, but only to take us as far as the nearest town. There we had ten minutes to change trains. Baggage carts were available but of no utility given the fact that the new train was reachable only by us running with our seven bags up one lengthy flight of stairs and down another. For us, in our late middle age—Lily still healing from a tendon repair of her ankle and I with chronic degenerative disease of my spine—this was no mean feat.

But we made it, and we got to Cardiff.

In planning the trip it had seemed to make sense to spend this first night in Cardiff. Was it not the largest city of Wales? The capital city? It did not concern us at first that we had never talked to anyone who had ever been to Cardiff. So what if the city looked unprepossessing upon our entrance by rail? Wasn't that par for the course of railway routes? And so what if we encountered the same problem of stairs to get from the train to the taxi stand? And so what if there was no taxi there? One would surely come along by-and-by. Besides, we knew that we'd soon be ensconced in the Angel Hotel, which our Fodor guidebook informed us was unquestionably Cardiff's best, with recently renovated, high-ceilinged rooms of bright pastel colors.

The renovation of the Angel Hotel, when we finally reached it, however, was incomplete. Its entire entrance and facade were under construction. This meant we had to carry our bags a block through and around all manner of scaffolding. There was no doorman. No bellman. It was hard for us to discern whether the young woman receptionist was speaking Brythonic or gum-chewing Cockney. The concierge desk at the other end of the grand foyer had clearly been vacant since the turn of the century. The elevator did not work. Carrying our bags up the palatial staircase, we finally arrived at our seventeen-foot-ceilinged nest. Its other dimensions were ten-by-ten. The walls were pastel brown. If the room had been renovated, the results vaguely reminded us of Calcutta. It was hot and stuffy. We threw open our second-story window that looked out, through the scaffolding, upon Cardiff's main and noisiest circle or circus. Our quarters were immediately filled with gasoline fumes. The cold I'd arrived with in London had turned into asthmatic bronchitis during our train ride and stair climbing. I unpacked antibiotics before anything else.

The hotel's sole redeeming feature was its central location—if the center of Cardiff could be considered redemptive in any fashion. It did mean that Cardiff Castle was just the other side of the circle surrounded by a large park. So, after unpacking and a failed attempt at a nap, we went for a walk. The park was as littered as Paddington Station. Its shrubbery was desperately in need of pruning. Those few paths that were paved were cracked and growing crops of weeds. We could discern that it had once been a fine park, just as the Angel had once been a fine hotel. It is sad to see a poor city. It is sadder still to see one that had originally been wealthy. It was clear to us not only that Cardiff was deep in an economic "recession," but that it had been in it for decades.

Around the square castle was a four-sided moat. Three sides were dry. The other, at its bottom, contained a modicum of parasitic sludge. From the outside, the castle itself was remarkable only because of its phoniness. In fact, Fodor told how most of it had been built by donations in late Victorian times so as to look like a medieval castle. The external result was colorfully ersatz. As to its inside, we cannot attest since there was an entrance fee.

But that was just the beginning of the problem.

We wouldn't have entered Cardiff Castle if it had been for free. The real problem, we realized, was that we wouldn't pay an entrance fee to get into hardly any castle, no matter how ancient, authentic, or historical it might be. Or palace. Or museum. It began to dawn upon us that we had stumbled into a potential predicament of alarming proportions.

My mind flashed back to my very first trip to Great Britain the summer I turned fourteen. My father was a cathedral buff, and as soon as we had docked at Liverpool he led my mother, four-years-older brother, and me on a circuitous route that included every possible cathedral we could reach in the allotted time. It was after dark at the end of the third day of this trek when we arrived at Salisbury. Both bored and exhausted, my brother and I were shortly asleep for what we assumed would be a lengthy rest.

Our father, however, was up at dawn, purchasing from the hotel a book entitled *The Cathedrals of England*. At seven o'clock he bounded into our room exclaiming, "Up you get. This one is the greatest of them all!" By eight we were on the lawn in front of the Salisbury Cathedral. While a few other tourists trickled in and large numbers of Englishmen passed by on their way to work, Dad opened his newfound guidebook and in his booming judicial voice began reading to us about the glories of the cathedral's nave and flying buttresses. I was squirming in early adolescent embarrassment. After what seemed an eternity the chapter was completed. Closing the book with a snap, Dad pointed to the great church and queried, "Now, isn't that the most magnificent building you've ever set your eyes upon?"

With great precision my brother responded, "I think it's the ugliest heap of stone I've ever seen."

"Me, too," I echoed.

Stunned, Dad dropped the guidebook on the grass, turned, and walked silently away, his shoulders slumped in dejection. "You boys have hurt your father very deeply," my mother said.

"We don't care," my brother and I simultaneously answered.

My recollection of this event was more one of family dynamics than cathedrals. Nonetheless, it set a tone. In the ensuing four decades, Lily and I were to enjoy discovering a few cathedrals and other famous monuments on our own. But by now we were well-traveled people who had quite had our fill of the world's roped-off showplaces. We'd also developed a distinct aversion to guides and significant concentrations of other tourists. We yearned for less traveled roads. But roads to where? Here we had come for three weeks to Wales and Scotland, famed for their well-visited castles and museums. We had deliberately set ourselves a leisurely schedule. What on earth were we going to do then except see some scenery? Why had we come? At this point we frankly didn't know.

We returned to the Angel where, because there seemed no better place in town, we ate a progressively inedible dinner. We attempted to console ourselves that the despair we were experiencing was the result of very temporary culture shock, which we would soon get over. After all, what else could be expected in entering a land where people spoke Brythonic? *Croeso i Gymru?* But as we finally drifted off to sleep, amid the noise and the fumes, we seriously wondered whether this trip had been even a slightly rational decision on our parts.

CHAPTER II

ROMANCE
MONDAY JUNE 1

Our day's assigned task was to pick up a rental car and get ourselves from Cardiff in the southeastern corner of Wales to St. David's on the tip of the far southwestern coast.

Assigned task? There are dozens of ways to plan and execute a trip. When we first thought about this one, our fantasy was that it would be great fun to just drift—going wherever we felt like going and simply finding a bed and breakfast place when we were ready to quit at the end of each day. The notion expressed our free-spirited sides. But it was just a fantasy. Our lives are complexly interwoven with those of hundreds of others. People would need to know how and where to get a hold of us. We would have to have a precise itinerary filled with fax numbers. There are times in life when it is simply not responsible to be free-spirited. So we had repaired to Joan, our trusted travel agent, for our assigned reservations.

We are also getting too old to be adventurous in certain respects. In my youth, it was fun—exciting—not to know where I might be sleeping on any given night. Today, searching for a bed and breakfast with a vacancy and hunting for a restaurant after a long drive seems more like a hassle. My stodgy side—my addiction to comfort and security—has definitively grown over the years.

In any case, we had given Joan certain broad parameters for the trip, leaving her the task of taking care of all the details. One parameter, however, was new for us. On our previous trips abroad, by virtue of limitations of time and money, we had always tried to cram in everything we possibly could. Now, older and wealthier, we had set a relaxed schedule for ourselves. This was to be a distinctly leisurely trip. Or so we thought.

Wales is a small country—perhaps the size of Pennsylvania. Joan and her British subagent had agreed with our estimation that three full days, even at a leisurely pace, was plenty to spend within its confines. The subagent had given us a computerized printout of travel directions with assorted castles, palaces, and museums to see along the way. His plan called for us to drive to St. David's by the southern coast. Our map, however, made it look like a slow way to get out of Cardiff. The quickest way seemed to first go due north to the mountains. Since our primary motivation on this morning was to escape Cardiff as rapidly as possible, we set aside the subagent's proposals. It was the last time we ever looked at them.

So we raced to get our car and headed north in the pouring rain. Within half an hour we were well out of the city and into the Brecon Beacon mountains. Lovely and clean they were amid the rain and clouds, their steep slopes often lush with pine. Even the very air had changed. "Praise God!" we exulted, realizing that our despair of the evening before was not culture shock—that not all of Wales is grimy and down at its heels— but merely Cardiff shock.

Driving farther north through a mountain valley we had a startling moment. Suddenly behind us we heard an explosive roar. Our fear hardly had time to register before we saw the cause: two jet fighter planes streaking ahead of us, wingtip to wingtip, no more than two hundred feet above our car and the valley floor. The occurrence would not be worth mention were it a singular incident. But it was not. We were to have the experience repeated in the days to come with sufficient frequency to eventually merit some analysis.

Deep in the center of the Brecon Beacons we turned west. Gradually, the mountains leveled off into seemingly endless rolling farmland, rich with sheep, hedgerows, wildflowers, and every hue of green in the continuing rain. We stopped for lunch at a prototypical pub in the town of Carmarthen, the supposed birth-place of Merlin. Merlin, more than hunger, was the drawing card, so after lunch we immediately walked to the information center to whet our deeper appetite.

The people of Great Britain are remarkably hospitable to tourists. Two dramatic examples are the well-marked public toilets and information centers in virtually all modest-sized British towns. Unfortunately, the lady at this information center had no literature about Merlin. She informed us, however, that there was a little road two miles back that would lead us to a field where there was a stone pointing to a cave on a hillside where he purportedly had lived.

Off we went, and soon were enmeshed in a maze of the narrowest paved roads we had ever driven. Giant hedgerows simultaneously caressed both sides of our newly rented compact. For the next two hours, in the still pouring rain, we drove at considerable risk through these little wooded tunnels, looking right and left for a supposed stone pointing to a supposed cave of a man who probably never existed except in people's imaginations. The search was a complete failure. We saw neither stone nor cave, and gave up looking only when it was well past time to head on for St. David's.

Who was Merlin? And why would a presumably rational late-middle-aged couple spend two hours in the rain dashing over hill and dale on dangerous roads to seek a glimpse of his mythical cave?

When the Romans departed Britain in 410 A.D., so did law and order. Angles, Saxons, and Jutes began to invade from northeastern Europe. English, Scottish, and Welsh tribal chieftains not only fought back but also fought each other and among themselves. Into this chaos there supposedly came a man, Arthur, who for a brief period purportedly established in England an idyllic, internally peaceful kingdom during the sixth century. That kingdom was called Camelot.

In our present day, fourteen or fifteen centuries later, with jet fighter planes roaring overhead, such peace seems generally illusive in the world. Back then, when we humans were apparently even more tribal than we are now, it would seem downright magical. Possibly "Merlin the Magician" played a most significant role in this magic.

There is no compelling historical evidence that King Arthur ever lived or his roundtable ever happened. Or Merlin. Camelot was probably but a dream. Nonetheless, an extraordinarily complex body of oral legend grew up around it in France and Great Britain. These legends began to be written down by the French and British in the twelfth century and have continued to be expanded upon to this day.

Although historical scholars seriously doubt the reality of King Arthur, literary scholars generally agree upon certain aspects of Arthurian legend. It is believed that the legends are primarily Celtic in origin. It is believed that certain parts of them came from Celtic folklore long predating the sixth century, and it is believed that the figure of Merlin was derived from specifically Welsh sources.

Who is Merlin? We don't know, because we don't know whether there is anything at all factual about Arthurian legend, and because he plays different roles in the various retellings. He is sometimes described as a prophet and sometimes as a magician and sometimes both. In some legends he is ascribed the magical role of engineering Arthur's birth; in others he served as a tutor to the young Arthur; in still others as an adviser to Arthur, the mature king. We further don't know because his personality as well as his birth, history, and demise have been defined differently in different versions. He has been variously described as the devil's son and unredeemably evil, as the devil's son redeemed, and as a Christ-like figure of miraculous conception and supreme goodness. He has been alternately portrayed as extraordinarily wise or stupid, competent or bungling, clean or dirty, sound of mind or insane, pure or impure, consistent or inconsistent. Some say he died a doddering old man in thrall to a malignantly seductive young woman; others that he merely copped out on his responsibilities by retiring. Still others tell that he retired gracefully without copping out at all, and some sources insist he was a man who never retired and will be resurrected again when needed.

Who is Merlin? All we can say with certainty is that he is a legendary wizard (whatever wizard might mean) who, from time to time, was reputed to live in caves. For reasons not yet understood, authors in the twentieth century have been writing more about him than in any previous one. It seems that King Arthur and his knights are becoming a little less interesting while Merlin, previously often a most peripheral figure, is becoming ever more intriguing to the modern psyche.

But the more compelling personal question is why Lily and I, fully adult children of the Age of Reason, should choose to make a hazardous two-hour detour in the rain on the off chance of catching sight of a mythical cave of a legendary wizard of doubtful character? On the surface it was not reasonable behavior.

The vast body of Arthurian legend is sometimes referred to as the Arthurian Romance. Herein lies, I believe, the essential clue to the mystery of Lily's and my seeming irrationality on this wet afternoon. The word *romance*, in this respect, has two meanings. One originated with the name of the Romans. From my perspective, the Romans were a notoriously unromantic people. But they knew how to write. And while the Celts—a most romantic people—despised the Romans, they did learn from them how to write down their tall tales, their oral traditions, on the printed page. Perhaps the greatest gift of Roman civilization was the Latin alphabet and the resulting so-called romance languages.

More to the point, however, is that the Celtic tales that came to be written down in these languages were filled with heroism, chivalry, ardor in battle and love, idealism, and a vision of the idyllic. The Arthurian legends are romance not simply because they were originally written in Latin and French, but because they are about romance. And Lily and I prowled about the byways of the Welsh countryside not simply because we were looking for the cave of the legendary wizard, but because we were yearning for our lives to be touched, yet once again, by romance.

I feel awkward. This is embarrassing. As a man of reason I am very comfortable talking about the mind and the world of ideas. But my need for romance is utterly *unreasonable*. It has nothing to do with the intellect. I must speak of the soul, and I must speak personally.

The world of the Arthurian romances is a world of castles. Malachi Martin (author of *The New Castle*) has proposed that the castle—so often depicted standing on a hill with its turrets and spires and ramparts reaching for the sky—is an archetype, a mythic symbol that captures a complex concept. Specifically, he proposed that the castle is the archetype of the meeting place between heaven and earth. And this I think—I *feel*—is what romance is all about. It is about the meeting of heaven and earth.

Ordinary life, our earthly existence, is often dull. Romance is exciting. Our moments of romance are those when a little bit of heaven seems, thank God, to impinge, to intrude upon our daily lives. I yearn for such moments. It is because I yearn for them so much that I generally feel this earth is not my true home. The yearning is particularly intense when I am bored for any length of time. I want to go home.

Heaven is the home of God. For years I have known that my only *real* romance is that with God. I want to be with God. I want to be in His or Her arms where I belong, and I hope I shall be when I die. But I am not ready to go home yet, and God does not come to me often. Certainly never on demand. She has Her own schedule. Her timing is not my timing, and I must content myself with that. I am not so good at being content, however, that I do not look forward to substitutes, even if they be but shadows of the real thing, even if I know I am being foolish.

Romantic love between two human beings is the most powerful and commonly sought after of such substitutes. But there is a big problem with it. In my first book I proclaimed human romantic love to be a temporary phenomenon, and its demise within the context of marriage (of any significant length) to be a human universal. I have received approximately twenty thousand letters in response to that book. Only one of them took issue with my proclamation. Its writer was twenty-two years of age.

So, after a while at least, marriage becomes a part of ordinary earthly existence and in some respects quite humdrum. Lily and I developed different ways of dealing with this dreary reality. Possibly one of hers was to resort to science fiction and fantasy literature. One of mine was to resort to sexual infidelity. It was a resort of which I am not proud. It was hurtful to Lily and hurtful to some other women. I would rather not have to mention it here. But it is too germane to the subject for it to be legitimately avoided—not only to the subject of romance but also the subject of this three-week trip. The trip was a journey together, and its account is, among other things, a reflection of our larger, longer journey of marriage.

My sexual infidelity is a glaring example of the unreasonableness of romance. I would never have been diagnosable as a full-blown "sex addict," but in some ways it was surely a compulsion. A purely rational human being would know better. I, however, am not purely rational, and this irrational part of me had to have its due. I might not have survived otherwise, but I always wished I could have been a different kind of person who did not need such an outlet. And I always knew that my infidelities were potentially dangerous and destructive, not only to others but to myself. In a very real sense I was engaging in them despite myself.

Remember, all symptoms are overdetermined. To what extent was my infidelity psychological? Spiritual? Biological? To what extent is our need for romance a genetic phenomenon that might vary in power from one individual to another? I don't know. I have spoken of my infidelity as something in the past, and so it seems to be. But I do not think this is the result of any moral, ethical, or spiritual growth on my part. Rather, it feels much more like a shrinkage of the glands. With my late middle age there has come a dramatic diminution of libido, praise the Lord. I am not nearly as horny as I used to be, and for me that is an extraordinary relief.

I labeled my infidelity potentially dangerous. There is an element of adventure in romance. An adventure is going into the unknown. If you know exactly where you are going, exactly how you will get there, and exactly what you will see along the way, it is not an adventure. After a while, no matter how imaginatively inventive and experimental you might be, marital sex pretty much ceases to be adventurous. The territory becomes old hat. Extramarital sex is another matter. There is a new body and a new personality to be explored. A new territory. It is also forbidden territory, and for some that might be a turn-on. For me it never was. Whatever else my psychology, the pure newness of another woman was my primary aphrodisiac.

Because they involve the unknown, adventures are inherently dangerous to a greater or lesser degree. Yet it is also only from adventures and their newness that we learn. If we know exactly where we're going, exactly how to get there, and exactly what we'll see along the way, we won't learn anything. Consequently, I cannot be utterly condemnatory of my affairs. For some I am deeply regretful and regretfully apologize. From others I have learned much and hope I gave as much as I got. But there are different ways to learn. Lily's forays into science and fantasy fiction, for instance, provided her with many valuable pieces of knowledge.

And there are other forms of adventure not only likely to be less dangerous but more educational. This trip, for instance.

One of the reasons my infidelity was so painful to Lily was her assumption that I was seeking—and might find—a better woman, a better mate. Except for a few brief moments at the nadir of our marriage fifteen years ago, that was never the case. In this respect, I was still very much a rational man. I knew perfectly well that I would never find a better woman—or even one as good. I was not looking for another wife. I was looking only for the newness, the freshness of romance. In this respect, my sexual infidelity was definitely addictive behavior. I was seeking what I knew full well would be an exciting but obviously ephemeral romantic "fix," a very temporary and temporal reexperience of the reunion of heaven and earth outside the boundaries of ordinary life.

I have used the word *seeking*. A final aspect of romance is the quest. I did not suffer from the Don Juan syndrome. *Conquest* was never a part of it, but there was an element of quest in my extramarital romances. While I always knew in my heart that what I really wanted was God, even in my most irrational moments, I never expected to capture Him by chasing after other women. Nonetheless, I was seeking a glimpse of Him on the ramparts. I was questing through sexual romance at least a brief visit to His castle. A major section of the body of Arthurian legend—derived from primarily French and obviously post-Christian sources—centers around the quest for the Holy Grail, the particular chalice used by Jesus at the Last Supper. Lily and I are both romantic people, but I would not go so far as to describe us as "romantics." In questing after Merlin's cave, the most we ever hoped to find was just a cave and nothing more. We did not expect the Holy Grail. In romantic literature, however, the important thing is not its object but the quest itself. It is the very act of human questing that is somehow romantic. So it was that when we finally gave up and returned to the main road we felt neither disillusioned nor significantly disappointed. No, we had not succeeded in finding Merlin's cave. But we had given it a damn good try and that was pretty much the point.

I do not feel awkward speaking of my need for romance and my infidelity solely because I am a man of reason; I also feel awkward as an author. Infidelity is a hot topic, a juicy subject. Indeed, it is a bombshell of sorts, and it is simply bad form for a writer to drop a bomb without picking up the pieces. Properly so. It is unkind to leave one's reader with loose ends.

In this instance there are all manner of loose ends. Questions abound. Did I tell Lily about my extramarital affairs? How else might she have found out? And then how did she respond? Was she vindictive? Did she reciprocate? Were my liaisons lasting affairs or one-night stands? Did they stop after my conversion to Christianity or did they continue? If they continued, was I not being a hypocrite? How could Lily live with such immorality? How could I condone it myself? The questions could go on and on.

Unkind though it might be to the reader, I am not going to even attempt to answer these questions or any others on the subject. I am going to be guilty of bad form. The fact is that I have little choice in the matter.

I suppose I could choose not to mention my infidelity at all. But there would be two major problems with such a course of inaction. One is that it would seriously shortchange any discussion about the issue of romance. The other is it would leave the reader with the false impression that I am a man of saintly self-control, and that while Lily's and my marriage may have a few amusing family sitcom quirks, we have somehow managed to rise above all the truly serious problems of matrimony. Neither is the case. I believe I owe my readers at least a minimum modicum of honesty and realism.

On the other hand, having raised the issue of infidelity, I could possibly choose to let it all hang out, so to speak, by making a thorough disclosure of each and every intimate detail. Much as the reader might want me to do so, however, that possibility is purely theoretical. The details are not solely my property. They very much involve Lily. Indirectly, they involve our children, other relatives, and many friends. Even if I might desire to tell all in the interest of literary taste, I do not have the *right* to do so. It would be a tasteless violation of many people's privacy.

Moreover, it would serve little purpose. Yes, it might satisfy the curiosity of some readers, but such satisfaction would likely be dangerous. The easily satisfied would conclude, "Ah, since this is the way Lily and Scotty handled these complex problems, and since they are such wonderful people, that's the way we ought to deal with them in our marriage." The conclusion would probably be fallacious. God loves variety and creates each of us differently. We are each of us unique people and we are married to unique spouses. Consequently, our marriages are different, and what's going to be the right thing for one marriage may be just the wrong thing for another. I can tell you how to guarantee yourself a bad marriage, but I cannot offer you any formulas that will guarantee you a good one. It is because of our extraordinary human variety that I once heard Tom Langford, dean of the Duke Divinity School at the time, make a most profound statement at a conference when he said, "Goodness cannot be stereotyped."

Realizing this, the less easily satisfied would still have a thousand questions no matter how many details I provided. It would occur to them that the problem of infidelity one way or another is an issue inherent in almost every marriage and a subject so complex as to merit an entire book in itself. This is a book about a three-week trip Lily and I took in Great Britain together. It is not intended to be a treatise on the extraordinarily deep ambiguities of fidelity. As a tale of our journey with each other, it will, among other things, deeply concern itself with our marriage. But not fully. Not completely. Not exhaustively. It is a slice of life of sorts and may even cut to the core, but in no way will it strive to be the whole pie.

So, speaking personally about the issue of marital fidelity inevitably places one on the horns of an insoluble dilemma, caught between the whitewashing sins of omission and the over-disclosing sins of indiscretion. This is not just a dilemma for Scott Peck. Nor is it just a dilemma for autobiographers. More than anything it is a dilemma of a strangely unbalanced society.

Marital infidelity is hardly abnormal. Study after study has demonstrated that the majority of married men have been *guilty* of it at least once, and such a substantial minority of married women that even among the "fair sex" it cannot be considered uncommon. Nonetheless, I emphasized the word *guilty* because our society generally considers this essentially normal behavior to be immoral. That in itself is not a spiritually incorrect assessment. We are all sinners one way or another. Who among us has not neglected our children to some degree at some time? Or abused our parents? Or been inconsiderate of associates? The fact that these sins of either commission or omission are statistically normal—even universal—and usually repetitive doesn't mean they are moral. But the peculiar power of sexuality leads us to a kind of national insanity over the issue of marital infidelity.

The insanity is most obvious in our treatment of public figures, particularly politicians. We expect them to not only be legally but sexually above reproach. Consequently, they must hide their sexual peccadilloes as best they can, pretending to a degree of sinlessness that only further feeds into our unrealistic expectations of them—until some enemy or spy reports a detail to suggest otherwise. Instantly, the politician's— or clergyman's—statistically normal sexual behavior becomes *news*, and investigatory reporters frenziedly compete to uncover every lurid detail of that which was once properly private.

Sin might be defined, among other ways, as unreasonable behavior, and it is not my intent to proclaim marital infidelity to be sinless. Something is seriously wrong with the understanding of the unreasonableness of romance in this Age of Reason, however, when there is no alternative between the pretense of completely rational sexual sinlessness on the one hand and the relentless exposé of intimate matters on the other. I do not choose to participate in this odd cultural charade. While refusing to portray myself as an utterly rational whited sepulcher of a man, I also refuse to make all the inherently private adventures and misadventures of my romantic life subject to the public domain. In charting this middle course, I hope I am making a bit of a public statement—and that readers will graciously allow me to stand unmolested.

Leaving behind the ambiguities of marital fidelity and, for the moment, those of Merlin, we now race down a much wider and less treacherous road. Although Joan had assigned us our destination, St. David's, we knew nothing more about it than what we had read over lunch in our guidebooks. As for the hotel there, one of them mentioned it without exuberance and the other not at all. Another parameter we had given Joan was that we wanted to spend our nights in the very best lodgings available in the area. Money was no object. The night before both she and the guidebook had failed us. Tonight we did not know what sort of place we were headed for. Nor did we know for what else we might be questing.

This tale began by asking the reasons why Lily and I were sitting in Paddington Station to begin a trip by going to Wales. Some prosaic answers were given. Now I offer one less prosaic. Willy-nilly, we were seeking romance in our lives. We were embarking upon an adventure into the unknown and a quest for that which we knew not.

We did know that St. David's was more or less the Welsh equivalent of England's Land's End. The only other thing our guidebook told us was that the town itself is the smallest city in Great Britain. The reason this is so is because it has a cathedral—a cathedral being the church of a bishop and the seat of a bishopric. The fact gives us a little glimpse of how much the Christian religion defined life back in the Age of Faith. No matter how tiny your town, as long as it had a bishop and his cathedral, it was a city. However large your town might be, lacking a bishop and cathedral, it was merely a town.

Half an hour beyond Carmarthen things changed. The rain became a drizzle. Gulls began to course the sky. Then gorse appeared in the hedgerows and the smell of the sea was in the air. Although the picture of its cathedral in our guidebook didn't look like much, we began to get a strong premonition that St. David's would prove to be the right place for our day's end. The premonition only grew as we abruptly hit the coast and then proceeded along the Pembrokeshire cliffs and downs.

By American definition, St. David's might not even be considered a town. Perhaps a village.

Its quaint and weathered stone houses clustered together on top of a hill or down in a small circle. I doubt that it contained more than a thousand inhabitants, including tourists. Our lodging, the Warpool Court Hotel, a converted manor house roughly four hundred yards from the "city" center, was well out in the country. Registering, we saw only omens of good taste. Our room, like the vast majority of accommodations in Great Britain, was minuscule by American standards, but it had a goodly sized window looking out across three hundred yards of fields, hedges, and cows straight to the sea. The drizzle was now but a soft and contented mist.

After settling in we took an hour's walk to the cathedral. Every other cathedral we'd seen was built either slightly above or at the level of its town. This one sits in a hollow several hundred feet beneath the town, behind the high dunes between it and the ocean. It was reputedly built there to hide it from seafaring marauders. In any case, its location makes it impossible to decently photograph. This was a precedent of sorts. We were to see little in Wales and Scotland that a camera could do justice to.

More typical of medieval cathedrals, St. David's has been rebuilt layer upon layer. There are vestiges from before A.D. 1000, but it is still very much alive and used. Adjacent to it in the hollow are the ruined choirs of its original bishop's palace. Atypical again, its substantial graveyard is built into a steep hillside—almost cliff—climbing up to the current bishop's manse and the "city."

A question hangs in the mist. Why should there be a rather small but greatly revered cathedral practically on the beach at the foot of this coastal village? The answer lies back in Celtic history and the fact that Christianity had two different origins in Great Britain.

It will be remembered that while Romans conquered and enculturated the Celts in the area that came to be known as England, they did not get far with the Celts in Ireland, Wales, and Scotland. In the mid-fourth century A.D., Christianity came to be the official religion of the Roman Empire. Immediately, waves of church officials were dispatched from Rome to bring the creed to England. The English were converted by government decree.

Not so the Irish, Welsh, and Scotch. Beginning with Ireland, they were converted by the evangelistic example of a few brave and dedicated wanderers largely operating under their own authority—men and women who have since come, formally or informally, to be considered saints. So legend has it that around A.D. 500 a Christian woman, Saint Non, sailed from Ireland and, landing on this point of the coast, first introduced Christianity to Wales. Her son, David—Dyfed in Welsh—carried on her work of evangelism from this base so successfully that until this day he, Saint Dyfed, is proudly celebrated as the patron saint of Wales. Although, with Arthur and Merlin, scholars are unsure as to whether Dyfed and his mother, Non, ever existed, it matters little. We now understand why the Cathedral of

St. David sits at the foot of this little village on the Pembrokeshire coast.

And we can also understand why there are some differences between English and Welsh Christianity. The English have little attachment to their pre-Christian roots. The Welsh are as passionately Christian as the English, but they retain an avid love for their pre-Christian Celtic history and legends. The resulting ambivalence was personified in the figure of Merlin.

Camelot is generally regarded as being in England and King Arthur as an Englishman. Merlin is a Welsh figure. If Camelot ever occurred in sixth-century England, it did so in a land that had been Christianized for two hundred years. Wales was just starting to be Christianized. In Arthurian legend, King Arthur and the knights of his Round Table are unequivocally Christian. Merlin, even when depicted as advising them, is not. Only in a very few versions is he identified as Christian. In the vast majority, he is identified as something else. Some of those versions portray him as pro-Christian, some neutral, and in some he is distinctly anti-Christian. Yet once again we find Merlin to be perhaps the most ambiguous figure in all of literature. But then, he is purported to have lived in a time of ambiguity. Possibly this is a reason for his increasing popularity in our own titularly rational age: that we, too, are living in particularly ambiguous times.

At this moment, however, Lily and I were not experiencing ambiguity but were possessed by a feeling far more strange. Walking the wet grass between the gravestones and the ruins, we shared the same irrational sense that we were as much in the sixth as the twentieth century. Specifically, we felt out of time. Although lacking my father's passion for cathedrals in general, this little one seemed a very special find, even magical in some way. The peacefulness of the place was palpable. Whether it was because of its strange location at the edge of the sea or because we visited it when it was enshrouded in mist or because of some other indefinable romantic factor, we do not know, but the Cathedral of St. David and its complex held for both of us a muted quality of holiness. Our visit to it was not unlike an interlude in Camelot.

As evening descended, we pulled away. Hand in hand we ambled back to the Warpool Court, shortly to discover it had an excellent restaurant. Unlike the previous night, our dinner got progressively better, culminating in rich but delicate fresh rhubarb ice cream embedded in a huge, crisp, caramelized cradle. In twelve hours time, mile by mile, we had gone from what seemed like the depths of hell to a poignant and gentle heaven.

CHAPTER III

ADDICTION
TUESDAY, JUNE 2

By this morning the mists had cleared, and our first serious venture of the day was a walk in the sun to the cliffs above the sea. On the way we stopped briefly at "Saint Non's well" and the tiny adjacent ruins of her chapel. We also stopped when Lily slipped on the wet descending path, tumbling three times over into a patch of stinging nettles. Saved by angels and her Gortex, she was unhurt except for one badly stung hand. The cliffs were lovely but we hurried back to dig out her anaphylactic kit just in case the nettles got to her. They didn't.

It wasn't until eleven that we started driving north along the west coast of Wales toward our evening's destination of Portmeirion, unaware that within the hour we were to have an experience that would change our lives.

One of our guidebooks told us that if we turned off the main road, just a few miles north of St. David's, and proceeded to Abercastle, we would find an unnamed, prehistoric burial chamber. We thought we'd give it a try. Abercastle, despite its fine- sounding name, proved to be but a hamlet of six houses at the edge of a tiny bay. It was a sweet little spot but no burial chamber was in sight. So we continued through it on the narrow road for a mile or so to where there was a lane with a sign identifying it as the entrance to Long House Farm. It occurred to us that the burial chamber might be on the farm—then again, it might not. Best we return to Abercastle and inquire as to its whereabouts. We did so and fortunately ran into a transplanted Englishman who lived in one of the houses and happened to be outside at its door. "Burial chamber?" he asked with puzzlement.

"How about some sort of prehistoric monument?" we suggested.

"Ah, yes," he told us happily. "There are some stones at Long House Farm. Just drive in and ask them. Nice people. They'll tell you where."

Back we went. British farms are quite unlike American ones. They tend to be large stone complexes with several courtyards and a somewhat foreboding quality. But the young lady who answered the door was perfectly friendly. She told us that if we went out of the complex we could park our car to the left near a gate into a field where we would find what we were searching for.

Slipping and sliding on the manure, as soon as we walked through the gate we saw it a hundred yards into the field, silhouetted against a broad bay in the distance: a tight cluster of six standing stones seven feet high with a huge boulder magically balanced on their tips. Although others might not see it that way, it was a castle of a sort—a meeting place between heaven and earth. For us it was a moment of epiphany. And while we did not quite realize it yet, we were addicted.

Addictions are overdetermined. In 1970–71, approximately half of the American troops in Vietnam tried heroin at least once. This statistic became a hot political issue. Inexperienced about such matters, members of Congress and other government officials assumed most of the soldiers would return to the United States as confirmed heroin addicts. My boss and I, representing military psychiatry in Washington during those years, doubted it. We had reason to suspect that much

49

more than a simple exposure to the drug was required to create an addict. Time proved us correct. A small minority did develop a real passion for it. But the vast majority, as soon as they were out of Vietnam, never sought after heroin again. In addition to the drug itself, sociological, psychological, spiritual, and biological factors are involved. Addictions are overdetermined.

As a small, personal example of such a probable biological factor, I like sedative drugs—"downers"—and am strongly habituated to one of them: alcohol. Although exposed, however, I have never particularly cared for stimulants or "uppers," such as Dexedrine, speed, or cocaine. Lily, who gets little to no enjoyment from alcohol, on the other hand, would practically kill for Dexedrine if she loosened her reins.

I said I am strongly habituated to alcohol. I eagerly look forward to my gin in quite hefty amounts at the end of a day. This habit has become more entrenched over the years. I dearly love the solace it brings me—the relaxation that results from having the edge taken off my consciousness—and I tend to adjust my day around the "cocktail hour"—or two or three hours. Despite my biological predilection to it and the power of the habit, I am not in the strict sense of the word actually addicted to the drug. I don't get ill or go crazy when I occasionally stop it. "No matter," my friends in AA would say, "anybody who depends upon it as much as you do is an alcoholic." Quite possibly they are right. But there are different definitions of alcoholism.

The World Health Organization, for instance, defines it in terms of the harmfulness of the habit—socially, physically, or economically. In this respect, I feel like Winston Churchill. Once when his wife criticized his drinking he replied, "My dear, alcohol has given me far more than it has ever taken away from me." My drinking has not significantly hurt me—not yet at least.

Tobacco is quite a different matter. I continue to smoke despite a serious bout of pneumonia that very likely wouldn't have occurred at all—or have been so serious—were I not a smoker. It is not a mere habit—something I do simply to keep my fingers busy. It is a full-blown physical addiction. Without nicotine for more than a couple of waking hours I become sick. The physical illness, the feeling that rats are gnawing at the inside of my rib cage, is the least of it. The mental illness is what is so devastating: I lose my concentration. I can no longer think. And, as the days go on, it becomes worse whenever I have attempted to quit.

The addiction is, of course, overdetermined. My mother was a smoker, and I got hits of nicotine in the womb. She was also the more spiritually mature of my parents. My father, who loved his cigars and at whom I was angry much of the time, routinely criticized her for her cigarettes. Growing up, I came to associate cigarette smoking with spiritual goodness. And with masculinity and maturity. In those days of the late forties I was actually grateful to the fifteen-year-old who taught me how to inhale the summer I was thirteen. In terms of genetic predisposition, my one sibling, a brother four years my senior, is also unable to quit despite having even more serious lung problems and being a less intense sort of person. For over forty years now I have used smoking, somewhat like alcohol, to take the edge of my consciousness, to provide me with brief respites from concentration and rewards for periods of hard mental work. No work requires such intense concentration as writing, and if I ever do kick this fierce addiction it will probably only be at a time I have ceased to write anymore. Finally, there is a major element of simple enjoyment. I know at least two people who started smoking not because I turned them on but simply from watching me smoke. Years later they confessed to me, "You looked like you were having so much fun I wanted to try it myself."

Oh, by the way, I also illegally smoked marijuana several times a week for over a decade. I stopped using it about a dozen years ago not out of any moral compunction but only because the drug ceased to have any beneficial effect for me.

A question seems obvious. Since I am a heavy drinker, an inveterate smoker, used to be an illegal drug user, and a bit of a philanderer to boot, do I have an addictive personality?

The answer is: "yes and no."

Yes and no? Where does the "no" come in? Is Peck in denial?

Obvious though the question might be, the answer isn't. The issue of "the addictive personality"—if there even is such a thing—is almost as complicated as the issue of marital fidelity. I cannot do it justice in a mere chapter. But having provided a few details in this case, it is necessary to throw in a few other facts to present an even slightly balanced picture.

A major part of the picture is the subject of nondrug addictions. Some have accused Lily, for instance, of having an addiction to crossword puzzles or, when she is home, to computer games. Many would consider such activities, like rose-gardening, to be harmless, often creative pastimes. And so they are, but most who are truly into them, like Lily, are able to acknowledge their addictive quality.

Unfortunately, many nondrug addictions are not so harmless and some far more destructive than the worst forms of drug abuse. Gambling and sexual addictions are two we commonly recognize. But others not so commonly recognized are destructive not only to the addict himself but practically lethal to the society around him: Addiction to money. Addiction to power. Addiction to control. Addiction to violence. These things can destroy entire civilizations, and may well be doing so to our own.

Yesterday I suggested that in seeking romance outside of marriage I was foolishly seeking a substitute for God. So it is with virtually all addictions. They are forms of idolatry. For the alcoholic, the bottle becomes an idol; for the heroin addict, the drug is his god. The nondrug addictions are no different. Our whole society may be going down the tubes because of its idolatry of wealth and security.

Many subtle idolatries are so common as to be essentially universal. One I have written about is the idolatry of family where family togetherness becomes an idol, where it becomes more important to do or say what will keep the family matriarch or patriarch happy than it is to do and say what God is calling you to do and say. Over half my audiences have had massive personal experience with this idolatry. Another I call the idolatry of human romantic love, where we look to our spouse or lover to be a god unto us—to meet all of our needs, to fulfill us, to bring us lasting heaven on earth. Of course, it never works, and among the reasons it doesn't is because when we do this, whether we are aware of it or not, we are violating the First Commandment. This first of the commandments, the prohibition of idolatry, is very specific: "I am the Lord, thy God. Thou shalt have no other gods before me." We are a naturally idolatrous people. It is very natural that we should want a tangible god, one we can see and touch, hold and embrace, and perhaps even possess. But God is not ours to possess; we are His or Hers to be possessed by.

So it is, when they understand these things, I occasionally ask of my audience, "Will everyone here who doesn't have any addiction please raise their hands?" No one ever does.

There are also, I believe, good addictions of a sort, and I have been blessed (or cursed) by one of them: an addiction to consciousness. It goes way back. "Scotty, you think too much," my parents used to tell me at least monthly during my younger years. I am a born contemplative, something that has generally been valued by the religious traditions. It is a lifestyle dedicated to maximum awareness, and like a gambler is drawn to the table, so I have been pulled to become ever more conscious of myself and the world about me. I can no more pass up a new insight than a cigarette.

Unfortunately, pain is an inevitable side effect of consciousness. The more aware we are, the more conscious we will become of our sins and imperfections, of our mortality and the aging process working in every cell of our bodies. We will become more effective as we grow in awareness of the manipulations of others and the games that people play, but we will become more conscious not only of their limitations but also their needs and burdens and sorrows. And more conscious of the sins and evils of society. People have spoken of nicotine as well as alcohol as anesthetics, and I told how I use both "to take the edge off my consciousness." I use them as medications to treat my side effects; they are, in a sense, counteraddictions.

All this may not make addiction to consciousness seem "good." Consider, however, its opposite. Carl Jung ascribed the root of human evil to "the refusal to meet the Shadow"—the Shadow being defined as that part of us that contains those traits we would rather not own up to, that we attempt to conceal not only from others but ourselves, that we are continually trying to sweep under the rug of consciousness. By the word *refusal*, Jung was implying something far more active than our usual passive resistance to criticism. So it is that one of the many possible definitions of evil is "militant ignorance." Militant unconsciousness. Certainly I believe some suffer from an addiction to unconsciousness. Or rather, they fail to suffer; it is the others around them who must suffer. Think of the ill-effects of those who are addicted to a high opinion of themselves, to complacency and self-righteousness!

Consciousness has many components. The drive toward it may be thought of as consisting of a number of "subaddictions"—really addictions in their own right. One of them I have previously written about as being thoroughly good. It is the addiction to mystery.

And that addiction is particularly germane this morning, as we stand in the manure in a moment of epiphany staring at a little-known prehistoric monument overlooking the sea in the midst of the field of the Long House Farm. For we are staring at mystery.

What is the reason for this strange cluster of six tall stones rooted in the ground and lifting an even larger boulder like a sacrifice to the heavens? Only one thing is obvious: They didn't just happen that way. People, presumably not aliens from spaceships, at considerable, even extraordinary, effort put them there, arranged them thus. What people? How? Why? For us the answers are romantically incomplete.

Through the ages people of most cultures, from time to time with greater or lesser degrees of fervor, have considered certain relatively small stones to have magical properties. A current, close-to-home example is the number of followers of the New Age movement who are enamored with crystals. Larger stones have always been used in the construction of walls, foundations, houses, palaces, pyramids, temples, and cathedrals, but their use was practical. The great religion of Islam is partially focused around a single and most unusual stone—apparently a meteorite that fell from space and comprises the center of the Kaaba in Mecca. But only one culture seemingly revolved about large stones or megaliths in themselves.

As best we can currently determine, between 4000 and 1500 B.C. a prehistoric people in north-western Europe and the British Isles were somehow driven to gather and erect megaliths in certain arrangements. It is as if they themselves were addicted to stones. Such ancient stone monuments are found no where else on this planet. Their arrangement is extremely varied. Most common is a simple, tall, solitary stone or menhir (long stone) placed upright in the earth. Often, however, these megaliths are placed in rows, circles, or semicircles or, occasionally, in far more complex arrangements. One such arrangements consists of two or more tall standing stones balancing a cross or lintel stone on top of them. This has come to be called a dolmen (stone table). The supposed "burial chamber" we had found in the field of Long House Farm was a dolmen.

Who were these "megalithic people"? By virtue of the fact that they were prehistoric, they raise far more questions than answers. We know that there were lots of them. They left a huge number of tombs, sometimes obviously associated with megaliths but more often not. From the tools buried with them they are classified as a Neolithic people. *Lith* is the Greek root for stone, but in this case it does not refer to the megaliths they erected; rather, it refers to the fact that although they did not yet know the art of making metals, they did have at their disposal relatively advanced tools of stone—axes and hammers of a sort. People with less advanced stone tools are classified as Mesolithic (middle stone age) or Paleolithic (early stone age). So it was a Neolithic people who erected megalithic monuments throughout a vast but specific region four to six thousand years ago.

They need to be put in perspective. At the same time, there were many other Neolithic people throughout the world who weren't erecting any monuments at all—at least none that have stood the test of time. In later millennia other cultures around the globe also erected megaliths, but never in such profusion or variety. Mysterious though it is to us now, there are reasons to suppose that the megalithic culture of northwestern Europe around 3000 B.C. was not only "advanced," but, as compared to more simple and local societies, in its range and complexity it was possibly the first human society to deserve the designation "civilization."

Another fact we know from their tools and remains is that these otherwise unique megalithic people were farmers. For the most part, unlike

Mesolithic and Paleolithic people, they were no longer hunger-gatherers. They tilled fields and domesticated animals. It is likely no accident that we found our first dolmen in a field—a location which had perhaps been a field for five thousand years.

Of their thousands of monuments, the most famous and studied is Stonehenge, a complex circle of multiple dolmens in the Salisbury Plain of southern England. Many things make it so famed. No other circle of dolmens is extant. The stones are far larger than most and were obviously quarried. Less obvious but well determined is the fact that they were quarried from two places— one quite close but the other from quarries two hundred miles away in western Wales (not too far from the dolmen at Long House Farm). Of all surviving megalithic monuments, Stonehenge is, in a sense, the most polished.

How did those Neolithic people transport such huge stones to that site? Despite all the study, we don't know. Before the Age of Reason people assumed it was magic. A number of the Arthurian legends credit Merlin and his magical powers for the feat. Today, with our science, we know Stonehenge was completed at least two thousand years before the alleged time of King Arthur and at least a thousand years before the arrival of the Celts in England. But we still don't know how.

Nor why. Because of the alignment of one of its stones in relation to the dawning of the solstice sun, scientists thirty years ago were proposing that Stonehenge was erected to serve either as an astronomical observatory or celebration. This was a theory, not a fact. There is a great deal of fashion in science, and often scientists themselves tend to blur the distinction. The public, hungering after certainty, blurs it even more. The theory trickled down, and many cultured people today will proclaim with great assurance that Stonehenge was a monument to astronomy. Over the past twenty years, however, scientists have seriously questioned that theory. The fact of the matter is that at the end of the twentieth century, we still don't know either the how or the why of Stonehenge. The mystery remains.

And in relation to the thousands of less studied megalithic "happenings" the same mystery also persists. Back now to our single, relatively small yet wonderful dolmen in the field of the Long House Farm, the question cries out: How did those prehistoric people find, transport, and erect these stones, and, above all, why?

Although impossible to answer with certainty, it is not difficult to guess at the "hows." Unlike those of Stonehenge, the stones of this, our first dolmen, are rough, irregular, and unpolished. They do not appear to have been quarried. We may guess that they were found nearby in their original state and selected to be dug up and transported. As to how they were moved to that central location, even prehistoric people can do extraordinary things with enough manpower. Evidence suggests they did not have wheels or wagons. It also suggests they were very proficient at cutting down trees one way or another. Quite possibly they rolled the stones there on logs. Then with deer antlers they dug holes to anchor the upright stones in the earth. One or two dozen pairs of hands could have lifted them into that position.

But how did they then manage to balance that huge boulder on the tips? Although they had ropes, it is unlikely they could simply have lifted it there. More likely they did it by planing. They may have filled the space in between the upright megaliths with dirt or rocks. With more rocks or dirt they could have built an upward sloping path or plane to the top. Finally, they could have heaved and rolled the boulder to the peak. Then removed all the dirt or rocks and voilà: a dolmen.

Such explanations are relatively prosaic. Less prosaic is the amount of work involved. All possible scenarios (other than aliens from outer space) posit many people working together very hard with great cooperation toward a shared goal. What was that goal? The guidebook called the dolmen a burial chamber. It is possible. But, like the popular pronouncement of Stonehenge as an astronomical observatory, the guidebook's pronouncement that this monument was a burial chamber represents another blurring between theory and fact. It satisfies a mind that needs certainty and cannot tolerate living with mystery. It also makes a number of highly questionable assumptions.

There are reasons for the theory. The megalithic people did expend an enormous amount of effort building tombs of many different kinds— some with giant stones, some with small stones, and some with both. There is no doubt they constructed various types of burial chambers using megaliths. These *obvious* chambers resemble dolmens with upright and lintel stones, closely fitted together, and scholars often refer to them as dolmens.

The stones of most dolmens, however, are not fit so closely together, and bodily remains have not been found within them. It has been suggested that some of their stones were simply destroyed. Just a few centuries ago we know that many more megalithic monuments existed in Great Britain than do today. Although lacking much in the way of verification, some have proposed that Christian priests had these monuments hauled down because they were pagan. More verifiable are accounts of their destruction for commercial purposes. But why destroy just some stones of a dolmen and not the whole thing? The suggestion makes little sense.

The more common suggestion is that dolmens such as the one we'd just found were originally entrances to large tombs of smaller stones. Such tombs abound. But if the Long House Farm dolmen was an entrance to a tomb, its size suggests it must have been a very large tomb indeed. What happened to it then? Where did the tomb go? If it was a typical but huge communal burial chamber, to where did the thousands of ordinary stones vanish? Lily and I spent a long time not only looking at the dolmen from a distance, but also walking underneath it and around it, touching the great stones, stroking and fondling them. We saw no trace of any grave or any other sign of additional construction.

I have referred to myself as a scientist. By this I mean that I am well trained in the scientific method and experienced in analyzing the results of scientific or scholarly research and using those results in certain ways, such as the practice of medicine. I must make it clear, however, that I am not much of a scholar or researcher myself. I am not patient enough. Good scholarship and research require an enormous amount of time. Let me use the question of whether or not this dolmen was a burial chamber as an example. I could have examined the records and deeds from the Long House Farm property as far back as they might go—perhaps back as far as the twelfth century. I might well have learned that there were once other stones on the property—piles of ordinary stones or more megaliths. I could also have spoken to all the Long House Farm neighbors, questioning them about local legends. I could have boned up on the history of Abercastle and the surrounding area. I might have hired a team of archaeologists at massive expense to excavate not only underneath the dolmen but dig up the entire field. Had I done this I might have unearthed conclusive evidence that the dolmen was indeed once part of a burial chamber.

But I didn't. I didn't have several years to spend in southwest Wales. We had to leave soon to explore other things. But with the major caveat that we didn't stay to thoroughly explore the question, I would like to offer my unscientific opinion that our guidebook was probably wrong: that *this* dolmen, at least, was not a burial chamber.

If the Long House Farm dolmen was not a burial chamber, then what was it? Why did our

Neolithic ancestors at extraordinary communal effort erect it? For what purpose?

We don't know.

Not knowing, as we shall repeatedly see, drives most people nuts.

There are two parts to the taste for mystery. One is delight in solving mysteries. As a scientist in the Age of Reason, this is a delight I share with many: uncovering the hidden reasons for things. The other part, however, makes the great majority of people nervous. Good scientists know that for every question they answer they will find at least three new questions to ask. And this doesn't necessarily make them comfortable. To have a full-blown taste for mystery one must take delight both in solving mysteries *and* in not solving them; in finding explanations for things *and* in living with things for which there currently is no explanation and which may be forever beyond explanation.

Lily and I have long been mystery addicts. Perhaps that is why we both became psychotherapists: We enjoy peering into the mysteries of the human soul in all its variety, unraveling hidden motives where we can, but content in knowing we could never get even one human being totally and neatly pigeonholed. In any case, it is precisely because we are mystery addicts that at this moment we are in the process of being turned into prehistoric stone addicts as well. What enchants us so much about the megaliths is not the little bit we know about them but all that we don't know.

There are often precursors to addiction, or what physicians call, in relation to a full-blown illness, prodromal signs—signs of the physical or mental imbalance to come. While we have never had any great passion for palaces or ordinary castles, we had long before this day a love of ancient ruins. The couple who came upon the stones in this Welsh field overlooking the sea had twice been to the Yucatán looking at the ruins of Mayan temples (and even discovering one for ourselves, which is not hard to do since the jungles of the Yucatán are chock-full of them). Although it had never before assumed the status of an addiction, Lily and I had been amateur archaeology buffs for over twenty-five years.

I know for sure that very few tourists would have been drawn off the main road and down little byways to such a field. And even if a busload of average people were to pull up at Long House Farm, most of them would curse at the manure, see only an unusual pile of stones, take a quick photograph, and move on toward grander sights—grander to them, that is. I say this not to put them down but simply to note how unusual, how statistically improbable, it is that this was a *mutual* moment of epiphany.

Things are interrelated. I've suggested that the addiction to mystery is intertwined with the addiction to consciousness. There are other connections. I analyzed our previous day's excursion to hunt for Merlin's cave, also down little byways, as resulting from a shared thirst for romance. Our equally odd behavior on this day follows the pattern. Mystery is very much an element of romance. And for me the mystery of these stones is as great a turn-on as the mystery of a newly revealed woman's body ever was. It is also a safer, healthier turn-on.

In mentioning my infidelity, one might wonder why or how Lily put up with it. How does a marriage survive such stresses. As for everything of significance, there is more than just one reason. A major one is shared tastes, passions, and, yes, addictions. There are many of them for us, ranging from spicy food to travel. But now we have a new one: our addiction to stones, our shared delight in their romantic mysteriousness. And our almost perverse glee that at the deepest level they will always be mysterious. As we journey ever deeper into mystery, there will be enough hints—clues—to eventually indulge in a little speculation. But the question of the "why" of megalithic monuments will continue to delightfully haunt us to the end.

In the meantime we must move on. Our next goal was Newport, only ten miles farther north on the main road. The reason for stopping here was because our guidebook identified it as the location of a whole circle of burial chambers. The woman in the town's information center knew what the book referred to. But she informed us that the site was sunken into the ground, virtually unfindable and unrecognizable. Learning of our interest in megaliths, she suggested that if we took a certain road off to the right a few miles farther on, we would eventually come to "some quite nice stones." She was a classy lady, and we took her advice. It proved a wise move. Four miles up into the hills on yet another one-lane Welsh road tunneling between the hedges was a marker and a gate through the hedge. Also a parked car and a space for ours as well. We walked through the gate and found another dolmen!

Although perhaps a foot shorter, this dolmen, in size, was at least as grand as the first. Its lintel stone was not as round or as high as that at Long House Farm, but it was longer, sharper, and just as dramatic. Again the huge stones were rough granite and did not appear to have been quarried. Ten yards in every direction medium-sized granite stones protruded a few inches to a foot out of the mown grass. There was a hint of regularity but no otherwise distinct pattern to them that we could discern. Clearly the site had once been something more than just a dolmen. As to what more, we had no information. Perhaps a burial chamber. Perhaps something else. We don't know. The whole site, roughly twenty yards in diameter, was fenced off. Beyond, fields and hedges and little copses gently undulated down toward a distant valley. It was a pretty and tranquil spot.

It was not, however, quite the epiphany for us that our first dolmen had been. Well worth the journey, but not ecstatic. Was this because it was our second dolmen and we were already jaded? Because we hadn't had to search for it as hard? Because it was marked and fenced off? Because its shape was somewhat different? Because we had to share it with three other tourists? Because the view was less spectacular? Who knows? Undoubtedly the answer was overdetermined.

I ask these questions primarily to introduce a significant principle. It is not so much an objective principle of archaeology as a subjective one of the soul. It pertains not only to megalithic monuments but also to the major ruins of any other ancient civilization, and is a significant cause for our pleasure in visiting both. Each such site is unique. For instance, Lily and I have visited six different Mayan ruins in the jungles of the Yucatán. The buildings are all identifiably Mayan. The surrounding jungle is monotonously the same. Yet each site has a different flavor, an atmosphere all its own. So it is with dolmens and other megalithic monuments. Some might feel that once they've seen one great, hoary prehistoric stone, they've seen them all. Not so for us. No two stones are alike. And when you add in factors of their arrangement, their location in the landscape, and even the weather, each site is memorable in its own way. We were never to know what would be around the next bend.

One specific difference in our dolmens deserves special mention. The fact that this second site was not only fenced off but had a sign on the road and its own little gate suggests that it was a National Trust (NT) site. The National Trust of Great Britain purchases such sites from landowners or, upon occasion, landowners donate them to the Trust. This means that the NT sites are protected and preserved and open to the public as part of the public domain, whether they be castles, Roman ruins, megaliths, or other spots of particular interest. By virtue of the fact that it was unmarked and unfenced, it is probably that our first dolmen was not an NT monument but part of the personal real estate of the owners of Long House Farm. The distinction is one of significance.

By now we had spent three hours covering the first twenty miles of our assigned day's itinerary. Yes, Wales is a small country and, yes, we had deliberately planned for a leisurely pace, but not quite *this* leisurely. To the benefit of our schedule, however, neither map nor guidebook indicated any other megalithic sites along our route. So now we headed straight up the west coast into the Snowdonia mountains of northwest Wales. They are more dramatic than the Brecon Beacons of the southeast, even steeper and occasionally more menacing. After a while, we turned west, gradually descending toward our lodging for the next two nights at the Hotel Portmeirion, back down at sea level on the gentle shore of an enormous tidal estuary (quite equivalent to the famed Bay of Fundy between Nova Scotia and New Brunswick).

From Fodor's we knew ahead of time that the four-starred Hotel Portmeirion would be either the best or worst of places. It was described as an "Italianate" theme park constructed in 1926 by Sir Clough Williams-Ellis. The guidebook was unclear as to whether it had originally been a hotel or recently restored as one (among other things). Much was made about the fact that it had been the site for the filming of a 1960s television series "The Prisoner."

We were directed to a slightly seedy registration center where we were assigned "The Prior's Lodging" and a porter to escort us to it. Following his motorized little cart we were led through an archway into an incredibly tacky conglomerate of gaudy buildings—the Prior's Lodging appearing the most tacky of all—swarming with British day visitors wheeling prams full of howling infants while their older children dashed this way and that playing rowdy games of tag. "I'm going to kill Joan," Lily screamed. "I'm going to kill her!"

I nodded in silent agreement, too sickened to even speak. Yet the moment the porter unlocked the Lodging door a miracle occurred. We were instantly transported into another world: a quiet and utterly secluded realm, perfectly peaceful save for the occasional screech of one of the very visible and neatly kept peacocks. Our elegantly appointed, black-and-white-decor quarters—huge by British standards—felt to us like a miniature palace with its crank-out windows looking down upon the estuary and across to the green hills beyond.

The genius of the place is that it manages to cater simultaneously to the most ordinary folk and to the wealthiest, most jaded (like us) situating them adjacent to each other without touching. I was reminded of a hall of mirrors. We had the sense of living in the midst of a splendid mirage. It is an extraordinary feat of architecture and design. Hats off to Sir Williams-Ellis and the restorers!

We had time for along evening walk on the

mile-wide sands of the estuary. Afterward, we ate at the hotel's excellent restaurant overlooking those same sands. Since they had been bare for hours now, Lily simply could not believe the tide would ever succeed in covering such a vast expanse. I wagered a pound to the contrary. She accepted. By the end of dinner, the course of our earlier walk was well submerged by the ocean, and we left the restaurant with me a pound heavier and a pound wealthier. But Lily had no regrets; nor did I. Having concluded Portmeirion to be the best of places, we had totally exonerated Joan and were to fall asleep feeling blessed by grace.

On the surface of things, the grace of Portmeirion was not terribly mysterious. Sir Clough Williams-Ellis had purchased it because it was a particularly beautiful spot. He had put a great deal of effort into developing it. Joan is a good travel agent and we had told her we wanted the best. Yet there is always mystery to grace, and I could talk about the combination of the mystery of God's creation and the mystery of human genius that made it such a special place.

But as I fell asleep it was not the grace of Portmeirion that haunted me so much as the grace of the dolmen back at Long House Farm.

We scientists are most interested in proof. Of the means used to establish proof, perhaps the most useful are the statistics of improbability. In terms of events we ask the question: What is the probability that this event could have occurred by pure chance? The lower the mathematically calculated probability, the greater the improbability and the safer we feel concluding that the event was not the result of chance alone but occurred because of a significant reason.

This is why, as a scientist, I have commonly spoken about grace in terms of a "pattern of highly improbable events with a beneficial outcome." It is also why I have concluded that in such patterns we can see the fingerprints—if not the actual hand—of God.

In this case, the beneficial outcome was Lily's and my unusual addiction to stone searching. We are unaccustomed to thinking of addictions as beneficial. When we consider how relatively safe and inexpensive this one is, however, we may make an exception. Particularly when we begin to examine the benefits, such as the experience and knowledge gained and the plain good fun involved. It beats extramarital sex, alcohol, and cigarettes. It even beats golf. Yes, I think there are a few profoundly healthy addictions. I think we may consider ourselves lucky—graced, if you will—to have developed this one.

Please remember yet once again how many things of significance are overdetermined. Sometimes we are more likely to discern the presence of grace in our lives the more willing we are to consider the multiplicity of reasons for an event. The improbability of an event caused by a single, slightly improbable factor is not striking, but that improbability increases geometrically when it is the result of many slightly improbable factors, all operating simultaneously.

I touched upon the improbability that Lily and

I should share the same relatively rare passion for prehistoric stones. Other improbabilities had also been in play this day. The dolmen at Long House Farm was not marked on our map nor was it mentioned in our Fodor. Our oldest child had come to England with her husband and infant son ten days before my nephew's wedding. They had picked up a somewhat unusual British guidebook. Unfortunately, given the rigors of traveling with an infant, it did not serve them well. Fortunately, however, they passed it on to us at the time of the wedding. Had they not done so we would never have known to go in search of a "burial chamber" just north of St. David's. It was a little bit of luck for us.

Suppose our search had been unsuccessful, as had our previous day's quest for Merlin's cave? Failed quests are not much a reward. They tend, as psychologists brutally put it, to "extinguish" our enthusiasms. Early success, on the other hand, tends to cement them or, in terms of an addiction, to get us hooked. I cannot say we would have given up so easily. Perhaps. Perhaps not. What I can say is that failed quests in this business of searching for stones were to prove quite common in the days ahead. And I am grateful to that transplanted Englishman who happened to be at his door in Abercastle to give us directions.

In a sense it was luck not only that we found the dolmen but also that it was there to find. I noted that most of the megalithic monuments of earlier Great Britain have been destroyed. Since this one apparently was not a National Trust site we probably wouldn't be wrong in crediting its existence to the good sentiment of the owners of Long House Farm. Who wouldn't want a Neolithic treasure in their backyard, you might ask? Lots of people. Perhaps farmers in particular. That dolmen not only made for difficult plowing, it took up a hundred square feet of perfectly good grazing or planting land. It was hardly cost effective. A little dynamite probably would have saved the owners a fair amount of money in the long run. No, I don't think we have the right to count on sentimental farmers.

Nor hospitable ones. I think it was *gracious* of the woman at the door to allow us to park and tread on her land. To be placidly interrupted by our ringing of her doorbell. To not have posted NO TRESPASSING signs. We were to meet other hospitable farmers, but not to come to count on them either. A number of our failed future quests would be the result of barbed wire, of posting, and even more ominous signs of unwelcome.

Finally and subjectively, the Long House Farm dolmen is an especially beautiful one. It is not one of a group, as in Stonehenge. It is not as tall or massive or mathematical as Stonehenge. It is neither quarried nor polished. But its very simplicity is part of its glory. Another part is its location. For Lily and me, two somewhat odd human beings, it could not have been more perfectly designed to be an ultimate turn-on so as to switch our brains into addiction status.

Is there meaning in all this? Who knows? Nonetheless, as I was falling asleep in our Prior's

Lodging, I was already pondering the mysterious grace of our first dolmen and the whole trip to date. Might it be possible that we were being guided? Could this trip—Lily's and my journey together and our mutual quest—somehow be touched by the hand of God in ways that had nothing to do with our own design?

CHAPTER IV

HOLINESS
WEDNESDAY, JUNE 3

With the Hotel Portmeirion as our base, we had the whole day to explore wherever we wanted. Actually, there were only two ways to go: east or west. East into the Snowdonia mountains or west to the Isle of Anglesey. Anglesey is apparently not much of a tourist attraction, because all the guidebooks advised the mountains with a plethora of possible slate mines to be visited. So, of course, we went to Anglesey.

The choice was overdetermined. Yes, our natural orneriness may have been one determinant, but there were many others. For one thing, we would have to go east through the mountains anyway on the morrow to get to England's Lake District. For another, slate mines were not our idea of a turn-on.

But the major reason was our burgeoning addiction to stones (not slate). We had purchased a new and larger map whose markings suggested two possible megalithic sites on Anglesey. There were no such markings in the mountains. This is not surprising. The megalithic people were predominantly agricultural, so mountains are not generally the place to look for their monuments.

The map placed one of those possible sites at the southwestern tip of Anglesey on what it designated as the Holy Isle. We did not know why it was so designated, but the name drew us. For whatever reasons, that which might be holy always draws us.

One final drawing card: The Isle of Anglesey is reputed to have been the last refuge of the Druids in Great Britain.

The Druids were a pre-Christian priestly class or cult of the Celts. We tend to associate priests with holiness, but it is a tendency that often gets us into trouble. While priests—or monks, nuns, and other clergy—may be slightly more likely to be holier than the rest of us, the vast majority of them are quite ordinary mortals. Sometimes clergy fall into the trap of thinking themselves holy merely because they're clergy. More commonly, we laypeople fall into the same trap with different but equally devastating results. By attributing holiness to the person in the robes, we may fail to pay attention to our own potential for holiness. Moreover, when clergy behave with a demonstrable lack of saintliness, we are prone to become profoundly disillusioned not only with them but also with the religion they represent.

Such disillusionment with Christianity is one of the roots of the New Age Movement. It is, I believe, a generally unhealthy root as opposed to some of its more constructive ones. Be that as it may, New Agers are flocking to almost any variety of spiritualism—ancient or modern—that is not Christian for their inspiration and nourishment. Strangely, the Druids have been one of their targets. A few are even declaring themselves to be Druids.

I say this is strange because it is most unclear what a Druid is. Or might be. Or who the Druids ever were. Yet, as a romantic of sorts, I can very much understand how easy it is in our yearning for the Holy to project holiness onto the blank screen of the unknown or to read it into anything that is deeply mysterious, including Stonehenge and other megaliths. Nonetheless, it seems it might be just as easy to become disillusioned with these pre-Christian priests of the past as with the Christian ones of the present.

What very little we do know about the Druids comes from the Romans, who apparently did not like them very much, even to the point of specifically invading Anglesey in A.D. 60 for the sole purpose of obliterating them. They reported that the Druids worshiped trees, particularly oaks, which is nice, and that they believed mistletoe to have magical properties—a belief they may have passed on to modern times since it also seems nice around Christmas time. The Romans further reported that the Druids practiced human sacrifice by burning people, sometimes in bulk. This does not seem so nice. We might remember, however, that the Christians of the Inquisition followed much the same quaint custom.

And there you pretty much have it. Some Arthurian legends hold that Merlin was a Druid. Since he is often designated as being pre-Christian, that might have been the case—if he ever existed. And as Merlin has sometimes been associated with Stonehenge, certain fantasy writers have written of the Druids using megalithic monuments—Stonehenge and other dolmens or stone circles—for their worship. Although there is no evidence to support it, this might also have been the case. We shall see down the road that the Celts did not totally ignore the great stones. But we need to bear in mind that the people who erected them were not Celts, and that the mysterious megaliths predate the Druids by at least a thousand years. If the Druids used the stones, it was only by virtue of the fact that they were already there, waiting like long-discarded secondhand clothes.

All this said and done, we still enjoyed the notion that we might find Druidic traces on Anglesey. In the rain once more. Anglesey is called an isle because it is separated from the rest of Wales by the Menai Strait, which at places is only a couple of hundred yards wide. After crossing the strait by bridge, we headed for the first monument at Moelfre, a pleasant village that provided us with both a picnic table overlooking its bay and a half hour respite out of the rain in which to eat our lunch. Afterward, a friendly inhabitant directed us back to a tiny sign we had missed that pointed toward the monument down another lane through the woods and fields.

The monument turned out to be—you guessed

it—a dolmen. It differed from the two of the previous day in a number respects. It had been marked on the map. The road to it had a sign. It was more in the woods, although the trees around it had been cut away. And it was encircled by an iron fence. While the lintel stone was huge, its dozen or so supporting stones rose only two to three feet from the ground. It was, in fact, a remarkably squat monument, almost to the point of being ugly. Here we could more easily imagine it to be the entrance to a burial chamber. It looked like the kind of thing dwarfs might pass through as they went to and from a mine deep in the earth. But we don't know. We don't know why this dolmen was so squat and low. For all we know its supporting stones may have sunk many feet into the earth under the enormous weight of their gigantic lintel over the course of forty centuries.

We also didn't know that this was the last dolmen we were to see on the trip.

From Moelfre we drove toward the Holy Isle. Although not densely so, Anglesey is more populated than we had imagined it to be. It may have little attraction for the ordinary tourist, but we found it a pleasantly gentle land, unmountainous and mostly agricultural, approximately a hundred miles in circumference by the main road.

It was to one side of that road, as the driver who had to be alert, I shortly spied our first standing stones or menhirs. They stood about ten feet tall, two of them thirty yards apart, anchored in a little patch of untilled moorland. We stopped to gape in awe.A part of our awe was their unpredictability. They had not been marked on our map. Nor mentioned in our guidebooks. They were not there to be searched for. They were simply *there*, just off a major road, nonchalantly waiting for anyone with the eyes to see.

They pointed to the sky. Once, perhaps, there had been more of them, but I doubt it because they seemed such a pair. They were of remarkably similar shape and size, and both were slightly slanted in the same direction as we were heading, almost as if to urge us forward. They looked like they possessed energy. We would have liked to have touched them, but they were well guarded both by thick barbed wire at the edge of the road and by the pouring rain. So we had to content ourselves with examining them from a distance. They appeared relatively smooth, and I wondered if they had been deliberately quarried as a pair.

Almost prayerfully now, we drove on to the Holy Isle. As Anglesey is separated from the mainland of Wales by a narrow strait, so the Holy Isle is separated from the rest of Anglesey by a tidal river that seemed hardly more than a stream. Yet it might almost have been an ocean, for the scenery and atmosphere abruptly changed as soon as we crossed it. No longer were we in gentle, agricultural country but in a bleak, wind-swept, rugged land. Even the quality of the houses was instantly altered. I was reminded, both by land and dwelling, of some of the wilder parts of Cape Cod.

Through a miscalculation of distance we drove past the turnoff to the other monument designated on our map and came to the end of the road at South Stack. It proved to be a grace-filled miscalculation that dumped us in a parking lot overlooking a cliff down to a dramatic lighthouse on the rocks below. The lighthouse seemed to be all there was to South Stack, and we assumed the view of it to be the sole reason for the parking lot. But even in the wind and rain we could still hear that raucous whine that comes from hand-held, gas-motored grass cutters. We looked toward the sound and saw three men on the other side of the road, knee-deep in the bracken, wielding these noisy tools. We were curious. Why on earth should there be three people mowing in the midst of what appeared to be a desolate and barren hillside? We walked across the road to discover a path with an almost invisible sign stating it led to a site of "hut circles" dating to A.D. 200. Farther up the path was a similar sign, except this one dated the same site back to 2000 B.C.

As we walked along we saw that the men were excavating from the bracken a large and indeterminate number of virtually identical stone foundations. These were not megaliths but small rocks that had obviously once served to support the wood or thatch of huts. Each foundation was shaped like a horseshoe and was about twelve feet in diameter. We examined well over a dozen of them while the men were excavating still others. We have no idea how many there might have been in all. We would have stayed for hours to attempt to ascertain the answer, but it was still raining, and cold and windy to boot. So we do not know whether the site was that of a large village or an entire city. Nor do we know whether it once housed Iron Age Celts—possibly Druids—as one sign suggested, or prehistoric— perhaps megalithic—people as the other proposed.

It really didn't matter much to us. Whoever it had housed, we knew for sure that we were standing on hallowed ground. We had discovered, to our satisfaction at least, one reason why this tip of Anglesey was called the Holy Isle. Even though we were being drenched in the driving rain, we were both experiencing the presence of God. And even though we couldn't stay as long as we would have wished, Lily and I will always remember those hut circles overlooking the sea as one of the most holy places we have ever visited.

I mentioned that the Cathedral of St. David's had a muted quality of holiness. I described the dolmen at Long House Farm as a meeting place between heaven and earth—as if it, too, was a holy spot, and so I do believe. And now, in the course of three days, I label a third place as the most holy of all. What's going on here? What do I mean by a holy place?

Some Catholics have a concept I much admire: the Sacrament of the Present Moment. It suggests that every moment of our lives is sacred, and that we should make of each moment a sacrament. Were we to do this we would think of the entire world as diffused with holiness. Wherever we might be would be a holy place for us, and we would see the holy, even sainthood, in everyone we encounter. For many reasons, I very much believe in this concept. Possibly I may even write more about it someday. For the moment, however, I must confess that the notion is purely an abstract ideal for me. Occasionally I remember to strive for it, but I never achieve it. While I intellectually acknowledge that everyone and every place may be holy, I actually go around experiencing the holy in very few places and people.

With that caveat about my dramatic limitations, let me analyze as best I can why I do find rare people and places to be so particularly special as to feel myself in the presence of holiness.

I very much appreciate places of pure natural beauty. Yet only one such place have I experienced as holy: certain groves of redwoods. This is not, I suspect, because I am a Druid at heart and worship trees in and of themselves; it has more to do with the silence and the light that those groves manage to capture. The day I drove with Lily and two of our children down northern California along the Avenue of the Giants was a particularly special day for me.

Every other place where I have experienced the holy has been not only one of natural beauty but also a site of human construction. This astonishes me. Why on earth should I need some sign of the past presence of human beings to feel the active presence of God in a place? I honestly don't know. But that's the way it is. The field at Long House Farm was beautiful in its own right, but it took a dolmen to make it a holy spot. And so it was for us with the hut circles at South Stack.

By themselves, little circles of ordinary stones in the ground are not holy. By itself the hillside overlooking the Irish Sea was not holy. But put them together and some kind of magic happened for us. I do not mean to imply that every conjunction of human construction and natural beauty is holy for me. Rarely is it so. I imply only that the conjunction almost always seems to be an essential ingredient. A meeting place between heaven and earth is somehow one between God and humanity.

I said it was no matter to us whether those hut dwellers at South Stack had been Iron Age Celts or Bronze Age peasants or the Neolithic erectors of megaliths. History, at least in the sense that we ordinarily think of it, is not an essential ingredient of the human element of holy places. Another of the most holy places that Lily and I share, not all that far from the Holy Isle as crows or gulls fly, is Tintagel on the coast of Cornwall. That holy place is not the tourist town of Tintagel but the ruins of an adjacent ancient castle that sits upon a promontory jutting out into the stormy ocean.

I cannot tell you what makes Tintagel such a holy spot for us any more than I can about the hut circles at South Stack: it is just the conjunction of natural beauty with ancient human ruins. Beyond that, it is mysterious—mystical. What I can say is that, like so many other such spots the mystical quality of the place tends to evaporate when there are too many tourists scrambling over its rocks and steep steps. And that this quality has nothing to do with the specifics of human history. The castle of Tintagel is reputed to have been that of King Arthur, but we couldn't care less. For starters, it is highly uncertain whether Arthur was an actual historical figure. Had the guidebooks surmised that the ruins of Tintagel were those of the castle of some Sir Ropdedop we'd never heard of, we would have been no less impressed. The age of those wonderful ruins would seem to coincide with Arthur's purported time. Beyond that, however, I wonder whether Arthur contributed to the holiness of Tintagel or the holiness of the place led to it being attributed to him of legend? I suspect the latter.

The same question arises in relation to another of my holy places: Assisi. Widely known as the birthplace of St. Francis, Assisi is not a deserted monument on a windswept coast but a still-living, breathing little city perched halfway up a mountain that arises out of a plain in central, inland Italy. When I climb to sit above the town, the spirit of peace pervading the place is palpable. And Francis has come to be known as a particularly peaceful saint. But each time I have been there I've wondered to what degree he made it a holy place as opposed to the degree that the holiness of the place made him a particularly saintly man.

Assisi is a religious shrine of sorts. So is the Cathedral at St. David's. Conceivably the hut circles at South Stack housed Druid priests. There may well be religious significance to dolmens, menhirs, and other megalithic monuments. Arthurian legends are spiritual one way or another, and whoever might have owned it, the castle at Tintagel undoubtedly once housed a little chapel. Must a holy place once upon a time have been a site of worship? I do not believe so. Not, at least, as we ordinarily think of worship.

In 1978, Lily and I had the good fortune to travel to Greece and those Greek isles known as the Cyclades. They are called this because they roughly form a circle, and at their center is the tiny, low-lying, uninhabited island of Delos. Because of its central location, the ancient Greeks considered Delos their "Holy Isle." Consequently, it is strewn with the ruins of great temples, but 2,500 years after its heyday neither Lily nor I felt holiness there. Indeed, we experienced it as perhaps the least holy of those wonderful islands. Back on the mainland we visited another famed religious shrine of the Greek embedded in the mountains: the temples of Delphi. They are beautiful mountains, but once again we had no hint of holiness. Where we did get a most strong mutual hint of the holy, however, was at the remains of the theater at Epidaurus. A theater!

I think we can extrapolate to people. Neither history nor religion nor the conjunction of them alone is sufficient to make someone holy. I have known a number of historically famous people, including clergy, who did not impress me with their holiness. I have also met some unknown women and men who were not overtly religious yet who clearly struck me as saints of some stripe.

It is high time for another caveat. I believe that holiness, like beauty, is at least partially in the eye of the beholder. We have often had the experience (and will again in the days ahead) of traveling to a place others consider holy only to find it left us cold. Conversely, others might visit the places I have mentioned and get nothing out of them. This is not a guidebook.

Similarly, I am aware that some of the people I've considered to be holy have been evaluated by others as the devil incarnate. Whoever else saints might be, we do not tend to feel neutral about them.

Still, I would not dare talk about holiness if it was utterly subjective. Were I to ramble on about some holes in the ground that I—and only I—considered very special, I'd probably be well on the way to being locked up. But Lily, who is quite sane, also felt the hut circles at South Stack to be one of the world's most special places. It was another mutual epiphany. One of the tests of proof, of reality, is termed "consensual validation." I'm not saying it would be the consensus of mankind that that site is a holy place. But whenever two or more very different people make exactly the same extraordinary assessment of a phenomenon, then it is truly a phenomenon, and it needs to be taken a bit seriously.

We've hit a theme. Consensual validation is remarkable only when it's between "very different people." That Lily and I are very different will become ever more clear. Yet, as noted, it is not entirely remarkable we should see things similarly. Why else should we have married and how else could the marriage have survived? I've alluded to it in terms of shared tastes. Now we can move into the area of judgment. What better foundation could there be for a marriage than a generally shared judgment of what is holy—and of that which is distinctly unholy?

The English root of the word *holy* is derived from the Anglo-Saxon word for whole. As a writer I find derivations often pregnant with meaning. In talking about holy places the key word I've used has been conjunction: a mysterious conjunction of natural beauty, past human construction, *and* a present beholder. The matter of holiness is, if you pardon the cliché, a *whole*, overdetermined ball of wax. I believe that human holiness also has something to do with wholeness. Those people I would designate as holy have generally been more conscious than most. In psychiatric parlance, they are more in touch with their Shadow-sides, and there is in them a more complete integration of their conscious and unconscious selves. If I am right about this, then saints are less self-deceptive than the rest of us, and in this respect, at least, more whole.

But do not think of them as perfect. In the arrogance of young adulthood I used to think of myself as a "whole" person. Now in late middle age I am profoundly aware of how unwhole I am. I am, for instance, well organized to a fault. This gift has allowed me to write books. It has also made me a mediocre parent at best, someone with a limited capacity for play and often not much fun to be with. Lily, occasionally disorganized to a fault, has flowed with our children and been much the better parent. She stops to sniff the flowers that I don't even notice unless she points them out to me, and she is wise in ways

I am not. Even together we are not whole. Our greatest learnings over the past decade have come from working intensively as a community with many others in a nonprofit organization whose success has been the result of the pooling of the diverse talents and visions of dozens of dedicated people. Only such a pool begins to become truly whole. We cannot stand alone.

So, there is a paradox in this matter of wholeness. It is at one and the same time a valid ideal and an impossible one. I do believe I have met some saints, but they have been imperfect and limited in their own ways. Indeed, I have come to distrust "perfect" people. There is an analogy in my love of stones. I have mentioned Stonehenge as the most polished and, in a sense, perfect of the megalithic monuments. I also find it relatively boring. The stones of the Long House Farm dolmen, on the other hand, were all different and uneven, yet they came together for me as a far more exciting whole, a real community of stones, so to speak. And as for single standing stones or menhirs, it is their unevenness of shape and texture that makes some of them so particularly beautiful. Or, in the case of the pair of menhirs we'd earlier spied to the side of today's road, their ever-so-slight slant. Is this not a principle of much great art—that its greatness often resides in some brilliantly studied or unstudied imperfection?

I have made the point that holy places and people are not necessarily religious in the usual sense of the word. This doesn't mean that they aren't spiritual. To the contrary, the matter of spirit is as crucial as it is mysterious.

I was once called upon to exorcise an evil spirit from a house. I did not find it there. I only found some evil in one or two of its inhabitants. But I have sensed an evil spirit in certain places. One was a church. I arrived early to give a lecture. No one else was there yet. It was a pretty church, but I felt within it an almost palpable spirit of oppressiveness. Although ordinarily very popular, I knew with certainty that on that evening my lecture would be ill-received. And so it proved to be with an audience feeling too oppressed in that place to laugh or even tap their feet to the music I used. Several years later I returned to the same church with trepidation only to discover that its evil spirit had departed.

When I talk about holy places I am speaking about a very good spirit that is hanging around them. Perhaps that spirit is fleeting. I do not know. What I do know is that it was not so fleeting in the two holy places I have visited more than once. I first happened upon both Assisi and Tintagel the summer I was nineteen. In 1980, twenty-five years later, I returned to Tintagel to find it as holy as I had left it. As I also found Assisi after twenty-nine years.

Occasionally it is possible to name either good or evil spirits with remarkable specificity. In the case of the holy places I have mentioned, I cannot be any more specific than to label it "the spirit of holiness." I think—I know—it has something to do with God. Whatever the reasons, I know that God was hanging around the hut circles at South Stack on this windy, rainy June afternoon.

The holiness of certain human beings is also a matter of spirit. It may be a good sign should you have a desire to be a saint, but only if you realize your desire to be nothing in and of itself. The spirit of holiness is not earned; it is a pure and mysterious gift. No one has written as deeply about the nature of sainthood as T. S. Eliot in his plays. In a sermon that is the centerpiece of *Murder in the Cathedral*, Eliot has his hero, Saint Thomas à Becket, speak these lines four days before his martyrdom:

A Christian martyrdom is no accident. Saints are not made by accident. Still less is a Christian martyrdom the effect of a man's will to become a saint, as a man by willing and contriving may become a ruler of men. Ambition fortifies the will of man to become ruler over other men: it operates with deception, cajolery, and violence, it is the action of impurity upon impurity. Not so in Heaven. A martyr, a saint, is always made by the design of God, for His love of men, to warn them and to lead them, to bring them back to His ways. A martyrdom is never the design of man; for the true martyr is he who has become the instrument of God, who has lost his will in the will of God, not lost it but found it, for he has found freedom in submission to God. The martyr no longer desires anything for himself, not even the glory of martyrdom. . . . so in Heaven the saints are most high, having made themselves most low, seeing themselves not as we see them, but in the light of the Godhead from which they draw their being.

Many saints are not physical martyrs; they often die quite natural deaths. I also suspect that not all martyrs are saints. Bearing these things in mind, Eliot's words apply to all saints. That's the way it is. Saints do not and cannot take credit for their sainthood.

From South Stack we retraced our steps—the only option available—and soon came to the little turn-off road we should have taken in the first place. At its end we arrived at a small farm. To its front was an open gate into a very wet field that held the original object of our quest to the Holy Isle: another pair of standing stones of the same height as our previous unmarked pair, but otherwise most different. These were closer together, perhaps only ten feet apart. They were thinner, less substantial, of rough granite that did not appear quarried. Without significant slant they pointed only straight to the sky. Even without our great good luck in stumbling upon the hut circles, they would have been well worth the trip. They looked incredibly ancient. Nonetheless, the previous pair, unmarked upon the map and unreachable, had been for us the more impressive.

There being no more designated monuments to see, we drove off the Holy Isle and straight back down the middle of Anglesey. As we crossed back onto the mainland the rain stopped and the clouds lifted, becoming shredded with piercing patches of early evening sun revealing the full glory of the Snowdonia mountains in the distance. We entered them by a different route— a country lane that marvelously meandered through all that Wales is most famous for: harsh mountains save where they glowed pale purple with whole forests of wild rhododendron; steep hillsides that rippled with cascades of white water from the all-day rain; rushing rivers that fed into flat, strangely rockless, valley meadows green as spring and soft as lawns.

Near the end of our day's journey, Lily—with my consent, I must grudgingly admit—misread the map, taking us away from instead of toward Portmeirion. The mistake might have been disastrous, forcing us as it did to drive a one-lane, three-mile causeway without police or electric light control. Had we met an enemy car in the middle it would have meant a two-thousand-yard backward retreat between the narrow walls. I doubt we would have made it. I was driving, but as a result of a surgical fusion of my neck there are 270 degrees behind me that I cannot directly see. Even if there had been room to open the car doors so as to switch seats, Lily is afflicted with a peculiar kind of brain deficiency that prevents her from accurately driving backwards no matter how far she turns or cranes her neck. But, by grace alone, we encountered no enemies, and at the other end of the causeway we ended up in the vicinity of a village called Harlech. The name rang bells.

Between the ages of eight and twelve I attended

a decidedly British private grammar school in New York City. The teachers took various harsh measures to instill in us unruly preadolescents some semblance of cooperative school spirit. One was group singing, and a favorite of their songs for us was the resounding march "Men of Harlech." Its original, ancient Welsh lyrics had been translated as:

Men of Harlech! honor calls us,
No proud Saxon e'er appalls us!
On we march, whate'er befalls us,
Never shall we fly.
Forward, lightly bounding,
To the trumpet's sounding;
Forward ever, backward ne'er,
The haughty foe astounding;
Fight for father, sister, mother,
Each is bound to each as brother;
And with faith in one another,
We will win or die.
Tho' our mothers may be weeping,
Tho' our sisters may be keeping,
Watch for some who are now sleeping
On the battlefield,
Still the trumpet's braying
Sounds on, ever saying
Let each bowman pierce a foe
And never stop the slaying,
Till invaders learn to fear us,
And no Saxon linger near us;
Men of Wales! our God doth hear us,
Never will we yield.

Fortunately, World War II ended before I reached the fifth grade in that school, and I never had to imitate the song's heroes. Also fortunately, we not only realized our mistake but somehow managed to make it back across the causeway, again without encountering a Saxon enemy auto in its midst—safe, sound, and wiser. We now had some experiential knowledge as a result of this unplanned detour as to why the Men of Harlech were so famed for their bravery if not stupidity.

I imagine it was necessary that those Welshmen should march forth against the Saxon invaders to protect their families and properties even as I imagine there might today be some more distant and abstract necessity for the Royal Air Force to be periodically sweeping over our heads. But I worry about the glory so generally attributed to such activity, then and now.

Glory is an attribute of God that we humans may reflect from time to time in a variety of ways. One of those ways may be in our courage. *May* be. I offered my opinion that not all martyrs are saints. The history of warfare is replete with examples of wasted martyrdom, like the famed Charge of the Light Brigade. Words such as "Theirs not to reason why, / Theirs but to do or die," may stir the souls of some, but not mine. I have been quick to point out that reason has its limitations, yet I believe it also is a God-given human faculty. There is a distinction to be made between smart courage and stupid courage. The saints I have known have all been women and men of courage; they also have all, like Thomas à Becket, been fiercely intelligent.

And the holy places we have seen—the Cathedral of St. David's, the dolmen at Long House Farm, the hut circles at South Stack—three already—were each pervaded by a spirit of peacefulness. I do not mean to imply that going off to battle is never the holy thing to do; only that we have seriously lost our wits when we think that there is something inherently holy about warfare. And that there seems to be a thin line between the courage of the Men of Harlech and their mindless blood-lust.

We returned to our bizarrely beautiful Prior's Lodging to find a nineteen-page fax from the Big Apple. Although we had left an itinerary for just such a purpose, it felt like an intrusion of unreality into an infinitely more meaningful world. After a hot bath and room-picnic, fax unread, I sat down to make some notes. Still unaware of quite how cemented our addiction to stones had become and never dreaming we were researching a book, we had already decided our journey was too rich to be entrusted to photo and memory alone. I wrote in the evening light. Only when we retired at eleven had it become too dark to do so any longer.

We were very much conscious of how far north we were, of how our days were rapidly approaching the summer solstice, and how we were headed much farther north still, even to the edge of the Arctic Circle. Might we get to see the midnight sun? We didn't know. What struck us thus far was not how long the days were—they seemed quite normal—but how long the evenings lingered; they just gently went on and on.

Lily and I are always conscious of light. It is a matter to which I have given some thought. Love, light, and truth are practically synonyms for God. This makes sense. Take but one of them away and civilization would vanish. The reality is most obvious in the case of light. No light, no photosynthesis; no plants upon which to feed; no people to build monuments and no light to see them by.

I mentioned that certain redwood groves are holy places for me because they capture silence and light. The forest is so dense as to exclude all external noise. It is possible to ignore their silence until a single bird sings within. When the single song has died not only do I realize I have heard a sound exquisite in its simplicity but also that I have heard it so precisely because it was embedded in pure silence. The same principle holds true for the very occasional ray of sun that manages to penetrate the grove's great green roof. Its light is so remarkably noticeable because there is so little of it, because it is so isolated in its purity. One does not take such light for granted.

I cannot say that other holy places have a unique light about them. What I can tell you is that I distinctly remember the quality of the light that glorified each one I have seen each time I saw it.

The matter is even more clear with holy men and women. However imperfect they might be, they have a light about them. It is no accident that the painters of the *Dark* Ages gave halos to the saints they depicted. I do not think saints to be the owners of their light. I believe it is the light of God. Why it is that God should especially reveal Her light at certain places and in certain people, I do not know. I do not expect to know. I may learn more, but I am old enough to doubt that even the midnight sun will be able to fully illumine such mystery.

CHAPTER V

CHANGING
THURSDAY, JUNE 4

When we awoke at sweet Portmeirion, the sun was shining. By the time we were in the mountains, two hours later, gloom had descended. I've talked about our sensitivity to light. In our combined 113 years, we have never witnessed such atmospheric gloom.

The slate mines we passed hardly helped. They all advertised tours, although I fail to understand why anyone on vacation would choose to visit the pits of hell. Slate is gray. At its best, this land has created stone towns of enormous charm and gentility. At its worst, the stone towns can be unrelievedly drab, often by virtue of Welsh slate without any attempt at adornment. The gasoline fumes that bothered us our first eve in Cardiff hung by the roadside in today's oppressive atmosphere and were to bother us many times again.

If Britain has emissions testing, it doesn't seem effective. But these things are notable only because the country is otherwise so humane.

I'd planned for a single stop on our day's journey to England's Lake District: the city of Chester, which sits just outside of northeastern Wales and just inside England. Indeed, it had originated as a Roman walled town designed to defend Britain against the Welsh Celts. It is most famous, however, for its half-timbered houses. I'd seen it with my parents forty-two years before and recollected it as probably the single greatest collection of such buildings in the world. In the early days of our marriage, Lily had exuberantly exclaimed over every photograph of every half-timbered house she spied in every magazine. She used to save the pictures for me. I also remembered Chester as being crowded and touristy, even back in 1950. I had no desire to see it again myself, but for decades I'd looked forward to the possibility of "showing" it to Lily. That possibility was now at hand. As we departed Betys-y-Coed, where the gloom was at its most intense and where the mountains begin to descend to the Welsh border, I said, "I sure hope it doesn't rain."

"Why?" Lily asked.

"Because it'll make it hard to see Chester," I answered.

"How so?"

"The guidebook says it's very crowded," I explained. "It advises that we park outside the walls and do the town on foot. That won't be too pleasant if it's pouring rain."

"If it's pouring rain, why don't we just skip it?" Lily suggested.

I was aghast. "We can't skip it," I said. "It's the greatest collection of half-timbered houses in the world."

"So what?" Lily commented.

"So what?" I echoed. "Your heart's desire has always been to see half-timbered houses."

"Has it? I don't remember."

I almost swore. I reminded her not only of the magazines but all the ersatz half-timbered houses she'd admired from a distance in the suburbs of Cleveland where we had lived when first married.

She was dubious. "Maybe I liked them then," she acknowledged, "but now a whole city of them would seem pretty tacky. If it's not raining, fine, let's go take a look. But if it is, I'd just as soon go on, if you don't mind."

People change.

No one is more of an expert on the subject than Lily herself. Twenty years ago, when we were both practicing psychotherapy—often with married couples, often with the same couples— she coined a crucial term: tenuousness. By this she meant that the adjustment of the partners to each other in a healthy marriage needs to be tenuous rather than tenacious, flexible rather than fixed. Husbands and wives should be prepared for each other to change and prepared to change themselves in response. Fortunately, she has taught me well enough that I did not continue, as some husbands might, "But you know you love half-timbered houses. You can't be that forgetful. Are you feeling all right? Of course you want to see Chester, even if it is raining."

Her feeling for half-timbered houses is perhaps the least of the things that have changed about Lily. I could talk of dozens of far more profound ways in which she has changed over the course of the thirty-three years of our marriage. From my point of view, the most profound has been the way she handles depression.

Lily began to suffer from pathological episodes of depression as soon as she entered her teens. Although seldom lasting long, these episodes were frightening in their intensity. She initially handled them by hiding them. During our court-ship and the first few years of our marriage, she succeeded remarkably well. My obtuseness helped her immensely. I was in love and could not imagine that there was any spot on her. If she vanished suddenly sometimes, I assumed it was her period or she was otherwise feeling ill. It also helped that, by virtue of the intensity of medical training, we were seldom together for long periods. I knew something was a *little* wrong, but nothing significant enough to worry about. Besides, Lily is a superb pretender when she sets her mind to it.

By the fifth year of our marriage, the pretense no longer worked. I was home more. I'd starting training as a psychiatrist. The bloom was off the romance. The episodes were more frequent and severe. They couldn't be hidden any longer.

The old-fashioned word for depression was melancholia—derived from the Greek for "black bile." As a psychiatrist I have seen many people more seriously depressed than Lily—more suicidal, more nonfunctional, more stuck—but I have never seen anyone with such black moods. They were frightening. Terrifying even—both for me and for her. The gloom that pervaded the Welsh mountains on this morning was nothing compared to the atmosphere which pervaded our house or apartment when Lily was depressed. I could literally tell whether she was depressed or not on any given evening as soon as I opened the door. I didn't have to see her or hear her. I could just feel it in the air.

I am a responsibility-holic. Throw some responsibility out on the floor, and I'll be the first to run to pick it up. Laboring under the illusion that it was my responsibility to make Lily happy in life, her depressions were almost daily reminders of my failure. The primary ingredient of the blackness in her was rage. I assumed I was the cause of the rage. Often that was, at least in part, the case, but it would be many years before I could even begin to understand how overdetermined her depressions were. I was a part of the stew, but then so were her parents and her brother, her fierce will, her childhood experiences, her psychological mechanisms, and her biochemistry. Maybe even her bile.

I am not going to go into the causes of Lily's depressions in any greater depth than this. It would be tempting to do so because it is a fascinating story. But it's not mine to tell. It is hers, and I can only hope she'll write it herself some day.

In the sixth year of our marriage, Lily was averaging two depressions a week, each approximately two days in duration. This meant she was depressed more than she wasn't. The lines of depression had started to be etched into her face even when she was feeling well. It was then, just after her thirty-first birthday, that she began intensive therapy with an experienced psychoanalyst. Entering psychotherapy with genuine intent is always an act of considerable courage. By virtue of various factors in her background, Lily's doing so was not merely brave, it was heroic.

The most painful thing for me back then was that she couldn't talk to me about her depressions. Her feelings were too overwhelming for her to talk, too overwhelming for her even to be able to think. Whenever I asked her what she was experiencing, she could only cry helplessly, or snarl "I'm not depressed," or dash out of the room. One of the happiest moments of my life occurred six months after she started therapy when, for the very first time, she was able to tell me with much gentle prodding about the complex of factors that had kicked off her depression fifteen hours earlier.

Because I was being sent overseas in 1967, Lily terminated this particular therapy after two years or three hundred hours. Although she still averaged two depressions a week, they each lasted eight instead of forty-eight hours. Over the course of the next seven years, working on her own, she got their duration down to four hours. She reentered therapy in 1974, and by 1976, with another three hundred sessions with a different therapist under her belt, the duration of her depressions averaged two hours. From 1979 to 1986, Lily spent several hundred more hours on a less intensive basis with a Jungian therapist. Today she still has two depressions a week. Each lasts about five minutes.

Psychotherapy has its detractors, and not without reason. Some psychotherapists are good, some mediocre, some poor, and some even harmful. Sometimes psychotherapy is attempted when the chances of success in the best hands are less than one in a hundred. Occasionally patients enter therapy with spurious motives. I once heard a "biochemical" psychiatrist proclaim, "Psychotherapy never cured anyone." He might have used Lily as a case in point. In 1965 she was suffering two depressions a week. Twenty-eight years later, after three courses of intensive therapy with three different therapists, she still "suffers" two depressions a week. See, no cure. But I can tell you from the bottom of my heart that there's a thousand light-years' difference between living with a spouse who's depressed ninety-six hours a week and one who's depressed ten minutes a week.

I said Lily shortened the duration of her depressions "working on her own." Substantial psychotherapy is successful—as it was in Lily's case—only when it becomes a way of life. Lily continued to examine and interpret herself after she left her first therapist, and does so to this very day. She reentered therapy twice more not because her first therapy had failed but because she thought she needed an extra boost to what she herself was already accomplishing.

When we married, Lily was an extrovert. Today she is an introvert. This is no accident. As psychotherapy becomes a way of life, one becomes a contemplative: a person who focuses at least as much upon her inner world as upon the outer one. Daydreams, night dreams, thoughts and feelings, insights, intuitions, and understandings all assume ever-increasing importance. It is not that external realities—other people, social problems, dirty dishes, and dead-lines—are neglected; it is that more time is spent in comprehending them. Contemplatives become more thoughtful. Yes, they need to with-draw from the world to a certain extent. They need, in comparison to others, much solitude. As a consequence, they may in some sense do less, but that which they do, they do thoughtfully, and in the long run they may end up actually accomplishing more.

I have in my books defined contemplation as a "lifestyle dedicated to maximum awareness." The reason Lily was able to decrease the duration of her depressions from roughly three thousand minutes to five minutes is simply that she grew more aware. *Simply*! She became aware of the strength of her will, her need to control, and her false expectations. She became aware of how best to look at herself when a depression was triggered, and how to quickly discern the steps she needed to take forward to come out the other end, and finally how to rapidly take those steps. Learning this depth of awareness has taken her thirty years. Over these years she has become very wise.

Not long ago, after a lecture I gave in Alabama, a distinguished-looking man came up from the audience. "I'm sure you don't remember me," he said, "but back in 1965 I met you and your wife when my son and I were staying at the same hotel as you in the Yucatán. I have a little gift to give you I thought you might like."

At that point I did remember him, and he was correct about me liking the gift. It was a photo he had taken of Lily and me standing on the porch of the hacienda during the first trip we'd ever taken together outside the United States. Two things about the picture were striking. One was how incredibly young we both looked. The other was Lily's face at the age of thirty. Although she was pretty in her youth and that vacation was a good time for us, I could see the depression in her face. In it there was a distinct hint of dullness and darkness, even harshness. As I write this Lily will soon turn sixty. She doesn't look it, but she hardly looks young anymore either. She is not always happy and very occasionally can be harsh. Most of the time, however, including when caught on camera, her face is now soft and filled with light. I think she may be a saint.

By the time we crossed the border from Wales into England, the gloom had burst like a water-filled balloon. The sky was now merely gray and it was pouring. Thus by virtue of the elements and Lily's changes, we were spared the half-timbered houses of Chester and the town of Chester was spared us.

The principle of tenuousness—that partners need to flexibly adjust to each other's changes—means that patterns of change are interdigitated. Indeed, they may be almost literally woven together in the ongoing tapestry of a marriage.

I mentioned that I am a responsibility-holic with a profound tendency to assume responsibility that is not properly mine. This tendency is not only harmful to me, it may be at least as harmful to others. For instance, feeling it my responsibility to see to it that those I love come to no harm, without even being aware I'm meddling, I often fall into the trap of trying to run their lives for them. To put it mildly, I tend to be overcontrolling. I wish I could say that I have made as much progress in overcoming the problem as Lily has made with her depressions, but I can't. I have, however, come a little ways.

In order to put this in perspective I need to point out that both Lily and I were born into sexist cultures and families where men were expected to be in charge and women, insofar as they wielded power, were expected to do so indirectly from behind the scenes. When we were married, we were only partly aware of this. Those parts of our sexism that were conscious, we gave up quickly, easily, and eagerly. Those that were unconscious, we clung to tenaciously.

Since I felt myself significantly responsible for Lily's happiness or unhappiness, it was hardly difficult for her to go along with that. Indeed, it's amazing that she didn't *totally* blame me for her depressions. But blame me somewhat she did, and when the Women's Liberation Movement came along, it gave an even clearer voice to her complaints. I was not only overcontrolling but specifically a male chauvinist oppressor. And she was right—up to a point.

A critical moment in our marriage occurred about a dozen years ago. For some time Lily had been thinking about seriously going back to school, but she wasn't getting anywhere in doing it. She accused me of causing her to spin her wheels. No, I wasn't overtly preventing her, but somehow I was subtly succeeding in oppressing her.

I was quite calm about it. "When you first began to point out ways in which I was chauvinistically oppressive, you were correct," I told her. "I'm grateful to you for making me more conscious. But for the past decade I've been working quite hard to purify myself of chauvinism or oppressiveness, and I think I've succeeded. I was willing to take the rap to some extent, because I was guilty. But that was then. I'm not guilty any longer. It's become a bum rap, and I'm not going to take it anymore. From here on in, if you're oppressed, as far as I'm concerned, it's because you're oppressing yourself."

Lily lay low for five years after that, contemplating. Then she exploded into the limelight of overt power. She did go back to school—not for literature or psychology but for management! She took over the management of "my" business. She announced she was no longer content to be an adviser to the board of directors of a foundation she helped to start, and that the time had come for her to be an up-front director herself. Shortly after that she took on the development and management of the foundation's national volunteer program. The little Chinese girl who was raised never to take charge of anything beyond the stove and pantry is now a major boss.

I think there is glory in this. You see, it is more than a story of someone learning new skills, more than doing something she couldn't do before, more than transcending her culture and tradition-ally assigned role. I began this story with the issue of real or perceived oppression, and by overtly assuming power Lily has declined the role of victim. But the change, and the risk, is greater than even just that. People have always come to Lily for advice. People have always loved her. Now she is a boss they can also hate for the first time.

After passing by Chester, we hit the great motorways of England, and they sped us along the corridor between the industrial cities of northern England. When we finally exited for the Lake District, our first stop was at one of the quite large shops catering to travelers that are commonly attached to Britain's gas stations. They are well stocked with guidebooks and local maps of fine detail. We didn't know whether the Lake District hosted any megalithic monuments, but if it did we were determined to find them. And not miss any.

Thanks to skipping Chester, we arrived at our destination, the Rothay Manor Hotel in

Ambleside at the eastern end of the District, by mid-afternoon. It was a most pleasant lodging with a fair amount of space by British standards. Since it was to be our home base for three nights, we appreciated the leg room. We also appreciated the fact that the rain had stopped, allowing us a leisurely stroll around the town. It is one of the "nice" gray slate towns, surrounded by green trees, with crooked streets and many bright windowed shops.

We used the extra time the rain had given us for plotting the course of our travels for the next three days. Although a significant part of the fun of travel, such plotting may at times be complex. This was such a time. What did we want to visit inside the Lake District? Was there anything to attract us in the environs outside the District? Were there some things to see on our way leaving the District? By this route? Or by that route?

The lengthiest portion of the plotting process is the map and guidebook research. This is my task because I enjoy it more than Lily. It is my version of doing crossword puzzles. Yet it's not entirely solitary. For instance, on this evening the guidebooks make a great to do about Wordsworth's cottage, which is not far from Ambleside. I sort of like Wordsworth's poetry, as does Lily, but neither of us is passionate about it. As for his cottage, I have zero desire to make a pilgrimage to it. I suspect Lily feels the same, but I'm not certain. So I interrupt her at her crossword puzzle by exclaiming with the utmost enthusiasm, "Oh, honey, we can get to see

Wordsworth's cottage! You remember how he was always writing about the Lake country?"

"Yuck," Lily mutters without even looking up from her puzzle.

Now I am certain. Wordsworth's cottage is not an avenue for further research.

When completed, I present the research results to Lily with my suggested routes, but taking care to list all possible alternate paths with their respective assets and liabilities. Then we begin the real discernment part of the process. I cannot describe how we do it; it is too mystical. It is almost akin to prayer. Occasionally the ultimate results are surprising. On this early evening they led us to a dramatically changed vision for the day ahead.

I have thus far talked much more of Lily's changes than my own, because they have been the more dramatic and perhaps the easier to write about. Still, I need to balance the account.

It is no accident I am an author. The word relates to authority. To publish anything other than the most scholarly of papers, a writer must be willing not only to assume authority but to do so most publicly. Even in the creation of fiction, an author is willy-nilly being up-front with at least some of his feelings, opinions, insights, judgments, and tastes. Unlike Lily, I have never hidden my light under a bushel or felt compelled to stay behind the scenes. In part, this is perhaps the result of being male in a male-dominated society. But only in part. The gift—or curse— of speaking with authority has been particularly pronounced in me from the beginning. At the age of twenty-one, in conjunction with a college psychology course, I was involved in something resembling a mild encounter group. During it an older, male fellow student commented, "I don't know whether this is a criticism or a compliment, but whenever you open your mouth, Scotty, it comes across to me as the voice of God."

I also already had high blood pressure.

Nine years later, a year after Lily did, I did, too, entered psychoanalysis—not because of depression, as in her case, but because of my intense anxiety. I was particularly anxious in relation to certain male authority figures. A part of the problem centered around my feelings toward my father, a famous judge and litigation lawyer who himself used to speak with great authority, albeit in a manner generally different from my own. Another part centered around my confusion over the sanity of my inner voices and opinions. When I was out of step with the leaders of society, including my direct supervisors, as was frequently the case, was this because I was a genuine prophet or simply a compulsive rebel? Was my authority godly or neurotic? I was extremely uneasy.

Had you asked me at the time whether I was a dependent sort of person, I would have answered, "Scott Peck dependent? Hell, no, he doesn't have a dependent bone in his body!" Indeed, I was one of those men so independent I couldn't even ask for directions. "You do it, hon," I'd blithely instruct Lily whenever we pulled into a gas station. Nonetheless, I considered myself mature and, after two years of psychiatry residency training, far too sophisticated to fall into the standard traps that psychotherapy patients stumble upon—like transference where they unconsciously get their analyst mixed up with their parents.

Knowing I would be reassigned in a year's time, at the outset I made a contract to see my analyst three times a week for a twelve-month period. After ten months my anxiety had gradually but dramatically subsided. I began a session by speaking of this. "I'm incredibly grateful to you for how much better I'm feeling," I told Dr. Akeley. "I know I made a contract to see you for a year, and I certainly wouldn't break it without your permission. But the past couple of days I've been thinking that maybe I've had all the therapy I need. I wonder if it isn't time to quit. Continuing to see you for the next two months feels like it might just be going through the motions. It seems stiff and formal at this point, given all the improvement I've made—thanks to you."

"Perhaps you feel like terminating treatment because you're angry at me for something," Dr. Akeley suggested. It was one of the rare times he spoke.

"To the contrary," I protested. "I've been having these thoughts only because you've helped me so much. I'm not angry at you at all. What I feel toward you, as I said, is nothing but profound gratitude."

"I wonder if something didn't happen during our last session to make you angry," Dr. Akeley persisted.

"No, of course not," I said firmly. "How could

I be angry when you've helped me? How could I feel anything but grateful? In fact, I love you."

"I still think you might be angry over something that happened in our last session," the man continued as if he hadn't heard me.

By now I was actually beginning to feel annoyed. "I'm not angry about anything that happened our last session," I proclaimed. "In fact, nothing happened at all last session. I spent the entirety of it talking about the paper I was writing on Buddhism. In fact, it was really a wasted session. But that was what was on my mind. I tried to shortcut it by asking you if you knew anything about Buddhism and you said you didn't. So I had to go off on this hour-long intellectual dissertation. Come to think of it, it's difficult to believe you didn't know anything about it. Anyone who's spent two years at the Jungian Institute in Zurich ought to know at least a little something about Buddhism. In fact, I bet you did know something about it, but you were just letting on that you didn't. That you were withholding yourself from me." My voice had begun to rise. "Withholding yourself from me the way my father used to do. The way he still does. You were behaving just like him. You're just like my father. You . . ."

Suddenly I heard myself.

The last two months of Dr. Akeley's and my work together were pregnant with insight. Through his help I came to realize that I did have some dependent bones in my body and that was okay. That, as a child, I had desperately wanted to depend upon my father, because he was such a charming and, in his way, loving man. But he was also such a dominating, overcontrolling man that I had come to realize he would steamroll my soul, that emotional dependence upon him would represent psychic suicide. Early on I had said to myself, "So who needs him? Who needs anybody?" And, without even being conscious of it, I became Mr. Self-Reliant with high blood pressure.

I was also unconsciously looking for older men to be father figures to me. Whenever these men—often supervisors—proved not to be the good father I was seeking, I'd become furious at them for not living up to my expectations. Thus my authority problem where I never fully understood my fury because those expectations were unconscious. Once they became conscious, however, I was able to deal with them realistically, getting from this man what I could and being able to forgive him for what I couldn't. I also became better able to discern when I was being neurotically out of step and when my authority was truly righteous.

I remain until this day grateful to my analyst for his self-discipline, gentleness, and discernment. I was a "good" patient but not an easy one. In any case, without that therapy there is no way I could even have functioned at all, much less adequately, either as an executive or a subordinate—roles I was to play (and learn from) many times in the ensuing years. And my blood pressure came down to normal.

Still, a neurosis is not like a little pebble one

kicks out of the path in front of him. As with Lily's depressions, it is more like a boulder one keeps chipping away at for a lifetime. I no longer have the slightest difficulty asking for directions. I remain until this day too slow to ask for help when I need it, however, and a bit reluctant to accept it when it's gratuitously offered. But I'm working on the problem. . . .

Until now I have made it sound as if depression has solely been Lily's struggle and never an affliction of my own. That is not true. I have suffered a significant depression of a sort, but it bore little resemblance to Lily's. Among other differences, she actively conquered hers through heroic work while I emerged from mine largely through the passivity of waiting.

From 1970 to 1972, while working at the U.S. Army Surgeon General's Office in Washington, I occasionally had to travel. I hated it. Resigning from the army in November 1972, we moved to the most rural part of Connecticut for me to become a country psychiatrist. We bought a rambling two-hundred-year-old colonial sheltered by ancient maples. For the next eight years, whenever I was outside, I'd exclaim to myself (or was it to God?), "It is so beautiful here. I can never leave this place."

In 1981, I began to be invited to lecture around the nation, and I found that I could leave the place. It was not a matter of substantial lecture fees or the excitement of the podium or pulpit. The reality was simply that the beauty of nature was somehow no longer essential to my soul. It was no longer the turn-on it had once been.

Within a year, great meals had also ceased to be a turn-on. I'd still rather have one than a Big Mac, but it was no longer important. In short order, great art similarly became unimportant. I appreciated it, but I didn't *covet* it anymore. By 1984, my increasing fame had shifted from being an excitement to a burden. It felt like a trap. And soon even beautiful women stopped looking so glamorous. Along about this time I began to feel depressed. It's hard to put one foot in front of another when nothing turns you on anymore.

In 1985, I went to see not a psychiatrist but a nun who had been my spiritual director for eight years. I recounted the changes inside myself. "If someone else came to me with the same tale," I told her, "I'd think it was depression. And I *am* depressed. I'm not suicidal, but I think about death a lot, hoping it will come early for me. I sigh the day long and wish I could sleep all the time. Yes, I'm depressed, but somehow that's not quite it. I haven't a clue what it is, but it's something more than depression. Or less."

"We have a name for your condition, you know," she said.

"Oh?"

"Yes, it's called the Dark Night of the Senses. It was first described in the sixteenth century by St. John of the Cross." She went on to say more. There was no question about the accuracy of the diagnosis.

"You've sure got me pegged," I responded with a grin of hope. "Now what do I do about it."

"Nothing."

"Nothing?"

"Yes, nothing," she answered emphatically. "I can't tell you anything to do. I can only warn you what not to do. That is to try to go back, which some people do by seeking after ever more beautiful women or greater art."

That made sense to me. "What do I do to go forward?" I asked.

"Nothing. Just wait."

"Wait? How long?"

"I have no idea," she replied. "Eventually, you'll come out the other side. It won't be the same as it was. It will feel better than it is now. But not as it was. It will be different, but I can't tell you how long it will take."

It took another year and a half, and it got worse before it got better. In the autumn of 1986 it felt like I was dying. Not physically dying—that I would have welcomed. It felt more like being in the Garden on the eve of my crucifixion, except that's an exaggeration. I wasn't sweating blood. I was, however, frightened and tearful.

And then around Christmas, in my fifty-first year, it ended almost as suddenly, and every bit as mysteriously, as it had begun.

This has been an oversimplification. More was involved than the Dark Night of the Senses. There were distinct elements of a midlife crisis. I was moving toward a still deeper commitment in my marriage. I became ready to abandon my career, if necessary, and I even took up the violin to prove the point. But I cannot, in truth, completely explain why my depression lifted. What I can say is that my spiritual director had

118

been absolutely correct. When it lifted, it was not like it was before. Before my joy had been the product of external events: a new romance, a new book, a great review, a dramatic stride forward by the foundation with which we worked, an accomplishment of a child. Now my joy, while hardly constant, was purely internal and unrelated to circumstances. Success didn't seem to do much to lift me up, and failure didn't bring me down. Some days, when my life seemed to be going badly and people asked, "How are you doing, Scotty?" I'd answer, "Great, although I've got no idea why."

The substantial separation of my joy from my senses has not been my only change in recent years. I have become less opinionated or else my opinions have become more convoluted. As I reread *The Road Less Traveled* almost twenty years after I wrote it, I am still struck by the truth that was given me; I am also struck by a kind of glib quality to its certainty. I am not as certain about many things as I used to be, and I am a bit less quick to judge. Perhaps my depression made me less sure of the simplicity of life and more sympathetic to some of the foibles of others. I don't know. There are other reasons for these subtle changes that will be recounted. But if Lily were to sum up the changes themselves, she would probably say that I've become more "gentled."

Settled in Ambleside on this evening, we are aware that this has been a day without stones. We would already be feeling the pains of withdrawal were it not for the fact that our map and guidebook research has made it clear that while there may not be any megaliths in the mountains of the Lake District, there are definitely some on the district's circumference. Our habit will be fed. Meanwhile, we digest those we have seen and begin to draw some morals from them—at least some morals for the process of seeking them.

Thus far we have seen six monuments. Two were in our guidebooks but not on our maps. One of those had a road marker and one didn't. Two more were on our maps but not in our guidebooks. Again, one had a road marker and one didn't. And then there were two that were neither on our maps nor in our books. Of the six, three had informational plaques and three didn't. At one site the information was contradictory. So what are the morals to be drawn from this confusion?

Confusion is the first moral. The search for stones is confusing. It is not certain that what is in the guidebook will be on the map or, we would learn, that what is on the map will be there at all. I said that I am not as certain about many things as I used to be. Obviously, I have become more comfortable with uncertainty and confusion. Indeed, I have even come to *enjoy* a modicum of uncertainty and healthy confusion. It seems quite possible to me that even if I had had the time and money, twenty years ago, back then I was not yet emotionally suited for the search. If a designated stone wasn't where it was supposed to be or what they said it was, well, damnit, I wasn't going to waste my time on a bunch of inefficient ambiguity! Perhaps stones are an addiction of maturity. Then again, maybe senility.

So this confusion will continue, and it brings us to a second moral: To be maximally successful the search process should be multifaceted. Maps alone are not enough. Guidebooks are not enough. You need to use both maps and guidebooks. And then to stay on the lookout even when there's nothing that either of them point to. Finally, if you come across a sign offering a historical explanation for a site, don't trust it completely. Keep your wits about you. Remember, in the case of great stones, we are dealing with *prehistory*.

I wonder: Is it an accident that these same rules also apply to the search for God? Inerrantist maps are useful, but not enough. The guidebooks of the mystics are not enough. Use them both, and when you're not using them, be alert for the unpredicted presence of God unexpectedly intruding upon your everyday life. By all means study, but don't believe everything you read. Think for yourself.

But back to stones and their confusion. It will be recalled that workmen were cutting away the bracken from the hut circles at South Stack. There are three types of ancient monuments: unexcavated, excavated, and restored. Those hut circles were obviously excavated or in the process of being so. Otherwise they would have been invisible. Were they restored? Certainly not to their original condition. Perhaps a stone had been replaced here and there; I don't know. It is possible to answer such questions if one seriously researches each site. But we are not serious researchers, and in the days ahead, as in the days past, we moved on too quickly to know. Except when the answer is obvious, issues of restoration of megalithic monuments will be left unearthed and the question itself unexcavated.

Is there another possible moral? We saw three dolmens in a row. Then two pairs of standing stones. Was this an accident or does there tend to be a pattern to the megaliths? The question is, for the moment, left hanging as darkness begins to descend.

As are other questions. Lily's and my changes that I've described have been for the better. Have I been holding back on ways, other than physically, that we've changed for the worse? I don't believe so. I believe we have both matured in the best sense of the word. But the sad reality is that not all people mature emotionally as life goes on. Some stay just the same. And some seem to actually deteriorate, changing for the worse, becoming ever more depressed or rigid and over-controlling or devious and manipulative with the years. There is no doubt in my mind that one of the major reasons—perhaps *the* major reason— our marriage has survived is that we have both grown through it and along with it.

We've been lucky. What would it be like to live with someone who's not growing, not changing for the better? I don't know. With someone who's changing for the worse? Sometimes when our changes have not been coming as quickly as we would have liked, both Lily and I have in our hearts questioned our vow to hang in together "in sickness and in health." The issue of physical sickness has never been an issue. But does sickness include unremitting spiritual stagnation or irreversible emotional deterioration? What about the marriage vows then? Had we both not grown, I suspect we would have checked out one way or another. But who can say what might have happened? We can only say that we're grateful for what has been. We also wonder what further emotional changes might lie ahead. Yet it's no longer much of a worry. The pattern of growth seems to have been set, and the omens look good.

CHAPTER VI

RELIGION
FRIDAY, JUNE 5

Having just ensconced ourselves in the Lake District, what we immediately did on this morning was to leave it. This might seem odd. Our research, however, suggested that the District could be adequately covered on the morrow, and our prayerful discernment of the night before had called us to *change*, to unexpectedly go east—east, away from the Cumbrian mountains and into the Pennines; east, above all, to the town of Sedbergh.

Sedbergh is sometimes referred to as the birthplace of the Quakers. About four miles outside the town is a hill (one of the Pennines) called

Firbank Fell. There, at the age of twenty-eight, an itinerant preacher, George Fox, gave a great sermon in 1652 on a fair-day to a thousand "Seekers." It was over three hours long. Reputedly, he stood on a rock on top of the fell talking to the multitude seated on the grass below. Our guidebook told us there was a plaque on that rock commemorating the event, and it was indeed an event. Many of the Seekers concluded that day that they had found what they were looking for. They, together with Fox, became the first Quakers. Ever since, the Quakers have had a beneficial effect throughout the world that cannot be accounted for merely in terms of their relatively small numbers.

The Pennines we crossed to reach Sedbergh are larger than ordinary hills yet gentler than mountains: massive rolls of windswept moorland. We sensed that they were very old. Bleak though they were, there was also a softness to them— perhaps the softness that sometimes can come with great age.

On our way to Firbank Fell, the other side of Sedbergh, we passed a mile-long caravan of gypsies parked on the edge of the road. Some of their vehicles were pickup trucks. Most were worn, little compact trailers. But intermingled among them was a substantial number of traditional gypsy wagons: quaint and tidy wooden barrels on wheels, brightly painted fore and aft. Small groups of men were gathered here and there in discussion. They didn't look particularly swarthy, and they certainly didn't look like they stole children.

While we got to see gypsies and probably got to see Firbank Fell—since we wandered little lanes in all directions around the area for over an hour—we never did succeed in finding the plaque we were seeking. But no matter. The ambience and just being there was more important. For what we were really seeking was not a plaque but one of our deepest spiritual roots.

I told earlier how between the Age of Faith and the Age of Reason there was a lengthy period of turmoil in Western civilization. That turmoil was at its height all over Europe throughout the seventeenth century. But perhaps its single greatest place and moment was England in 1652, and its sweetest symbol may be Firbank Fell.

The greatest blow to the Age of Faith had occurred over a hundred years before, in 1517, when a Catholic monk, Martin Luther, nailed ninety-five theses or grievances on the door of the Cathedral of Wittenberg in Germany. They protested multiple abuses within the Church and argued for reform, thereby beginning a movement in human history called the Reformation.

Many of the abuses Luther attacked were fund-raising practices, such as the selling of indulgences and the sacraments. Eventually, the Catholic church was to clean up its act in this regard. But what it has been unable to stomach even to this very day was Luther's protesting the role of priest as intermediary between God and ordinary human beings. He held that all humans can have—and should have—a direct line to God. In other, over-simplified terms, we can think for ourselves. Those who agreed with this protest came to be called Protestants, and the reformation specifically the Protestant Reformation.

In England, a lesser blow to the Age of Faith soon followed. King Henry VIII wished to divorce his first wife, Catherine of Aragon, to marry Anne Boleyn. Catherine, to whom he had been married by arrangement, had had many miscarriages and produced only one living girl child. Henry was convinced that he needed a male heir and that the flirtatious Anne would provide it. He was to be proven wrong on both counts. In any case, he was a good Catholic and for over three years steadfastly petitioned Pope Clement VII for an annulment. More for political than moral or religious reasons, Clement persistently refused. Finally and desperately, with Anne pregnant, in 1533, Henry got what he wanted after declaring himself rather than the pope to be head of the church in England. Thus, overnight, the Anglican church was born.

To this day the Anglican and Roman Catholic churches share the same theology; their only essential difference is the issue of authority. Initiated for purely sexual and political reasons, it remains somewhat questionable whether the Anglican church is a Protestant one—and even whether its genesis should be considered a part of the Reformation at all.

Back to the *real* Protestant Reformation based on the belief each individual can have a direct relationship with God. Allow such individualism, encouraging people to think for themselves, and you open a floodgate. In short order there was not one Protestant denomination, the Lutherans, but many. The largest in Great Britain came to be the Presbyterians.

Thinking for themselves, there were a number who felt that the Lutherans and Presbyterians did not go far enough, that the Reformation needed to be more radical and the church further purified. In their yearning for ecclesiastical purity, they became known as the Puritans. We tend to think of the Puritans as stodgy conservatives. They were, in fact, the left-wing radicals of their day.

This is important to understand because the Quakers sprung from Puritan soil. It was English Puritans who had settled in Massachusetts in 1620. George Fox was born a mere four years later, in 1624, not into a Puritan family but into Puritan times. A Puritan he was to become and, as such, one of the most effective social and ecclesiastical radicals in history.

There are principles of group behavior that can be extended to very large groups, even nations. In their most primitive form, groups are what we call pseudocommunities. Everyone seems to believe the same thing. Conformity is the order of the day. Individual differences are hidden and conflict is avoided. So it was in England during the Age of Faith. Everyone was Roman Catholic or seemed to be. It was a time of religious uniformity.

Whenever the individual differences of the members are encouraged (as they were by the Reformation) a group evolves—or degenerates, depending upon your point of view—into a stage called "chaos." While the underlying premise of pseudocommunity is the pretense that there are no differences, once they have surfaced, the underlying premise of chaos is that differences should be obliterated. If the differences are religious, then conversion is the means of obliteration. Each group member believes he has the one and only true faith, and everyone is trying to convert everyone else. It is not a civil phase. It is noisy, antagonistic, and confusing. It is chaotic.

The turmoil of seventeenth-century England was a time of such chaos. The Roman Catholics believed they had the one true faith and tried to convert everyone back to Catholicism. The Anglicans wanted every English person to be Anglican. The Presbyterians thought everybody ought to be Presbyterian. The Puritans were no different, trying to bring about a Puritan world. And they all thought they could somehow make it happen by decree. It was not a period of religious toleration.

Nor was it yet a time of much separation between church and state. Consequently, the religious chaos of the day was mirrored by political chaos. King James I (1603–25) and Anglican, was distinctly anti-Catholic and anti-Puritan. Charles I (1625–49), while titularly Anglican, was distinctly pro-Catholic and antipathetic to all Protestants. Because of his anti-Protestantism, Charles was beheaded, and from 1649 to 1659 England was primarily governed by a commoner, Oliver Cromwell, and his son Richard, Puritans who strove for religious toleration of a sort. The royalty was reestablished with Charles II (1660–85), another Anglican who returned to policies in favor of Catholics and antagonistic to Protestants. James II (1685–88) was an open Catholic who attempted to destroy the Anglican church. For his trouble he was deposed by Parliament in favor of a foreigner, William of Orange (1689–1702), to protect British Protestantism. Confusing? If you sometimes had troubled back in school, as I did, with English history, don't feel bad.

Now to George Fox, citizen of this time of turmoil, whose life spanned all these reigns. Son of a lower-middle-class family, he was intelligent but not formally well educated. He was neither a good writer—there is considerable reason to believe he had a form of dyslexia—nor was he eloquent in the ordinary sense of the word. In his early teens, he was apprenticed to a wool merchant. Evidence suggests he was good apprentice, clever and honest, and he seemed to be headed for a successful career in business. But suddenly, at the age of nineteen, for no discernible reason, he "dropped out." The next three years he roamed the British midlands, mostly sleeping by hedges in the fields, alone and doing nothing. Nothing except thinking, that is. It is mysterious how he was financially supported, but then that would remain mysterious for the remaining fifty years of his life.

At age twenty-two, his behavior changed. He began to wander out of the fields and into the towns and churches to debate with clergy or others learned in religion—men he called "professors." People were impressed by his surprising knowledge of the Bible but generally regarded him as a noisy nuisance. He interrupted church services. He proclaimed that the light of Christ was in each and every human being. Because of this he seemed to have no respect for authority or class distinction and the rigid customs then associated with such distinctions. He refused to take off his hat in the presence of his "betters." He insisted upon referring to everyone as "thee" or "thou" when these pronouns were customarily reserved solely for children and lovers. He wouldn't pay the mandatory tithe to the Anglican church. Nor would he take oaths as required by government officials. He was imprisoned twice during this period and beaten an unknown number of other times.

On a brilliant early summer afternoon in 1652, he climbed to the top of one of the southern Pennines, Pendle Hill, and there received a vision that he was to preach to the multitudes. In obedience he moved north to Sedbergh, known to be the center of the Seekers, women and men seeking a satisfactory spiritual path in the religious confusion of the times. At Firbank Fell, his vision was soon fulfilled. For the first time, and ever thereafter, George Fox had converts and friends—very good friends. Indeed, the organization he founded came to be known as the Religious Society of Friends.

But he never stopped moving. For the next thirty-nine years he traveled incessantly, preaching or visiting and encouraging other Friends, first throughout England and later in the American colonies and Holland as well. He is credited with conducting a successful exorcism and two miraculous physical healings during his travels. He was imprisoned at least six more times, once under the most inhumane conditions and once for more than two years. He seemed to have had absolutely no fear of prison or beating or illness or hardship or death—no fear whatsoever for his safety. Although his "church" soon had over forty thousand dedicated members, he steadfastly refused to allow it to be called a church or himself to be in charge of it. He came to be deeply concerned with organization, but only for organization without hierarchy. At the age of forty-five he married a fifty-five-year-old devoted wealthy widow and Friend. She had a beautiful house, Swarthmore Hall, but now they were both too busy traveling to enjoy it for long or even often to be together. In January 1691, two days after preaching on a trip to London, he peacefully died at age sixty-nine. From its description, the ultimate cause of his death would simply seem to be that he was totally worn out.

Many have tried to explain George Fox without much success. The explanation of his historical context is quite sensible, but that doesn't explain the man. Why did he drop out of a successful career? How was he supported financially? Why was he so oblivious to comfort and safety? Not well read except for the Bible, possessing neither literary nor oratorical skills, how did he manage to inspire thousands of others to not only believe his message but also to match his own bravery? A number of his contemporaries answered this last question: It was his integrity, an integrity that left them almost breathless. But from where did such extraordinary integrity come? How did he manage never to succumb to bitterness? To the temptations of fame? Of power? How did he stay so balanced?

Some have suggested that he was mad, mentally ill, even though mental illness is usually characterized by a lack of integrity or balance of one sort or another. There is a condition, however, that has been called "divine madness." Here I believe we are on the mark. It doesn't sit well in this Age of Reason, but the only explanation I can offer for George Fox is that he was a saint—a person who had inexplicably but heavily been touched by the direct hand of God.

Although we failed to find the plaque on Firbank Fell, we did manage successfully to seek out the Briggs Flat meeting house just the other side of Sedbergh. It is the second oldest Quaker meeting house in Great Britain, built in 1675, when the new Quakers were being imprisoned in droves for precisely such crimes as constructing meeting houses or meeting at all—as well as for imitating George Fox by their "theeing" and "thouing" and their refusal to tithe to the Church of England, bow to magistrates, doff their hats or take oaths. It is the smallest of the many meeting houses I have seen. Otherwise it is typical with its quadrilateral "facing benches" on the ground floor and around the tiny balcony. Unlike most churches, this distinctive Quaker architecture allows—encourages—everyone to look at each other. Tastes differ, but I find many of these plain meeting houses strangely beautiful in their simplicity. The one at Briggs Flat is additionally beautiful by virtue of an equally simple and sweet tiny English garden that surrounds it. Also, across a narrow dirt road, there sits another compact little seventeenth-century building. This was not a meeting house but a "living house." Behind it, hidden in the shade, is an ancient, almost miniature graveyard that contains the remains of several dozen of those courageous first Friends. The whole spot was another sort of holy place for both of us.

It had not originally been intended as a holy place. Among his other fundamental ideas, George Fox so loved God and Christ that he was certain they didn't reside in a building. From the beginning he referred to ordinary churches as "steeple houses," and while in their unsteepled meeting houses the early Quakers developed a unique type of internal design, they regarded these buildings as utilitarian places and never as holy places.

It is unclear how they came to be called Quakers. One tradition holds that they shook or trembled, so great was their religious passion. The other is that their passionate integrity caused the magistrates they defied to tremble and quake in *their* boots. No matter, the early Friends were an earthquake on the seventeenth-century religious scene. And later Friends, from time to time, have continued to cause social earthquakes ever since, as they did by leading the fight to abolish slavery for almost a hundred years. The mainline

Protestant denominations have been referred to as the legitimate children of the Reformation, and the Religious Society of Friends as its love-child.

But what about Lily's and my passion? We are nondenominational Christians. Hence we are not Quakers any more than we are Catholics or Methodists. What then led us almost precipitously to Sedbergh so far out of the Lake District? Why not to some Presbyterian or Anglican shrine? Why not down to Liverpool, birthplace of the Beatles?

The most consuming passion of our lives over the past decade—yes, yet another shared passion—has been "community." Working with hundreds of others over this period we have devoted a third of our time and a third of our savings to the Foundation for Community Encouragement (FCE). The purpose of this foundation is to teach the principles of community, by which we mean healthy communication within and between groups. These principles have recently become so specific that they can be considered to constitute a technology—a technology of people rather than things. It is a technology that transcends denominations, transcends religions, and even transcends culture. We see the salvation of the world as depending on the degree that the human race is going to be willing to learn this technology. The outcome is quite up for grabs. It is not easy learning.

The various parts of this potentially saving technology have evolved from many sources: Christian monasticism, the Oxford movement, AA and the Twelve-Step programs, the sensitivity group movement, the Tavistock model, and management consulting practices. But the deepest and greatest source has been the Quakers.

Remember, the first major teaching of George Fox was that the "light of Christ" resides within every human being. Their faith in this shared divinity led the Quakers to the radical egalitarianism that caused them so much persecution. It is perhaps their only doctrine that is crucial, and why another one of their early names was "the Children of Light." Although the Quakers remain essentially Christian, gradually the doctrine came simply to be called "the inner light."

The Quakers place a greater emphasis upon practice than doctrine—another virtue, I believe—and gradually their crucial doctrine of the inner light evolved into a practice that is most odd in our frenetic, nominally Christian culture: the silent meeting. At such a meeting they will gather together for an hour-long "service," and absolutely nothing may happen. There is no minister, no sermon, no psalms, no songs; only silence. The silence may be broken by anyone present who feels "moved" by his or her inner light to speak on any subject. Often such spontaneous speeches are very brief. Unfortunately, they are sometimes quite long. But when no one speaks, after an hour of total silence together, the congregation may feel more satisfied than if they had had an "active" meeting. No one's inner light may have shown forth in words, but everyone has had an hour to quietly listen to her or his own.

The Quakers have also done much to promote education, and I had the opportunity to spend my last two years of high school at Friends Seminary in New York City. It was there I had my first taste of community. And my first experience of silent meetings. In fact, it was out of the silence of one of those meetings, at the age of seventeen, that I myself first began to preach—that I felt my own inner light moving me to say things wiser than I knew I had in me to say.

This Quaker experience came to be directly translated into the technology of community. FCE teaches organizations to begin their business meetings in silence. At community building workshops for the public we start with a list of instructions. The final one goes: "Community has to do with communication. Among the innumerable sins of communication, one of the greatest is to speak when you are not moved. We all know people who do this—or else somehow seem to be continually 'moved,' thereby monopolizing the airtime. Another great sin is to fail to speak when you are moved, which is a form of disobedience. We are now going to go into three minutes of silence. Then, out of silence, you will begin to speak as you are so moved."

In one sense, George Fox and the early Quakers were no different from other religious folk of their day; they, too, believed they had the one and only true faith. Theirs was an evangelistic vision of a world where all would be Friends. But as they were sucked into the Age of Reason, they realized it was not to be, and in the eighteenth century the Quakers became leading advocates of religious toleration and peacemaking. Many since have been pacifists, but hardly all.

The greatest contribution of the Friends to peacemaking, I believe, has not been pacifism but their experience in the fine art of consensual decision-making. I have labeled the technology of community as saving precisely because it is a technology of peacemaking, of reconciliation. A major ingredient of this technology is the practice of consensus, and I must credit George Fox as its major originator.

Achieving genuine consensus often requires a great deal of time. Recently, ten women and men from across the United States convened at their own expense for a meeting of FCE's volunteer management group. Just one of many of the volunteer activities this group manages is the conduct of a large annual public conference. The 1993 conference had originally been scheduled to be in Denver, Colorado, but several in the group now questioned the integrity of holding it there. The principles of community are antidiscriminatory. One of them is inclusivity wherever possible. The preceding autumn Colorado had passed an amendment discriminatory to homosexuals. Homosexuals across the nation had responded by asking organizations to boycott Colorado as a place for their conferences. Would it not be promoting exclusivity to hold the conference in Denver as planned? On the other hand, couldn't the process of boycotting itself be interpreted as a practice of exclusion? The short-term economic consequences of the decision were negligible. Nonetheless, many seemingly more important agenda items were dropped by this group of busy executives to discuss the integrity of the issue in total depth. Individuals wavered this way and that. Finally, after three and a half hours, consensus was reached to hold the conference in Denver as planned. The group was extremely pleased not only by its decision but also by the way it had spent its time.

This is strange organizational behavior in the world's terms. But then the world may well be dying, which is why in teaching the principles of community we are attempting to teach groups how to be organizations that are "in the world but not of the world." But how? Even if it can be demonstrated to be most cost-effective in the long run—and I believe it can be—how can you possibly teach worldly people to take the time, when appropriate, for such ethical discernment through consensual decision-making?

George Fox had the key. In fact, he seemed to have it by the age of twenty. In writing about how he had dropped out at nineteen to roam the countryside seeking answers, and later while arguing with "professors," he described himself as "waiting upon the Lord" (a phrase he perhaps borrowed from Isaiah 40:31). I suspect he taught early Quakers how to do likewise. And that it was out of this teaching that the Friends' practice of consensual decision-making arose. Such decision-making is not hasty. It can be done only by men and women who have learned how to wait.

This is why the executives of FCE's volunteer management group felt so pleased with their consensus. They knew that they had succeeded in waiting on the Lord. And it reflects an even broader reason we are so indebted to George Fox. A major part of the technology of community is the technology of waiting. In teaching consensus we are teaching people and organizations how to wait—how to not speak until moved, how to wait for the voice of their inner light, and ultimately how to wait on the Lord.

That was the why of our spontaneous pilgrimage to Sedbergh.

Still, all things are overdetermined, and it so happens that our guidebook designated three megalithic sites twenty miles to the northwest. Off we went from the Briggs Flat meeting house along more one-way lanes again in search of stones. Our first quarry was the Gamelands stone circle just before the village of Orton. Ending up in the village we figured we'd overshot the mark, turned around, and drove back a mile to where there was a dirt track heading through the fields toward a gentle hilltop in the distance. It had dangerously deep mud holes. There was no sign. But there was also no other turn-off in the vicinity. Hoping our rented car would survive the path, we took it, peering to the right and left. Nothing was to be seen except the high stone walls so characteristic of Scotland and northern England. A thousand yards up the hill the track came to a dead end. It had clearly been the proverbial wild-goose chase.

Disappointed, we turned around. But then, thanks to the elevation and her sharp eyes, Lily was able to spot the otherwise hidden site behind the walls in the corner of an ordinary field. Down we went. There was a little gate in the wall. We opened it and trudged through wet clover to rejoice in the find: not standing stones but thirty or so smoothly rounded, low-lying boulders forming a perfect circle approximately forty yards in diameter. We danced in celebration and sopping shoes.

The site itself, buried in the countryside, was reason enough for celebration. Again, however, all things are overdetermined. We also celebrated because it truly was a find. Like the dolmen at Long House Farm, we really had to seek it, look for it, and work for it. And then there was a bit of just plain luck; it was so easy to overlook. Only from that small dead-end spot was it visible. And in retrospect we continue to rejoice. We knew already in the days to come we would be seeing other stone circles. What we didn't know, however, was that we had discovered the one and only *low-stone* circle of the trip.

Soon we sought out another site, the Crosby Lodge Settlement. This time we easily found a larger lane with a clear sign pointing to Crosby Lodge. Ah, this would be simple! The "lodge" turned out to be a huge, gloomy stone farm compound at the end of the lane, not unlike Long House Farm only even more foreboding. It appeared deserted. Something more than civility and respect for privacy kept us from driving into the compound or knocking on a door in inquiry. Parking outside, Lily unexpectedly complained of fatigue and decided to wait in the car while I prowled the perimeter. I walked down a path to one side of the compound to where I had a good view of some of the farm's fields. No large stones or anything else to suggest a ruin could be seen; only fields. I returned to the car. "I couldn't see anything," I said. "Maybe we should see if we can rouse someone in the lodge."

Lily looked strange. She pointed out the side window. "What's that?" she asked.

"What's what?"

"*That*! Whatever it is that's on the fence."

About ten feet to the side of the car was a barbed-wire fence. When I first looked I wondered why she was pointing at it. Then I began to suddenly feel queasy. Every three inches a small something was dangling from the top strand. My initial instinct was that they might be some kind of flags placed there for God knows what reason. But there was a slight breeze, and there was no movement in them. My next instinct was that they might be sleeping bats, hanging upside down—a flock of them that had somehow chosen that spot for a daylong nap. I moved in cautiously lest I awaken them. Three feet away the horror began to dawn on me. Two feet and the reality was unmistakable. Each little "thing" hanging down was a dead mole or shrew, each embedded by its upper jaw from the top spike of every barb for thirty feet along the fence. There were about a hundred of them in a row. Each body was moderately decomposed and withered. My guess was that they had been dead for perhaps a week. All killed at the same time. How? Impaled there at the same time. Why?

We drove away. It is the only time in my life I

141

have avoided trying to answer my own questions. Although a Christian, as a scientist and a child of the Age of Reason, I had never before until this day been tempted to cross myself.

A half-mile down the paved road there was a much friendlier-looking farm and a farmer forking manure into a spreader. We stopped. "We're looking for a prehistoric monument that's supposed to be quite close to here," I explained. "Do you know where it might be?"

"No," he replied, "I don't know of any ruins around here."

"I have no idea of what kind of a monument it might be," I said, "but it's called the Crosby Lodge Settlement."

"Oh," he answered, pointing, "there's a farm just over there called Crosby Lodge. What I'd suggest is that you drive in there and ask them."

We did not take his suggestion. There are some mysteries, I believe, that should not be explored by an unarmed couple alone. And some stones perhaps best left unturned.

So we skipped to our third and last megalithic quarry of the day: the Standing Stones of Shap. We found the village of Shap quite handily but no markers in its environs. We stopped for directions at a little bakery in the village center, paying 88 pence for a couple of meat pies to justify our inquiry. The most knowledgeable of its three attendants (with a degree of disinterest in their own esoteric megaliths we were now coming to expect from most "locals") told us, "Well, if ye turn right at the fire station over there, and then immediately left at the surgery, ye'll come to the gate of a field. If ye climb up the field and over the hill, on the other side ye'll find a stone. Or so I'm told. I've never seen it meself.''

Her directions were splendid, but there were two problems. One was that the gate in question was wired shut, obviously for posterity. Being in late middle age, our gate-climbing skills are no longer what they used to be. The other problem was that, once we did get into the field, the large herd of neanderthalic North Yorkshire sheep therein all seemed to be deep in heat—for me. But we made it through more wet clover and manure over the brink of the field and, sure enough, in a plowed plot several high stone walls farther on there stood a single, massive, squarish stone—crowned not at its six-foot top but at its base with a halo of unplowed grass sparkling green against the brown earth in the late afternoon sun. While left in doubt by what was meant in our guidebook by the "Standing Stones of Shap" in the plural, it alone was sufficiently satisfying for us to depart for our hotel and temporary home in the Lake District after another day of high adventure.

In the ordinary sense of the word, Lily and I are not gamblers. Two of our best friends, a well-to-do couple in their forties, go off for long weekends in Las Vegas twice a year. Much as we love them, we cannot empathize with their behavior. We simply do not understand why anyone would want to play craps or blackjack for more than an hour or two, much less travel to such a ghastly and faraway place to do so. But, as already mentioned, upon occasion we do make a modest wager with each other. Some of these are ritual occasions. Annually, for instance, we have a dollar riding on just when the large lake in front of our house in northwestern Connecticut will freeze over and another one on when it will melt. Although the stakes are small, there are elaborate arguments about parameters: Is the lake truly frozen when there is still a thermal hole in its middle? Has it actually thawed when a thin rim of ice remains on a cold early spring morning? Most of our wagers, however, are spur of the moment affairs. I had been so impressed by the North Yorkshire sheep and the frequent signs advertising them that I commented on our way back that we must have been in Yorkshire on our day's travel.

"I think we were in Cumbria all the time," Lily said.

This did not seem reasonable to me. Cumbria *is* the Lake District from which we had wandered far afield. It's mountains are called the Cumbrian mountains. We had gone to the Pennines. Why would they need another name? And why weren't the sheep called Cumbrian sheep? "I'll bet you we were in Yorkshire," I countered.

"How much?"

"A pound."

The bet was sealed. Back in the Rothay Manor Hotel I pored over our best map with escalating chagrin. I also poured out some gin, but the alcohol could not obscure the inescapable reality that Cumbria extended much farther eastward than I'd assumed, even to include Sedbergh. We'd been about three miles from the Yorkshire border but no closer. Reluctantly I had to hand over to Lily the very pound I'd won a mere three days before over the flooding sands of Portmeirion. Since I do all the map research, how had she ever known? She wouldn't tell me. She hasn't told me to this day.

I'm feeling a bit sad. Not about losing the bet. About the Quakers. And about all of Christianity in Europe and North America. The magnificent spirit those early Quakers had in the days of persecution, so similar to that of the earliest Christians in the days of their persecution, seems to have faded away, almost totally evaporated. The Quakers have since had schisms among them. Many don't want silent meetings and don't have them. Some don't even have meeting houses anymore; they have steeple houses and robes as if George Fox had never lived.

This is not all bad. A dozen years ago a good Quaker woman came to see me with a vague malaise. After listening at length, I told she was liturgy starved. At that point in her life she needed robes and chants and incense. I advised a retreat at a convent, and soon afterward she became an Episcopalian.

I'm glad for the religious tolerance in Western civilization today. I'm sickened by the religious wars that continue elsewhere. I'm sickened by the Christians in the Age of Faith who reputedly pulled down some of the great standing stones because they were pagan.

Yet this wonderful toleration of the modern era in most of the West seems to have left us with a vapid religious life. With the separation of church and state, Christianity has, perhaps inevitably, become *privatized*, meaning something that is practiced only in the privacy of one's head. There is no room for religious practice in school, in the marketplace, in government. In the Age of Reason there has been a glaring failure of praxis, namely the integration of theology with practice, with our day-to-day behavior, the kind of practice for which the Quakers were once justifiably famous. The Christian church in the West has become so lukewarm and the faith of Christians so neatly compartmentalized that we have degenerated into a kind of passionless blasphemy. Where are we headed?

Like George Fox and the early Quakers, albeit with less obvious courage, Lily and I are working to "save the world." In the technology of community we believe we have found *the* answer, and we have a vision of a society where everyone will practice it. FCE definitively is an evangelistic organization. It is not, however, a church. It is utterly nonsectarian. Indeed, we teach people to stop trying to convert each other, to listen much more than to speak, and our principles encourage toleration within specifically but broadly defined limits. Yet it is not a secular organization either. The technology of people that it teaches is a distinctly spiritual technology, a spiritual practice. Indeed, the concluding sentence of FCE's mission statement reads: "As we seek to encourage others we remember our reliance on a *spirit* both within and beyond ourselves."

The two hundred or so of us most deeply involved with FCE feel *called* to its work. There is no other way we could have the passion necessary for it. But two hundred is a tiny number. Thousands exposed to our work do not seem to feel such passion. Our teaching tends to look soft on the surface, but it is tough in practice. It cannot be practiced without passion, and it is completely unclear how well we will succeed in this strangely passionless Age of Reason. Who knows? We must wait and see. We are waiting on the Lord.

I am always waiting on the Lord, whether I like it or not. Sometimes I whimsically wish I could write a book that *wasn't* about religion, but I can't. For me, God is always lurking in the background, waiting also on me. For instance, can we talk about stones without speaking of God? We know much about the early Quakers. We know practically nothing about the megalithic people. Yet there is one thing we do know about them for sure, and that is, like the early Quakers, the prehistoric erectors of great stones obviously shared some burning kind of communal passion. Can there be such a passion that is not religious, not spiritual, not of God?

CHAPTER VII

AGING
SATURDAY, JUNE 6

On this only full day in the Lake District our first target was not the lakes but more stones: specifically the Castlerigg stone circle near Keswick.

It proved an easy target. It is not a low-stone but a standing-stone circle, the stones standing high enough to be spotted over the walls of their hilltop field. A clear sign points the way down a paved road to where there is a great gap in the wall and significant parking space alongside.

The circle appeared exactly the same size as the one we found the previous day—roughly forty yards in diameter—with much the same number of evenly spaced stones—about thirty of them. But rather than being rounded boulders these are jagged and far more diverse. Some rise to seven feet, others to only three or four. I am reminded of a mouthful of teeth—a giant's mouth—with molars and canines and incisors rising out of the jaw of the earth. An old giant, perhaps, because these stone teeth look as if they had developed some serious cavities over the centuries. I would not call them pretty. What makes the site is not the beauty of the stones but their placement on a hilltop framed by the Cumbrian mountains in the distance.

A large, well-kept National Trust plaque pronounces the site to be "one of the principal Neolithic monuments of England, just secondary to Stonehenge." Certainly such would seem to be its reputation. Another couple was there when we arrived. Two more showed up within the next five minutes. And as we were about to depart a huge bus disgorged a flood of camera-bedecked Japanese visitors who flowed out over the well-cropped field. It was such a swarm we had to dodge them and felt like we were wading upstream to get back to our little Ford.

Although not a holy place from our point of view, we weren't disappointed. But while the plaque may have declared it a principal site just secondary to Stonehenge—perhaps because it was so easy to find, because it was not off the beaten track and we had to share it with others— we far preferred the hidden Gamelands stone circle we'd discovered on our own the afternoon before.

Besides, in but another day's time, we were to learn that the plaque's assessment of the site was nonsense.

The remainder of the day we spent in the Lake country itself. We covered it well. Basically it is a gigantic national park, roughly equivalent in size and variety to Yellowstone but with many differences. One is the extraordinary plethora of beautiful three-star hotels, like ours, as well as lovely two- and one-star ones and innumerable B&B's (private homes that take in a few guests for bed and breakfast). It is clearly Vacationland England, but without anything the slightest bit tawdry about it.

It is mountain country. They are craggy and glamorous mountains. Throughout the valleys are mossy, deeply shaded copses. And, of course, lakes—lakes of many sizes, all with pristine shores and sparkling clean water. It is postcard pretty.

The mountains are of two qualities depending upon where you happen to be at any given moment: either relatively verdant or stark, bare, and foreboding. They were not always that way. Their barren aspects are the result of massive deforestation by human beings. The evidence seems conclusive that the humans responsible were not the English, not the Romans, not the Celts, but our prehistoric, megalithic people. Why? Why, five thousand years ago, did these people need so many trees? Just for their fires? To roll their stones upon? We don't know.

It is a clear, almost hot day, the kind of day we've learned that the British exult in as glorious, they have so few of them, but so common for us that we'd rather it was cooler. Still, it's a perfect day to see the District, and the only metaphorical cloud on the horizon is that, after five days of driving, my back is starting to hurt.

Actually, my back is always hurting a little bit. What I mean is that the pillow I keep behind it when seated is not enough to compensate, and now my lumbosacral area is beginning to burn somewhat. It's also becoming more difficult than usual to get out of the car and straighten up.

There is a principle we are taught in medical school so significant that it's in Latin: *locus minoris resistentiae*—LMR or the place of least resistance. It means that almost every human being has a particular organ system that is more prone to problems than others. Lily's LMR is her gastrointestinal system. Mine is my spine.

At age nineteen I woke up one morning with a stiff, painful neck. I'd heard the expression "wry neck," and I assumed it would go away in a few days, and so it did. But every year or two I'd have another one. My X-rays did not look remarkable. At age thirty-five I began to have lengthy periods of dull pain in my shoulder blades. At thirty-seven, lifting some bricks, I felt as if my lower back was hit by lightning and had to be hospitalized for three days. It was a month before I was back to normal. Lesser episodes of lower back pain followed annually. At forty-one I began to have tingling and numbness in my left hand. At forty-four I could no longer straighten my neck. The X-rays had stopped looking so normal. I had degenerative disc disease, and that year the neurosurgeons did a laminectomy, removing one of the discs from my neck. At fifty-one I had severe pain in my right arm. The surgeons removed another disc from my neck and did a cervical fusion. At age fifty-three I had another episode of severe lower back pain, but this time the pain was also in my right leg, which rapidly became partially paralyzed. Now the surgeons removed two discs from my lumbar spine.

A cautionary note: Back pain is almost always best treated by bed rest and prevented by a specific exercise regime. Surgery is a treatment of last resort. Let me also thank God for it. Without it I'd long since be dead. And before that insane from pain.

Like most diseases my spine problem is psycho-somatic, which means overdetermined. One determinant is heredity. A milder variety of the problem runs in the family. My spine is also where I work out my tension. If I look in the rearview mirror and see a police car behind me, I can feel my back scrunch up like an accordion. It is probably no accident the disease began in my neck. Even as a child I'd fearfully developed a penchant for "sticking my neck out." It's become something of a lifestyle for me, and life wears us down.

Once or twice I've already referred to Lily and me as a "late-middle-aged couple" at fifty-six and -seven on this particular trip. That might surprise some, but I find their surprise amusing. The denial of not only death but aging in our culture is often down-right humorous. Most Americans seem to think that "middle age" begins at sixty. If such language and mathematics were correct, then "old age" would properly begin at a hundred and twenty.

While I laugh at the age-denial of others, the truth is that I've participated in some of it myself. I deferred my first neck surgery for a month, surprised that a famous surgeon should have proposed it with such alacrity for such a minor problem. Afterward he told me, "I've never seen anyone look more debilitated." Me, debilitated? At forty-four? So what if I couldn't hold my head up and hadn't been able to see the sky for three months?

Ah, yes, denial. As far as I was concerned that surgery took care of everything, and I continued my life as if I were invincible. I never considered the possibility that there might be something wrong with lecturing in a city for eight hours and getting on a plane that evening to lecture in another city for eight more hours the next day. And the next and the next . . . At forty-eight I came down with a "little" case of pneumonia. I went on smoking, drinking, and working for eight days, convinced that my mild antibiotics would take care of it. Then I ended up in the hospital with three different types of bacterial infection in my lungs simultaneously, turning blue and short of breath at rest. It is a terrifying thing not to be able to breathe. That was when I ceased acting like an iron man, and I've never been tempted to act like one again.

Perhaps because I had a brother four years older whose life seemed to be much more glamorous than mine, throughout my "young age" I always wanted to be older. That was why I started smoking at thirteen—not so much from peer pressure but because back in 1949 it looked like the mature thing to do. And I succeeded in my wish to be older. What with smoking and drinking and living with the tension of chronically sticking my neck out, I am an old fifty-six on this trip. When I look at my contemporaries dashing off to the next city immediately upon the conclusion of an absolutely depleting conference, a part of me admires them for being in better shape than

I. But in another part I wonder about the degree to which they are still trying to deny their limitations, and what it will be like for them when their denial ultimately comes crashing down.

In any case, I no longer have anything like the stamina I used to have. It is not just my spine that makes it increasingly difficult to get in and out of cars and sometimes to even make it up the stairs at the end of a long day. It is everything: eyes, hearing, teeth. It is weakness in my left ankle from an old rupture of an Achilles tendon and aches in my right from an old fracture. I forget simple words and names, although it is unclear to what degree my memory is failing or that I just have so much more to remember. Hemorrhoids have to be cleaned. I dribble my pants several times a day as a result of an enlarging prostate (called "old man's disease"). It takes me an extra hour to get started each morning what with flossing my gums to keep my teeth from falling out, gulping down Metamucil to keep my colon diverticuli from acting up and, above all, doing elaborately dull back exercises lest I become within the year a frozen pillar of calcium.

I'm not seeking sympathy, because I get plenty from Lily. A decade ago we used to joke about how indestructibly healthy she was even though almost two years older than I. No more. Her cholesterol is precarious. She's lost two teeth to aging gums, and other teeth are starting to shift. She, too, is addicted to Metamucil. She had to have a gall bladder full of gravel removed the same week I had my last spinal surgery. Estrogen and calcium pills should not be forgotten. Her recent ankle surgery was required because she was falling from an old sprain that had not seemed so bad twenty-five years before. She has arthritis in her fingers. Each time she goes to the oculist he tells her that the lens of her left eye has become a little more cloudy. "You mean my cataract?" Lily asks.

"Let's just say it's cloudy," he responds, accustomed to catering to the denial of his clients.

Seven years ago, when I was in my depression and Dark Night of the Senses, I was greatly consoled by a little book of quotes and cartoons, *Who Needs Mid-life at Your Age?* One of its quotes was: "Middle age is when you keep thinking in another couple of weeks you'll be back to normal." By that definition, Lily and I are no longer in middle age but at the onset of old age. It is not fascinating fun to sit around swapping aches and pains. But thank God we have each other to share them with.

Perhaps the thing that has surprised me most about aging is the pure *physicality* of it. Whatever one's attitudes about it—however different its individual schedule and distant it may seem, however much it may be denied—it comes. It is inexorable. My surprise at first was gentle. When I was forty I visited the aforementioned oculist. "Within the next three years you're going to need bifocals," he commented.

"How can you tell that?" I demanded skeptically.

"You've just got those kind of eyes," he enigmatically answered.

I didn't believe him. Two years later I got my

first pair. Last year I noticed a small gray-brown blotch—a benign seborrheic keratosis—on my left temple. "Oh, shit," I exclaimed, no longer naive. Before he died in his eighties, my father had a similar colored but inoperably huge and unsightly blotch—on his left temple. Over the past year my little blotch has doubled in size. I'm not big on cosmetics, but I think I'd best soon make an appointment with a dermatologist to get it removed while it is still manageable, even though I realize the notion of physical cure is largely an illusion.

Next to its inexorability, the thing that impresses me most about aging it the increasing rigidity of the body. It is not just the rigidity of my spine. Jet lag that once could be shrugged off can be so no longer. The biological clock is less flexible, less adjustable. Yet even at home, sleep is more problematic. The day's problems are not so easily forgotten or shrugged off. This rigidity is akin to brittleness, and the brittleness to fragility. I spoke of my spine as my place of least resistance. But in old age everything begins to become brittle: bruises bleed more, hernias happen, lungs don't clear, ears don't hear. Such fragility reveals the imminence of death. Most people do not die because of a single organ system but because all of the systems have become fragile, and whatever treatment may help sustain one will hurt another until nothing works anymore.

For many, along with this physical rigidity and fragility, there comes a distinct psychological rigidity and fragility. But this is not so inexorable and certainly not inevitable. There are ways that Lily and I have become less adaptable. We are more than ever attached to our creature comforts—to these lovely hotels we are staying in, me to my gin at the end of the day and Lily to her crosswords. On the whole, however, I believe we are less rigid in our thinking. Our opinions are less dogmatic. We are better able to work with others. Our leadership skills are more flexible. We do have to grow old physically; all of us will become decrepit and die. But we do not *have* to grow old mentally—a bit fuzzy perhaps, but not with a rigor mortis of the mind. We have seen spiritual youthfulness in some other elderly, and I think we can also see it in ourselves. But then I also think we have been lucky.

For several years before she died my mother had a little wall hanging in her bedroom that read, "Old age is not for sissies." I used to think she was being dramatic. I have since changed my mind and regret my lack of empathy. Indeed, one of the difficult things about aging for us is the subtle lack of empathy we experience from the more youthful, including our children. Our younger friends sometimes do not quite under-stand when we retire early, when I'm not willing to play iron man or Lily superwoman, as if we were being perversely withholding. In March 1992, I went to Texas to see our two-month-old grandson, a lovely and alert but restless ("colicky" seems to be a no-no word these days) infant who would usually cry unless he was being continually walked. Because of my back, ten minutes at a time was all I could hold him before trying to put him down or sit down—which wouldn't work—or hand him back to his mother. I explained this. She knows I have a bad back. She even knows that I can't stand behind a podium for more than fifteen minutes and must lecture mostly from a chair.

But I could sense in her eyes an assessment that I was being an unhelpful father and undoting grandparent.

It would be unnatural to actually welcome aging. It is a process of stripping away. Eventually a stripping away of *everything*. Ultimately, however, it is our choice as to whether or not we are going to be willing to be stripped away.

In the later days of my practice I was consulted by four remarkably similar women in their late sixties and early seventies who came to me with the same chief complaint: depression at growing old. Each was secular-minded. Each had either made money or married money. All their children had turned out golden. It was as if life had gone according to a script. But now they were getting cataracts, requiring hearing aids or dentures, and facing hip replacements. This wasn't the way they would have written the script, and they were pissed. I saw no way to assist them without converting them to a vision of old age as some-thing more than a meaningless time of watching themselves simply rot away. I tried to help them "buy it" as a spiritual period of their lives, a time of preparation. It was not an easy sell. In attempting it I kept saying to each of them in every possible way, "Look, you're not the scriptwriter; it's just not your show." Two of them shortly left my ministrations, preferring to be depressed than come to terms with the fact that life was not solely their own show.

Although she was the more depressed, I had a much easier time of it with another elderly woman who had a distinctly religious, Christian mindset. In her mid-sixties she had suffered a detached retina in each of her eyes. The ophthalmologist was unsuccessful in reattaching it in either eye using the most advanced laser treatment. She was furious at him. Although there was no evidence for it, she was convinced he had botched the job and was guilty of unprovable malpractice. Ninety percent blind, she was incensed at her fate. A theme emerged at the beginning of her second session with me. "I just hate it when they have to take hold of my arm to help me out of the pew or walk me down the steps at church," she ranted, and "I hate being stuck at home. I know that lots of people volunteer to take me places, but I can't be asking my friends to drive me around all the time."

"It's clear to me," I told her, "that you've taken a lot of pride in your independence. You've been a very successful person, and I think you needed that pride for your many accomplishments. But, you know, it's a journey from here to heaven, and it's a good rule of journeying to travel lightly. I'm not sure how successfully you're going to be in getting to heaven carrying around all this pride. You see your blindness as a curse, and I don't blame you. Conceivably, however, you might look at it as a blessing designed to relieve you of the no longer necessary burden of your pride. Except for your eyes, you're in pretty good health. Likely you've got at least a dozen more years to live. It's up to you whether you'd rather live those years with a curse or a blessing."

When she returned for her third session her depression of four years' duration had lifted.

I wish that all cases could be so easy. And I'm not sure that I'd be able to be as graceful as this woman. But what I am utterly certain about is that I'll not be able to deal decently with my aging without relying on my relationship with God. It is not solely a matter of faith in an afterlife that is my true home, and faith that aging is a process of preparation for it. I need something even more personal. I need God as well as Lily to complain to about the violence of the stripping away. And I need God upon occasion to answer in Her peculiar way, sometimes seemingly through spirits and angels of a sort. In that strict British private grammar school where I was urged ahead by the violently chauvinistic "Men of Harlech," I was also urged forward by as soft a song as ever written (no matter how racist it may sound today):

> I hear those gentle voices calling,
> I'm coming, I'm coming,
> for my head is bending low;
> I hear those gentle voices calling,
> "Old black Joe."

Seven years ago, facing the delicate surgery of my cervical fusion and a bit spaced out on narcotics for the pain, I was lying in bed one night talking to God. Typically, I was functioning on two levels, not only praying but listening to myself pray. And what I heard myself say was, "Darling, I'd do almost anything for You." Then I had to laugh. It was absurd. *Almost* anything! Because I knew even then that it was not enough, that I still wanted it to be at least partially my show. God doesn't want part of us; God wants all of us. So it is that the stripping away of old age is not partial. It is not just physical; it is total.

The stripping away of health and physical agility is not as painful for me, and I suspect for others, as the psychological stripping away. The stripping away of illusions, hundreds of them! That's all to the good, but it still hurts and may leave many distrustful, cynical, and embittered. The loss of heroes! I actually see more heroism in people these days, but it is an everyday kind of heroism that generates respect and admiration, not adoration. I have no more big heroes to look up to. The loss of mentors! Some are still alive, but I have outgrown them. Now I have the pleasure of being a mentor myself for many in limited ways, but it is not the same. There is a real sadness in outgrowing one's best teachers. Soon, if I live long enough, I shall be losing more and more friends to death. I may even outlive Lily. Everything will be stripped away except for God before whom I shall finally be naked.

Yet another kind of stripping away is that of interests. It began with the Dark Night of the Senses, that stripping away of some of my appetite for beauty and art and elegance. Television bores me. Very few books—poetry, novels, works of wisdom—hold my attention for long. I feel as if I've read it all before, and in a sense I have. Into this vacuum of my mind our sudden fascination for stones has come as a surprising, most wonderful gift. But this, too, shall probably pass, and the day will likely come when a great standing stone will look merely like a rock. For the moment, however, I am very grateful.

And I am not whining. There are great virtues to aging that I shall be recounting.

At midday we drove near the Cumbrian coast away from the mountains. There we spied one of Britain's few hitchhikers and stopped to pick him up. He was a young Scotsman who'd come to those parts from Aberdeen six years before to do construction work on a nearby nuclear power plant and had stayed to wed a local lady. He told us that the beauty of the Lake District would pale before the beauty of the Scottish highlands we'd soon be visiting. It was hard to believe, and we assumed this outrageous assessment to represent mere national pride. His thick Scottish accent did not bode well for our future communication in those highlands. We were still able to ascertain, however, that he'd been apprenticed in carpentry and "joinering," and now was attending school in the hope of becoming a lecturer in these same subjects. By lecturer he meant a high school technical teacher, a position which he felt would offer him a brighter future than the construction business. One virtue of aging is that we do not envy anyone anymore. We do not miss our youth. Having been fortunate enough to have had a successful career, it is impossible for me to feel anything but compassion for a young person who is still trying to carve one out.

After dropping off our hiker we did pass by his nuclear power plant. Its environs, he had assured us, were still highly radioactive from a little spill a decade or so previously. It was the third such plant we'd driven by on our trip to date. Each is dramatically marked and exuberantly offers free family tours. We are not educated enough on the subject to have a thoughtful opinion as to the relative wholesomeness of nuclear power, on which England is obviously more dependent than the United States. But all these gigantic plants have an eerie, futuristic quality that reminds us somehow of Mordor, the mythical evil kingdom of J. R. R. Tolkien's writing. This plant, the largest of all, looked ominous indeed in the distance.

We turned inland to Wast Water, one of the District's least-visited lakes. It was nice. But once you've seen one of these lakes you've pretty much seen them all. Of course, we're jaded once again. We live year-round on a large lake nestled in the hills that, in its slightly different way, is just as beautiful. When we travel it is Lily's specialty to write the postcards home. She is already preparing her evening's message about how silly it seems to have flown six thousand miles to be in the Old England lake country as opposed to sitting in our own New England lake country.

But these mountains are much higher, and on our way back to our hotel we cross over the Hard Knott and Wry Nose passes. They are aptly named. The Roman road across them is no more than six feet wide for thirty miles, often at a twenty-five-degree incline with corkscrew bends. The Romans were famous for building straight roads. As far as we know, this was the only curved road they ever made. Operating much of the time in the first of its five gears, our little Ford will never be young again.

Guarding the tops of the passes are the ruins of small Roman forts—square piles of rocks without any visible redeeming feature. As far as Lily and I can discern, the Romans were a remarkably unimaginative race who, except under the direst of circumstances, such as the Cumbrian mountains, were utterly enamored of the straight line. We are not the only ones to feel this way. Several scholars have lamented the assets the English have poured into the archaeological investigation of their Roman ruins, which all look much the same, while neglecting adequate study of the infinitely more interesting and varied prehistoric megaliths.

Also trudging up and over the passes with backpacks in the hot sun were groups of sweating British, German, and Outward Bound youth. No, we do not envy their age or stamina. They did not look as if they were having all that much fun. In our work with the Foundation for Community Encouragement, Lily and I get to experience a sense of community all the time, but that is because we are meeting a spiritual challenge together rather than a physical one. We don't have to sweat outwardly. In our imagination it was easy to transform the obviously driven hikers into driven Roman legions desperately trying to extend or preserve the boundaries of an empire.

It is a relief for us to not feel compelled to build empires anymore.

I have alluded to another relief associated with my personal aging. Men differ enormously in this regard and, as I have said, I am an old fifty-six. For the past two years I'd experienced a dramatic diminution in libido. I am simply not very horny anymore. As a traveling speaker continually exposed to beautiful and occasionally eager women, this loss of libido has made my existence pleasantly less complicated and upsetting. It has liberated me from many previously potent temptations. I'm aware of how the average man would likely find such rapid waning of his sexual drive and potency to be disheartening if not downright terrifying. He might well even seek out a physician for treatment. I don't want any treatment for myself, thank you, and I know of a few other men in my position who have similarly experienced this "disease" of aging much more like a healing.

Having managed over the passes, we arrived safely back at our comfortable hotel—more like an elegant inn—in Ambleside. Over gin and maps we are acutely aware not so much of aging as the simple passage of time, and that this is the end of the first week of our trip. Two weeks to go, all of them in Scotland. If it seems strange that we'd spend two-thirds of our time in Scotland, it might help to know that Scotland is quite large— larger than all of England and Wales combined. And England it is not. Like Wales, it is Celtic and more foreign, a land to which we have never been before. Will it be wild? Dark? Dangerous? We do not know, but we are excited, particularly since we shall be going very far north and to a place or two that tourists don't usually visit. That we are doing so seems a bit frightening in the fragility of our early old age. On the other hand, it is precisely our age that has made such outer reaches so comfortably accessible.

Given our culture's distaste for the reality of aging, there may be some who have not found this an uplifting chapter. So I shall end it with an uplifting bedtime story that may or may not be related to the aging process. At least I think it is uplifting. It is a rather bizarre story, and it is possible that the intellectually complacent may find it as unsettling as the subject of aging itself.

The story has to do with spirits. In the early 1980s, involved with several cases of demonic possession, I'd had some experience with evil spirits. Personally, I had never been attacked by one, but I knew a few people who clearly had been and I had prayed against those spirits. To the subject of good spirits I'd never given any thought. I believed without doubt in the reality of the Holy Spirit as a bringer of wisdom, but I did not envision Her as being separate from God. Certainly I'd not considered the possibility of there being good spirits with distinct identities.

Then in the spring of 1986 I was going to bed one night. This was when I was deep in the Dark Night of the Senses and near the worst of my depression. I was feeling not merely gloomy but quite convinced I'd never feel uplifted again.

Once in bed, too depressed to read, I reached up and turned out the light. And at that first moment of darkness I was accosted by a spirit.

There is no way to describe it other than metaphorically. It was as if a metaphorical blast of wind had somehow entered my bedroom and struck my body. Without even asking I knew instantly that it was a good spirit. I cannot tell you how. It not only struck me but stuck to me as if wanting to get inside me. I knew with certainty that I'd been accosted by a good spirit and that it was entirely up to me whether I was going to let it in.

The first thing I did was to wordlessly ask what kind of a good spirit it was. No sooner was the question asked than the answer came back with equal utter certainty: it was a "Spirit of Mirth."

That was when the battle began.

I waged the struggle on two levels. The first was intellectual. The scientist in me, the skeptical man of Reason, immediately went into action. Just because it said that it was a spirit of mirth, how did I really *know* that to be the case? Might it be tricking me? I had no sense that was so. But what would be the long-term consequences if I let it in? It was then I realized for the first time in my life the meaning of the expression "Don't look a gift horse in the mouth." Here I'd been offered a gift and I was checking it out like a veterinarian. Were its teeth okay? Might one of them be abscessed? Might there be some unexpected bills to pay in the future? My behavior began to seem increasingly silly.

So I switched the battle to a deeper, more

167

emotional level. I was depressed. I had every reason to be depressed. People were starting to regard me as property. They wanted more and more from me: read my manuscript, sign my book, help me find a therapist, give me a promotional comment, grant me an interview, be on my show, tell me what to do about my son who's taking drugs, explain what you meant when you said . . . and on and on. So what was this stupid spirit of mirth doing hanging around? I had no reason to be mirthful. Why should I let it in when I had every reason for only depression?

But finally that, too, struck me as silly. I gave up, let it in, and giggled myself to sleep. For the next two days I experienced some surcease from my depression. Thereafter I was depressed as usual until I came out of it about nine months later.

What to make of this? The average psychiatrist, if he didn't lock me up, would conclude that there must have been some sudden shift of neurotransmitter levels in my mid-brain. Fine, but why such a shift? It is not much of an explanation when there was no discernible stimulus for a radical neurophysiological change. Yet emotions are internally generated, are they not? They can hardly be caused by external "spirits," can they? And whoever heard of such a thing as a spirit of mirth floating around in the ether, independent of a human body? I could continue in this vein until twisted, lost, and paralyzed in a morass of questions. The whole thing simply doesn't fit in the Age of Reason.

Instead, I choose to take the experience at its

face value: At a time when I needed it, I was inexplicably assaulted by a spirit of mirth which I finally recognized as a gift and elected to let inside me. I believe that it is still inside me. It is not that I was never mirthful before or that I am always mirthful now. But I do tend to take more delight in life's incongruities these days. Just one such incongruity is the mystification of totally rational minds when confronted by certain stones. Or spirits. As I age, I seem often to be finding life less frankly exciting but also subtly more humorous.

CHAPTER VIII

PARENTHOOD
SUNDAY JUNE 7

We departed the Lake District over yet another pass, but then lingered in England for three more hours in the environs of Penrith—searching for stones, of course.

Our first site, the Mayborough Earthworks, was so poorly marked we passed by it four times. Our ordinance survey map placed it very precisely adjacent to an underpass of M6, the great motorway to Scotland. A hundred yards into the unkempt field we kept passing was a hillock. Ordinary though it looked, we finally decided it might just be what we were seeking. We scrambled through the fence, walked the field, and climbed the hillock. It was indeed the site.

The hillock turned out to be a twenty-foot-high rim of bracken-covered rocks enclosing a perfectly circular meadow a hundred yards in diameter. In the very middle of the meadow stood a single great stone of a most distinctive shape.

Exploring the site we realized that, invisible from the road, there was an entranceway through the rim into the enclosure. And leaving it we discovered an exit stile through a hedge back onto the road. The hedge had almost entirely overgrown the stile. Next to the stile, on the inside of the hedge, was a large but utterly hidden information plaque identifying it as a three- to four-thousand-year-old Neolithic period monument. There was even a map on the plaque showing how until recently there had been seven other standing stones therein progressing from the entranceway to the remaining central stone. It did not tell what happened to them. Perhaps they had been used in the construction of the adjacent Concrete Period motorway. Finally, the plaque authoritatively informed us that the enclosure had served as a meeting and trading place.

We chuckled. Already we had come to realize the fact that no one knows the purpose of *any* megalithic site, save for those truly obvious burial chambers. But so many people, including National Trust officials, simply cannot tolerate the "emptiness of not knowing." In the days ahead we were to chuckle again as guidebooks or plaques definitively told us that this or that monument was used for astrological sightings, the prediction of eclipses, fertility celebrations, marketing, dancing, theater, government, and so on. Over and over we were reminded how newspapers almost daily offer us similarly authoritative explanations for the previous day's stock market fluctuation. Whatever would we do if the authorities simply told us they didn't have an explanation in this Age of Reason? Sue them or fire them, I suppose. Maybe even execute them, we'd be so upset.

Only a quarter mile away was another prehistoric monument, King Arthur's Round Table, hidden behind high stone walls at the corner of a village. This time, however, the stile was well marked, although there was no information sign. Constructed by the megalithic people, it is a monument without stones. Indeed, it was an absolutely stoneless, close-cropped, bright green field surrounded by a circular earthen rim only a few feet high. Inside the rim is a wide, gentle ditch resembling a grassy, shallow, waterless moat. And encircled by the ditch is an absolutely flat, absolutely round, forty-yard-wide "table" of earth, almost like a polished emerald on this June day. Hence the name King Arthur's Round Table, although the site had nothing to do with King Arthur or his knights.

Later we were to learn that this type of earthwork of rim, ditch, and inner table is called a henge. Indeed, Stonehenge is so named because its great stones stand on such a table encircled by a similar ditch and rim. Twenty miles northeast of Stonehenge is another much larger henge in the town of Avebury that is also famous for it stones, although they are menhirs without lintels. There are many henges that do not have stones, however, and apparently never did. King Arthur's Round Table is one of these. Why did the megalithic people build henges, either with or without stones? For what reason or purpose? No one knows.

From this, our first henge, we drove five miles along gentle lanes to the isolated site of Long Meg and Her Daughters. The "daughters" part is a stone circle in a flatlands field bordered by ancient trees. It is the widest circle of stones we had seen to date—or were to see—on the trip: approximately sixty yards in diameter. At one corner the road actually transects it, but the circle is so large one has no feeling that the road violates it. Its stones are somewhere in between low stones and tall standing ones; mostly rugged, granite boulders four to five feet high and almost equally as broad. They are lovely stones, but because of its great width, the circle itself is not as impressive as it would be if the stones were closer together. Yet it is one of the most impressive of all megalithic sites, and what makes it so is Long Meg. She stands about a dozen yards outside the circle, perhaps the finest single menhir in all of England, about fifteen feet high but bent at her top, probing into the blue sky like a sharp and crooked, upturned witch's nose.

A spirit of peace akin to holiness pervades the place, and we lingered for over an hour to soak it up. It could not have been more different from yesterday's Castlerigg stone circle. Throughout our whole time there only one other couple was present, quietly sketching the scene. Although grateful for it, we were puzzled by its lesser renown. Certainly, despite Castlerigg's pretentious claim, this was for us much the greater site.

We carefully inspected Long Meg up close. Unlike her daughters, she is not of granite. Another deficit in my scholarship is my total ignorance of geology. I can only suspect she was of a kind of sandstone, and appeared to have been quarried with her sharp-edged and flat smooth surfaces. Her color was not granite gray but light brown, almost bronze. On one surface a modern barbarian—unfortunately by the name of Scott— had etched his pathetic moniker. I hope he is doing at least some penance time in Purgatory for such a sin. The only other markings on another surface were two virtually identical foot-wide swirls. These did not look modern. We guessed them to be prehistoric, but it would be two more days before the accuracy of this guess would be confirmed.

What is the meaning of Long Meg standing just outside the stone circle? We don't know. While we would not see a similar configuration on this trip, we would later learn from research that it is hardly unique. Outside the circle of Stonehenge, for instance, there sits a huge megalith called the Heel Stone. But it is still not as distinctive a stone as Long Meg, and the purpose of such configurations remains obscure to the best of scholars. Long Meg and Her Daughters is undoubtedly a relatively modern name for a prehistoric monument that probably had nothing to do with families. But it is an appropriate name for the site, and we are left thinking not so much of mothers and daughters as the topic of parents and children.

It is not an easy topic for me to write about for many reasons. For one, this is a painful time for us in our lives as parents. Our relationship with all three of our children is currently not great, and my relationship with them is particularly poor. It is unclear at the moment whether this is just a very difficult phase or something more permanent. It is also unclear to what extent the problem is due to us being terrible parents or maybe due to the possibility that we've been almost too good in some ways. And while we are striving for healing, it is furthermore still unclear how much healing is probable or even possible.

Another reason is that I may be too close to the subject to write about it coherently. Indeed, one of our questions is whether or not this closeness is excessive, thereby requiring our children to keep their distance from me.

Finally, I cannot write too personally. Our children have their own lives to live and their own stories to tell. They deserve their privacy—particularly in relation to me. It is difficult enough to be a child at any age. It is uniquely difficult at their age to be children of a famous man whom many place on an absurdly high pedestal. That also may be a part of our problem.

I've indicated that Lily and I are not big gamblers. In some respects, however, that simply isn't correct. In a couple of common and a couple of uncommon ways we've been big-time betters.

One common way was in getting married. We bet that our marriage would work. It was a bet that has really paid off, although there were times when it seemed an awfully close call. It's not all been a matter of good luck. Both of us brought to our marriage some characteristics such as loyalty and pertinacity that have allowed us to hang in together over the rough spots. Still, getting married was a huge gamble in the sense that we didn't have the foggiest idea what we were doing at the time we stood before the altar. We knew nothing about what marriage would really be like, and we were too innocent to even know that we didn't know. In this we were hardly unique. I suspect the vast majority of couples—perhaps all who are young as we were then, in our mid-twenties—are operating on equally blind faith. This is not to be decried. I do not believe that all ignorance is bliss. But were it not for such blissful ignorance, I doubt that there would be many marriages.

Or many children. We wanted our three children. Each was the product of a well-planned pregnancy. We can likely even remember each utterly deliberate moment of conception. But that doesn't mean that we really knew what we were doing. We did not know they would be born healthy. We did not know *who* each of them would be. We did not know at all what it would be like to be parents. No matter how common childbearing might be, it was another huge gamble.

Among the things of which we were blissfully ignorant was the plain matter of how much work children are. I have defined mental health as "an ongoing process of dedication to reality at all costs." We psychotherapists strive to destroy illusions. Yet we are also aware that there are such things as "healthy illusions," and I have survived much of the past thirty years by virtue of them: I used to think that the children would be easier when they got out of diapers; then I had the illusion they would be easier when they went to school; then when they got their driver's licenses; then when they got into college; then when they got out of college; then when they reached thirty. Now I believe they'll be easier when they're in their forties, and please don't anyone tell me differently!

I ramble on this way even though I was not the one who bore the brunt of the work. I've said how we were born and raised in sexist cultures, and through all but the first eighteen months of our marriage I've been the primary breadwinner and Lily the primary homemaker. But I do not think that this has solely been the result of our stereotypical cultural upbringings. Lily and I are so very different and have such different gifts. Specifically, she has the gift of flowing and I the gift of paragraphs. Although occasionally disorganized to a fault, she has always had the flexibility to flow with the children's ever-fluctuating needs and schedules. It was, until very recently, doubtful that she was capable of writing books. Conversely, I am organized to a fault. For instance, I can be insufferable when I actually speak as well as write in paragraphs, saying, "First of all . . ., second . . ., third . . . and now on to part B." My gift of paragraphs has made us a good deal of money, but it has not made me the best of parents. It wasn't easy for me (as it was for Lily) to spontaneously play with children when my mind was contemplating the structure of the chapter I was writing on the stages of religious transformation. Given our gifts, Lily generally likes homemaking; I don't. I generally like to write and balance the checkbook; Lily doesn't.

Satisfactory though this division of labor has been for us, our children have not been so happy with it. They resent me for being the lesser parent, seldom as available to them as Lily. In part their resentment is justified. I have hardly been the best of fathers or as attentive as I both could and should have been. Yet in part I also resent their resentment. Raised in the time of women's liberation it is easy, I suppose, for them to see Lily's and my differing roles not so much resulting from our gifts as my male dominance. But I wish they could realize that poor though I've been at it, I've probably been a more attentive parent than my own father (who was reputedly out on the golf course when I was born).

Anyway, children are a lot of work. I mentioned as one of the great blessings of our aging that we don't envy anyone anymore. We don't envy our daughter and son-in-law as they have to deal day in and day out with our one-year-old grandson. We don't envy the young woman we see on the airplane with two toddlers in tow. Or the young couple. We don't envy parents whose children are in the throes of adolescence or who are struggling to pay college tuition. We've been there. We are glad we did it, but we are also glad that for us those parts of parenting are done, and we've no desire to do them over again.

If children are so much work, why bother? It's fine to speak of life's mystical yearning for itself, to re-create itself. Or the social responsibility of the well educated to procreate. Or the desire to achieve immortality of a sort through the production of progeny. All of these probably were determinants of our blind urge to thrice deliberately set aside contraceptives. But they are not today the reason we are glad we did so. We do not see our children as a social responsibility we have fulfilled. Nor some straw of immortality at which we can grasp. And certainly not as re-creations of ourselves, given the fact that they are so different from us. No, we are not glad for these reasons. We are glad for the learning. If you seriously want to learn about life, having and raising children is probably the single best way. Ignorant though we still are, it is hard for Lily and me to even imagine how much more ignorant we would be of ourselves and others had we been childless.

The learnings have been so great it is impossible to touch upon more than a few of them.

We have learned that our children are not our creations. They bear little resemblance to us or to each other. This learning was highlighted by the fact that our first two children were both girls born less than a year apart. They looked much the same the day they were born. Four or five days after their births, however, we brought very different creatures home from the same hospital. They sucked differently. They cried differently. They required that they be held differently. They slept differently. As a psychotherapist I have focused a great deal on how good or bad parenting can affect personalities. But it is as a parent I have learned how deeply one's personality, or at least one's temperament, is determined by pure biology: by the unique combination of the genes of a unique egg and a unique sperm.

So they were both human and unique, as was their later born unique younger brother, and we learned from both the differences and the similarities of their development in infancy, through childhood, through adolescence, and into young adulthood. I have a friend, a child psychiatrist, a single man who has never had children. Loving and empathetic, he is an excellent child psychiatrist—far better than I could ever be. The reason he is so much better than me is that he is more detached and objective. Yet I think I know more than he about the human condition. I know it is possible to fully learn about the human condition without being a parent, but I'm not sure it's probable.

Putting it another way, I'm not sure how fully I could have joined in the human race (which, for parents, often feels like a rat race) without being a father struggling to fulfill at least the minimum responsibilities of parenthood. Our children have radically connected me in ways to Lily as a coparent, to my parents as their grandparents, to other parents as fellows, and most recently to a particular infant because he is my grandchild. I appreciate many things about our children, such as their unique sense of humor. But what I am most grateful to them for is the learning they have wittingly or unwittingly provided me. And are still providing.

The learning these days is all about separation.

I was not prepared for it.

It is standard psychiatric knowledge that it is the task of children to separate from their parents not just geographically but psychologically—to "individuate," to become individuals who are no longer emotionally tied to their parents' apron strings, who can fully think for themselves. It is also common knowledge that psychiatrically disturbed parents can interfere with this separation process so as to retard it or to even make it impossible. The professional literature (as opposed to fiction and theater) tends to imply that in healthy human development this separation process is completed by the child and its parents by the end of adolescence. Otherwise the subject is not afforded much importance. There is amazingly little in the scientific literature to suggest that it may be normal for a child to continue struggling with separation issues throughout his or her twenties. Much less through the thirties and into the forties. Nor is there much about how the child's parents must struggle as parents with these separation issues when they are in their fifties, sixties, and even seventies. Finally, the professional literature doesn't talk about how much it can hurt for all concerned.

I should have been prepared because I didn't

finish emotionally separating from my own parents until I was in my early forties.

One weekend when I was twenty I taught myself to ski in the mountains of Vermont. That is to say, I learned how to turn sufficiently that I could go down the more modest trails at a fair pace without hitting a tree or anyone else. Gliding down one of those trails, feeling like a real athlete, I caught myself thinking, "Gee, I wish my parents could see me now!" I laughed at how ridiculous it was. My parents were three hundred miles away, and wild horses couldn't have dragged them to a ski area. Here I was, twenty years old and still wanting their approval like a five-year-old screeching, "Look at me. Mommy, Daddy, look at what I can do!"

Laugh though I did at myself, I still didn't stop almost desperately wanting my parents' approval. This meant that I was chronically angry with them. For the most part, I had already very much become an individual in my own right, even to the degree that I was so radically different from them that it was virtually impossible for them to approve of anything that I did. Overcontrolling, hidebound WASPs, they had a fixed agenda for me that had nothing to do with the person I was— and little to do with the times in which I lived. They disapproved of my marrying Lily, of us having children so early, of my entering the army, my entering psychiatry, and my leaving the army. They disapproved of the house we bought. They disapproved of me wasting time writing books. Each of those times and many more I was furious at their disapproval. Only when I was forty-two

181

did I switch to being amused at it. And then it was not that I no longer wanted them to approve of me; it was just that I no longer *expected* or *needed* their approval. And only then was I fully separated from them.

So why should I be so surprised that our children at ages twenty-three, thirty, and thirty-one, all successful in their own right and financially independent, are very angry with me for unclear reasons and giving both of us clear messages that they want us to keep our distance from them? Particularly since Lily and I are strong-willed people who would also run their lives if we could, albeit with the very best of intentions?

Intellectually, I know it would be disastrous for us to run their lives. In my head I have no desire to control them. But their recent animosity has revealed to me depths of supposedly benign parental despotism I never knew existed. And I feel as if I am doomed to repeat history.

Thirty years ago, at the end of a luncheon with my father, who was a famous attorney at the time, I inquired what he would be doing right after we parted. He told me he had an appointment with a young lawyer who was asking him for advice about a career choice. I stifled a desire to laugh. My brother and I had long since learned never to go to my father for advice about anything. My father did not advise us what to do; he *told* us what to do. My first instinct was to pity the young lawyer for his ignorance. But then it occurred to me that my father might actually be quite good at advising young lawyers; he just wasn't adept at advising his own children: There were too many "hooks" for him with us. It was perhaps the first time I ever realized that not only did my parents have emotional hooks into me, but I had similar hooks into them—buttons I could push, even unwittingly, that were utterly guaranteed to drive them mad or at least temporarily suffer a severe lapse in judgment.

And now, with all four of our own parents finally and fully unhooked from us by the grave, Lily and I find ourselves just as emotionally tangled up with our children. We'd had the fantasy that when they were grown our role as parents would easily evolve from caretakers to that of comfortable friends. Instead, in their presence, we feel we must walk on eggs. Our most idle remarks or facial expressions may evoke their scorn or precipitate a hurtful silence. Recently, we had two new friends, a young couple, as house guests for three days. It was great fun. But it was poignant at the end for us to realize that this couple was the same age as our children, and yet throughout the long weekend we'd been relaxed. There were no hooks.

I suppose this is inevitable.

Shortly after we were married, a couple with whom we were quite close in medical school lost their two-month-old infant to crib death. Wanting to return to their roots for a few days to grieve, they asked us if we would care for their cocker spaniel puppy until they returned. We were happy to be of help in this small way. Ben was a friendly pup, but he was not yet house-broken. He was also accustomed to awaken in the middle of the night to be present for infant

183

feedings. By the end of the four days we were ready to kill Ben. And we thought, "My God, if we can't even stand taking care of a young dog for a few days, how on earth can we ever be decent parents?"

When our first child was born about a year later, however, it was no problem. Ben had no hooks in us. He'd solely been a burden. But our new daughter had hooks in us from well before her birth. Although difficult as a very young infant, attending to her every need was as natural for us as breathing. She had been born to be loved by us, and we had been born to care for her. And so it was with our other children. And so it continued as they grew and their needs changed from diaper changing, to story reading, to camping, to carpooling, to driver education and college selection.

Only now they don't want our caring. That is to say, they do and they don't. They want our admiration and gifts and money, but they don't want *us*. They don't want any of our wisdom. Certainly they don't want any of our advice. They also don't want to hear our stories. Partly that may be because they suspect some word of advice to be hidden in our stories even when it isn't. And partly it's because they're simply not interested. They have their own lives to live. They do want us to be interested in their lives, as long as there's no hint of desire to help, much less control. But at this point they really couldn't care less about our lives. In a sense, they want us to like them but not to love them anymore. And sometimes, even though they're our own children, it's not so easy for us to like them when they're so different from us, when they no longer want our concern, and when their desire for our liking is so much of a one-way street.

Am I feeling sorry for myself? Yes and no.

No, because I realize that, in a way, they need me to stop loving them since I do not yet know how to love them without caring for them, without wanting the best for them so desperately that I slip now and then into advice offering. I have not learned how to love neutrally. Maybe I am starting to learn. I don't know. Maybe is the most optimistic I can be at this point.

But yes, I am feeling a bit sorry for myself—and for Lily—because it feels a bit unfair. I'm not saying that it is unfair. To the contrary, I think it *is* simply the necessary way of things. But that's my head speaking. On an emotional level it feels heart-wrenching. It feels unfair that God should have called me to passionately love my children for thirty years and now, rather suddenly, should be calling me to a neutered kind of love. It feels like I must almost *stop* loving them.

I was eight years old when I was first exposed to the story of God calling upon Abraham to kill his beloved son Isaac, the very child God had given him in the first place. I thought it was a crazy story. I thought God was crazy for asking Abraham to do it, and Abraham was crazy for going ahead with it. I still don't think it's a very good story for eight-year-olds. But at fifty-six it now hits home. I am Abraham. I know I have to hand my children over to God and that they are totally His to do with as He wishes (within the limits of their own responsibility and free wills). But I wonder about Abraham. How could he have led Isaac up to that place of sacrifice, in obedience to God, if he still loved the boy? Did he not first have to somehow stop loving Isaac? At least on some deep level? And if so, how?

I have spoken of aging as a process of stripping away, suggesting that the stripping must be ultimate so that the soul is eventually utterly naked before God, before his true Beloved. Oh, how nice and poetic that sounds! God is my Beloved, and I have long yearned to be naked for Him. But I never bargained for the possibility that I might have to have stripped away from me even my accustomed kind of love for my own children. I cannot imagine any part of aging to be more painful than that. Nor can I yet imagine what it will feel like when such stripping is finished.

From Long Meg and Her Daughters we drove to the aforementioned motorway and sped up it into Scotland and through Scotland's unremarkable (for us) lowlands to Glasgow. We had a good map of the city that led us straight to our lodgings without having to see hardly anything of the town. The lodgings proved to be considerably more abysmal than Cardiff's and a shocking come-down from those of our previous six nights. They were in a hotel with a false front of Georgian elegance. Behind the front wall it was a 1970s cement box with its entrance in back. Our eight-by-twelve-foot room was decorated in plain light brown, plain medium brown, and plain dark brown. Its solitary window looked out upon a parking lot, but even this view was visible only by standing. It being stuffy without air-conditioning, we immediately opened the window to let in some tepid air and a swarm of flies. We have stayed in some extremely primitive conditions during our more youthful travels, so this was hardly the worst accommodation of our lives. Still, it was down near the bottom of the list.

It was so depressing we immediately repaired to our Fodor to discover how Joan had done us such a wrong. That famed guidebook listed One Devonshire Gardens as being Glasgow's only good hotel, having some eight guest rooms, which may well have been all booked before we'd even begun to plan the trip. Fodor said it also had the city's finest restaurant. Our spirits being in need of an uplift, we called to find that it was within walking distance down the very street of our hotel's false front, and that they could take us. Off we quickly went.

The street down which we walked was lined by once lovely Georgian houses without false fronts, but every other one had a FOR LET sign, every fourth one some boarded windows, and many had garbage piled high before their basement entrance. The sidewalks were badly cracked, and grass was growing in the cracks. It was not hard to guess that Glasgow was down at its heels.

One Devonshire Gardens, however, was not. We were ushered not into a dining room but an elegant living room where we were offered cocktails. Along with the drinks came menus. Then our orders were taken. Ten minutes later we were led straight to our table. The meal, of course, was excellent, although not quite memorable. What was memorable was the decor. It was the most exquisitely decorated dining room in which we've ever eaten.

We also remember it as the place where it began to dawn on us that the practice of offering cocktails and menus in a living room and the taking of orders before seating guests in the restaurant is a practice common to many of Britain's best restaurants. We'd first experienced it at Portmeirion and were to experience it again. It not only struck us as a civilized sort of custom but an efficient one. It seemed to require fewer waiters and waitresses and, by the time we got to our table, everyone clearly knew what they were doing. Perhaps it is a custom that will spread to the United States.

One of the pleasures of dining at sidewalk cafés is people-watching. Sometimes this is also the case with fine dining. On this evening our dinner companions were remarkably varied, as often happens in out-of-the-way, great restaurants: a handsome Scots couple in their late thirties; a quartet of distinguished and genteel Texan ladies and gentlemen in their early sixties; a punk rock couple in their late twenties who seemed utterly out of place, yet were quiet and mannerly; a dapper and self-satisfied middle-aged Japanese man with his obviously depressed Japanese wife; a trio of men around age fifty all associated with the same international business conglomerate— one American, one Scottish, and the other indeterminately British—all trying to one-up each other for over two solid hours. From every word they quite loudly said you could tell that each man was a very important person—except that very, *very* important people don't talk that way and hopefully can enjoy their food more.

What our dinner companions might have thought of us we have no idea, but we had fun. We spoke of how it was still light outside the restaurant even though it was very late dining for us. We knew there was a scientific explanation for this, and Lily diagrammed the relationship between the sun and the earth at this time of year by comparing the diameter of the mouth of her wine glass to the greater diameter of its bowl. The explanation made a great deal of sense, although in the morning we were not able to exactly remember what that sense was. We could, however, remember her proposal that stone circles perhaps had served as prehistoric helicopter landing pads.

On a more serious note, after we returned to the dreary reality of our hotel room, I reviewed the day in my mind as I fell asleep, as was my custom. Its highlight had been not the restaurant but Long Meg and Her Daughters—particularly Long Meg herself. I identified her as much with fathers as with mothers, with myself as much as with Lily. Why didn't the megalithic people put that beautiful stone inside the circle? In the center? I don't know. A few times they did erect central stones, but the menhir outside the circle was their more common arrangement.

If the arrangement was at all meant to symbolize families, the common position of the "heel" stone makes sense. Parents should not be the center of their children's lives. It is up to the children to find their own centers and, ultimately, perhaps, to create their own circles.

So Meg stands beside, outside, and aside.

It is our task as parents, at least when our children are young, to stand *beside* them: to brood over them, to walk beside them so as to protect them from harm whenever possible.

But we cannot be them. We cannot be inside their souls. They are foreigners to us. No matter that they issue forth from our loins, no matter how many years we walk beside them, guarding them, we are inevitably *outside* them. They are separate. Lonely though it might be for both them and us, as parents we are outsiders in relation to our children.

Finally, however well we may have trained ourselves to care for them, and however many years we may have exercised that care, there comes a time, gradually or suddenly, subtly or dramatically, when we need to step *aside*. It's impossible to know how to do it right. Children are likely to blame us for doing it too soon or too late, too gently or too abruptly. They are unlikely to have any appreciation for how difficult it may be for their parents to drastically change roles. But so what? It's not an issue of ease. It's simply of what needs to be done. Hopefully, Lily and I have done it. We have stepped aside, and if all goes well for us and our children, we'll be staying aside forever.

CHAPTER IX

MONEY
MONDAY, JUNE 8

Today was a dreary day—neither hot nor cold, neither cloudy nor sunny—in a dreary city.

Glasgow is not all bad. It isn't, however, much of a tourist attraction. We strolled through a large park, as unkempt as Cardiff's, and from a distance saw a few fine buildings, notably the university. But mostly Glasgow is grimy and littered. In the interest of our son, an artist, we visited the city center to stop by the somewhat renowned, albeit unrelievedly drab, Glasgow School of Art. The three unenthusiastic clerks in the registrar's office were at a loss to tell us any reason he might want to come there to school from the United States, much less from San Francisco. By the time we had completed this visit our spirits had sunk so low we even lunched at a Burger King in hope that a taste of home might cheer us up. It didn't.

The problem, of course, was not so much the city as its poverty. Our guess of the night before that Glasgow was currently down at her heels proved accurate indeed. It is not pleasant to see someone down on his luck, and certainly not a whole city. That was the pain greater than the sight of litter and decaying buildings: the sight of decaying people. Many looked hearty enough, but, whatever the reasons, Glasgow seemed to have far more than its share of physically crippled or otherwise sickly looking citizens.

In planning the trip I had suspected that Glasgow was no beauty spot. Then what were we doing in it? An overnight stop on our way to the Highlands might have made good sense, but why had we scheduled two nights and an entire day? The answer is that it exists. We had never seen Scotland before. We wanted to know something about it. It didn't feel right to visit it for a fortnight without seriously seeing one of its two largest cities. Still, I'd also suspected we'd be seeing poverty there. Why travel to see poverty? Again, because it exists.

It was not the first time we have been guilty of such foolishness. In 1969, when we were stationed with the military in Okinawa, Lily and I went on vacation to Bangkok, Singapore, and India. In going to India, we had deliberately scheduled two full days in Calcutta because we *wanted* to see its poverty, a devastating poverty that makes Cardiff and Glasgow look like habitations of splendor. No matter that we spent most of our time in Calcutta trying to get out more quickly; we have seen it. At our home in rural northwestern Connecticut there is a small brick patio thirty yards to the side of the house. It is shaded by ancient maples and looks out over our well-tended flower gardens. From May through October I spend much of my time sitting on that patio writing, dictating, making phone calls, meeting with people, or simply looking at the beauty surrounding me. I call it "my anti-Calcutta spot." It is an antidote to ugliness and decay and despair. I am very grateful for it, and my name for it bespeaks of a depth of appreciation that would be lacking had I not seen Calcutta.

My father was a self-made man. The son of a small-town Indiana haberdasher, he graduated from college at nineteen, Harvard Law School at twenty-two, and by the time I was born, he was a major partner in New York City's most prestigious law firm. I was raised in security and comfort and provided with the best education money could buy. I am therefore *not* a self-made man. Enveloped by affluence, I grew up on Park Avenue.

What most people do not realize, however, is that there are two Park Avenues in Manhattan. The one we hear about, where I was raised, extends southward from 96th Street—an almost four-mile-long canyon lined by impressive apartment buildings, each with fancily uniformed doormen. It is a wide canyon, the widest avenue in New York City, four lanes heading downtown and four headed uptown separated by a rectangular block-long garden on every street. These gardens are filled with flowers in the spring. Deep below them lie the tunnels of the New York Central Railroad. Sometimes you can faintly hear the trains rumbling underneath, even feel them vibrating by, but it is all very muted and civilized.

At 96th Street the trains come out from their tunnel going north to clack noisily upon tracks elevated on ancient, rusty steel girders. It is still called Park Avenue, but the parks are gone, instantly replaced by this maze of grimy metal. Just as instantly the tall apartment buildings are also gone. More narrow, the avenue is now lined by row after row of tenements pressing in, their windows boarded up or used for the hanging of laundry. The doormen have suddenly become junkies and panhandlers and prostitutes and muggers. Within the course of a city block the traveler has gone from a part of New York City famed for its white-skinned affluence and entered Harlem, a part almost equally famed for its dark-skinned degradation. Ninety-sixth Street and Park Avenue is one of the most dramatic juxtapositions of financial wealth and financial poverty in the world. Attending a private boy's grammar school near the junction and riding the 4:02 train north on weekends to our "country home," I could not help but see it. That juxtaposition haunted me as a young child, and it has continued to haunt me.

Such matters are not to be simplistically analyzed. But I know nothing better to credit than this haunting for a certain sense of social responsibility that has also haunted me ever since. From early on I was profoundly aware that, financially at least, I was advantaged through no fault of my own. It wasn't something I had earned; it was something I was born into. Financially, I was born lucky, and I knew it. It led to a sense of gratitude and also to a sense of guilt of sorts. I felt obligated to somehow pay the world back for my mindless good fortune. But how?

Not by going into Harlem myself, or any other ghetto of poverty. The battle between the rich and poor has hardly begun, but I was one of those to early on have a little foretaste of it. Back in the 1940s, affluent adults were safe in New York City and could still walk in Central Park at night. But children were not safe. I was almost accustomed, by the age of ten, to being assaulted the closer I got to Harlem, both in the park and in the streets, by small gangs of youths from north of 96th Street whose pastime was to prey on little rich kids. I was never physically hurt, but I was knocked down and robbed on a number of occasions. It was not a useless experience. By an early age I had learned how to feel my fear and smell danger when it was still a way off. And I certainly learned not to go into Harlem. It was a learning that has stood me in good stead. The very few times since that I have walked into a ghetto of poverty and violence have been only when I had a ghetto guide and a reputation as peacemaker that preceded me.

It is not just a matter of fear for my physical safety but also fear for my spirit. I personally experience the discomforts and shabbiness of poverty as both depressing and oppressing. Mind you, I know that the spiritual poverty of those who dwell above the tracks on the "good" part of Park Avenue is at least as great as those who dwell under the tracks on the bad part. But my own very being seems to *need* a certain modicum of beauty and softness, security and comfort for my health. I am not very tough in this way. Having felt as if I would die if I did not escape the contamination of Calcutta within forty-eight hours, I look upon Mother Teresa as a powerful figure. I cannot imagine myself having the toughness to voluntarily live year after year in the midst of such squalor.

The best I am able to do is to not ignore it. There are certain people who seem to have trained their eyes to not see poverty. Some are the poor themselves, and while their blindness may be a curse to keep them in poverty, it may also be a blessing that enables them to survive. Others are wealthy. Somehow they are simply not able to notice the 96th Street juxtapositions of this world. They are kept out of sight and out of mind. I think this blindness is a curse in itself, because it causes people to think of their wealth solely as their right. I find such people hard to love in their arrogance and complacency. This is what I mean by their spiritual poverty, that they are paradoxically impoverished precisely because they are not poor in spirit and have become emotional fat cats.

So this was not a pleasant day. I would not have wanted to stay in Glasgow longer. But I am glad to have at least seen it. And Cardiff. And Calcutta. And 96th Street.

Addicted to my comforts, I am a careful money manager. Yet from time to time, even with money I have made a big gamble. Perhaps the biggest such gamble was marrying Lily since my father, who disapproved of her because she is Chinese, vowed he would disinherit me if I did so without waiting at least the four years until I finished medical school. For a few months I tried to wait, but it didn't seem right. It didn't seem right to not marry, and it didn't seem right to let my father try to control my life with money. So we were married on December 27, 1959, during my first year in medical school. We had paid up one month's rent on an apartment in the attic of the True Sisters Nursery School in Cleveland, Ohio. I had purchased a used bed, bureau, and hot plate. The apartment had a small, old refrigerator but was otherwise unfurnished. We had $800 in the bank—our life savings at twenty-three and twenty-five—no car, and a $1,200 tuition bill coming due in two months.

Our first fight occurred four days after our wedding when Lily went out and bought a cheap eight-piece place setting that was on sale. I saw no need for more than four. Another agony occurred shortly thereafter. Our little garret was a mile from the nearest grocery market, and our greatest hardship that first winter was carrying heavy bags of groceries back along Cleveland's poorly shoveled, icy sidewalks. After several weeks of debate, we broke down and for $25 purchased at Sears a small cart to wheel the bags behind us. The first time we used it, as was the custom, we parked it inside the entrance of the store, and used a real grocery cart for our shopping. When we finished that shopping we discovered that our own little cart had been stolen. It felt a bit like rape, as being robbed often does. Given the state of our finances, it also felt close to tragedy.

Lily was an experienced laboratory technician, and within a few days of arriving in Cleveland had landed a forty-hour-a-week job at University Hospitals. In addition, we both worked two to three nights a week in the labs. We could have made it. Indeed, after three months when my father offered to reinherit me to the tune of paying my tuition in addition to a stipend of a hundred dollars a month, we were quite tempted to tell him to take his money and shove it. Fortunately, we had an older couple for friends. They suggested that money might be the only way my father knew how to communicate (a perspicacious assessment) and that by rejecting his offer we might forever be blocking communication with my parents. So wiser heads prevailed, and we bought another little shopping cart that we guarded more closely. Otherwise, our lifestyle didn't change until our first child was born a year and a half later.

Just as my father's reinheriting me permitted us to have children two years sooner, so I suspect many years later his generosity played a major role in my becoming a writer. In early 1975 he made us a gift of fifty thousand dollars that allowed us to pay off our mortgage and have a few extra dollars in the bank as well. Six months later I had the notion to write a book about discipline, love, and grace. The notion stuck. I began reorganizing my practice to limit it to four days a week, and in January 1976 I used the other three days to begin writing *The Road Less Traveled*. I am not sure that the notion would have come to me in the first place, much less be acted upon, had I had the burden of mortgage payments hanging over my head. I do not think the timing was accidental. I think his gift of money gave me the freedom to follow my calling.

I suspect that for some years my father felt he

had reason to regret his generosity. "What are you doing writing a book? You know books don't sell," he admonished me on several occasions. "You're a psychiatrist. You've got a good practice going. Stick with it. Shoemaker, stick to your last."

He was wrong in a sense, because I was hardly writing the book to make money; I was doing it because I was under orders of a sort. He was right, however, that books generally don't sell. Indeed, it was six years from the time I had begun writing it that it had made me more than the minimum wage. And the three years after it was published—during a period of rampant inflation when all three of our children were either in college or private school—was the first time since the end of medical school that we not only didn't save a little bit of money but were spending more than we were making.

But things turned around, and in 1983 we began making more money from *The Road Less Traveled* and my other books than we had ever dreamed. That has continued, with the result that this day in Glasgow in our late middle age we are a relatively wealthy couple.

At the age of nineteen, on a trip to Naples, I took an American Express bus tour to Pompeii. At one point the bus stopped in the midst of the ruins and the guide announced that the men and women would need to separate for twenty minutes. He was going to take us men up the street to see some artwork that was illegal for women to view. He suggested the ladies would like to go down the street where there was some fine shopping. We all piled out of the bus and separated as instructed save for an elderly nun who either did not speak English or hadn't heard the guide. She trotted right along with us men. I will never forget the frantic anxiety with which the American women cried out, "Sister, don't go. Come back. Sister, come back right now!" Eventually they did succeed in saving her from venial sin. Ah, those were the obedient fifties.

My other memory that day is of the art. The larger amount of it consisted of human figures painted with Roman accuracy lining the walls of a small room, depicted in standard positions of copulation. More memorable for me, however, was a single painting on the outside of the villa. It was protected by a box with a little door that the guide slyly unlocked to reveal the figure of a middle-aged man holding out in front of himself a simple scale. On one plate of the scale was painted a pile of gold coins. On the other, protruding from the man's toga, lay the bulk of the man's enormous but somewhat flaccid phallus. Impressed by the size of this member, one of my fellow tourists commented, "No wonder the Romans conquered the world!" But what impressed me more was the caption beneath the painting. I cannot remember the Latin, but it roughly translated as, "In youth one has a powerful penis; in age a lot of money; and their different virtues balance out."

I would not recall this experience of almost forty years ago with such clarity had not the message of the medium been quite meaningful in its accuracy. But the matter is also considerably more ambiguous than the artist had let on. The sexual potency of youth, as I've suggested, can be something of a mixed blessing. Moreover, one does not necessarily have much gold in old age. Finally, if we are fortunate enough to come into money with aging, as Lily and I have been, we are also likely to discover that wealth, too, can be a mixed blessing. Sexuality and money are two of the most paradoxical things I know. Remember that all blessings are potential curses, and all curses are potential blessings, and the greater the one the greater the other.

You should perhaps realize that we are probably not as wealthy as you might think. Our net worth is just about four million dollars. That's handsome, but it doesn't put us in a league with the really big-timers. Moreover, given appreciation and inflation, almost half of that wealth has come from my parents by gift or inheritance. I have not earned any more money as a famous author than my father did as a famous lawyer. Except by inheritance, the only way to amass a truly great fortune is through extraordinary success in the business of industry. One might think of my books and lectures as being a part of the entertainment industry, and it is true that a few entertainers make as much money as the other greatest business moguls. The entertainment they provide, however, is considerably more glamorous than treatises about psychology and religion.

I must say this because the overestimation of

wealth by others is one of the burdens of money, and why many attempt to keep their wealth secret. But if your name is Rockefeller or on the bestseller list it cannot be kept secret, and one instantly becomes what the legal profession refers to as "deep pockets." By this lawyers mean that the individual is particularly liable to suit for particularly large sums simply because he or she is known or assumed to be wealthy.

Liability to litigation is not the only problem of the "deep pockets syndrome"; one also becomes a target for fund-raisers. This in itself is not bad. I believe in philanthropy and fund-raisers. But it can be bad when the philanthropy is *expected*, when one is criticized for not giving to a particular charity or for not giving more. Moreover, when one does contribute substantially to a charity one is likely to create even greater expectations, and that can be quite destructive. It is not always easy to get such a charity to refrain from thinking, "Well, there's plenty more where that came from."

One reason for the frequent overestimation of wealth is the underestimation of the expenses of wealth. I think people who are not self-employed (which is most) are more likely to be prone to this. A couple of years ago my program manager received a letter from a clergyman in England requesting my services as a lecturer and inquiring as to my fee. Gail wrote back that my standard fee was $10,000 U.S. for a lecture day or any part thereof, plus travel expenses. She added, however, that there might be some flexibility in this were he to cooperate with others in setting up a lecture tour in Great Britain. A letter quickly returned from him that he was "absolutely outraged" a supposed man of God should charge "a daily fee half my annual stipend." Gail replied that she understood there was a culture factor involved. We knew that the British were not accustomed, like the Americans and Australians, to paying significantly for hearing lectures, and she doubted they could reach accommodation. "But it may help to salve your sense of outrage," she commented, "to know that Dr. Peck pays his own benefits such as housing and health insurance, that he pays ten times your annual stipend for staff salaries and operations, another ten times your stipend for taxes and gives away yet another ten times to charity in addition to a third of his time." Gail did not hear back from the gentleman, and we doubt he was much mollified.

Being in the "entertainment industry," our wealth and my fame are deeply intertwined. Fame sells books and lectures. Lectures and publicity sell more books and lectures. This has necessitated many ongoing decisions, some a bit agonizing, and we are never certain we have made them well. Just how many media interviews should I do? None or all have been tempting solutions, but it's generally seemed best to set some kind of middle course. What course? How? Which to do and which not to do? Should I put my address in my books? Which letters should be answered personally, which by our staff, and which not at all? How far should we go in offering help to those who request it? What manuscripts should I bless as others have blessed mine? How much protection do I need from predators? How is it best effected?

For ten years, until early 1982, we had the services of a part-time secretary and a one-day-a-week maid. I answered all our mail and paid the bills. Lily minded the children while also seeing some patients. We had a single phone line with a listed number. I figured out our own taxes. In retrospect, in many ways, life was remarkably uncomplicated.

Now we have six different phone lines and three different fax lines; a full-time staff of three, a part-time staff of two; the regular services of a real estate lawyer, a tax lawyer, and a publishing lawyer; a hard-working accountant who tells us what to sign; and an unusually conscientious literary agent. We are utterly dependent upon all these people and their talents. There is no way we could handle the complications of our lives without them, much less be here in Scotland on holiday with only a rare fax to deal with. We have been truly blessed by their gifts and dedication. But this wonderful human conglomerate did not just happen by accident nor does it continue to work smoothly without glitches. It all has to be "managed." And while it has allowed us to lead infinitely more complicated lives, this management has required not only some of our time but also that we do a little bit to learn "management skill." In other words, the real grace of such support is also a responsibility that is itself a complication which requires time and attention and represents yet another hidden cost to fame and wealth.

Moreover, money itself needs to be managed, and this, too, takes time. If you're fortunate enough to have savings, you can put them under your mattress, but it's not smart and hardly what would be called stewardship. So where and how do you invest your nest egg? Do you invest it yourself or let others do it for you? Should you go for high-risk/high-yield investments or low-risk/low-yield ones? How much should you get into tax shelters? How much should be tied up and how much liquid? How diversified should your investments be? How much research should you do in making these decisions? Obviously, the more money you have the more such decisions you will need to make and the more complicated they may become. Paradoxically, now that we are relatively wealthy I worry much more about money than I did a decade ago when we had very little of it to brood over.

The most complicated financial decision we've had to make was whether to incorporate our business. The reasons to consider it were mostly the tax shelters available at the time to "professional corporations" (many of which were shortly abolished leaving us with a more cumbersome financial bureaucracy for little pay off). For us, the greatest complication of that decision was its ethical aspects. I was concerned about the ethics of the shelters available to the wealthy and how much they contributed to the tendency for "the rich to become richer while the poor become poorer." Ultimately, we decided to take the advice of a wise and older couple who suggested one formula for living: "Make as much money as you can so that you can give as much of it away as you can."

So a year later we began to think about how best to give a substantial amount of our money away. No charitable organization existed to do what we believed was the most needed in the world: to teach people the principles of community—the dawning technology of healthy communication within and between groups or organizations. So, in conjunction with nine others, Lily and I decided to start one. Thus, in 1984, the Foundation for Community Encouragement (FCE) was established. For us it has been very much like having children. We never dreamed of how much work it would be. We also never dreamed of how much we would learn from it.

It can be either very easy or very difficult to give away money. A number of FCE's small donors and a few of its large ones have simply said, "Here's my check. It seems like you're doing good work and we'd like to help you out, but this is as far as we want to get involved." We're very grateful to them. But others who donate large sums feel it may be incumbent upon them to see to it that they are managed well, and if so they may discover it can actually be more complicated to give away money than it is to make it. Paradoxically again, it may also be more emotionally rewarding—as it has been for us.

When we started FCE we were a bunch of do-gooders who didn't know anything about how to do good in terms of running a nonprofit organization. Had you asked me back then what strategic planning was, I might have told you it was probably something the air force did over Cambodia. Most of what we have learned these past eight years has come as a result of working with many others in the management of FCE, and it has often been painful learning. At one point or another we have made almost every managerial mistake in the book. And far and away the most agonizing financial decision we've ever had to make was not in regard to our personal finances but in regard to "charity." FCE was hit devastatingly hard by the 1990–92 "recession," and survived only because over the course of six months we downsized its annual budget from $750,000 to $250,000. This meant the laying off of ten employees. There are relatively few things in life more dreadful than assuming the responsibility for laying off competent people.

FCE also not only survived but thrived thanks to the ever-increasing generosity of its donors and other volunteers. Donors are volunteers, and volunteers donate not only their money but also their time. That time is money and money is time is a well-known equivalency. Lily and I have given FCE over a million dollars these past years. In addition, as recounted, to protect or enhance that investment, we've given it approximately a third of our time. Others have given it hundreds of thousand of dollars, but, more importantly, many have given it as much time as we. Currently, FCE has only three full-time employees. Yet its influence is greater than ever because a hundred are working for it for free.

This has also added to our necessary learning

of management skills. Recently a renowned organizational psychologist (who had already been a financial donor) decided to become more deeply involved through his time as well. He was briefed about FCE's many problems for which he initially had textbook solutions. After learning, however, that it is compromised of not only a board and staff and financial donors but also of a body of leaders who sometimes work as independent subcontractors for fee and sometimes for free, as well as paid and unpaid consultants in addition to a host of other volunteers, he opined that "While FCE is relatively small, perhaps by necessity it may just be the most complex organization on the face of the earth."

Money is also power of a sort, and power is dangerous. It can give one control over people, which may make them afraid or dishonest, which is neither good for them nor for you. It may also make them improperly dependent, leading to all manner of resentment and destructiveness. Or to a psychology of entitlement where it is simply assumed that "the Pecks will provide." Consequently, along with our philanthropy has come the responsibility to do our damnedest to empower others in the organization. Sometimes this has seemed like an endless uphill struggle. But now in our late middle age one of the greatest joys of our life is that we seem to have succeeded. FCE has finally become independent from us financially and managerially. It now stands on its own two feet and, insofar as we want, we can step aside and take our rest.

More recently we have also been giving our

money to our children. This, too, is our delight, and it, too, is problematic. Not only are money and time rough equivalents but also money and freedom. So it is our delight because we believe we are helping to give them greater freedom just as my father's gift gave me the freedom to write *The Road Less Traveled.* But along with this delight has come the same set of dilemmas of power associated with organizational philanthropy. How does the donor discourage dependency and a sense of entitlement? At what ages and levels of maturity should money be given to children directly or in trust? What responsibility, if any, do parents have to teach their adult children financial management skills? How should such teaching be accomplished? Given our children's and our own separation issues, giving money to them has, upon occasion, led them to feel controlled and less rather than more free: The very opposite of our heart's desire for them.

Of all the paradoxes of money, the greatest quirk for us personally is that giving it away has turned us into fund-raisers. Wanting our number-one charity, FCE, to become independent of us as quickly as possible has meant we have had to work long and hard to find and enlist other major donors. It seems to me one of God's best ironies in our lives that at the very moment we became wealthy, He also put us in the position of being beggars.

It is not an easy position. Raised to be a supposedly good WASP, one way or another it was drummed into me that becoming a beggar would be the ultimate degradation, that asking someone for money would not merely be the most tasteless, egregious thing I could do to them but the most humiliating thing I could do to myself. Overcoming these profound, built-in inhibitions has been difficult.

There is also a tendency for the rich to be profoundly stingy. On the average, those who make relatively little money give away a larger percentage of their income to charity than those who annually make six figures or more. That is a sad fact of life—at least the life of those of us called to fund-raising—and a pathetic commentary on what wealth may do to people. Even worse, there are those of the wealthy who are willing to entertain us fund-raisers (and themselves) primarily because they enjoy toying with us and the apparent sadistic pleasure of saying, "No," after encouraging us into their lair. Fund-raising is an enormously frustrating business. And, in a sense, it is degrading when we begin to allow it to propel us to look upon others as mere potential "targets."

From time to time, however, we do meet wealthy people who are extremely generous, even to the point of giving away half of their income each year. (Average them in, and it means that most of the rich don't give anything away.) Whenever this has happened I have felt touched by grace. I was particularly touched by one such incident.

Eight years ago, when FCE was struggling to get started, I did a speaking engagement in Fort Worth. A woman came up to me in the book-signing line afterward explaining that she didn't have a book but wanted to deliver a letter to me from a friend of hers. I thanked her and, because many were waiting in line, I simply slipped the envelope into my coat pocket. When the book signing was done the promoter of the engagement drove me back to the hotel. During the drive he handed me a check for $6,000, my fee for lecturing in those days. At that moment I remembered the letter in my pocket, fished it out, and read:

> Dear Scotty: I'm sorry I was tied up and couldn't come to hear you talk today. You probably don't remember me, but six months ago I heard you speak in San Antonio about community and your new foundation. Please find enclosed a small donation to its work. I wish it could be more.

So I was sitting there in the car with two checks on my lap. One was made out to me by contract for services for $6,000. The other for $500 to FCE was a total surprise. Which check, which sum, more uplifted my spirits? It was the lesser. Should you wonder why, you might remember that grace has sometimes been defined as "the gift unearned, the gift unexpected." I believe it has been good for us that at a time when we could have begun to totally rely upon our predictable investment accounts we were pushed to rely on such unpredictable providence.

Fund-raising is itself community building, and while we may initially have sought some of them out as targets, over the years many of FCE's significant donors of time and money have also become our dear friends. It is hard not to love someone who is consistently willing to share the load with you. Given its frustrations and my own inhibitions, I could not even have done it unless I envisioned begging as a spiritual discipline of sorts (for which there is a long religious tradition). It has seldom paid off in the ways and times we expected. But in the long run it has paid off handsomely. Through fund-raising we have been blessed not only by the grace of dollars for FCE but even more by the grace of good friends.

To continue with its paradoxes, it is often recognized that money is perhaps more likely to be enslaving than liberating. It is a seductive mistress. I've mentioned that I worry far more about money than I used to when we didn't have much of it, and have explained why this is proper to a degree. What I haven't said is that I worry about it more than necessary—and in ways that I shouldn't. It can easily slip into an obsession. Partly this is because just thinking about it can relieve boredom and anxiety. It is almost fun to obsessively count the numbers, to review over and again our various bank accounts and their daily fluctuations.

I am perhaps more prone to this obsession than most. Born in May 1936, I am very much a Depression baby. Throughout our good side of Park Avenue childhoods, my father would not only expound to my brother and me, "You boys have got to learn the value of a dollar," but also repeatedly proclaim, "We're going to the poorhouse." Part of me knew at the time that this was laughable. Partly, however, it also sunk in. As an adolescent, when I took my dates to dinner I would sit in silent anguish if they ordered anything other than one of the least expensive entrées. I was able to get over that, but to this day I'm not entirely certain we're not going to the poorhouse. What if the bottom falls out of the stock market? What if inflation runs rampant? What if? What if?

Money and security are also equivalents of another sort, but great security is an illusion. Life is an inherently insecure business. At the age of fifteen, terrified as I quit a prestigious prepatory school and walked away from a golden WASP track that had been all laid out for me, I was granted a revelation that "the only real security in life lies in relishing life's insecurity." I have preached this revelation, yet to this day I continue to need to relearn it. Savings are a security. Indeed, a certain variety of them are called "securities." But enough of them is never enough—at least not when we are chasing after the illusion of total security. Annoy me though they might as a fund-raiser, I know perfectly well that those very wealthy who never give away anything have been damned to chase after that empty illusion.

I know because a part of them is in me. I may not have fallen prey as completely as they to the idolatry of money, but the fact remains that nothing continues to interfere more with my prayer life than book sales statistics. Some spiritual writers have diagnosed the human race as suffering from a "psychology of scarcity" and urged us to what they call a psychology of abundance—a mind-set where we feel that there will always be enough and that God will plentifully provide. I believe in this teaching. It's just that as a Depression baby I'm practically never able to follow it, try as I might.

Occasionally, however, I do receive an inadvertent assist from our beloved accountant when he advises us to switch funds from here to there or roll them over from this into that. He used to try to explain these things to us. Now, familiar with the limitations of my mind, whenever I ask, "Why do you want us to do that, John?" he replies, "Just do it, Doctor, just do it." At such moments I do begin to feel that it is all merely paper; it is funny money. And, on a strange level, money is funny. If I can only momentarily catch a glimpse of this level of reality, I imagine it must be impossible for those who have no wealth to laugh about it. But I, for one, desperately need reminding that money is not the most serious thing in life.

Another seduction of money is the insulation it can provide. It can keep us well south of 96th Street, but that can also mean we are kept well south of reality and oblivious to the winters of the world. Such oblivion may lead us not merely to the ignorance of poverty but the ignorance of ideas, even to the ignorance of the present. My father hit his professional and financial stride in the early 1940s, and there he stayed by and large. He stopped growing. His little Park Avenue world insulated him from Vietnam and the hippies, from Head Start programs and the Women's Movement, from Watts and Watergate. The world was changing, but though he did much good with his money, it allowed him to not change along with the times. This is why in the last two decades of his life Lily and I came to refer to his Park Avenue apartment as "the mausoleum."

Still, there is paradox, and not all insulation is to be decried. We used the expensive opulence of One Devonshire Gardens last night to soften the blow of the ugliness of our hotel and Glasgow's poverty. I do not think this was bad. Such softening allowed us to stay and experience Glasgow more deeply rather than immediately retreating from it, as we had from Calcutta. We need a certain amount of such insulation, just as we need shelter and clothing. It may be used to provide necessary and quite justified relief.

Another kind of justifiable relief is the wonderful relief from endless comparative shopping. Lily and I will assiduously research the cost/benefit ratios of various houses or automobiles before purchasing one. But thank God we no longer have to look around for the least expensive onions or drive ten miles farther for a slightly less costly screwdriver. Such shopping is a form of enslavement and often a compulsive psychological addiction. We have been sadly amused to watch certain people whose time is worth over thirty dollars an hour spend two hours and two dollars of gas to save three dollars on a "better buy."

Disagreement over money has superficially been the death of countless marriages, although often it is but a symbol of deeper, divisive issues.

All things are overdetermined. Conversely, agreement over money has been one of the many determinants of the sometimes surprising strength of Lily's and my marriage. As in other areas, there has been considerable division of labor. I am the one who does the obsessive counting and loves to do the banking, but I'd never make a significant new investment without Lily's concurrence. As primary homemaker, she handles most of the consuming but never makes an extraordinary purchase without my agreement. Roughly half of our assets are held jointly and the other half divided very evenly between us. This policy is a radical departure from that of my father, who, for some reason I never understood, maintained total control over my mother's finances. Even before the days of the Women's Liberation Movement, from the very beginning, Lily and I were in agreement that her homemaking services were of at least equal worth to my "breadwinning" ones.

The most basic reason for our agreement is that we share the same *values* (with a little exception now and then). We both think that Jaguars are lovely cars, but neither of us has felt that the money couldn't be spent better elsewhere. Our top priorities have been responsible savings, education for ourselves as well as our children, staff development, travel (itself, hopefully, a form of education), and effective philanthropy plus a modicum of sustaining beauty.

Tonight we do not have such beauty. But we did at the restaurant last night and perhaps tomorrow we shall have it again. That's enough.

So we sit in our infinitely brown, cramped, and airless room, picnicking on meat pies, occasionally looking out the small window over the uninviting back alleys of Glasgow on another evening that is ever more endless the farther north we go. Like Cardiff, it has not been an easy day. Yet, overall, we realize that on this trip we thus far have generally been having great fun together.

And together, each in our own way in our late middle age, we are toying with a complex notion. Maybe we don't have to leave *more* money to our children than we ourselves received. The point may not be to start or enlarge a dynasty. Maybe we don't have to give ever more to philanthropy in the attempt to save the world. Maybe, within the limits of reason—charting a fine course between self-indulgent profligacy and self-abnegation—one of the many potential virtues of money is that it is simply to be enjoyed.

CHAPTER X

DEATH
TUESDAY JUNE 9

Our escape from Glasgow was remarkably similar to our escape from Cardiff, only even more dramatic. Needless to say, we departed the city as early as we possibly could, and within an hour, in the pouring rain, we were already halfway up the western shore of Loch Lomond.

Loch Lomond! Reverberations from my childhood swept over me the way the sheets of rain and mist were sweeping over our car. As I noted, back in that English grammar school not all the songs we sang were songs of battle. Some were of tender, bittersweet romance, and the one I piped out in my prepubescent voice with as great vigor as Men of Harlech was:

> Oh, ye'll tak' the high road
> an' I'll tak' the low road,
> An' I'll be in Scotland before ye;
> But me and my true love will never meet again
> On the bonnie, bonnie banks o' Loch Lomond.

Yet here, almost fifty years later, I was together on the same road with Lily—more my true love than anyone other than God—on those very bonnie banks of which I had once so lustily intoned.

We could barely make them out in the swirling mists and showers. But they were lovely. More than lovely. And this is something those who have not been there will simply have to take on faith, because I cannot explain it. I cannot explain how, when we couldn't begin to see the mountain tops or the other shore in the fog, but we knew with total certainty that we had entered the most beautiful land on earth.

The scientist in me shrinks from such hyperbole. The *most* beautiful land on earth? Why not New Zealand? Why not the Greek Isles? Why not the Tetons, the Grand Canyon? Why not Wales or the Lake District? Besides, beauty is in the eye

218

of the beholder. Isn't everything relative? Who are we to absolutely declare this the most beautiful land on earth?

I cannot answer you. Let's just say that Scotland is divided into its islands and mainland, and its mainland can be divided into north and south. Glasgow sits between the north and the south. Let's just say that a few miles north of Glasgow the land undergoes a transformation into something that will haunt us for the rest of our days—as it has haunted many before us and will haunt many to come.

One thing that makes the northern mainland of Scotland so haunting is its lakes or "lochs." The traveler is seldom for long out of sight of one of these bodies of water. Some, like Loch Lomond, are true lakes—large inland bodies of fresh water. Others, like the nearby Loch Fyne, are long inlets that give way to the sea, as do the fjords of Norway. And in the case of still others, like Loch Ness, it is hard to tell which is which since one type will not infrequently flow into the other. But no matter. The Scotch are right to call them all lochs because each and every one of them has a similar pristine glory that overwhelms such minor geographical considerations.

There were two ways to play the day. We could have stopped on the bonnie banks of Loch Lomond—or in the exquisite town of Inveraray that juts out into Loch Fyne—and waited for the rain to stop. But we didn't know how long that might take. Besides, while we were certain it would eventually clear, we were not sure we would then ever have left.

So instead we proceeded on to emerge from the downpour into a drizzle and from the mountains into the less dramatic but marvelously gentle landscape of the Kilmartin Valley. It was not solely a weather-based decision. By now we were becoming experienced researchers with ever more specific guidebooks and ever more detailed ordinance survey maps. Over these we had whiled away a few of our Glasgow hours to realize that this valley, about twenty miles in length, had been one of the greater centers of megalithic civilization. And after a day without them, we were once again starved for stones.

The valley is not famous only for its stones. When mysterious enough, we can also devour a site that is not quite prehistoric. Rising out of the bogland of the valley floor, like a landlocked Mont-Saint-Michel, is a steep, 150-foot-high hill crowned with boulders. When we climbed the hill, just below the top, we marched through a natural passageway between the great rocks to enter the hollow of the crown. This was Dunadd Fort, the central fort of the Dalriada, a Scots tribe from around A.D. 500. It was also where the tribe reputedly crowned its kings for the ensuing five hundred years. It did not feel to us like some idle legend. The spot reeked of history. It took us little imagination to be transported back more than a thousand years into that hilltop hollow and feel the presence of a throng of fur-clad warriors gathered there to pledge their lives and loyalty. Indeed, were I to choose between Westminster Abbey and Dunadd Fort, the latter would be far and away my preferred place to conduct a coronation.

The fort is additionally noteworthy for the Boar Stone. Nestled among the boulders at its very top are two slabs of stone. The larger contains a deep carving of a footprint and a shallow carving of a footprint and a shallow carving of a wild boar. Although so shallow as to be barely discernible, we were astonished by the realism and artistry of the animal. It would be another week before we would have some understanding of this artistry. In the smaller, adjacent slab there was carved a simple, round depression or "cup." We knew enough at this point to realize that the boar carving was posthistoric and the simple cup, a typical mark of the megalithic people, was probably prehistoric. The Dunadd Fort, dramatically overlooking a part of the valley and its river, is a naturally "holy" spot, appropriate not only for the crowning of kings but for any kind of great solemn ritual. It is probable that the Dalriada had appropriated for their historic fort a site that over two thousand years before had also been sacred to the prehistoric, megalithic culture.

And it is that older culture which has left the greater mark on Kilmartin Valley. We spent an hour exploring the fort; we spent four exploring megalithic remains.

One type of such remains was exemplified by the sculptured stones of Achnabreck. They were well marked but not easily accessible. After parking at the end of a dirt road, we hiked along a marvelously mossy path through a Merlinesque wood of dripping, druidic oaks. This eventually led us to a gate into the backyard of a farm. Crossing it, we followed where the grass had been trod into a long meadow and hence climbed through its herd of sheep toward a mountaintop pine forest. Just inside the forest we finally found a clearing containing several great ledges of bare rock. These natural rock formations were extensively carved with almost mathematically precise sets of concentric circles that are called, quite simply, "rings."

Some rings contained only three concentric circles and were but a foot wide. Others had up to seven and were close to a yard wide. Occasionally the rings overlapped, giving the effect of flowing into each other. Many were open-ended and might better be termed *swirls* than rings. We immediately recognized that the two figures we had seen carved into the side of Old Meg back in England were the same brand of art. In fact, with the exception of primitive hollows or "cups" and the stones themselves, rings are the most significant form of art remaining from the megalithic culture in the British Isles.

Modern sophisticates might be tempted to say that sets of concentric circles should hardly be labeled "art." I doubt, however, that they would fall prey to the temptation once they had actually visited a few sites containing them. The rings somehow bespeak of their great age, and there is something strangely impressive about them. Frankly, they are a bit exciting.

A number of similar sites of carved, natural rock faces dot the Kilmartin Valley, but we did not visit them. We'd spent over an hour on the sculptured stones of Achnabreck, and it was all we could afford—particularly given the fact that it was still drizzling and our feet were already utterly soaked. And given the fact that the valley is also dotted throughout by menhirs or standing stones of extraordinary variety. Twice there was a pattern to them. At one place six formed a close, regular row in a distant field. At another, five were more widely separated, spanning the corners of three, now separate, fields in an apparently straight line. How we would have loved to have paced each row! But they were across multiple barbed-wire fences and acres of useful grain we would have trampled. Besides, we were already calculating the number of hours we would need to spend this evening with the hairdryer aimed not at our heads but at our shoes.

Most of the menhirs were simply single stones, standing in their aloneness and uniqueness. One that we touched, having found it marked in its solitude on our survey map, we discovered in the back wall of a cemetery, a lichened old corpse of a megalith embedded amid the gorse. Another, because it was marked on the same map at the very foot of Dunadd Fort, we searched for in vain for almost half an hour until we finally realized it was sitting under a clothesline in the backyard of a farmhouse. It was not surprising we'd over-looked it. Although incredibly accurate as to their location, survey maps don't indicate the size of the stones. This one was but three feet high— hardly even a hitching post. I roared with laughter when I eventually identified it. A workman in the backyard heard me and inquired as to the source of my mirth. I pointed to it and opined it might be the smallest identified menhir in all of Great Britain. "Aye, it's a bit wee," he agreed.

On the other hand, another menhir down the valley was at least as tall as Old Meg and strikingly phallic, but sadly unreachable. Still others were less sizable but dramatically hoary and closer to the road. We embraced several of them.

But the main attraction of Kilmartin Valley is its many megalithic tombs. They are all over the valley. Their greatest concentration, however, is a two-mile-long row of them collectively named the Nether Largie Cairns. They comprise a four-thousand-year-old necropolis.

The most obvious thing we know about the megalithic people is that they considered death to be a matter of considerable import. In this respect alone, they were not unique. Three ways they behaved, however, conspire to make their fascination with death quite remarkable.

One is that they were megalithic. Just as they manipulated huge stones for other purposes, so they used them to construct tombs. Stones remain, and the larger they are the more clearly they remain to tell us something of what these people were up to. For all we know they may simply have dumped most of their dead into the ground or the local river. But to house a considerable number of them for a time they constructed chambers from huge slabs of rock.

A second factor is that they did not seem to be very much focused upon a dead individual. Into these megalithic burial chambers they usually put the remains not of one but of many. To what extent the intermingled skeletons belonged to the same small family or the same large tribe we do not know. What we do know, relative to other cultures, is that the megalithic people distinctly favored a kind of group entombment. And perhaps that is partly why they went to such effort to build tombs that would last—the monuments were cost effective.

Neither of these factors alone, or together, are unique. Lily and I spent three wonderful years on the island of Okinawa. The Okinawans have an ancient culture that centers, to a considerable extent, upon ancestor worship. Profusely dotting the island are both ancient and modern huge cement-sculptured, womb-shaped tombs—some of them even lining the fairways of a golf course—into which they place the bones of the family dead in urns over the span of multiple generations.

Different from Okinawa, the third, and most decisive, factor is the extraordinary variety of these megalithic, communal tombs scattered in profusion throughout Great Britain and northwestern Europe. Some were built belowground but most are aboveground. Of all those aboveground, many were covered by circular mounds of ordinary stones to form the cairns and "tumuli" that dot much of the countryside—albeit often almost invisible except to the discriminating eye with a survey map in hand. Others were so covered but then the covering was extended for many yards—for no useful purpose that is discernible—to form long, narrow rectangular mounds or barrows. Others were covered not with stones but simply earth. Others weren't covered at all, and remain in the form of certain dolmens or quoits, starkly protruding into the sky. Some tombs have a single chamber, others have many. The variety is almost infinite.

The remains that have been found therein make for a similarly variegated picture. Some bodies appear to have been left out in the open to decompose before the bones were entombed; others appear to have been put in from the start. Some remains were clearly cremated first, and others were not. Some tombs contain both burned and unburned bones. Moreover, the bones have been found in all manner of postures and configurations. Sometimes the hands and feet are missing, sometimes the skulls; and sometimes they've just been separated, with skulls in one part of the tomb and the other bones in another. The megalithic people would appear to have been great experimenters with their dead.

Of the fraction of the Nether Largie Cairns we visited, two particularly interested us. One was the Dunchraigaig Cairn, a thirty-yard circular mound of stones that had been excavated but not restored. What impressed us about it was the partially collapsed structure of megaliths at its center, protruding up out of the small stones. It had clearly been the entrance to the tomb proper. This structure was not what one would call a dolmen, but it was sufficiently close in appearance for us to realize why scholars believe that at least some of the British dolmens had originally been either burial chambers or the entranceways of such chambers.

Still more impressive to us was the Temple Wood circle, another cairn, or pile of rocks, also thirty yards in diameter. It had not only been excavated but so well restored that its rocks were almost prissy in their neatness. In the very center of these rocks was a small rectangular, gravelike cyst. What made this site remarkable, however, was none of these: It was the four-foot-tall megalithic slabs rising out of the rocks to form a most precise stone circle approximately twenty yards in diameter. Moreover, one of these large stones was quite clearly carved with two open-ended rings or swirls. The prevailing opinion of the scholars is that the stone circle was erected by early megalithic people around 3000 B.C. and it wasn't until over a thousand years later that others decided to throw in a bunch of rocks and make a tomb or cairn out of it.

I wish they hadn't. For me the stone circle by itself would have been considerably more striking and beautiful if they'd just left it alone. This assessment is partly a matter of aesthetics. I rejoice in the *purity* of the megaliths and hate to see them cluttered up with mere rocks, no matter how neatly restored. It is also, I suspect, a reflection of my personal, philosophical disinterest in the matter of tombs.

Clearly, through the ages, a number of people have sought to ensure their own immortality through certain funerary practices which they have dictated in advance of their earthly demise. The pharaohs of Egypt were the most notable example, ordering the construction of gigantic pyramids to house their embalmed remains in sacrosanct chambers elaborately hidden from potential grave robbers. Even today there are some people with a distinct interest in the notion that they might have their bodies freeze-dried at the moment of death. I suppose they hope that at some future date interested parties will simply add some water and bring them back to life. Do they ever consider the possibility, I wonder, that there might be no interested parties?

I find it hard to empathize with such behavior. One reason it strikes me as downright silly is its materialism. It would seem to identify life solely with the body—the corpus and ultimately the corpse. It expresses no hope that the spirit or soul might eventually exist independent of the flesh. This (to me despairing) attitude is remarkably common. It is reflected in the strange Christian (and Muslim) doctrine of the resurrection of the body. Although I have become, to my immense surprise, a middle of the road Christian for the most part, this doctrine is one I still cannot subscribe to. It seems primarily a way for Christians to hedge their bets. They say they believe in the immortal soul, but apparently they want to have their body around, too. Not me, thank you. For me, the notion that we will rise from our graves on Judgment Day and pick up our corpses to slog along is distasteful to say the least.

I look forward to being liberated from my body. Mind you, I see great virtue in bodies. It is probable that nothing much gets done without them, for good as well as ill. Both God and Satan seem to *need* human bodies to do their work, and mine is an *incarnational* religion. As just one example, the vision of the Foundation for Community Encouragement (FCE) would be worthless were it not for the fact that there is an organization—a literal *corporation* or body of paid and unpaid, living human beings—to translate (or incarnate) that vision into action within the world.

Nonetheless, I do not worship bodies. In that divine play of sex, I have worshiped *at* bodies. But my glands have also driven me to indiscretion and, as I have said, I find the diminution of their potency these days to be, on the whole, a relief. Colds make me miserable and influenza is a nightmare. Forty years of an aching back has left its toll. When I think of myself I do not essentially think of my body, nor do I think of Lily as a body. I think of her uncapturable spirit, so uniquely different from my own equally uncapturable one. No, we are more spirit than flesh, and my own hope is for a day when I do not have to carry this corpus around anymore, when I can travel freely with neither luggage nor jet lag.

The other thing that strikes me so silly about a concern with one's own embalming or monumental tomb is the hubris of it all. What is its motivation except the desire to beat death? With the exception of my addiction to cigarettes, which in part is another burden of my body, I have no desire to court death. But never in my wildest imagination have I thought that I could beat it. Even Jesus didn't beat it. All he did was painfully hang around for a little bit in an ethereal, barely recognizable form to make a point. The point of resurrection is not that we can beat death; it is that there is more to us than our death, than our mere bodies.

That said, the primary reason for tombs has never been so much to cater to the desires of the deceased as the desires of the still living. The megalithic dead didn't haul great stones any more than the modern dead drive hearses or write checks to the mortician. We survivors do it. Why? Why do we do all this stuff? It is, of course, over-determined behavior.

Mostly, I suspect, it is our own, multifaceted denial of death. If we keep some bones around, then *something* is left. Perhaps the spirit is dead, but the very bones are evidence that the material-istic obliteration of death is not total. Not for a long while, at least. I myself do not find this particularly consoling, but it would appear that many do. Then there is the possibility that if the spirit is not dead, it will be benignly disposed toward us by virtue of our show of respect for its mortal remains. It will not haunt us into an early demise. Indeed, it may somehow even protect us into longevity. It is a kind of quid pro quo. If I respect you, you'll respect me. Moreover, if we honor the bones of our parents, perhaps our children will honor ours.

Finally, this fiddling with bones gives us some-thing to do. The reality is that we are utterly helpless in the face of death. Not even with the best of modern medicine do we ultimately have any control over it—even though one of the illu-sions of the modern world is that if we just improve our medicine a little bit more we might indeed be able to beat death. Meanwhile, as long as we can fiddle with the bones of those who have died we may be able to obtain some slight surcease from our feelings of absolute help-lessness. We still retain some semblance, some vestige of control.

But all this is false magic. While I can under-stand its motives from my psychoanalytic perch, as a child of the Age of Reason such motives seem pathetic. I am not, therefore, empathetic.

There is, however, one aspect of tombs that does seem a bit more reasonable to me. We humans get attached to each other. At their worst, such attachments can be killing. At their best they are not only life-giving but an exemplification of what it truly means to be human. Forget the pathological ones. The interruption by death of even the healthiest of attachments is likely to leave us feeling an intolerable void. I am not into intol-erable pain. So what if priestly anesthetics dull reality? I am all for them if they can help us in making healthy transitions, and tombs may serve us well as healthy "transitional objects" (a psychi-atric term) in this regard.

As Lily and I age, as her cholesterol level goes higher and my lungs become wheezier, we wonder more about which one of us will die first. Children of the Age of Reason, we will, of course, have no fuss, no muss cremations. But if Lily is the first, I daresay that I shall want the little, almost pretty, package of her ashes to also be placed in the ground at a pleasant spot and identi-fied by some kind of marker so I can easily find it again. I imagine that, as I make the transition into widowerhood—if I can make it—I will at first, from time to time, want to go to that spot when the weather is good, sit there for a while, and say, "Hi, Hon, it's me. How are you doing? I miss you, but generally I'm getting along okay. Let me tell you about . . ."

But that's it. No big monuments. No fiddling with bones. Not Lily's, and please not mine. I'd rather be free not only from the confines of my body but also from the constraints of society, for which I've done my bit. Let me go. Indeed, my disinterest in tombs runs deep and goes way back. Almost thirty years ago I wrote a poem, paradoxically entitled "Life Wish" because it expressed my yearning for liberation:

> *When I die*
> *I will no longer*
> *Belong to you.*
> *Do not enclose me*
> *In your midst*
> *But carry me*
> *To some open spot;*
> *Relieve me*
> *Of belts, buckles*
> *And leave me*
> *Naked there.*
> *The gentle insects*
> *Will play amid my hair.*
> *Beasts and great black birds*
> *Will find my flesh cool*
> *In the afternoon.*
> *With evening*
> *My shriveled eyes*

Will calmly reflect
The distant light
Of stars,
And I will thank you then.

Do you think me cold-hearted? A number of people have upon occasion, and I am a highly analytical, rational man. But I do mourn. I just don't do it the way most people do. I'm a bit different in that I generally do my mourning before the fact, while they generally do it after the fact.

I first became aware of this in terms of places. The three years we spent on Okinawa, from 1967 to 1970, were extraordinarily happy ones for us. Four months before we left there, on reassignment to Washington, I was sitting on a hilltop one afternoon, and I realized I was already saying good-bye to the island. When the time came for us to depart, I did not look back. I had no regrets. Not conscious ones at least, I must add, because twice a year I'll dream I'm still back there or going back.

I said that Lily and I think about each other's death. In earlier years, during the rough spots of our marriage, such thoughts were usually "death wishes." "Suppose she got leukemia," I'd think. "Of course I hope she doesn't. But what if she did? I'd support her to the end. Then what would I do? Would I start dating again quickly? Probably. Who might I date? Hmmm, let's see now . . ." But now our thoughts are not fantasies of freedom; they are the work of preparation. In a sense, we have already begun our mourning and we're already preparing to say good-bye.

It is painful to watch someone die a protracted death. Both my parents died slowly with considerable unhappiness, so I not only got to mourn each of them for five years before the fact, but when the end finally came I truly saw it as a cause for rejoicing. My grief was minimal. At the time of my mother's death I was about to conduct an exorcism. Helping me from the sidelines in this somewhat daring endeavor was a mentor of mine, Malachi, a brilliant Irish Jesuit. Four days before the exorcism was to begin he phoned to inquire how I was holding up. "I'm really doing very well, Malachi," I informed him. "The only thing is that my mother died last week."

"Oooh, I'm sorry to hear your Mimmy died," he exclaimed.

"I'm not," I said definitively. "She was unhappy and she'd been ill for a long time. I'm glad she finally got it over with. The only thing that makes me sad about it was that I wasn't with her at the time and she had to die alone."

"Oooh, I knoo how you feel," he commiserated. "But we never die aloon. There are hoondreds there—thousands there—they coom from all over."

Ah, well, Malachi's Irish, and he's not only done a lot of exorcisms but he probably believes in leprechauns! Still, it was consoling.

Although I am not the least turned on by tombs, the fact is that for most of my life I've had a romance with death—particularly my own. Death was one of many things my parents, who advised me to think less, themselves did their best to avoid pondering. For me, however, it was, and still is, a fascinating subject for contemplation. By the time I was an adolescent I had concluded that death was perhaps the most important fact of life—that this life is temporary and, physically at least, we are temporal creatures. My romance with death has done more than anything else to give me a sense of the meaningfulness of our temporary existence. Indeed, I have written much about this and lectured widely on the subject.

The fact that I am freer than most from the denial of death doesn't mean that I'm not afraid of it. Intellectually I find the prospect of death in many ways comforting. Emotionally, I find it terrifying. My terror takes two forms: major and minor.

The minor form relates to my writing. In all respects but one I am quite disposable. My children don't need me much any more, and Lily is a strong person who can survive quite well without me. There'll be enough of an inheritance to keep the wolves from the door. FCE has blessedly become fiscally and managerially independent of me. My lectures are mostly recorded or edited. But whenever I am in the midst of writing a book, like this one, that is dear to my heart, I am terrified that I will die before it's completed. The proofreading can be done by others. A final polishing can be accomplished by editors. But until it's in a full draft form that's acceptable to me, I don't feel disposable. There is no one else who can write it. It's not the proceeds that might be lost nor the investment of time. It's that a hopefully well-conceived work of art will be stillborn and never see the light of day; that's my terror. I am told that other authors suffer a similar form of death-anxiety.

But the BIG terror is not the demise of my work; it is the death of *me*. I believe in an afterlife. I can even give a half dozen different fairly cogent reasons for this belief. But believing is not the same as knowing, and at the very core of my being is the unmitigated terror of nonbeing. Call it narcissism; call it attachment, call it the survival instinct, call it whatever you want, but the plain fact of the matter is that I am terrified of dying. It is not that my body will cease to exist; it is that I will cease to exist. There will no longer be any Scott Peck. There will be nothing. No matter that it is probably an illusion, it feels that when I die I will be face-to-face with the abyss of nothingness.

I recounted how nine years ago I had three different kinds of bacterial pneumonia simultaneously. On my second afternoon in the hospital I suddenly said to Lily, aghast, "I can't breathe." She ran out and got the nurse, who saw that I had turned blue. Respiratory therapy was at my bedside in a matter of seconds, and I was shortly a bit better. But even with their ministrations and continuous oxygen it was several days before I was no longer blue and weeks before I was no longer short of breath at rest. It is very scary not to be able to breathe. It was a long time before I would let poor Lily out of my sight except when I was asleep. I had come close to the abyss. I don't want to be there again even though I know I shall be. Relatively soon.

Freud hypothesized that we have both a life wish and a death wish. To me it is not a hypothesis. The death wish is obvious. For the moment I would rather continue to smoke my beloved cigarettes with the surcease they bring than to live an extra painful year or two. And I am close to being ready to go home. Every so often in a question-and-answer period someone will ask, "Dr. Peck, would you give us yet another example of grace?" And I will reply, "Yes, we get to die. I don't know about you, but at fifty-six I am starting to get tired, not so tired that I am ready to give up, but if I thought of myself as having to wade through this crap for another three or four hundred years, I think I might cash in my chips sooner rather than later." Sometime in the next few decades it is obvious to me that either my body or my spirit or both will become sufficiently fatigued as to outweigh my terror of dying. Not take away the terror, unfortunately, just outweigh it.

Presently, however, my life wish is still more obvious. Except for golf and walking, I don't like to exercise anymore. I particularly dislike—I hate and always have—calisthenics or exercise for the pure sake of exercise. It is so boring I can hardly bear it. Yet each and every morning these days—once I've had a cup of coffee and a cigarette or two and a few moments of prayer to screw up my courage—I spend fifteen minutes getting all out of breath doing my stupid back exercises. Because, if I don't, my spine will be frozen within a few weeks and not long thereafter I'll be dead. There are still a few things I want to do and sights I want to see. I still love life. But it is quite unclear, in doing these unpleasant, seemingly interminable stretching exercises, to what extent I am motivated by my love of life or my terror of dying.

As I said, there are things I want to do and see, and so it was on this afternoon. We had places to go. By the time we departed the Kilmartin Valley with its row of tombs and all its marvelous stones, it had stopped raining. And by the time, an hour later, we had reached our day's final destination of Oban, the early evening sun was shining.

Utterly unlike Glasgow, Oban is an ideal place to bed down. More than a town yet slightly less than a city, its Victorian buildings line a lovely bay on the west coast of the Scottish mainland. None of its buildings could have been more Victorian than our lodging, the Hotel Columba, an almost bizarre, six-storied edifice, taller than it is broad, protruding like an upturned coffin from its own tiny point right at the middle of the bay. We were assigned a room on the fourth floor. It was all we could do to fit our two selves and luggage into its three-by-three foot antique elevator that escalated us at a rate of one story every two minutes. Not unexpectedly, our room was also remarkably compact. But it had a wide, heavy, pre-Edwardian window that we eventually managed to shove open so as to let in the wonderfully pungent, salty sea air.

The window looked out, at just the right angle,

across a corner of the bay, to Oban's impressive south quay. Many people were strolling it, and there was a touch of holiday atmosphere. It was low tide, so the little, brightly colored fishing boats were sitting on the sand in cockeyed poses. The gulls were screeching, and the moment we began our picnic supper they flocked to the windowsill. There was nothing they didn't like— even Stilton cheese. We had a good deal of stale bread left over from Glasgow, and they flapped their wings on the sill with competitive delight at their windfall. No sooner had we and they finished our repast together than the sound of bagpipes began in the distance. We tried to guess where it was coming from, but the wild whine was strangely diffuse. After ten minutes we realized why when we saw orange-kilted pipers, four by four, emerging simultaneously from different streets to assemble on the quay. There was to be a kind of concert!

For our age, Lily and I practically bounded down the stairs, unwilling to waste the time we knew the creaky elevator would make of its passage. The concert lasted a good half hour. The pipers—all men, of course—were members of an ancient and formal association, magnificent males with fine faces as well as lungs. They did solos and duets and choruses, everything that bagpipes can possibly do, and they did it with joy and as much skill as we'll ever hear again. When they passed the hat at the end, Lily and I gave them all the coin we had between us, which was well over five pounds. It was money well spent. We only wished they'd played for longer.

Strolling back along the quay to the Columba in the evening light we felt it had been the perfect end to the perfect day.

But not quite the end. There is always the matter of falling asleep, a time I usually relish. It is a time of prayer. No one has ever adequately defined prayer, but my favorite definition is that of Matthew Fox: "Prayer is a radical response to the mysteries of life." I am not doing much responding as I fall asleep, but I am generally pondering mysteries, large or small. I am playing with questions, particularly those the day has raised, and much of the fun of traveling for me is that it gives rise to more than the ordinary number of questions.

The information plaque at the Temple Wood circle had opined that its megalithic stone circle was constructed more than a thousand years before the little tomb inside it. But do they *know*? In fact, they don't. Through carbon dating we can assess the age of human, other animal, or plant remains, from bones to seeds. Through another technique we can assess the time at which clay was baked, so we can tell the age of any piece of pottery. But we cannot date stones—or, more precisely, we cannot date when they were quarried or when they were erected. We can only guess by the age of the remains of life that might be found in their vicinity. In regard to a stone circle and grave complex, there are three possibilities: the grave came before the circle, the circle came before the grave, or the grave and the circle were constructed at roughly the same time. But which of these possibilities is the right one, we cannot know for sure. The mystery will remain.

Mostly tonight I am not pondering such technical questions. Probably because of the tombs we'd seen that afternoon, I'm thinking about aspects of the deeper mystery of death. How will Lily die? How will I die? Will it be a slow death like my parents or will I have a sudden death? As a psychiatrist I know that the time of a human death is usually not wholly an accident; there is a certain, slightly discernible interaction between God and the individual human soul that helps determine it. But what about the type of death? Is this pure accident? Could it be that those who have a lingering death which gradually strips them away, which breaks them inch by inch, may somehow need such stripping and breaking? Or that those who suddenly drop may not? Or is there some other dynamic involved? What about me? How much more stripping and breaking might I need before I am prepared to give up the ghost?

What a wonderful expression: give up the ghost! To finally let the spirit separate from the body, to surrender so it can leap free!

But not all is death. My thoughts return to our first stones, the dolmen at Long House Farm, which the guidebook identified as a burial chamber but which looked much more like an altar of sorts. Having seen the collapsed megaliths of the tomb at Dunchraigaig Cairn, I can understand how some archaeologists might assume that *all* dolmens were once burial sites. But then archaeologists tend to have a certain preoccupation with burial. This is natural. After all, it is in graves and tombs that they are most likely to find human remains and the artifacts that provide them with the most telling information about prehistoric human cultures. Their investigations tend to make it sound as if the megalithic culture totally centered around tombs and possibly ancestor worship. But it is not unlikely that the archaeologists by virtue of their profession are more preoccupied with death than these Neolithic people were.

Probably the stone circle at Temple Wood did precede the tomb. For as far as we can tell, most of the stone circles had nothing to do with graves or tombs. The henges were not burial sites either. There is no evidence that the menhirs were giant grave stones. Cups and rings have been found on the inside walls of a few megalithic tombs, but all those at Achnabreck and carved into the other rock faces of Kilmartin Valley seemed to have no funerary significance. Then what were they for? What reason or reasons lay behind the carvings, the henges, the stone circles, the rows of standing stones, the pairs of stones, and all the thousands upon thousands of single solitary menhirs of the megalithic people?

We don't know.

There is no question that the megalithic people had a certain fascination with death. But their greatest communal efforts and largest and finest stones were reserved for something other than tombs. Something they must have considered even more important. With what we know about anthropology, their interest in death is not puzzling. It would appear, however, that death was not their primary fascination. Their primary cultural focus seems to have lain elsewhere in a realm of thought, feeling, and behavior that is still utterly mysterious to our rational minds five thousand years later despite the best efforts of modern, scientific archaeology.

CHAPTER XI

PILGRIMAGE
WEDNESDAY, JUNE 10

It is 7:30 A.M., and Lily and I are standing beside our car on Oban's pier waiting to board a ferry. Shades of Paddington Station, we are there a good thirty minutes earlier than we needed to be. The guidebooks warn that having a prepaid ticket does not assure one's car access to the Scottish ferries; it is still on a first-come, first-served basis. So our car is second in line. Free though I feel to disregard all other recommendations of guidebooks, these cautionary notes about time and schedules somehow become holy scripture for me. God forbid that we should ever literally or figuratively miss the boat.

We are off on our first of several planned visits to the Hebrides. They are a large complex of islands off the west coast of mainland Scotland, and are divided into the Inner and Outer Hebrides. The ferry for which we are waiting will take us this morning for a forty-minute ride to the 350-square-mile Isle of Mull, the second largest of the Inner Hebrides.

Why do we want to go to the Isle of Mull? We don't much, although we'd heard it was quite pretty. The reason we are going there is to drive straight across to its far side, park our car, and get on another ferry for a thousand-yard crossing to a tiny, six-square-mile island called Iona.

Why are we taking such a laborious trip just to get to a tiny island out in the middle of nowhere? It is because Iona is reputed to be a holy island. We are making a pilgrimage.

The reason for Iona's reputed holiness is St. Columba (after whom our funny hotel in Oban is named). Columba was an Irish abbot who landed there with a band of disciples in A.D. 563 with the deliberate intent of Christianizing Scotland. He himself apparently thought the little island was such a holy place that there he largely stayed—or so legend holds. By all accounts he was indeed a most saintly man. Certainly he had a genius for training and inspiring missionaries, and by the time he died thirty-five years later most of Scotland had become Christian. Off and on ever since, Iona has been a destination for pilgrims.

In making a pilgrimage on this day, Lily and I were doing something that is profoundly and characteristically human—and a practice of every major religion. Indeed, twenty-three years before, we ourselves had visited Varanasi (Benares), a city in India sacred both to Buddhists and Hindus, where we watched Hindu pilgrims praying along the bank of the Ganges at dawn and Tibetan Buddhist pilgrims kissing Buddha's statues at a nearby shrine. A pilgrimage to Mecca is one of the "Pillars of Islam" and almost an obligation sometime in the life of a Muslim.

In Christianity the practice of pilgrimage reached its height during the Middle Ages. The greatest destination was, and still is, Jerusalem and the Holy Land. But there were many others: Rome, Santiago de Compostela in northwestern Spain (supposedly the site of relics of St. James, the "greater" apostle), Canterbury (where St. Thomas à Becket was martyred), and even little Iona.

The reasons for making a pilgrimage have often been far more complex or overdetermined than simply that of visiting a holy spot. Going to do battle against the Muslims in the ill-fated crusades was generally considered a form of pilgrimage. The medieval Catholic church granted all manner of "indulgences" to pilgrims, with complicated formulas for the number of days of release from purgatory they might obtain by virtue of their journeys. Certain sinners, from commoners to kings, were ordered by the church to make a pilgrimage as penance, and others made them quite voluntarily for the remission of sins.

Perhaps the most famous place of Christian pilgrimage in modern times is Lourdes, a French town in the foothills of the Pyrenees, where in 1858—well into this Age of Reason—an uneducated, lower-class, asthmatic fourteen-year-old girl, Bernadette, had a series of visions of the

Virgin Mary. Shortly thereafter miraculous healings seemed to occur around the site of her visions. Today, over a hundred thousand people each year make the somewhat arduous trek to that otherwise obscure town, not out of devotion to Bernadette nor to the Virgin but primarily for healing—their own or others. Or just to get "help."

Close to where we live in rural northwestern Connecticut there is a little derivative, still more recent shrine that advertises itself as "Lourdes of Litchfield." It is not much visited except on the third Sunday of May when hundreds of somewhat frightening-looking, leather-jacketed bikers descend upon it each year from all over for "the blessing of the motorcycles." Laugh if you want, but for me the phenomenon gives bikers a bit more humanity than I might otherwise ascribe to them. It may be no accident that a few years ago, totally lost, my driver and I were led out of the least desirous bowels of New Jersey by a remarkably saintly biker.

New sites of pilgrimage are arising all the time, no matter how deep we are into the Age of Reason. Knowledge of them spreads by word of mouth, and the people come. The most dramatic of this generation is Medjugorje, where six youths began having a series of visions and dialogues with the Virgin Mary in 1981 in what a few years ago used to be Yugoslavia. I have received dozens of letters from people who have already visited it and returned in awe. And sometimes old sites become resurrected. By 1800, Iona had become totally neglected. But after World War II various church people began to repair and rebuild it and monks quietly began to return. As did the pilgrims. There has been no promotion, no advertising. It has all been a matter of word of mouth. So we are headed to little Iona on this morning because a number of disparate friends and acquaintances have said, "Go there; it is a holy place."

Eventually the waiting ferry sleepily opens its gorge and we drive in. And eventually it departs, no more than a third full for all our waiting. We have locked the car and ambled to the upper decks. The morning is crisp and clear, and we are excited. It is a pretty ride—not thrilling, but we are sure that thrilling things are ahead of us.

When the boat docks, we drive into a scrawny hamlet and hence onto the single-lane road across the isle. I am reminded once again how beauty is in the eye of the beholder. The man who had told us that it was a pretty island had different eyes from ours. There is not much we can say about Mull. It is mountainous. Very few people live there, which is not surprising since there seems to be little to support human life. The mountains are barren. The valleys are, too. The only relief was provided by several of the reforestation projects which are characteristic of much of Scotland, mainland and islands alike. These we applaud. As on Mull, the pines of the projects are generally too young to be beautiful. But someday these investments in the future will be fine forests, and Scotland will have a thriving timber industry if it so chooses.

After an hour's drive across the wastes of Mull, we arrived at its southwest coast and a place called Fionnphort. We are not sure why the place has a name, because there was nothing there except a dock and a growing row of the parked cars of other pilgrims. Iona is clearly visible across the strait, a miniature sort of Mull save for the fact that there is a fine-looking church to interrupt its starkness.

The ferry gets us there in no time. There are a couple of small houses near the pier. A little road quickly brings us to the ruins of a medieval convent. We snap a few pictures and move on to a pleasant, tiny graveyard shaded by cedars. Then to the church or current abbey. It is quite old but well restored. Inside, and also in the adjoining, more modern cloister, it is quiet. Outside is a sweet flower garden, and scattered here and there in the surrounding fields of sheep and wildflowers are a few more undistinguished hunks of ruined medieval walls. Lily and I sit for a while in a field looking back toward Mull. The sun feels good. We can hear an occasional bird, and it is a pleasant spot. But for us it is just another little island, and less inspiring than dozens that dot the coast of Maine. We experience no awe and do not sense the holiness we had hoped to find.

We have a choice. Mull is not renowned for its stones, but our survey map shows a few in its southeast corner. We can leave quickly to look for them or we can spend another two hours on Iona hiking across its rocky spine to explore the other side and ocean shore. We elect to search for stones, and we are already gone from Iona by noon.

Although we were able to find none—not one—of the stones we were looking for, it was probably the right decision. That little south-eastern corner of Mull had more vegetation than we'd seen on the whole rest of the isle, and the narrow lanes we leisurely explored on our unsuccessful search were lovely. At one spot the exploration was leisurely indeed when we ran head on into two men driving a herd of twenty long-horned and long-haired Scottish cattle down the road. It took a long time for these magnificently shaggy, literally golden beasts to squeeze by our car. They were beautiful, almost holy—an unforgettable sight.

As we boarded the ferry back to Oban the sky clouded over. By the time we were reensconced in our room it was looking ominous. It seemed it would be raining again in the morning. After cocktails and picnic, we strolled the quay, so vibrant the evening before, but now it felt gray and lifeless. We waited in hope of the bagpipers, but they did not appear. All in all it had been a disappointing day.

We'd been pilgrims long enough to keep such things in perspective. So what if, for us, Iona had lacked the quality of holiness we'd anticipated? We'd not come to Scotland just for it. The fact is that all travel is pilgrimage. This entire trip is a pilgrimage, and in making it we are behaving no differently in essence than many of the pilgrims of Europe in the Middle Ages, no differently from most of the pilgrims who ever were or ever will be.

Chaucer's *Canterbury Tales*, about a group of medieval British pilgrims traveling together on their way to the shrine of Canterbury, is illustrative. Of the group, the most experienced pilgrim is the Wife of Bath who had been three times to the Holy Land as well as on a number of other pilgrimages. Why? Was she doing penance? Apparently not. She was hardly a guilt-ridden lady. Was it because she was particularly pious? Possible, but doubtful. The most probable reason for her repetitive behavior was simply that she liked to travel. And here we have a key. Travel was not easy in the Middle Ages. One did not undertake it lightly. Nor was travel for the sake of travel culturally sanctioned as it is today. There were inns, but they were generally places of such ill repute and danger that two new monastic orders were created for the specific purpose of providing safe shelter to pilgrims along their journey. Thus were the first hospices invented. But the travel industry as we know it had not yet been invented, and travel still had to be justified, one had to have a reason. The most common justifiable reasons were either war or pilgrimage, both of which could enlarge the scope of men's and women's minds.

Even today it is nice for those of us who are socially responsible workaholics to have justification for travel. It is doubtful we would have made this trip at all had it not been for our family social obligation to participate in my nephew's wedding. Our side trip today to Iona may even have added a superficial note of piety to the venture. But the real reason we have come to Wales, Scotland, and the Lake District has been to travel.

Perhaps it is our definition of piety that needs broadening. Perhaps in her thinly disguised but otherwise unadulterated love of travel, the rather bawdy Wife of Bath was the most pious of the lot. It seems to me a part of our collective death wish, which I very much share, to want to stay where we are, to not seek out new and challenging experience, to remain in our ruts of the accustomed. To venture forth, on the other hand, to deliberately court the different and foreign and unexpected as we do when we travel, no matter how gently, seems a part of a grand life wish and a strange yearning to enlarge the scope of our minds. Yes, perhaps it is indeed a holy activity, and all travel is a pilgrimage.

There is another little noted but dramatic similarity between Lily and me and the Wife of Bath and many other pilgrims: We are well into middle age. It is no accident. In young adulthood, although we have the vigor, seldom do we have the money or time for travel. When elderly we are more likely to possess the time and money, but often we lack the vigor. So it is that late middle age is a time for travel. This was so in medieval Europe. And it has been so elsewhere.

From time immemorial the Hindus of India have tended to divide one's life into stages. The stage of early adulthood is that of the "householder." Here it is proper to stay put, devoting oneself to home and hearth, to making money and otherwise providing for your children and the generations to come. In late middle age, however, it is quite proper and sanctioned for men—at least—to leave their families to become "wanderers" or pilgrims. In a different form, the same understanding of the stages of life was recognized in medieval Christianity. He or she who was embarking on a pilgrimage first needed to seek the blessing of the church, and that blessing would not be provided unless the pilgrim could give evidence that he was leaving his family reasonably well provided for.

In my sophomore year in college I took a sociology course taught by a professor who was considered to be a bit of an oddball. Strangely, the thing I remember best from that course was not any great principle of sociology but an offhand, seemingly irrelevant comment he made one day. "We are all of us in a rut," he said, "and there are two ways to get out of it. One is to travel and the other is to work in a mental hospital." Perhaps I took him at his word, and he was partially instrumental in my going on to become both a psychiatrist and something of a traveler.

While I am grateful for his word of wisdom, I believe it deserves two major qualifications. One is that it is quite possible for someone to travel extensively or be a psychotherapist or both and still stay in a rut. I have known several psychiatrists who have not appreciably "grown" or personally developed over the course of a thirty-year career. As for travel, I spoke of how my father used his money, among other ways, to mentally insulate himself. My mother and he did a lot of traveling in their later years, but it was always to wealthy places, staying only in the very best and most proven of hotels. Although I in no way begrudge him his comforts and the pleasure he took in travel, I never saw any evidence that his travels had significantly broadened his mind. Lily and I know others who have traveled to the most exotic places, sometimes impoverished like India, and never saw the poverty or anything deeper than the architecture. It is possible to travel with one's eyes or mind barely open.

Indeed, it worries me that I may be becoming like them and very much like my father. When I traveled as a college student I did so on a shoestring with little thought of where I might bed down for the night. Consequently, I stayed in some of the damnedest places, where I had a lot of surprises and much interaction with the local people. But now, like my father, in our age we are attached to our comforts and want to sleep in distinctly good, if not ritzy, hotels where we're likely to meet only those employed in the travel industry. We do, however, still manage to keep our eyes open. . . . I hope.

The other major qualification is that geographical travel and the practice of psychotherapy are hardly the only things that may broaden one's horizons. Marriage may do it. Having children may do it for you. Prayer can do it. Alcoholism and depression may do it. Most recently it has been our volunteer work with FCE far more than travel that has done it for Lily and me. There is hardly anything that can't do it. On the other hand, there is no guarantee that anything *will* do it. It is possible for us human beings to remain largely oblivious to life, learning little from it over the years.

What I am saying here is that life is a pilgrimage. Or rather, that it can be one if we use it as such.

The notion that all of human existence can be a pilgrimage is as ancient as the written word. It is contained in the Hindu concept of reincarnation. Mystics of all ages, cultures, and religions have known it. Many of the early Christians—the Desert Fathers, for instance—knew it. The Pilgrims who settled at Plymouth Rock identified themselves as such not so much because they envisioned themselves on a pilgrimage to the New World as because they were early, radical Protestants who thought of their entire lives as pilgrimages. Their vision reached its height of popularity six decades later through the services of a contemporary of George Fox—and an amazingly similar man—John Bunyan. Bunyan was a lower-middle-class tinker who fell in with some devout Christians in his early adulthood and underwent a dramatic conversion to radical Protestantism. Shortly thereafter he began to preach, and soon, for his troubles, like Fox, he was imprisoned. Although not imprisoned as frequently, he spent the longer time in jail—twelve years, or a fifth of his life. While in jail he wrote a book, *Pilgrim's Progress*, about the dynamics of the spiritual journey. This book was published in 1678 and became an instant best-seller of its day. Over three hundred years later it remains a "classic," translated into over a hundred languages.

But not a much read classic in this Age of Reason and supposed Enlightenment. It does seem a bit quaint these days. C. S. Lewis tried to rectify the problem by writing a kind of updated revision more suitable for our modern tastes, *Pilgrim's Regress*, published in 1944, but it is one of his least-known works. It would seem that *The Road Less Traveled* may have been more successful in reintroducing the notion of life as pilgrimage into public consciousness. If that's the case, it had a number of assists in doing so.

One was from its publisher. My working title for it was "The Psychology of Spiritual Growth." The editors said, "It's a great book, Scotty, but the title's got to go." I sat for a week making a long list of more poetic possibilities. Number thirty-seven on the list was *"The Road Less Traveled."* I do not know whether I would have come up with it without an assist from Robert Frost working through my unconscious. What I do know is that as soon as I'd written it down I recognized that it had a Frostian ring to it and immediately checked my old copy of his collected poems to find "The Road Not Taken," which begins, "Two roads diverged in a yellow wood," and concludes, "I took the one less traveled by, / And that has made all the difference." Actually, Frost left it utterly ambiguous whether the choice of the less traveled road was, in fact, the better one. That was not his point; his point was simply that our seemingly inconsequential choices can often make a great difference in our lives.

Nonetheless, the poem reeks of his understanding of life as traveling, as a journey if not a pilgrimage.

So one assist came from the publisher who insisted upon a better title and another from Robert Frost who gave a familiar ring to the one that eventuated. But the biggest assist, as I analyze it in retrospect, came indirectly from two most disparate and unlikely quarters: from Sigmund Freud, an atheist who was threatened practically unto death by the whole issue of spirituality, and Bill Wilson, an alcoholic stockbroker who eventually came to perfect terms with spirituality but remained extremely leery of "religion."

In a sense, Freud invented psychotherapy and Bill Wilson, through Alcoholics Anonymous and its Twelve-Step Program, invented the self-help movement (which may be looked upon as psychotherapy for free). Most people who get into therapy by either route (or both) do so because they want to get from where they are psychologically to some other place. And when they succeed in doing so they move—they have a sense that they have traveled—and the sense that they are still traveling. As noted, mystics of all ages and cultures have seen life as a pilgrimage, but until recently they have been a tiny minority. Therapy, however, is the best means for people who are not born mystics to come to a realization that their existence is a journey.

Frieda Fromm Reichman, a famous psychoanalyst (who served as the model for the therapist in Joanne Greenberg's *I Never Promised You a Rose Garden*) long ago told a story illustrative of this. She had been working intensively for a year with a severely ill young man. It was her custom on the anniversary of the onset of treatment to review the progress of her cases. In the case of this patient, for whom she had great respect, she felt discouraged by his almost total lack of progress over the year. She seriously wondered whether she was the right therapist for him, and decided to raise the issue with him sometime in the next week of their work together. But he began their very next session by saying, "You're probably not aware of it, Dr. Fromm Reichman, but I've been seeing you for exactly a year now, and I really want to thank you. A year ago I would never have dreamed that I could ever have gotten from where I was then to where I am today, that I could have progressed so far in such a short time. Indeed, if I have any concern about our work together its only that sometimes I'm frightened by how fast we're moving."

Many of my own patients made no discernible progress, and most of the rest traveled less far and fast than I would have liked. Of my many failings as a therapist, I think the greatest was perhaps my impatience, and I apologize to those who may have been hindered by it. But the point is that when people do move in therapy, as that young man, they develop a sense of life as a journey—and one that continues after formal therapy has been terminated. They have become pilgrims.

Both the practice of professional psychotherapy and Alcoholics Anonymous didn't really begin to get off the ground until the 1950s. But then they hit their stride, and one result was that when *The Road Less Traveled* was published in 1978 there was an ever-growing number of more or less experienced pilgrims out there waiting for it and wanting to spread the word. It is no accident that the very first fan letter I received began, "Dear Dr. Peck: you must be an alcoholic. . . ." Its writer found it difficult to believe I could have written the book without first having been humbled by alcoholism and then having spent years of traveling with AA.

Nonetheless, the road less traveled still remains less traveled, and while my books may have hit the nonfiction bestseller lists, preaching pilgrimage has hardly put me anywhere near the top of the entertainment industry. Mostly, the media preaches a less effortful, more comfortable brand of amusement, and ancient though it might be, the notion of life as a spiritual journey is not all that prevalent in this Age of Reason. The secularism of our public schools pretty much prevents teaching of the notion therein. I like to imagine a different educational mandate, but I am doubtful how willing most teachers or professors would be to grapple with the obvious question from their students: "Pilgrimage to where?"

I am willing to grapple with it, but even for me it would be an embarrassing process in a typical academic setting. Think about it. "Professor Peck, you've suggested that we should look at life as a pilgrimage, but where is the place we are traveling toward as pilgrims?"

"I don't know for sure. Hopefully heaven."

"You believe in a heaven?"

"Yes."

"What does it look like?"

"I don't know. I'm not sure it looks like anything. Maybe we won't even need eyes there."

"But you still believe in it?"

"Yes."

"Professor Peck, I seem to recollect hearing you say that even though you believe in an afterlife, you're not absolutely certain about it. You've even admitted that you're terrified of dying and spoken of it as jumping into an abyss."

"That's true."

"So where again is the destination of the pilgrimage?"

"As I told you, I don't know for sure. Maybe Death is the destination. Maybe we are pilgrims to the abyss."

"That doesn't seem very pleasant."

"True, but maybe when we leap into that abyss of emptiness we'll find something beyond the nothingness, something very worthwhile, something worth dying for."

"And what might that be, Professor Peck?"

"I don't know. Maybe the Kingdom."

"The Kingdom? What's that?"

"It's something that Jesus talked a great deal about."

"But what is it exactly?"

"I'm sorry, I can't put it into words. He kept trying to tell us, but he didn't succeed very well. The best he could do was to give us hints in a whole bunch of paradoxical parables."

"So it's all very vague, isn't it?"

"Yes. But it has something to do with holiness. Pilgrims travel to holy places. You might want to think of life as a journey toward holiness."

"Would you please define holiness, Professor Peck?"

"I'm afraid I can't. It's too hard to capture, except to say that I think it has something to do with light."

"Do you mean to say that we are on a pilgrimage toward sainthood."

"Yes. Thank you. You've got it."

"No, I don't have it, Professor Peck. I remember you telling us that God creates saints, and that we cannot achieve sainthood by our own volition."

"That's correct. But I think we can cooperate in the process. Or refuse to cooperate. I don't believe it's predestined. I think God somehow sets us up for it, but then it's our choice whether we travel toward it or run away from it. I think we're somehow cocreators with God."

"Very interesting, Professor Peck. But would you tell us the rules for this cooperation? And how we can tell whether we're choosing rightly or wrongly?"

"Well, there's this thing called prayer. Now I can't define exactly what prayer is, but . . ."

So it goes in this Age of Reason. And so it is that we preachers spend almost all of our time and energy preaching to the already converted. But it is also the already converted who sustain and uplift us. One of those already converted, a great contemporary preacher who has spoken and written eloquently about pilgrimage in every way possible, is Frederick Buechner. Years ago he penned a sermon he entitled "To Be a Saint." He began it by telling how he and his wife were sitting outside at their farm in Vermont with another couple on a lovely summer evening. The Green Mountains were turning purple in the dusk and a horse was prancing in a nearby meadow. "It's so beautiful here!" the wife of the other couple exclaimed. "Why do you ever leave here, Freddy?"

Buechner wrote of how he gave her an inane answer. But the question haunted him. "Why *do* I leave here?" he pondered. "Why should anyone leave anywhere?" And the answer he finally reached was: "to be a saint."

Buechner's writings have helped sustain me. I do not proclaim myself to be a saint anymore than he does. But also having a beautiful home in rural New England, I, too, often wonder why I ever leave it. The behavior is overdetermined. The most common reason I leave is to preach— albeit, unlike George Fox and John Bunyan, usually for considerable sums of money. But it is not solely the money. I also receive gifts on these trips from my audiences. Invariably the most valuable ones are those given most anonymously. A powerful gift was recently handed me in Canada by a woman who, without saying a word, simply slipped a page into my hand. The page was not credited. For all I know, the woman, the gift-giver herself, wrote it. In any case, it also spoke of the problems of "pilgrimage education":

THE LESSON

*Then Jesus took his disciples up the mountain and
     gathering them*
around him, he taught them saying:
*Blessed are the poor in spirit for theirs is the Kingdom
     of heaven*
Blessed are the meek.
Blessed are they that mourn.
Blessed are the merciful.
Blessed are they who thirst for justice.
Blessed are you when persecuted.
Blessed are you when you suffer.
Be glad and rejoice for your reward is great in heaven.
*Then Simon Peter said, "Do we have to write this
     down?"*
And Andrew said, "Are we supposed to know this?"

And James said, "Will we have a test on it?"
And Philip said, "What if we don't know it?"
*And Bartholomew said, "Do we have to hand this
     in?"*
*And John said the other disciples didn't have to learn
     this.*
And Matthew said, "When do we get out of here?"
*And Judas said, "What does this have to do with
     real life?"*
*Then one of the Pharisees present asked to see Jesus's
     lesson plans and*
*inquired of Jesus his terminal objectives in the
     cognitive domain.*

And Jesus wept. . . .

John Bunyan is also known for writing a hymn, "Who Would True Valor See." Even today in many churches people sing its verse:

> *There's no discouragement*
> *Shall make him once relent*
> *His first avowed intent*
> *To be a pilgrim.*

Whether they know what they are singing or not is another matter. Church or synagogue or mosque attendance or the profession of religion does not, in my experience, guarantee that one will see herself as a pilgrim. Clergy may be no more effective than schoolteachers in preaching the concept of life as a journey, in reaching the hearts of their often only superficially converted congregations. But as the hymn suggests, once someone is captured by the notion of life as a pilgrimage, she is unlikely ever to let it go. And then she will remain open to learning all the lessons there are, like the beatitudes, that teach the principles for successful journeying. In fact, the world is full of travel tips.

One of the most obvious is to travel lightly. I already mentioned this in regard to the blind woman who was burdened by her pride. But often we are simply weighed down by mere things. A Hasidic story makes the point. Around the end of the nineteenth century, a tourist from the United States visited the famous Polish rabbi Hafez Hayyim. He was astonished to see that the rabbi's home was just a simple room filled with books.

The only furniture was a table and a bench. "Rabbi, where is your furniture?" asked the tourist.

"Where is yours?" replied Hafez.

"Mine? But I'm only a visitor here."

"So am I," said the rabbi.

Lily's and my home in Connecticut is quite large and filled with furniture. It has needed to be with three offices and three children, along with a waiting room or two, and space for guests and group meetings and business entertainment. But now our children have left home. We long ago ceased our psychotherapy practices and no longer need waiting rooms. Most of the business meetings have become too large or complicated and are being shifted to hotels and retreat centers. For the first time in twenty years we are beginning to think about selling the place. There are many reasons not to. The real estate market is down. The flower gardens are beautiful beyond words. There is still a lot of business that goes on in the house. But are we dragging our feet simply because we feel so well settled? I'm not sure that's the case yet. What we are sure of, however, is that sometime over the next decade or so we are going to need to dump our beautiful home that is still deeply beloved to us. And dump almost all of the furniture. And, yes, even dump the books.

Assuming that both our minds remain clear, we shall be making this decision conjointly. It will be a most bittersweet moment on our pilgrimage together.

As in Chaucer's *Canterbury Tales*, pilgrims tend

to travel together. They make new friends and find companionship, which is another hidden benefit of the journey. I am not seriously concerned that we're not meeting people on this trip. It is a vacation, and we meet more than enough people in our work. And thanks to our involvement with community and FCE, we are blessed to have as many friends as we can possibly handle at this point. Besides, the companionship of each other is all we need for the moment. Neither of us would like to be traveling alone, however. Not now, not on vacation, not on this vacation. We are moving as a pair.

It was the pilgrimage of life that first brought us together in a Columbia University physics class almost exactly thirty-four years ago, and our marriage itself has been a pilgrimage. Perhaps the majority of marriages are "failed" pilgrimages, but what surprises me is how many of them succeed. Certainly, given the intensity of some of our struggles with and against each other, it feels surprising not only that we can still cohabit the same very small British hotel rooms but also that we're having such fun. I've been dropping a few hints as to why our marriage seems to have been successful, and I'll continue to do so. One is that each of us has the capacity to travel alone. Much of the time Lily is going to geographical and psychological destinations without me, and I am doing likewise without her. There is nothing cloying about our relationship. The same principle holds true for convents and monasteries and successful communes. It is a well-established saying among them that "You're not ready to live in community until you can live alone."

So there is a complex interweaving of individual pilgrimages and the pilgrimage of a marriage, and there needs to be a kind of art to it. Right now we are weaving the threads tightly together. The time will shortly return for us to loosen the weave. For the moment, however, as we explore Scotland, we also have the opportunity to explore our marriage. And to go, as pilgrims, ever deeper into its mystery.

And into the mystery of the stones as well. Although we saw no stones today, we learned several things. One is that we are in relation to them as pilgrims. It was clear from the start that we were headed for Iona as pilgrims. When that pilgrimage proved disappointing, we immediately headed for stones. The instinct was the same. In searching for stones, we are searching for something that might be holy, a place where we can feel in the presence of holiness, just as the pilgrims to Mecca may feel in the presence of holiness at the black stone of the Kaaba or medieval pilgrims apparently often felt at the relics of St. James at Santiago de Compostela. Sometimes we miss, as we did today at Iona or yesterday at the tombs of the Kilmartin Valley. But with stones we score at least as often, as we also did yesterday with the sculptured stones of Achnabreck and the scattered menhirs of that same valley.

We have further learned that a miss, a "failed" pilgrimage, is only a failure in appearance. Today we not only missed the presence of holiness on Iona but failed to find the stones we were looking for on Mull. Yet in looking for those stones we traveled the prettiest part of Mull and stumbled upon that herd of Scottish cattle. Perhaps the greatest virtue of stone chasing is that it takes us again and again over strange little byways we would not ordinarily have traveled and provides us with sights and experiences we would not otherwise have had. Today was the cementing of a learning that had been dawning on us from almost the very start of the trip and that we'd been hearing for many years: namely, that one's destination is quite likely to not be nearly as important or meaningful as the journey itself. This is another profound and ancient truth of pilgrimage.

Our first grandchild, Ian, was born five months ago. In their travels my parents took two of our children, when they were early adolescents, on trips to France and Great Britain. Should our health be up to it, when he's ten or twelve, maybe we'll be able to take Ian to Scotland and show him a herd of golden, long-horned, long-haired cattle. Along the way we might also show him a few stones, although perhaps it would be considerably better for him to discover them by himself.

CHAPTER XII

GRATITUDE
THURSDAY, JUNE 11

It never rains but it pours," they say. I am enamored of these old proverbs for the truth they capture. Life's "bad stuff" does seem to come in bunches. It may be a reflection of our entitlement mentality, however, that I know of no proverb for the more remarkable converse: It's amazing how well things generally click together.

Despite the gloomy omens of the evening before, today we awoke to a perfectly clear morning with Oban's quay sparkling in the sun outside our window.

Then we had a leisurely breakfast of kippers— a variety of broiled herring seldom served elsewhere. British kippers come in three varieties: good, excellent, and out of this world. These were out of this world. Possibly this was because Oban is not far from Loch Fyne, and Loch Fyne kippers are reputedly the world's best. On the other hand, it may have been just good luck.

Next we departed Oban by driving inland and north past Loch Linnhe. Within three miles our impression of two days ago amid the clouds that north, mainland Scotland is the most beautiful land on earth was confirmed under blue sky. Everything glistened: mountains, waters, forests.

We expected no stones this day. Yet as we rounded a corner twenty miles inland on our way to Loch Ness, Lily suddenly screamed, "There's one!" One, indeed. Smack in the middle of a large, golden valley meadow, silhouetted on all sides by mountains, stood a single fifteen-foot-high menhir, as proud and straight and strong as any that could ever be seen, dwarfing the sheep and cattle that grazed in its meadow. It was unmentioned in our guidebooks. It was not marked on our best map. There was no preparation for its simple magnificence. It was pure gift.

Whoa! It's well before noon and I've already stumbled into murky intellectual territory. To label something a gift means that there must be a giver. Who or what gave the sight of this beautiful stone to us on this beautiful morning?

There are only two ways to deal with the question. One is to declare it ridiculous. Humans give gifts to each other. Even then we may look at their gift-giving behavior as some mere, and often perverse, instinct, like that which propels our cats to dump the chipmunks they have killed on our doorstep. Regardless, the megalithic people who erected the stone five thousand years ago certainly did not have Scott and Lily Peck in mind. There is no connection. The generations of farmers who left the stone standing ever since perhaps did so because it was too much trouble to move. Most tourists wouldn't have noticed it, and of the few who did, most couldn't have cared less. The fact that a couple happens to come along who happen to share an esoteric interest in the rock is a nonevent, an occurrence without the slightest significance. Gift? Come on now, this is the Age of Reason. To look at this sort of thing as a gift is an extraordinarily self-centered, hypothetical construct without any rational basis. Pure gift? Get real; it is but pure accident, devoid of meaning.

This way of dealing with the matter is very rational. Completely rational. There is only one problem with it: It offers no reason for thankfulness. There is a name for the accompanying attitude: It is called "nihilism," derived from the Latin word *nibil*, for nothing. When it is played out, nihilism ultimately holds that there is nothing of any worth. In accounts of exorcisms over the centuries, when allowed to speak, demons have consistently espoused nihilism. But that comment itself smacks of hocuspocus, inquisitions, and the Dark Ages. The fact is that nihilism is utterly rational and hence, in the guise of cosmic cynicism, a most acceptable and common "philosophy" in this enlightened age.

The other way to understand the issue is much more iffy and, from a rational point of view, full of holes. It posits a superhuman giver, God, who likes to give gifts to human creatures because He/She particularly loves us. Whether this God has anything to do with the downpours in our lives is uncertain, although in retrospect they often seem to have been blessings in disguise. As to the recognizable gifts, some of us see a pattern of beneficence to them far greater and more constant than any pattern of misfortune. For this beneficent pattern of gift-giving we have a name: grace.

I've said this "theory" can be shot full of holes by even the most half-baked rationalist. Let him ask, for instance, "But how does grace work?" and we religious folk must answer, "We don't have the foggiest idea." In other words, grace is a miracle. Because miracles are events that are unexplainable by natural law, rationalists deny their existence. Here, however, they have their own little hole. If something happens that cannot be explained by natural law, it doesn't mean it didn't happen. It doesn't even mean that miracles are lawless. The possibility exists that miracles are quite obedient to certain natural laws but that we simply don't understand those laws yet.

Anyway, grace is a true gift. I spoke of this in relation to fundraising when I told how I once had two checks sitting on my lap, one in payment by contract for services rendered and the other an unasked for, unanticipated donation. I generally support the expression, "There's no such thing as a free lunch." But that was one of those moments of exception when I sat with an earned meal on one knee and a delicious, surprise repast on the other. If something is earned it is not a true gift. Grace, however, is unearned. It is for free. It is gratis.

So we have these three words: grace, gratis, and gratitude. They flow into one another. Perceive grace and you will naturally feel grateful. We did not earn this morning's great stone. We hadn't even spotted it on a map and gone off in search of it. We didn't lift a finger. It was simply there for us, glittering in the sunlight, and we were profoundly grateful.

While I cannot prove the existence of grace to a total rationalist, as a psychotherapist I must heartily come down in favor of the "theory." Appreciating pleasant surprises, like unsought megaliths, as gifts tends to be good for one's mental health. Those who perceive grace in the world are more likely to be grateful than those who don't. And grateful people are more likely to be happy than ungrateful ones. They are also more likely to make others happy. Feeling given to by the world, they feel predisposed to give back to the world. Thus my one coauthored book is entitled *What Return Can I Make?*

A decade ago I was participating in a colloquium at a small Christian conference with theologian Ted Gill. In an evening talk I told the group I thought a grateful heart was one of the prerequisites for being a genuine Christian. "Last night Scotty said that a grateful heart was one prerequisite for being a Christian," Ted began the next morning, "and right off the bat I want to say I disagree with him. It is not one prerequisite. It is *the* prerequisite."

Let me backpedal for a moment—and I suspect that Ted would be backpedaling right along with me. We were addressing a Christian audience, and for the purpose using a kind of shorthand. There are lots of people who identify themselves as Christians who do not seem to have particularly grateful hearts—or be particularly good Christians. Conversely, millions upon millions of Jews, Muslims, Hindus, Buddhists, agnostics, and even atheists do have grateful hearts. A relatively persistent sense of gratitude is not a Christian monopoly; it is an utterly nonsectarian phenomenon.

And a *strange* phenomenon! Why do some people have such obviously grateful hearts while others have distinctly ungrateful ones? And still others fall in between who seem relatively bland in both their gratitude and their resentment? We don't know. The science of psychology doesn't have much to offer on the subject.

It would be simple to believe that children from nurturing homes will automatically grow up to be grateful adults and that deprived homes regularly turn out malcontents. The problem is that there's not much evidence to support it. Exceptions abound. I've known many who were raised in the midst of neglect, poverty, and even brutality who seem to quite naturally live their adult lives praising the Lord, or at least praising life's munificence. Conversely, I've known a few from homes of love and comfort who seemed born ingrates. Can biology tell us more? I used the term *born ingrate*. Could there be a gene for a grateful heart? Possibly, but we certainly haven't yet located it on any chromosome, or determined whether the gene for gratitude is a dominant one, a recessive one, or perhaps a mutation. And even if we did we'd still be left pondering why this human being happened to be blessed by such a gene while another poor soul lost out.

There is a way to look at the matter that at

first glance appears bizarrely paradoxical, but it's where I place my bet. I think that a grateful heart is a gift. In other words, the capacity to appreciate gifts is itself a gift. And, by extrapolation, faith is a gift. The ability to perceive the miraculous in the ordinary is a gift. Perhaps even the awe of stones is a gift.

The early Christian theologians took the Greek word for gift—charisma—and justifiably made much of it. They spoke of a number of charismas of which the quality of being charismatic—the gift of eloquence or persuasiveness—was but one. They focused primarily upon those charismas that seemed to have a distinctly miraculous or supernatural flavor—the gift of speaking in tongues, the gift of prophecy, the gift of healing, and so on—and developed quite a lengthy list of them, these "gifts of the Holy Spirit." I think their list of more than a dozen charismas was much too small. I think there should be hundreds on it. Quite possibly thousands. And at the very head of the list I think I would put the gift of a grateful heart.

To look at our human talents as gifts—gifts that are presumably from God—is realistic. The nature versus nurture debate has raged for centuries without the slightest resolution. If you are blessed with a pleasant disposition, you would be on shaky ground to simply ascribe it to your upbringing. It would be equally shaky to just ascribe it to your heredity. Or even some mathematically indeterminable mixture of both. The reality is you just don't know, and in any case you've been lucky. Moreover, you don't even know that nature or nurture are the only possible explanations. So why not regard your pleasant disposition as a mysterious gift that may have come from God through routes you don't understand? Such an attitude of realistic intellectual humility tends to encourage a grateful sense of wonder.

It is emotionally as well as intellectually humble. If I regard my talent for writing as the result of a good private school education (nurture) or a good gene (nature), I am likely to think of it as an accidental self-possession. "It's my talent," I will feel. "I got it through the luck of the draw. There's no deeper meaning to it, and it's entirely my business what I do with it." If I think of it as a gift that is from God, however, then I am more likely to believe that my talent is not entirely my own, that it has been given into my stewardship and I have an obligation to use it insofar as I can for the greater glory of the giver.

There is a worse trap than thinking of our gifts as accidental self-possessions, and that is to believe that we have earned them. This is a temptation to which the rich, famous, or powerful are particularly prone. There are people who have a talent—yes, a gift—for making money, for investing. But they are likely to think, "I earned this money (or power or fame). It is my money. It is mine, all mine." It is because of this temptation that the majority of the very rich hoard their wealth. It is a relatively small minority who realize their talent for making a vast fortune is a gift that has been given to them and conclude: "This is my money on paper, but that is in name only. In reality, it was given to me; it is God's money. I am here to steward it and, as best I can, to give it back."

I've suggested that all blessings are potential curses. This business of gifts is not all a bed of roses; there are side effects. I have already hinted at the downside of the gift of a grateful heart: It is a chronic sense of obligation. For instance, our sense of obligation propelled Lily and me into our work with FCE, and it has caused us a lot of headaches and heartaches. Mind you, the pain's been worth it, but while our lives have been enriched by our gratitude, they've also been less comfortable as a result.

Another example. Right below a grateful heart on my list of the greatest blessings that can be bestowed upon a human being comes a strong will. A strong will does not guarantee success; it may create a Hitler. But a weak will pretty much guarantees failure. All who do well in psychotherapy, for instance, have that mysterious will to grow which the apathetic lack. There is a side effect, however. The down side of a strong will is a bad temper. It is strong-willed people who wrap golf clubs around trees because that damn little ball won't go where they want it to. Any strong-willed person has a lot of learning to do to effectively manage her anger.

A grateful heart and a strong will are relatively common gifts. Less common ones may also be quite crucial in their own way. One day in 1980, when *The Road Less Traveled* was just beginning to become known, a patient of mine recounted how the week before she'd happened to be at a cocktail party where my mother was also a guest. The patient told of overhearing a conversation between my mother and another elderly lady who said, "Oh, Mrs. Peck, you must be very proud of your son, Scotty."

"No, not particularly," my mother responded in the tart manner those in their last years may have.

The other lady protested, "But he's written this wonderful book that everyone's starting to read."

"Yes, but that's got nothing to do with me," retorted my mother. "It's his mind, you see. It's a gift."

I think my mother was both right and wrong. I think she was wrong in believing it had nothing to do with her. She was also wrong about it being my mind—assuming she was talking in terms of IQ. But I think she was right about it being a gift. Actually, a combination of a whole number of gifts. One in particular, however, stands out.

Many years ago Lily and I became friends with Tom, a younger man in the army. He and I had grown up in the same little WASP community during the summers. I hadn't played with him because he was just a baby at the time, but I'd played with his older brothers and his mother had known me as a child. A few years later Tom came to have dinner at our new home in Connecticut. He was visiting his mother at the time and the night before he'd told her, "Mom, tomorrow night I'm going to have dinner with Scott Peck. Do you remember Scott Peck?"

"Oh, yes," she answered, "he was that little

boy who was always talking about the kinds of things that people shouldn't talk about."

As you can see, the gift goes way back.

It also illustrates how all gifts or blessings are potential curses. As far as Tom's mother was concerned, my outspokenness was hardly a gift; it simply made me an obnoxious little brat. As an adult, it has propelled me to be unnecessarily impolitic at times. Furthermore, it caused me a fair amount of stress to be out of step with the WASP culture in which I was raised—a culture where tastefully talking about unimportant matters is encouraged while the raising of important ones is usually considered tasteless because it rocks the boat. Nonetheless, it has been mostly blessing. The one response I've received more than any other to all my books is not so much that I've said anything new but rather that I've written the kinds of things readers have been thinking all along but were afraid to talk about. "What a relief it was to know I wasn't alone," they've told me, "to know I wasn't crazy."

Phyllis Theroux, who, through her *Washington Post* book review, deliberately set *The Road Less Traveled* on the path toward fame, also did more than anyone else to prepare me to handle that fame. Early on she reminded me, "It's not your book, you know." I immediately knew what she was talking about. Still later she commented, "It's as if God happened to be walking in northwest Connecticut when He decided He wanted a book written." This kind of thinking does not lead to arrogance. To the contrary, it predisposes us to humility. Phyllis and I do not mean that

The Road Less Traveled or any of my other books are channeled material. They are not the Word of God. They contain imperfections for which I am totally responsible. I am only partially responsible for their virtues, however. They are better books than I could have written myself. I had assistance. They were gifts to me.

So I'm grateful to God for my books. But I am also grateful to editors. There are different types of editors, and they tend to exist in a hierarchy of prestige. At the top of the hierarchy are the broad-brush acquisition editors. They "acquire" draft books for their publishing company and will usually suggest (occasionally require) major or sweeping changes for the better. In the middle are the line editors. They suggest medium-sized changes: further elaboration of a point or a character, the addition of a paragraph here or deletion of a paragraph there, maybe some modest cutting. Then at the bottom of the heap are the lowly creatures called copy-editors.

I didn't know about these sorts of things when I sold the first draft of *The Road*. A few major changes were suggested that seemed constructive (including the title). I made them and a number of others that occurred to me. The manuscript was judged to be complete and acceptable. Then one afternoon I went to our mailbox to find a bulky package from the publisher. I opened it to find my manuscript returned to me. My heart sank as I concluded that even though I'd been paid a small advance they must have decided not to publish it after all. But as I searched for a letter of explanation to that effect I quickly discovered that it was not my manuscript. It was my manuscript with about twenty blue marks on each of its four hundred pages along with approximately sixty pink slips stuck to those pages. Actually, there was a note. It read: "Dr. Peck's use of footnotes is extremely sloppy. Otherwise I thought it rather good." The note, which was to the editor, was unsigned. I had no idea back then that these were words of high praise, but it did begin to dawn on me that I had fallen into the hands of a copyeditor.

The blue marks were her suggested single-word alterations, reconstruction of my semicolons, undangling of my participles, and the like. The pink slips were her major "queries," questioning my meaning or even my facts. My first and prolonged reaction was one of profound shame that I should have produced a manuscript deserving ten thousand different corrections. My next reaction, also prolonged, was one of rage that any human being could possibly be so nitpicking. Only after twenty-four hours did I come to a set of more balanced realizations. One was that her suggested minute changes, with very few exceptions, made it a better book. Another—and this was crucial—was that she and I had different personalities and hence different gifts. Had I possessed her extraordinary attention to detail I probably wouldn't have been able to write the book in the first place. On the other hand, if she possessed my capacity for "big picture" thinking she probably wouldn't have been able to be a copy editor. I needed her nit-picking, and she needed my book to pick on. We needed each other. Her gift of nit-picking was, in fact, a gift of love, and ever since I have been profoundly grateful for the service of copy editors. They may be regarded as being at the bottom of the heap, but for me they have been partners.

Our talented staff teases me that I never mention their great gifts in the text of my work. All right. Valerie tells neat jokes and has a vase of flowers at our bedsides whenever we return from a trip. Susan balances a checkbook better than I and is a computer whiz who always knows what to do with the infernal machines when something goes wrong with them. Gail is a skilled people pleaser who has yet to negotiate a speaking engagement where she hasn't created goodwill in the process. I don't know what we would do without them. Thank you. Of course, as I've taken pains to point out, all gifts have their downsides. Gail is so quick to please that she glosses over an important detail now and then. Simply because I'm computer-illiterate, Susan usually treats me like an ignorant dolt in all respects. And while Valerie will remember the flowers, she's likely to forget to empty the waste-baskets. No. Don't hit me. No. Please. . . .

In our work with community and FCE, the same lessons have been brought home to me a thousand different times in a thousand different ways. Will has a gift for business wisdom, Mary Ann for waiting for consensus, Gay for discerning when issues are being avoided, Dick for listening, Ellen for speaking up. And so it goes. In any group where women and men struggle to authentically communicate, their individual gifts will eventually emerge just as flowers will blossom in sequence in a well-tended garden. This person will dream for the group, that one will be the grain of sand in the oyster, this one will capture the group's joy, and that one expresses its sorrow with an eloquence that I could never have. Community reveals both our gifts and our limitations. Through it I have become not only more grateful for my own gifts but ever more grateful for the gifts of others—gifts that I do not possess but which the organization desperately needs. In my first book I took pathological dependency to task, and I still do. But these days I am more into championing and celebrating healthy interdependency.

I have made it sound as if I go about my days in unending, mellow-yellow gratitude. Not so. Take the matter of shopping, for instance. I hate to shop for presents. Usually I am maturely grateful for the way things work out, but whenever I go Christmas shopping (if I have to) my maturity goes flying right out the window. I become an arrogant little prince. If there are three presents I am looking for and I find them all on a single morning in a single shop, I'll feel as if my royal right has been served and I'll return home unperturbed. If I find two of them, I'll be seriously annoyed. If one, I am outraged at my poor fortune and life's inefficiency. And should I happen to not score at all, I'll consider myself one of the world's greatest victims. Instead of thinking, "Into every life a little rain must fall" or even "It never rains but it pours," I'll become obsessed with fantasies of outlawing Christmas by royal edict.

Lily, on the other hand, is a superb shopper. My gift of paragraphs is a gift of organization, of moving methodically toward a goal. I am an enormously goal-directed person. So when I shop I have to have a precise goal in mind, and when the vagaries of stores (over which, unlike my paragraphs, I have no control) prevent the attainment of my goal I feel enormously frustrated. I spoke of how Lily has the opposite gift of flowing. The downside of her gift is an occasional lack of organization. But her gift has not only allowed her to flow with the children to their great benefit, it permits her to flow through stores as one sniffs the flowers, seldom looking for anything in particular yet constantly discovering unexpected gems. Of course our different talents in this regard might also be looked upon as a reflection of the infinitely mysterious gift of sexuality. As one wag put it, "Men go shopping for objects; women for relaxation."

Some might consider this a dreadfully sexist analysis, and I have met a few women who hated to shop every bit as much as I. But only a very few. In any case, I pretty much depend upon Lily to do our shopping. Look at this as my male chauvinism, if you so choose, or her codependency. But the fact is we're both doing what we like, and we do it well. I choose to see it as interdependency.

Lily and I also share gifts in common. Perhaps these are the most important ones. Just as faith, hope, and gratitude are somewhat separate gifts, so also are they very much interconnected. Now I am talking of gifts of pertinacity, loyalty, and commitment that are also interrelated. And I am very glad indeed that we share them. I'm unsure our marriage could have long survived had just one of us had them. More than anything else, it is because we have both been fortunate enough to have been granted these quiet, seemingly unglamorous gifts that the marriage has not only survived but become something of a mystical body.

Can gifts be taught? Learned? Developed? Yes, within certain limits—and with one large caution.

Five years ago, I took a few violin lessons. To my amazement I discovered I could play the thing a little bit. It became clear to me that were I to practice assiduously for a few years—something I decided not to do—I could actually learn to play it reasonably well. It was also clear, starting at age fifty-one, that no matter how much I practiced I would never be a virtuoso. Whether I could have been had I started at age five is questionable. Actually, my mother did take me for a cello lesson at that age. Although I may have possessed some incipient talent, the issue was irrelevant since I possessed no will to be a cellist. I had no calling.

At age ten I did receive a calling to be a great tennis player, a calling so strong I practiced and practiced and practiced. The result was that by twelve I had become the preteen scourge of the courts with a good serve and a superb forehand. I had a weak backhand, however, and for the next twenty years I did what's called "running around your backhand." I emphasized my strong suit and attempted to avoid my weak one. I was very good, but I was not great. At thirty-two I realized that if I was ever going to have a whole tennis game—be the best that I could be—I was going to have to work on my backhand. This meant instead of avoiding it I'd need to use it at every opportunity. I did so. It was profoundly humiliating. I lost to players I could easily beat. People watched me play and sniffed, "I can't understand why they told me Peck was any good." But after three months of such humiliation I did succeed in developing a much stronger backhand and hence a much better game. That was when I decided to take up golf, which is truly humbling.

So gifts or talents can be learned or developed, but usually only with a great deal of practice and often only with the maturity required for the humility to work on our weak sides. Even then we probably won't become virtuosos. Moreover, none of us has the time or energy to learn all skills, develop all talents. We need to be selective. I took violin lessons not to become a violinist but to see if I could become one if I wanted to badly enough. There were, in fact, other things I wanted to do more.

Life's learning is not always hard work. Perhaps it is no accident that, after thirty-three years of marriage, Lily and I have the same Myers-Briggs personality type (INTJ for those familiar with the test). I doubt we started out that way. There is no question I have learned to become much more intuitive under Lily's tutelage. And she has definitely become more introverted as some of my shyness and need for solitude have rubbed off on her. This has not taken any conscious exertion on our parts. Perceiving the virtue of some of each other's traits, without even being aware of doing so, we gradually and effortlessly imitated them. Given our profound and remaining differences, this "growing together" does not worry us. It has been all to the good. We must admit to finding it a bit scary, however, that somehow over the years we have come to develop virtually identical signatures!

I promised a note of caution. In defining charismas as gifts of the Holy Spirit, the Church has meant it literally: They are gifts from God given to us for God's own purposes and with God's own timing. From early Old Testament times until today there have always been people who have sought to obtain, maintain, or enhance certain supernatural gifts—miraculous healing powers, the ability to predict the future, the capacity to commune with the spirits of the dead, and so on—to serve their own ambitions whenever they willed it. This behavior is referred to as magic. Its practitioners attempt to distinguish between white magic and black magic, but the Church's position is that our capacity for self-deception in regard to our motives is such that all magic should be considered potentially black. I agree with this assessment. I have seen people who have dabbled in magic who have hurt themselves and the world. It is no accident that one of them was deep into both magic and insider trading in the stock market. They are analogous activities.

In this Age of Reason the prevailing psychology

is that our gifts are our own. We think we are our own creators, and that our lives are totally our own to do with as we please. While I have no desire to see us return to the excesses of the Age of Faith, I believe this prevailing modern view is a false psychology. Eventually it can become downright pernicious. By all means, seek to improve yourself. But in doing so may I suggest that you also consider a currently less popular world view: namely, that we ultimately belong either to God or to the devil.

This day continued to be one that belonged to God. I think all days do, but this one was particularly blatant about it. Needless to say, when we reached Loch Ness we stopped at length to pay homage to Nessie. Although we looked for it, the monster was nowhere in sight. This did not surprise us. One associates Nessie with the fog and the mists. Certainly we'd never heard of a supposed sighting on a clear day. There are degrees of clarity, and on this noon the Loch sparkled in a way I'd never seen before. On several occasions I've had to watch out for snow blindness. This was the first time I'd ever had concern over the possibility of water blindness.

Almost halfway up the Loch we turned west to head over the highlands toward our eventual destination: the Isle of Skye, the largest of the Hebrides. On the way we took a planned two-hour detour to visit stones of a sort, the Glenelg brochs. Brochs are not prehistoric megaliths. They are, however, quite ancient and mysterious. Pre-Christian and pre-Roman, dating to around

150 B.C., they are tall, round stone fortresses about twenty yards in diameter. No one knows how high they were originally, since all of them have lost their tops to war or time long before the beginnings of archaeology. The best preserved today rise to forty feet, but one might guess that at one time they rose to at least eighty. For reasons not understood, the remains of these impressive structures, perhaps the most impressive of any extant structures in Great Britain predating the medieval cathedrals, are found only in northern Scotland.

The brochs reminded us of the post-Christian round towers we'd seen in Ireland, except that even though they'd been built almost a thousand years earlier they were of more complex construction with double instead of single walls. The Glenelg brochs are particularly remarkable because the two of them are hardly more than a stone's throw apart. To our knowledge, this profligacy in broch building occurred nowhere else. Most remarkable of all was their setting. Although, as obviously defensive structures, there was nothing holy about them per se, they were nestled together into a sweet valley, shaded by huge old oaks. It being June, the little fields of the valley were rampant with wild foxgloves in flower. The sun was hot and it was so quiet we could hear the insects buzzing in the air. One English couple and a single man were the sole other visitors. Once more we were privileged to be present at the holy conjunction of ancient human remains, natural beauty, and relative solitude.

Another holy spot, and again we felt blessed and grateful.

From the brochs we drove to Kyle of Lochalsh, where one gets the ferry to Skye. On the way we passed a two-star hotel, and I commented to Lily that while I'd prefer a three-star one, I'd still be happy if Broadford Hotel, our lodging for the next two nights on Skye, had two stars. We took the ferry without incident across the narrow strait to the isle (strange they built brochs two thousand years ago but haven't yet built a bridge) and drove eight miles north. We spotted the Broadford Hotel with ease from the road. Its sign had no stars. We didn't need the sign to tell us it had no stars. A hundred yards away one could discern its starlessness. A starless hotel in Great Britain is generally a quite visible dump.

There are occasional no-star hotels in Britain that are surprisingly decent once you get inside, but the Broadford was not one of them. Its entrance was being repaired. Perhaps great things will come of it in the Third Millennium. But the 1992 result was that we had to carry our luggage through the seedy bar to the seedy reception desk next to the seedy lounge and seedy restaurant. Thence we carried it up seedy hallways to our assigned eight-by-eight-foot seedy cubicle overlooking the seedy parking lot. It was our ultimate moment of shared claustrophobia. I dashed back to the reception desk in panic to beg for a room somewhere with a view. I was firmly told that the hotel had only two rooms with any view, and both were occupied.

At that moment there was a phonelike sound

in an alcove behind the reception desk. The firm but dreary-looking lady receptionist instantly vanished into it. I hung around waiting for her return, thinking to ask her about other lodgings on Skye—even a bed and breakfast home within an hour's drive. I waited and waited, unable to face returning to the airless cubicle. After ten minutes the manager, a genial giant of a man, suddenly came out with some papers in hand. It was a five-page fax for me from New York City that had just been received. Handing it to me, he said, "I understand that you'd like to have a room with a view. I've found out that a client has canceled, so we can give you one after all."

The new cubicle was as cramped as the first, but—blessing of blessings!—its window looked out over the road to the sound and across its waters to the mountains of the mainland. What a difference for us a view makes! By it alone an utterly uninhabitable space had been transformed into a reasonably habitable one—at least habitable for two nights. Moreover, the breeze was blowing straight in from the bay.

Just as it was unthinkable to have stayed in the airless and viewless cubicle to which we'd originally been assigned, so it was unthinkable to even consider dining in the Broadford's unutterably grimy dining room smelling of stale lima beans. Yet we'd run out of picnic supplies. What to do? We had noted a plain building fifty yards down the road that looked as if it might contain some little fish and chips sort of place. We walked over to it and, sure enough, found a five-table restaurant that was plain but not the least bit grimy and served decent if not exotic fare. The waitress, an Australian lass in her thirties, was competent and most friendly without being intrusive. Thing had ended up much better than we'd dreamed two hours before.

After dinner we strolled along the bay for a bit and then back to our cubicle to retire. Before sleep we pondered a mystery other than that of the stones for a change. How was it an unavailable room with a view had suddenly become available? As with any mystery, we couldn't answer it with certainty, but we could hazard a good guess. We guessed it was the fax. It was not unreasonable to suspect that this was probably the first time in its history that the Broadford Hotel had ever received a fax for one of its guests. And that as a consequence the manager had concluded we might be Very Important People, even royalty in disguise, deserving of the best it had to offer. Thank God for the timing! Although the Broadford, save for its two rooms with a view, was far and away the worst British dump in which we'd stayed to date—worse than Cardiff, worse than Glasgow—we fell asleep feeling graced and grateful.

CHAPTER XIII

PEACE
FRIDAY, JUNE 12

Another clear and sunny, almost hot, day for a leisurely seven-hour drive around the circumference of the isle of Skye. We stopped when we felt like it: Portree, the isle's largest town, for Lily and me to shop a bit; the Museum of Island Life to see some old thatched huts and nineteenth-century artifacts; the Clan Donald ruined palace and gardens to stroll amid the flora.

None of it was dramatic. On the other hand, it was not boring either. Similar though it was to Mull in terms of external geography, the most memorable thing for us was its pervasive peacefulness. Skye is called "the misty isle." We are unsure whether this is because it is more usually shrouded in fog or because, on atypical, clear days like today, its cliffs and mountains seem to rise from the sea out of a faint film of mist clinging to the water's edge. We, however, would call it "the peaceful isle."

Peace fascinates me.

My earliest memories are primarily ones of peace. Another little poem I wrote seems to set the stage of my life:

In the autumn of the year that I was three
My mother
Wakened me from a dark sleep to see
The Northern lights dancing in the cold.
In her warm night arms
I danced all the way to China
Before she carried me in.
I still dance, and I do not know
If I can ever forgive her
For such love.

The following autumn contains my first memory of war. I can remember standing at the top of the stairs in my pajamas, although I was supposed to be in bed asleep, peeking down into the living room where my mother was sitting with a veritable crowd of other women, knitting. They were engaged in a communal project called "Bundles for Britain." Britain was at war with Germany, and the knitting of socks and sweaters was a way Americans could support the British well before the United States entered the war. The memory symbolizes my relationship with that war: I watched its drama from the top of the stairs, safe and secure in my soft, flannel pajamas.

Of course America did shortly join World War II and my childhood is full of memories of it thereafter. The two strongest are opposites. One is of my friendship with Tommy Bernheim. I can't be certain why Tommy was my best friend of those years, but I suspect it was because he had the finest collection of toy weaponry in all of New York City. From age six to nine he and

I gleefully spent endless hours going "ack-ack-ack" at each other in Central Park and his family's apartment.

The other strongest memory is of making speeches. In my bedroom after the lights had been turned out I would huddle upside down deep underneath the bedclothes, so as not to be heard, delivering lengthy, eight-year-old speeches to the combined nations of the globe exhorting them toward world peace.

The roots of vocation run deep. In one sense or another I have been making speeches ever since, and often as not on behalf of peace. I've long had a distinct calling to peacemaking. I've also always enjoyed a good, clean, intellectual fight, often, too, on behalf of peace, when there's been no actual violence or real hatred involved. These two, paradoxical sides of my nature may be a reflection of the fact that I am a Gemini, but they do not, I think, mean that I have a split personality. Most truth and all great issues are chock-full of paradox, and the matter of peace is paradoxical indeed.

And, of course, profoundly overdetermined. Peace is not just one thing with a single cause. Peace is many things; among them a spirit, a gift, a condition, a process, a decision, a victory of love over evil, an ongoing task and the predictable result of a great deal of highly disciplined hard work.

I have no idea why the Isle of Skye struck us as so much more peaceful than the Isle of Mull or than most other places. I do not know how or why the spirit of peace had happened to descend upon it. There is much about peace that is mysterious. As a scientist, however, I do know something about the causes of a spirit of peace among human beings.

In 1981 I led a workshop on the supposed topic of spiritual growth for sixty people in Washington, D.C. For reasons I did not understand at the time, a spirit of peace entered that otherwise ordinary university room where we were working and bathed the sixty of us in its glow. It felt like a miracle. In speaking of grace yesterday, I offhandedly suggested that miracles, defined as happenings that cannot be explained by natural law, may be quite lawful but seem miraculous simply because we have not yet discerned the laws by which they operate. Asked to lead other workshops, I wondered whether the powerful miracle that had occurred on that 1981 November afternoon could be repeated. In other words, could I discern its laws? I found that I could, and three years later Lily and I banded together with others to establish the Foundation for Community Encouragement (FCE) to teach these laws of the miracle of peace.

We came to call the process of our workshops community building and labeled them "community-building workshops" or CBWs. They were so labeled because that's what they seemed to be: a process of taking a group of relative strangers and assisting them in building themselves into a community. As part of the lawfulness of the miracle, we discerned there were fairly predictable stages to the process that we named "pseudocommunity," "chaos," "emptiness," and "community." Some knowledge of these stages is essential to any understanding of peace among humans and the task of peacemaking.

Pseudocommunity is an apt name because it is a false community—something that looks like a community but isn't. Gather a group of people together for virtually any purpose and they will begin by pretending that they are already a community. The basic pretense is that there are no significant differences between them. This pretense is maintained by an unwritten set of rules they all know—"good manners"—whereby they can gloss over their differences. Although it bores me to death as an ex-WASP, I don't want to say that pseudocommunity is useless. Nor deride good manners. They are real, albeit primitive tools of peacekeeping, and they, along with the pseudocommunity they create, allow us to maintain peace and coexist peacefully when there aren't any major issues between us.

Still, it is a pretense. We humans are not all the same. And when our differences are forced to the surface one way or another, the group will immediately degenerate into the stage of chaos. Now that the differences have surfaced, what characterizes this stage is the attempt to make everyone the same. Everyone attempts to heal or convert one another back into a false uniformity. Occasionally, the members do succeed in "stuffing" their differences so as to regress into an even stronger form of pseudocommunity or cult. More commonly, the "healing" and "converting" become progressively angrier until war or group self-destruction results. I used the word *degenerate* into chaos. The more proper word is *evolves* into chaos. While it feels like war and may become war, chaos is actually one step closer to reality, and it is a stage that cannot be skipped in a deep peacemaking process.

If a group of people are of goodwill (which they usually are) and have good leadership (which they usually don't), then they can evolve out of chaos into the stage we call "emptiness." This is the hard part. Pseudocommunity and chaos come naturally to us humans. Emptiness does not. But it is crucial (if you'll pardon a not so accidental pun). In the stage of emptiness the members of the group will sacrificially empty themselves of whatever it is that stands between them and real community.

The list of "things" that must be emptied can seem almost endless: fixed expectations and rigid agendas; prejudices or simplistic instant likes and dislikes; quick answers arrived at without listening; the need to heal and convert or "fix" others; preset positions and notions of what winning might look like; needs for certainty and control and looking good; intellectual equanimity and the appearance of sophistication; excessive emotional detachment; sexism, racism, and other "isms"; a fondness for fighting on the one hand and a desire for peace at any price on the other. . . . I could go on and on. The task would seem impossible were it not for the fact that with the right type of leadership, groups of all kinds and sizes can routinely accomplish it over the course of a day or two.

Two factors in paradoxical tandem make it so possible. One is the extraordinary power of group pressure to cause change for better or for worse. In the case of community building, it is for the better because of the leaders' insistence upon integrity. That is the other factor. The message is not "Sacrifice everything for the group." Instead, it is "Empty yourself of what you don't need." Consequently, a critical sentence of our mission statement reads, "FCE's approach encourages tolerance of ambiguity, the experience of discovery, and the tension between holding on and letting go." Allowing themselves to experience this tension, people are amazed to discover all that they can let go of while still holding on firmly to their integrity.

When the participants have become sufficiently empty, then the miracle of community happens. Suddenly, without warning, there will be a marked shift in the whole tone of the group. The members begin to speak far more authentically. And concisely. There are periods of lovely silence. People listen. In terms of content, twice as much gets said in half as many words. That which was irritating often becomes endearing. It is as if the members are all operating in sync. It feels like music, and complex consensual decision making becomes both extraordinarily efficient and wise.

While the shift from the stage of chaos into the stage of emptiness is usually gradual by fits and starts, the shift of the group from emptiness into community is usually instantaneous and dramatic. Some experience it as if the door had suddenly been thrown open and God had walked into the room. Even more commonly that moment is felt as the entrance of a palpable spirit of peace. Peace—pure, deep, soft, ever so gentle peace. It is an enchanting, enthralling experience.

I said that I was speaking as a scientist. We scientists not only conduct experiments but repeat them. Indeed, scientific proof requires that an experiment produce the same results in as many different laboratories as possible, conducted by different experimenters. Each community-building workshop (CBW) might be considered an experiment. To date, FCE has conducted almost five hundred CBWs with about a hundred different leaders in a wide variety of settings (for the public, for organizations in conflict, for civic leaders, for prisoners, for scholars from different faiths, etc.) in six different nations. Approximately ninety percent of these CBWs "reached" community. Twenty thousand people around the globe, often in cross-cultural groups, have now experienced the spirit of peace I have described.

Much as I enjoy the spirit of peace, my primary interest is in peace itself. The spirit is usually felt only when a group enters community for the first time. Thereafter its intensity wanes, yet the group is able to continue its peacemaking work as a result of the skills it has learned. Indeed, community is usually required for effective peacemaking.

In hierarchical organizations an individual may dictate a decision to a group. When a group itself makes a decision—as it must in most situations of conflict—it has in essence only two decision-making modes available: adversarialism or consensus. Voting is the most common form of adversarial decision making. It is often not very effective. Because it is a kind of win/lose decision making, it leaves the minority dissatisfied, resentful, and often soon undermining. Genuine consensus (as opposed to pseudoconsensus) is win/win decision making that achieves "buy in" from all the members of the group. It may take more time, but it is more likely to eventuate in wise, lasting decisions.

When the issues to be decided are major, true consensus can generally be achieved only by a group that is in community. This is the reason for one of FCE's motto: "Community building first, decision making second." It is also the reason my book on the subject, *The Different Drum*, is subtitled "Community Making and Peace." Community building should take precedence to peacemaking. The fact that it usually doesn't accounts for the poor track record of professional diplomats who, as a class, have no knowledge or understanding of genuine community.

People will often talk about the extraordinary amount of "unconditional love" that seems to be floating around the room once a group has gotten into community. There is a lot of love in fact, but I would hardly call it unconditional. Indeed, it is there only because the members of the group have met a whole number of conditions. In particular, they have done the work of emptiness and, in a sense, have earned it. In another sense, community is beyond pure earning. It is a gift.

So it is that FCE instructs its leaders: "Your job is not to lead a group into community; it is to lead it into emptiness, and when a group is sufficiently empty then community will come in as a gift of the Holy Spirit."

This use of the term *Holy Spirit* makes it sound as if FCE is a specifically Christian organization. It is not; it is nonsectarian. But it *is* spiritual, and we envision peacemaking as a spiritual sort of process. Most of us have the sense that we could not succeed at this work if left solely to our own devices, if we did not have help from God (as we understand Him). So it is that the last sentence of FCE's mission statement reads: "As we seek to encourage others, so we remember our reliance upon a spirit both within and beyond ourselves."

I promised paradox, and here we are face-to-face with it. Almost all the great religions struggle over and again to embrace the paradox of grace and works. In the Judeo-Christian tradition we say, "God helps those who help themselves." Muhammad phrased it, "Trust in God, but tie your camel first." These sayings remind us to do our homework, but many of us workaholics need more reminding to not leave God out of the picture. For when we forget God we fall into heresy, tying twenty-six knots in the tether of our camel and still not feeling secure. Nor achieving either much peace or community, both of which require a considerable amount of trust and risk.

Mind you, I am talking of God, not religion. All manner of absurd wars have been fought over religion, but mostly by people who have forgotten about God. I believe that serious peacemaking

301

(as opposed to sham negotiations) requires community, and community requires that we seriously attempt to not only be in community with each other but also with God, that we actively welcome God to the table while accepting that it will be Her choice when and whether to appear and that Her presence will be a gift.

Grace is mysterious, work is not; it's just hard. I've already alluded to the work of building community, which is primarily the work of "emptiness," of people stretching themselves for one another. But this work is just the beginning. The greatest work for groups over the long haul is maintaining community once they've got it. A group never stays in community for long. Within a few hours, days, or weeks, it will lapse back into chaos or pseudocommunity. What characterizes a healthy group is not that it is always u"in community" but the rapidity with which it will recognize that it has fallen out of it, and the group's willingness to then do the work of regaining it. "We've lost it," a member will proclaim, and add, "I wonder what we need to empty ourselves of this time?" In other words, maintaining community is an ongoing process of rebuilding it—and rebuilding and rebuilding it over and over again.

So we arrive at some tough lessons. Peace is a lot of work. And it's not a one-shot deal. Preserving the peace is every bit as hard as achieving it in the first place. The plain fact of the matter is that on an intellectual and emotional level war is easier than peace. In waging war we

302

will physically often work around the clock in preference to doing the intellectual work of peace, and will gladly risk our physical lives rather than risk ourselves emotionally. In other words, war comes quite naturally to human beings while peace does not.

To put it another way, we generally resist peace. I used to think the major reason people resisted community was their fear of deviating from the "ethic" of rugged individualism, their terror of losing their composure and exposing their brokenness. But I have changed my mind about this. People do resist community for this reason, but the greater reason, I've come to realize, is their even more primitive laziness. What has caused me to change my mind has been the experience of watching organizations resist the work of community maintenance.

Much as we try to tell the otherwise intelligent executives of organizations that building community is not a quick fix, they generally persist in believing that it will be one. And then, when their newly built community falls apart, they will discredit the process even though it worked. Three times now I've had the excruciatingly sad experience of watching an organization achieve dramatic goals through community building only to lose the community, refuse to work to regain it, and ultimately give up the goals it had achieved. Why? Why on earth would an organization purchase a pearl of great price and then throw it away after it was demonstrably effective? We asked them, of course. The words were different each time, but they all translated out as "It's too much trouble."

I am not yet addressing the issue of a "just" or necessary war, only unnecessary war: the issue of why we humans frequently go to great lengths to kill one another in situations where a most decent peace would be quite feasible if we simply worked at it a little bit. In *The Road Less Traveled* I suggested that laziness might be the essence of what theologians call original sin. By laziness I did not so much mean physical lethargy as mental, emotional, or spiritual inertia. And I'll stick with that as the most fundamental analysis of our absurdity.

Casting an additional particularly American and paradoxical light on the matter, perhaps the simultaneously most profound and silliest words ever written were: "We hold these truths to be self-evident; that all men are created equal; that they are endowed by their creator with certain unalienable Rights; that among these are life, liberty, and the pursuit of happiness." I believe that these words of the Declaration of Independence constitute a magnificent and holy vision that accurately captures the essence of the human condition.

They are also horribly misleading.

We are all equal in the sight of God. Beyond that, however, we are utterly unequal. We have different gifts and liabilities, different genes, different languages and cultures, different values and styles of thinking, different personal histories, different levels of competence, and so on, and so on. Indeed, humanity might be properly labeled "the unequal species." What most distinguishes us from all the other creatures is our extraordinary diversity and the variability of our behavior. Equal? Just in the moral sphere alone we range from the horribly demonic to the gloriously angelic.

The false notion of our equality propels us into the pretense of pseudocommunity, and when the pretense fails, as it must for any intimacy or authenticity, then it propels us to attempt to achieve equality by force: the force of gentle persuasion followed by less and less gentle persuasion. We totally misinterpret our task. Society's task is not to establish equality. It is to develop systems that deal humanely with our inequality—systems that, within reason, celebrate and encourage diversity.

The concept of human rights is central to the development of such systems, and I wholeheartedly applaud the Bill of Rights amended to the U.S. Constitution and specifically interpreted by the courts. I am much more dubious, however, about the sweeping rights claimed by the Declaration of Independence: the rights to life, liberty, and the pursuit of happiness. Rapidly approaching old age, for instance, I am increasingly dubious about my right to life in certain respects. As an author and teacher, I must question my liberty to lie or even subtly distort. As a psychiatrist and theologian, I'm not sure how worthy a pursuit that of happiness is, knowing happiness to be either a side effect of some deeper pursuit or else the result of self-delusion. My still larger problem is with the aggregate of these rights. Add the rights of life, liberty, and the pursuit of happiness together, and it sounds as if we have a right to peace. As if we are entitled to peace.

One side of the paradox is that peace is a truly proper human aspiration. There is a difference between lethal and nonlethal conflict. We need the latter. If managed properly it actually tends to promote human dignity. Despite its supposed glories and songs like "The Men of Harlech," war generally destroys our dignity. Defining peace as the absence of outright war, it is indeed noble to aspire to it, and we cannot aspire to something we feel we don't deserve. In this sense we should regard peace as a "right."

The other side of the paradox is that we have no right to deserve peace without working for it. All that I have said about community and everything we know about peace indicates we have no reason whatsoever to effortlessly expect it. Or expect that once we have, through sacrifice, won peace, it will stay around for long without us having to lift a finger again. The greatest problem of the notion of rights is the psychology of entitlement. Calling the rights to life, liberty, and the pursuit of happiness "unalienable" may well serve to exaggerate the problem. Volumes upon volumes could be written about the subject. Suffice it to say that while a psychology of entitlement can have its virtues, it also has extremely dangerous pitfalls. Perhaps no pitfall is more dangerous than the assumption we are entitled to peace.

One way the notion of entitlement to peace

can work itself out is the assumption of vast numbers of Americans that all conflicts can be peacefully resolved. It is naive. Yet many others operate out of the opposite assumption that no conflict can be resolved except through force, through violence or the threat of it. This assumption is cynical and self-fulfilling. The paradoxical reality at this point in human evolution is that some wars are unavoidable or "just," and some are unjust, unnecessary, and waged at horrifying cost out of sheer laziness and stupidity.

I recounted my formative years during what Americans now refer to as "the good war." While it might earlier have been preventable, by the time America entered it World War II was unavoidable. Japan was in the grips of nationalistic insanity and Germany possessed by the demonic. Both had to be stopped, and could only be stopped by the brute force of war. The word *good* seems inappropriate for the slaughter of battle, but that particular battle was necessary.

In a very real sense, however, I came of age twenty years later. By early 1965 it was apparent that there was a great deal of lying surrounding the United States's involvement in Vietnam. My first reaction was to think, "Yes, but my country must know what it's doing." As the lies continued, my next was: "It looks as if my country *doesn't* know what it's doing, but not being privy to CIA and other government information, I couldn't possibly understand the complexities of the situation." But the lies went on, and by the end of that year I concluded that I had to at least try to understand it. After only three weeks of evening reading about Vietnamese history, I could understand it. What America was doing in the war was incredibly stupid and downright evil. Most frightening of all was the realization that after three weeks of research in my spare time as a psychiatry resident I knew more about Vietnam than the men who were making our policy there. My government was waging war in a nation it hadn't even taken the trouble to study!

Hard to believe? One of the premises upon which the United States was waging war in Vietnam at the time was its belief that the burgeoning communism there was an extension of Chinese communism—an export from mainland China located to the north. Only in the first few days of my reading I discovered that the Vietnamese and Chinese had been traditional enemies for over a thousand years. On the assumption they were collaborating with the Chinese, which couldn't have been further from the case, the United States inadvertently pushed the Vietnamese nationalists to the only place they could go for help: the waiting arms of the Russian Communists. This was but one of the multiple, mindless stupidities that governed America's insistence upon maintaining massive and useless carnage for a decade. Yes, some major wars are the result of sheer laziness, and can be easily avoided by combining integrity with a small amount of intellectual homework.

I've spoken of conflicts that can and cannot be peacefully resolved. There is a third type: the conflict that cannot be resolved but can be *tran-*

scended by "agreeing to disagree." The result can be peaceful coexistence between groups as large as nations and small as a marriage.

We were standing in the tiny bedroom of our attic apartment over the True Sisters' Nursery School in Cleveland. It was a summer day in the first year of our marriage. The sun was beating down on the eaves and we were awash with sweat. Strange I should recall these details and not what precipitated the issue. But I remember clearly telling Lily, "I don't believe there should be any secrets between us," and I can remember her retorting, "Well, I do. I think there is a place for secrets in marriage, and I intend to keep some from you." Our horns were locked, and in a way they've been locked ever since.

In another way, however, we've consistently unlocked them. Part of our doing so has been our realization that this divisive issue between us is a very real one. In the early days I used to think that Lily was simply wrong in her attachment to secrecy, and it was my task to help her to see the light. She in turn hoped that I would rapidly outgrow my obviously immature need to be a blabber-mouth. But gradually, without deserting our own inclinations, each of us came to realize the validity of the other's position, and indeed today could argue forcefully on the other's behalf. Lily now appreciates my outspokenness as a gift—mostly—and I usually appreciate her need for privacy as well as her gift of being more politic than I. The issue is real because it's one of life's innumerable paradoxes, and we slowly learned to respect our opposite positions as sides of a greater reality. Transcendence of an issue is thus accomplished.

It was also accomplished because we came to modify our positions to the point that they are seldom positions anymore. One of the "rights" of age seems to be speaking one's mind, and Lily has come to exercise that right more and more over the years. Meanwhile, I have learned something about how to keep my mouth shut, and occasionally these days can be almost reticent.

The conflict between secrecy and outspokenness has hardly been our only struggle of long standing. In speaking of our different styles of shopping I quipped how men shop for a specific object while women shop to relax. A recently popular way of looking at such matters is through the lens of "sociobiology"—a theory that much of our social behavior is determined by our genes. It suggests that back in Paleolithic times there was distinct survival value in men being good hunters of game and women being good gatherers of edible plants. The hypothesis is that through the survival of the fittest evolution has bred modern man to be a hunter and modern woman a gatherer. Some pooh-pooh this theory. Observing Lily shop, however, I am not ready to dismiss it out of hand. She does seem to be a born gatherer. I myself do not feel like a born hunter, yet in looking at the fierce concentration with which I often pursue an idea, Lily can perceive me as one who is stalking his prey.

But things are hardly ever black and white. Take our behavior on the golf course, for instance. I am so goal-directed my eye is always on the hole, and as a consequence I am a very poor lost ball finder. I'm as impatient hunting for golf balls in the underbrush as I am when shopping. Not so goal-directed, Lily is likely to "pick up" every other hole after she's made a bad shot or two. When she does, while I'm playing out the hole, she's wandering around the rough and the woods gleefully picking up my lost balls and those of dozens of golfers who preceded us. She's very good at this, and her passion for the search is a gift to me. A lousy golfer, on an eighteen-hole round I'll lose as many as six balls, but when we play together, thanks to her foraging, we're likely to return with at least twice as many balls as when we started out. But in her foraging is she hunting or gathering? Certainly she's hunting for the stupid little things, yet she's so good at it she makes it look like simple gathering—as if she was simply collecting an apron-full of forget-me-nots from a field of wildflowers. The distinction between hunters and gatherers is not all that clear.

Anyway, gender differences are so routinely divisive that the conflict they *engender* has long been referred to in terms of war as "the battle of the sexes." Although never with a vengeance, Lily and I have chronically engaged in this battle with as much vigor as most. By and large we have transcended it, too, but that doesn't mean it is resolved. While I accept the behavior, to this day I have no empathy with Lily's need for makeup and hairdressers, and she has none for my tendency to still look at other women occasionally with a hunter's appreciative eye. In such respects, we've not yet been able to walk in each other's shoes.

When we can do it, walking in another's shoes is the best producer of empathy and conflict-resolution technique there is. Or driving in another's feet! Unaccustomed as I was to the peculiar British custom of driving on the left-hand side of the road, I'd been continually wandering too far to the left out of what Lily had assumed to be a combination of clumsiness and inattentiveness. For most of the past twelve days she has been intermittently screeching at me whenever I drove the car up against the left-hand curbs. Today on Skye, because my back is seriously beginning to hurt, I asked her to take over the wheel. As she now careened us over the curb with equal frequency as I, she acknowledged a sudden increase in empathy. Ahh, it's nice to be vindicated! And to be peaceful.

I've been speaking of peace between people. But what of peace within oneself, that much-yearned-for condition called "inner peace"? The same sort of paradoxical principles hold. Although we have the right to desire it, we are no more entitled to inner peace than we are to outer peace. Moreover, in order to possess it we are frequently called to forsake it. Only those who can constantly lie to themselves without qualm have constant peace of mind. But if we do not want to be brain damaged in this manner, we need to remember that there is something far more important than inner peace: integrity. To remember this myself, it helps me to think about Jesus, who so often

312

felt frustrated, angry, frightened, lonely, sad, and depressed—a man who clearly desired to be popular but would not sell out for it and taught us that life is something more than a popularity contest, a man who did not seem to have much "inner peace" as the world is accustomed to imagining, yet who has been called "the Prince of Peace."

So it is I used to tell my patients, "Psychotherapy is not about happiness; it is about power. If you go the whole route in here, I cannot guarantee that you will leave one jot happier. What I can guarantee is that you will leave more competent. The problem is that there's a vacuum of competence in the world, so what happens as soon as people become more competent is that God or Life will give them greater tasks to do. So you may well leave here worrying about far bigger things than when you came in. On the other hand, there is a certain joy—a kind of happiness or inner peace, if you will—that comes from knowing that you're worrying about the big things and no longer getting totally bent out of shape over the little ones."

As I've suggested, this paradoxically real brand of inner peace is a derivative of integrity, and the subject of integrity brings us back to community. I noted how there's an old adage among monks and nuns that you're not ready to live in community until you can live by yourself, and at FCE we talk about being in community with yourself. By this we mean knowing yourself, being in touch with all your different parts, including your vices as well as your virtues. I've told how Carl Jung ascribed the root of human evil to the "refusal to meet the Shadow"—the Shadow being defined as that part of us containing those traits we'd rather not own up to, that we're continually trying to hide not only from others but also from ourselves, that we're continually trying to sweep under the rug of our own consciousness. By refusal to meet the Shadow, Jung was implying a radical avoidance of being in touch with oneself. We individuals each have our shadow side. So do groups. One of the definitions of a true community, as opposed to a pseudocommunity, is "a group that deals with its own Shadow." Wars tend to be started either by individuals or by groups lacking integrity or wholeness, who are out of touch with their own sins, who are filled with pride over their strengths but lack the humility to see their weaknesses and deal with their Shadows.

Three years ago at a conference on community I had the privilege of moderating a panel of five speakers who had alternately addressed the topics of "Community with Yourself," "Community between Rich and Poor," "Community in Education," "Community and Race Relations," and "Community in Business." In addition to moderating it, I had the role of making an impromptu summation at the end. My task was made easier by the speaker on "Community between Rich and Poor," when she commented, "You cannot build community from a distance." Oh, how profound! We wealthy cannot build community with the poor while totally remaining in posh developments sequestered by security guards. Blacks, Caucasians, and Hispanics, for example, cannot be in community without daring to be in the same room together for a prolonged period. Teachers cannot be in community with students if they consistently maintain their academic aloofness. I can't teach a business executive how to build community in her corporation without learning about her business and stretching myself to be in her shoes. A "hands on" approach is required. It is the same with this business of inner peace. Just as there is pseudo-community and true community, so there is a false kind of peace of mind that derives from being out of touch with yourself and a true kind which requires us to be close and intimate with every facet of ourselves.

All this may seem far removed from the subject of stones—none of which we've seen today. But it isn't. The major reason we're so enamored with them is their mystery, and one of the great unanswered questions about the megalithic people is the mystery of what happened to them. When the Celts came to Britain around 500 B.C., they tinkered with the great stones. But they did not erect them. The megalithic culture was long dead by the time they arrived. Why? Why did the culture lose its extraordinary vitality?

Lily offers a pregnant hint. I told how I tended to meet my need for romance through infidelity and Lily through immersion in science fiction and fantasy literature, and how her path was probably the more constructive. One of its constructive results emerged today as we talked, while driving up and down the curbs of Skye, about the relationship between myth and prehistory. "You know how I've always loved elves and fairies," she commented. "Together with leprechauns and maybe some others they're referred to as 'the week folk' or 'the little people.' There's a theme that keeps popping up about them. They hate iron. Well, maybe it's not so much that they hate iron as they're afraid of it. You tell me that the Celts brought iron to Britain. I wonder if the wee folk weren't pre-Celts or the megalithic people."

There was no doubt in my mind that she was on to something. There are, however, some caveats. For one, the human remains of the megalithic people unearthed by archaeologists indicate that they weren't all that much shorter than we are today, and were just as tall as the Celts. Another is that the megalithic culture had begun to decline well over a millennium before the Celts came with their iron. What that decline may have been more related to than the advent of iron was the advent of bronze.

As best we can discern, between 2000 and 1500 B.C. is called the Bronze Age, as distinct from the ensuing Iron Age. The Bronze Age people in Great Britain did build a few stone circles and stone rows, but only a few, and the stones were mostly short and small—two to four feet tall instead of ten to twenty, better measurable in pounds than tons. It was as if they were going through the motions without any of the amazing communal energy or dedication of their ancestors.

There were other dramatic changes. Before 2000 B.C., as noted, the tombs were primarily communal. Such Bronze Age tombs as have been discovered seemed to primarily be those of individuals, and by the bronze implements buried with them archaeologists believe they were individuals of particularly high status. The Bronze Age people in certain parts of Great Britain built a great many stone walls, suggesting land ownership. They also began to build even higher walls encircling their villages or collections of hut circles—walls that seem to have been defensive structures.

Since we are talking about prehistory, it is still a matter of conjecture, but the leading theory for the decline of the megalithic people is their transition from a communal culture to a culture much closer to our own present one: a society characterized by distinct social stratification, private property ownership, war, and thievery. This transition seemed to coincide with the introduction of usable metal, namely bronze, into the culture. It would further seem that this introduction was equivalent to introducing money and the competition for wealth.

We think of elves and fairies as idyllic folk, living in sweet harmony with nature and one another. Whether the megalithic people had true "community" in the sense I've used the word, I have no idea. We do not even know if they were particularly peaceful. What we do know with certainty, however, is that they communally built extraordinary monuments in Great Britain and northwestern Europe that would not again be matched in magnificence in that area of the globe for over three thousand years. And that with the coming of bronze they somehow lost their communal greatness. It would seem that the legendary wee folk were right to be afraid of metal.

We ate again this evening at the same clean little restaurant just down the road from the grimy Broadford Hotel, and again we were graciously served by the same waitress. Old customers now, we got to chatting and told her how we'd be leaving early in the morning to catch the ferry for the lengthy trip to the Isles of Lewis and Harris, the largest and most northern of the Outer Hebrides. "Oh, you'll have to see the Stones of Callanish when you're there," she exclaimed without even knowing about our addiction. "They're wonderful!"

With this encouragement, after dinner we once more strolled down along the bay. Until now I'd not been able to predict the British weather. But this evening, after three solid days of sunshine, we watched high clouds rising in the west. It was unmistakable that a very large storm was approaching to coincide with our sea voyage on the morrow to the outermost reaches of the British Isles. We went to sleep with a sense of anticipation tinged with a certain amount of forebiding.

CHAPTER XIV

ADVENTURE
SATURDAY, JUNE 13

It is 9:00 A.M. and we are in the unpronounceable hamlet of Uig, twenty miles northwest of Broadford. It is the Isle of Skye headquarters of the Caledonian MacBrayne Company, which seems to own and operate all of the innumerable ferries in Scotland. This time our car is *first* in line, and we will have a long wait since the incoming boat has not yet arrived. But we are not bored. It is blowing a gale and I am wandering the pier, mentally clocking the gusts at 50 mph, hoping they will get even stronger and that our two-hour crossing to Lewis will be dramatically stormy. Dramatic, but safe.

I love storms. This, too, goes way back. When I was five years old my parents built a home on top of Sharon Mountain in the foothills of the Berkshires. It had a little well house with a weather vane on its roof. For the next seven years I would climb that roof on hot summer afternoons and sit there, clutching the weather vane as if I could somehow control the winds, and watch the great thunderstorms broil up over the Hudson River valley fifty miles to the west. I have been a weather watcher ever since.

I particularly love the wind. No line of poetry

had held more meaning for me than the one of Shelley in his "Ode to the West Wind" where he begs, "Make me thy lyre, even as the forest is." Well before I knew that line, when I sat on our well-house roof, I was already seeking to be the wind's lyre, to be played upon like the leaves of a maple or the fronds of a palm.

In September of the year that I was eight, the hurricane of 1944 blew itself out over the Berkshires. The night it did, without informing any adult, I clung to the roof with exultation in the darkness. For years afterward it was my dream that when I grew up I would spend my vacations in Florida in September because that was when and where hurricanes seemed most likely to hit. By the time I was grown up I had better sense.

Yet in a way my dream was fulfilled. One of the reasons the three years we spent in Okinawa were so wonderful for us was that they were tinged with the excitement of the fact that the island sits right in the middle of an area of the Pacific Ocean known as Typhoon Alley. For weeks each summer and autumn we would be in what the military government called a "Condition." Condition 4 meant simply that there was a typhoon somewhere around a thousand miles away. Condition 3 signified a typhoon five or six hundred miles away. Condition 2 meant it was within a day's distance. Condition 1 was declared when it looked as if a typhoon might hit us that day. Condition 1 was, in turn, subdivided into Normal, when you'd best be taping your windows; Caution, when sustained winds of 35 to 75 knots were being experienced and nonessential personnel (like psychiatrists) were let off work; and Emergency, when winds of over 75 knots were at hand. Five times we were in Condition 1 Caution during our years there, and twice in Condition 1 Emergency— once for twenty-four hours in a slow-moving storm that hit us dead center with seventeen inches of rain. Ah, that was a storm!

But I do not like destruction. Okinawa's houses and foliage have for centuries been acclimated to easily withstand the *Dai Phoons* or Big Winds. Indeed, its primitive and odoriferous open sewer system even seemed dependent upon a massive flushing out every few years. I have no love for the likes of 1992's Hurricane Andrew, however, or for tornadoes that only wreak a devastation, like war, for which there can be no real preparation or decent acclimatization. I like the big winds of the world to be within reason.

Still, to acknowledge my Shadow side, there is in my love of storms not a desire for destruction but a definite delight in their capacity to overpower the ordinary social order of human beings. In its most childlike and rebellious form, it is the delight of seeing school called off—shut down and perhaps even buried under ten feet of snow. In a more mystical sense, it is my joy in being caught up in a power so obviously capable of overwhelming our little temporal desires. Whenever I stand in the wind of a great storm, I feel intimately a part of something much larger than myself. Frankly, I feel in touch with God.

Someone, I can't remember who, once suggested that our basic attitudes toward storms are a reflection of our different spiritual natures. Those who adore, almost worship, storms, the theory goes, are people possessed by a powerful spirituality with which they are comfortable. Those who are always terrified by storms also have a powerful spirituality, but one with which they are fearful and uneasy. Finally, the more normal people who are relatively disinterested in storms are said to be those with seemingly lukewarm spirituality and generally secular nature. Whether there is any truth to this theory I do not know, but in my case it seems to fit, and it's fun to play with.

Anyway, we are about to venture forth into the stormy North Atlantic, and the primary reason is for adventure. All travel to new places is adventure, and in one sense this has been the most adventuresome of all our trips. Why had I been four times previously to England but never once to Wales or Scotland? Circumstance? I think not. My parents, like all the WASPs of yesteryear, were distinct Anglophiles. They worshiped at the shrine of English culture. Not British, but *English* culture, and like the English themselves they considered Wales and Scotland to be slightly inferior, off-center parts of the British Empire, a bit beyond the reaches of true civilization and gentility. Somehow they communicated this to me, and in making this trip we were deliberately setting out for the dark parts of Great Britain, the wild terrain of the unpredictable Celts and not the gentle land of the English. It so happens that to date we have found the Welsh and Scots to be extremely hospitable and at least as civilized as their flatland, Romanized cousins. But we hadn't known this when we started out, for these places unjustifiably held a tiny bit of fear for us.

In planning the trip we were aware that these next two days would be the most adventurous. We'd both seen movies of the Hebrides and had been touched by their romance. We wanted to feel them for ourselves. But we were also propelled by our sense of adventure. The inner islands alone would not suffice; we had to go to those as far out as we could get. This might not seem terribly adventurous to younger, more intrepid travelers, but consider this: We'd not yet seen a decent hotel in the Inner Hebrides; what in God's name kind of lodging could we expect to find on Lewis this evening in the Outer ones? We didn't know.

All adventure is a going into the unknown. As I earlier pointed out, if we know exactly where we're going, how to get there, and what we'll see along the way, it isn't an adventure. It is human— and smart—to be afraid of the unknown, to be at least a tiny bit scared when embarking on an adventure. But it is only from adventures that we learn much of significance. So our primary motive for today's journey is not the excitement of jeopardy but the excitement of learning and stimulation by the new and unexpected.

One of the common responses I receive from my readership is an expression of gratitude for my courage. It always takes me by surprise, because I seldom think of myself as courageous. I'm far more accustomed to feeling like a coward. But then I need to remind myself that they're talking of intellectual as opposed to physical courage. Early in the game of life, for reasons I cannot explain in the slightest, I seem to have made a trade-off between these two types, because I am one of the physically least adventuresome people who ever existed.

In swimming, I was the last among my peers "to reach the float" because I was so terrified that I would drown while getting there. For the same sort of reason I was embarrassingly late in learning how to ride a bike. I did my very best to avoid fisticuffs, and when they were upon me nonetheless, I would simply curl up as best I could into a ball, instinctively protecting both my face and genitals. By adolescence, my self-image was distinctly that of a "chicken." I stayed away from "body contact" sports in favor of tennis. When I finally learned to ski at the age of twenty, I became the world's safest skier, one who would never fall much less careen into a tree. No, I was never much of a "man."

And as I got older my timidity only increased. At seventeen I was a skilled and exuberant body surfer. At twenty-seven one afternoon, when we were stationed on Hawaii, we went to the beach at Makapuu, famed for its waves. They were indeed lovely waves, and I would have exulted in them a decade before. But with a wife and two young children and an already stiffening spine, they seemed so monstrous I quickly retreated before them and we raced back home. As for modern "hobbies," such as rock-climbing, bungee jumping, hang-gliding, and sky-diving, I can only look upon them with an actuary's eye as bizarre forms of mass hysteria or personal insanity.

I guess I could be called "intellectually adventurous," but this has never seemed to me so much a matter of courage as a very low tolerance for boredom. "Mommy, I'm bored," may not have been the first words I spoke, but they were certainly the most frequently spoken ones of my early childhood. I recall my mother being remarkably patient with this, although I'm sure she was greatly relieved when I became an early and voracious reader.

Underlying my poor tolerance for boredom lies an even deeper gift or curse: a thirst for meaning. As far back as I can remember, any activity that seemed meaningless to me bored me figuratively—and sometimes even literally—to tears. To this day, whenever I find myself in a role that feels meaningless, I either have to rapidly find a way of re-creating that role into something meaningful or else get the hell out.

Often when people thank me for my courage, they are referring to my outspokenness. I was "that little boy who was always talking about the kinds of things people shouldn't talk about," but that was not because I was brave but because I was already bored by the inanities of WASP conversation.

Without question the bravest thing I ever did was at the age of fifteen when I quit Exeter, a prestigious prep school, thereby defying my parents' fondest expectations. Even I am amazed at my courage when I look back on that event. What was so gutsy about it had nothing to do with it being an act of defiance, but the fact that in doing it I was not only walking off a golden WASP track that had been all laid out for me but walking out of WASP culture entirely. And there was no other culture back then for me to go to. I was fully aware that I was treading way out on a limb and I was, frankly, terrified. But less terrified than afraid of dying. For somehow I knew that I was dying in the culture of Exeter and would die in the culture it was attempting to prepare me for—a culture that, for me, was essentially devoid of meaning.

I have written several times of that event because it was, in a certain sense, the beginning of my life. Until very recently it has been a life beyond culture. In many ways I've had to make up the rules as I went along. I don't mean I've not been law abiding. To the contrary, I greatly respect the law and, with but one or two minor exceptions, I'm almost excessively scrupulous in obeying it as I am train and ferry schedules. I'm one of those people who takes note of tags on mattresses that state, "Do not remove under penalty of law," and would dare not do so even though the mattress is my own property. It's another one of the ways I am a chicken. No, I'm not talking about laws but the informal rules and conventions of society when they make little sense: such rules as you should never ask anyone what they've paid for their house; you shouldn't eat ice cream for breakfast; and that in a good restaurant it would be egregious to order two appetizers and a dessert while passing on the entrée.

These kinds of rules can be broken with such impunity that I'm surprised by the energy it took me to learn so. Others, soon to be mentioned, may have their price tag. My attitude toward them is much like that toward storms. In many ways I've been excited by, and very much enjoyed, being on a cultural cutting edge. It's analogous to being in the teeth of the wind. But I've never sought destruction and have always tried to be careful. I haven't wanted to hurt anyone, although in this I've not always succeeded. One of our children was chronically embarrassed by having such an unconventional father. Even Lily and others of our close associates have lived in almost constant trepidation of what I might do or say next. They've also gained a fair amount. In any case, while I've made some mistakes, the fact of the matter is that I have twin streaks in me: unconventionality and cautiousness. I've never been too inhibited to intellectually go out on a limb, but my own trepidation has caused me to do my damnedest to make sure it's never been a broken limb.

In the eyes of some, my most dramatic rule-breaking was my involvement with two cases of demonic possession and their exorcisms. Possession is not a diagnosis recognized—or even to be considered—by the predominantly secular psychiatric establishment. Hence exorcism is not regarded as an acceptable practice, and one hospital gave some thought to expelling me from its staff when it learned of my participation in such a bizarre activity.

Actually, in both cases I conducted my involvement very carefully. It was six months or more from the time I first suspected the diagnosis of possession until we proceeded with the exorcisms. Psychological testing was obtained. Psychologically trained clergy were consulted who agreed with the diagnosis. The patients were thoroughly informed that exorcism was a treatment beyond the pale in the eyes of traditional psychiatry, and they signed elaborate consent forms. The exorcisms were finally conducted by teams of seven to ten, including not only clergy but psychotherapists and physicians in addition to myself.

Once more, as an author, I am in an overdetermined bind. The subjects of possession and exorcism are so provocative in this Age of Reason that their very mention is tantalizing. Yet they are also extremely complex and cannot be adequately addressed here without creating an imbalance in the whole book. Indeed, I have elsewhere written an entire chapter of twenty-nine pages about them (*People of the Lie: The Hope for Healing Human Evil*, 1983) and even that has left readers dissatisfied. It may help to know that there is a whole book on the subject that is more worthwhile than others: *Hostage to the Devil* by Malachi Martin (also the author of *The New Castle*). By virtue of the fact that Malachi is a priest—and neither a psychologist nor a scientist—the book has great limitations and leaves many questions hanging in the air. Nonetheless, it was sufficient to propel me to look more deeply into these matters. I could tell the man knew what he was talking about.

There is another problem still greater than that of page space. In my caution, before uninvolving myself with these adventurous issues, I asked Malachi what the major effect upon me might be if I participated in an exorcism. Instantly he responded, "It will give you greater authority and make you more lonely."

Although I was willing to take the risk, it was only several years later that I fully understood what he meant and why it was so. As a result of my participation I have *seen* things that most people have not. Therefore, I have greater authority because I know things they don't, yet it is lonely because I can never fully share these things.

The problem is that "seeing is believing." When I say that the northern mainland of Scotland is the most beautiful place on earth, I am asking people to take me on faith. Even if I had far greater literary skills than I possess, I could not describe the countryside well enough to actually convince them; I can only encourage them to go see for themselves.

So it is with demonic possession, only the problem is magnified in this Age of Reason when it is generally assumed that demons do not exist, that they are figments of the imagination of deluded, unscientific minds of those who had the misfortune to live way back in the Age of Faith. We know scenery exists, but not demons. The problem is further magnified by the fact that genuine possession is an extremely rare phenomenon. And still further because the two possessed patients of my acquaintance remain so embarrassed by their involvement with the demonic that they have not yet given me permission to write about their cases with the kind of detail that can help to make things come alive for a reader. I am restricted by the sacrosanct rules of psychiatric confidentiality.

But even if I could write in such detail, most rationalists would stay unconvinced. People do not become converted to a deep belief in God unless they have had a personal experience with the deity. How can it be any different with the devil? Particularly when God touches lives frequently and Satan seldom?

Nonetheless, propelled initially by intellectual curiosity, as a result of Martin's book, I went out to see if I could possibly find a case of possession, skeptical that I ever would. I was fully converted only at the time of the first exorcism, which is itself an uncovering process, when I actually had the opportunity to see the demonic. I have seen an ugliness that is distinctly inhuman, and ugliness in two human beings that properly did not belong there, an ugliness they eventually chose to renounce and expel with the team's assistance. But I do not expect the reader to believe the reality of this incredibly ugly spirit of malignity unless he or she has been one of those few who have had a similar opportunity to stare in the "face" of the demonic.

Eventually, more than mere intellectual curiosity was involved for me. But whatever courage was required from all of the participants—most notably the two patients in question—was dictated by almost titanic forces. In preparing for one case I agonized with a consultant over the possibility that the patient might die during the exorcism. "That's true," the consultant replied, "but it's certain that she'll die without it."

During the exorcisms, those of us on the teams knew very little about what we were doing. We were profoundly aware of operating in the dark. Yes, they were indeed adventures. We also learned a great deal. And while we were very much out on a limb, I think I can accurately claim that we knew more about what we were doing than the otherwise perfectly good traditional psychiatrists who had previously attempted to treat these patients without success.

Those experiences were most meaningful. Although seemingly less dramatic, our adventures with FCE have been far more prolonged and, for us, even more meaningful. When we started the organization in 1984, we on its board of directors were a bunch of do-gooders who wanted to do good but didn't know much about how. In particular, we had no idea how to run a business, which a nonprofit organization, every bit as much as a profit-making one, must be if it is to be successful. Again, we were operating in the dark. I had to learn. We had to learn. We had to learn not only about strategic planning but all about marketing, conference coordinating, management of volunteers, upsizing and downsizing, fund-raising and development, computer systems and mailing lists, mission and vision statements, accounting procedures, and so on. We also had to learn even more important things, such as how bigger isn't necessarily better, how to coordinate, and how to clarify role and power issues. Given our ignorance, it is amazing to me that FCE has survived and is currently flourishing. Grace has been a major element.

Integrity has been another. While we made all the mistakes in the book, we made them with integrity, and somehow that seemed to save them from being total disasters. Our primary value of integrity also meant that we had to integrate good business principles with our principles of community. This integration was not cheaply achieved. It required that we learn still more about management and the nature of organizational culture and consensual decision making. And learn more deeply about community itself. One of our informal mottos became "FCE goes deeper." So we ventured ever farther into the depths of what community is all about, discovering both the profound limitations and equally profound virtues of community in the workplace, and beginning to learn how to sort them out.

It was good that we did so. When we started FCE, the market for community building was that part of the general public interested in a temporary, individual experience of personal growth. Gradually, however, as more people had the experience of community, the primary market shifted to businesses seeking greater organizational effectiveness and creativity. We were able to meet this growing demand with integrity only because we knew something about the complexities of integrating community principles with business operations—largely as a result of having practiced on ourselves.

I've spoken of our adventure with FCE as if it were in the past, but that is only because we don't know what the future holds. In fact, we are in the midst of the adventure. We are still learning, discovering. For all I know, we may just be beginning to learn. One thing is very clear, however. I stated that until recently mine has been a life beyond culture where I had to make up the rules as I went along. Although we had no such grand vision when FCE began, lately it has become more and more apparent that what our work is about, on the deepest level, is forging the outlines of a new planetary culture. What an adventure that is! And what a relief to no longer be a man without a culture. Some of the rules are in place now. Others we are still making up as we go along, but we're not doing so alone; we're hammering them out together.

On this morning it is the Caledonian MacBrayne Company that is thankfully making the rules and declaring them in no uncertain terms. The great ferry arrived, seemingly unfazed by the building storm. We boarded it and, after parking the car in its bowels, Lily and I climbed to the upper deck to be greeted with bellowing instructions as to which lifeboat station to proceed to when which combination of horns blew. They are standard instructions on all the ferries—even the dinky little ones that carried us across the straits, narrow as streams, from Mull to Iona and from the mainland to Skye. We hadn't listened before. Great though this boat is, however, as it pulls out from shore into the gale, the instructions about lifeboats suddenly seem to shriek of realistic possibilities, and we attend to them carefully.

Fortunately—or unfortunately—the storm got no worse. Once out to sea, we pitched and rolled a bit, but we'd found two seats up top protected from the wind. Had we been inside and down below, we would undoubtedly have felt queasy. Next to Bonine, however, fresh air is the best preventative for seasickness, and we survived the trip with neither mishap nor discomfort. Even when it began to pour halfway across, wrapped in our Gortex and behind the bulkhead, the crossing remained easy.

Sadly, the rain was so blinding as to largely obscure our entrance into Tarbert, one of the more dramatic harbors of the world. We slid into it through innumerable rock-ribbed islands, a convoluted fairyland of stone and sea. This advent alone would have made our adventure to the Outer Hebrides worthwhile.

Being first in line this day was also worth our while. It meant ours was the first car off the boat and hence first to arrive at the tiny information center to purchase local survey maps and then at a little shop to stock up on edibles. At each we were pursued by an oil-slickered horde from the ferry.

Ensconced in the car and munching on Hebridean ham, we poured over the maps to learn that what looked just like Lewis in our atlas back home was actually two islands, Lewis to the north and Harris to the south—each renowned for their tweed. The narrow harbor we'd snuck into separated the two, and immediately beyond it was a short bridge connecting them. Lewis, where we'd be lodging thirty miles up the coast, has the vast majority of megaliths. It is not good to hunt for them in a downpour. So our course seemed clear. This afternoon we would drive around Harris in the rain, leaving most of Lewis and its monuments for the morrow when the storm would presumably be over. It was unquestionably the right decision, albeit one that would long plague me with a tinge of regret.

The reason for regret is geological. Although separated only by a few yards of sea water, geologically Harris and Lewis are extraordinarily different islands. Except for its southernmost tip where we landed, Lewis is mostly brown bog. Harris is mostly light gray stone. In fact, it is incredibly stony. Incredible means not to be believed. Like the Tarbert harbor, I had a hard time believing it even as I saw it. And it was not easy to see through the almost blinding sheets of rain. But much of what I spied fascinated me.

The stoniness of Harris takes two forms. Almost every hillside is streaked with stone. Or, one might say, the hills *are* stone but streaked with thin veins of vegetation. The other form occurs when the land flattens out into fields of heaved rock. I got an impression that there was so much more stone than the hills could hold that they'd been required to shed their excess into the valleys as a giant might scatter monstrous flakes of dandruff into the creases of his clothes.

The same giant also made puddles, for every field of rock held at least several little ponds in its midst. Either it rained like this every day or else the stone somehow squeezed the water out of the land. For me this bizarre landscape had a haunting beauty, as did the seascape of countless coves and an occasional sand beach that oddly seemed to glisten despite the gloom. In the midst of such bleakness there were a surprising number of tiny houses, and now and then we were even more surprised by an actual plot of green grass or copse of rhododendron.

It only took us a couple of hours to circle Harris. Had it not been for the continuous sheets of rain we would have wanted much more time to explore the distinctly otherworldly island. And to walk to Clach Mhicleoid, a menhir so gigantic it was photographable from our car window even though half a mile away. But to stroll out to its windswept promontory in such weather would have been folly. Much as we love stones, and adventurous though we might be, we're not fool-hardy. Still, it was not easy to pass by a megalith probably more massive than any single one we'd seen to date.

There being no other alternative in the rain, we left Harris largely unexplored, passing across the same little bridge by which we entered and drove through the seemingly endless bogs to Stornoway, the capital city of the Isle of Lewis. Just as we were surprised by the number of houses on Harris, so we were surprised by the size of Stornoway. It was at least as large as Oban and likely the largest town we'd seen since Glasgow.

It was also large enough to be confusing, and we had to stop to ask directions from a man on the street as to how to get to the Caberfeidh Hotel. Successfully following them, we were initially dismayed by the hotel's low-lying, dumpy, Scotch-modern exterior. Pulling in, however, we noted a three-star rating that was confirmed when we got to our room, a simple space but palatially large in comparison to anything we'd had for a week. It also had a view over a bit of lawn to some trees that were waving in the tail end of the storm.

We may have an instinct for adventure, but, as must be clear by now, we also have an extremely strong nesting instinct. At the end of a day of adventure we desperately want a safe nest, and tonight we have one. A decently sized nest. Views make a difference, but in these "tight little islands," so does space, and there is an enormous difference between this room and our no-star cubicle on Skye where, despite the view, Lily and I could not help but ineffectually entangle ourselves like the Hindus do in the village shops of India.

Once ensconced, we learned that the Caberfeidh is a Best Western Hotel. I had to laugh. God is always playing little jokes on me, and this seemed like one of them. Best Western, which we previously assumed to be an exclusively American phenomenon, is our favorite motel chain back in the States. How surprising, in contradiction to my dire imaginings, that we should discover such a familiar nest in, of all places, the Outer Hebrides! Could someone have been saying to me, "Oh, ye of little faith"? Promising that there will always eventually be a safe haven and admonishing me to adventure a bit more boldly in the future? Perhaps. Perhaps not. But I do believe there are little lessons to be learned from travel.

So much for the seemingly little things. In terms of the big picture, it is almost silly to look at this day or these three weeks as an adventure. Life is an adventure. Or should be.

My adventures with possession and exorcism were a distinctly part-time matter, a brief dabbling. Our adventure with FCE began only eight years ago. But the adventure with our children has lasted over three decades and still continues. It started with unknowns. Would Lily survive the perils of pregnancy and delivery? Would each child be a girl or boy? Healthy or unhealthy? Then it was to be other unknowns all the way. Would they survive their illnesses and accidents? How to deal with this one's eating problems? That one's shyness? Dropping out of school? Are we being overcontrolling, overprotective? Too forceful or not forceful enough? Although no longer our "responsibility," new questions persist in haunting us. Should we offer unsolicited advice about child raising? Money management? When advice is solicited, how should we respond? Deeply or superficially? Are we too close or too distant? Where there is hurt and resentment, will there be reconciliation? How long will it take?

We cannot live their lives for them, and those

lives have always been far more their own adventures than ours. Then, too, Lily and I must lead our own lives, though we're committed to lead them together. But how much together? What should this togetherness look like? Are we striking the right balance between separateness and togetherness? Does the balance need to change as we age? The adventure of our marriage also goes on and on.

Lily is as adventurous as I, but our styles of adventuresomeness couldn't be more different. It might be said that my style is radical and fundamental, while hers is superficial—although that in itself is a superficial analysis. In any case, when it comes to the little things of life, I am a creature of habit. When I arise I squeeze my orange juice, drink it while feeding the cats and skimming the newspaper, make myself a cup of instant coffee, take it back to bed with me for my first cigarette of the day and a bit of prayer time. Then I floss my teeth, shave, do a precise sequence of eight back exercises, brush my teeth, bathe, and so on. This is all done in exact order, and God forbid that anyone should interfere with my routine. The fact is that much of the time I am frankly stodgy. When driving, except in search of stones, I stick to the roads that are tried and true.

Lily is different. Give her a new locale and she will immediately be off exploring every little byway in the county, gleefully getting lost and wandering about until she locates herself—only to get lost again in a different location. On these forays she discovers all manner of surprises, including some tangible ones that she'll present to me with pride at the end of the day. She gathers these presents with the same uncanny proficiency with which she gathers lost golf balls. Or with which she shops, or finds four-leaf clovers, one right after another. Or exquisite shells on the beach. She can do things by routine when she has to, like her share of the constant packing and unpacking on this trip. But she'd rather not. What time she retires at night is more likely to be determined by what's on late-night TV than biology, and as for her sleep pattern, there generally isn't one.

When I am tired or depressed, Lily's delight in small "unimportant" things annoys me, and I feel bored by her seeming superficiality. Most of the time, however, I am amused by it. I find it entertaining. And enriching. It relieves me of boredom and causes me to chuckle—at her and with her. It tends to pull me out of ruts and broaden my horizons. Her little discoveries add as much color to my life as hers, and make our adventure together generally jolly.

Moreover, I do not mean to imply that Lily *is* superficial. To the contrary, when necessary, she can rise to the occasion out of depths deeper than mine. I am reminded of FCE's first Leaders' Roundtable. One is designated an FCE leader because she or he has been carefully selected and trained to lead community-building workshops as a "vocation" and spare-time activity. The leaders come from a wide variety of full-time occupations but are selected for certain things they have in common: a sense of humor, calling, dedication, sensitivity, flexibility, integrity, courage, and a capacity for sacrifice. Not surprisingly, therefore, they tend to be men and women on the cutting edge of their professions, in often stressful positions, frequently burdened and overextended. The Roundtable was initially designed as a renewal time for them when they could find sustenance through their own community-building workshop, letting their hair down with their peers. Lily and I were designated to lead this first Roundtable.

Shortly after it began, one of the leaders, a clergyman, recounted how that past week a parishioner had shot two children to death. Although not quite of the same magnitude, other "horror stories" followed, tumbling one after another. Much of the task of leading a group into community is the task of doing nothing, so Lily and I sat there hour after hour listening to this unburdening, not saying a word. For the first day I was not worried. Although in this case remarkably unrelieved, such unburdening is essentially required before the authentic joy of community can emerge.

But on the second morning there was no sign of any joy emerging, and we had only two days. About a third of the leaders—fifteen of them— as individuals looked clinically depressed, which was understandable given the immediate circumstances of their lives. What was starting to seriously concern me, however, was that the entire group seemed mired in a swamp of despair. "It seems to me that the group is depressed," I finally commented, ever so wisely.

"Duhhh," the group resounded. "You're

really brilliant, Scotty. Of course we're depressed." And they went on with wave after wave of despondency.

I broke in again after another hour. "I'm confused," I said. "I've worked with depressed groups before. When I pointed out to them that they were depressed as a group they've always responded in one of two ways. Either they denied it and went on being depressed or else they accepted the diagnosis and got out of it. This is the first time I've ever seen a group that acknowledged it was depressed, but seems to have no interest in getting out of it."

"And just what do you suggest we do to get out of it, smarty pants?" the group sarcastically queried. Knowing it wasn't my role to answer such a question—and I probably couldn't anyway—they almost enthusiastically continued despairing.

Another hour went by and I tried again. "I may not have worked with a group this depressed before," I interjected, "but I have worked with seriously depressed individuals. Their biggest problem is not their depression per se but the fact that they regard their depression as a friend. It's okay if you're depressed as long as you see depression as an enemy, as something you want to be rid of. But it's not easy to help someone who likes their depression. I'm getting really worried about this group. It's almost as if you're *choosing* to stay depressed."

"Will you just bug off?" the group retorted. "As our leader you're supposed to have some empathy. You don't know what it's like to be in our shoes. Leave us alone! We've got every right to be depressed."

I was despairing. The Roundtable was supposed to be an uplifting experience, not a downer. But it was clearly going to be a downer. I'd given it my best—and last—shot, and they seemed to have made their choice. Irrevocably. Knowing nothing else to do, I felt hopeless and even began to be sucked into their depression myself.

It was at this point, with only two hours left to go, that Lily spoke for the first time. "As some of you may know, I like science fiction and fantasy stories," she said. "It's the strangest thing. One of those stories has been in my mind all day today. I don't know why. I keep trying to put it aside but it persists in coming back. Maybe it's what some of you Christians might call the Holy Spirit. I don't know, but perhaps I ought to tell it."

The group was naturally all ears.

"Well, okay then," Lily continued. "As best as I can recollect it, it was about a man who heard a legend of paradise. According to the legend, paradise was located on an island in the midst of a very large and distant lake. Most people didn't take the legend seriously, but this man believed it and decided to go and seek the island. So he set off on his travels. He went through jungles and across deserts and over mountain ranges. Finally, after years of journeying, he learned that on the other side of the very next range of mountains there was a huge lake with an island in it, an island that was indeed paradise."

The group was listening intently, almost

enthralled. I was doubly enthralled. Like the group I was intensely curious as to what would come next in this adventure story and why Lily was so moved to tell it. Unlike the rest of the group, however, I knew she was lying. She is a very good liar when she needs to be—so good, in fact, that only someone who's lived with her for many years can tell. What the others didn't realize was that she was making almost all of the story up. At best she'd read a little germ of it once. Probably she'd been making it up all morning. Certainly she was continuing to make it up as she went on. Aware of her fabrication, I was even more intrigued as to what the hell was happening.

"As he began climbing that last mountain range," Lily continued, "a strange thing occurred. He started hearing an odd sound. It was very faint at first, but he imagined it to be like a wail. When he got to the top of the range it seemed even more clearly like a wail. Not only that, but down below was the huge lake with the island in its middle, and he could have sworn the wailing sound was coming from the island. By the time he climbed down the mountains and reached the shore of the lake he was certain. The never-ending, woeful wail was obviously emanating from the island.

"He was puzzled. The island didn't sound like paradise at all. It sounded like a place to be avoided. But he'd traveled for so many years and come so far, he was not going to be deterred. He began swimming. The farther he swam, the louder the wailing became. By the time he finally, breathlessly, reached the island it was almost a deafening shriek. No, this couldn't possibly be paradise. Now he was driven not by yearning but by pure curiosity. He had to find the source of this ghastly whine. He started to walk the beach of the island toward it."

Lily paused for a moment. We were as breathless as the swimmer, hanging on her every word in anticipation.

"Halfway around the island," she proceeded, "he came upon an old woman sitting on the beach wailing her lungs out so intently she didn't even see him. He tapped her on the shoulder. She stopped and looked up. 'Excuse me,' he said, 'but why are you wailing?'

" 'Why?' She appeared confused. ' I'm not sure why. I'm not sure I can remember. My memory's not what it used to be. I'm an old woman, you know.'

" 'But there must be some reason,' he persisted.

"A light of recognition came over her face. 'Oh, yes, I remember now,' she answered. 'It's because I'm a Banshee.'

" 'A Banshee?'

" 'Yes. We Banshees mourn for the world. It's our job, you know. When I was young there used to be lots of us, so we didn't have to do it all the time. But now there are only three of us Banshees left. And somebody's got to do it. So I'd best get on with it. Ahhheeeee!' "

With this concluding wail Lily stopped, the story over. Ever so gently she had simultaneously dignified the Leaders' mourning and called them a bunch of Banshees.

The group sat in dead silence for three minutes.

Finally, the clergyman, whose parishioner had murdered the two children, broke the silence. "I think I'll take Saturday nights off," he said.

There was another minute of silence, and a second leader added, "Me, too."

"Maybe a whole weekend now and then," chimed in a third. There was laughter. And bubbles of joy. And a spirit of peace. The group was out of its depression, and the day was saved.

Oh, Lily has her depths, and they can be adventurous indeed.

I spoke of the relationship between my need for adventure and my low tolerance for boredom. In order to be healthy we need be able to tolerate a small amount of boredom now and then. There is something wrong with needing excitement all the time. It can turn us into compulsive trouble-makers. And I believe I myself could do a bit better in this respect. On the whole, however, I suspect the feeling of being bored is very much a God-given emotion.

A decade ago Lily and I were having cocktails in Montgomery, Alabama, with a great and gracious elderly lady, Louise More, a sophisticated evangelist who had served me as a mentor. I can't remember the context, but Louise suddenly pronounced, "As far as I'm concerned, the greatest sin is to bore God."

I think that when humans are feeling significantly bored for a substantial period of time, it is probable that we are also boring God. Such boredom is a sign that we need to change, that it's time to move on, time for another adventure.

I do not believe that either Lily or I are boring people. As we occasionally bore each other, it is possible that Lily may now and then bore God with her frivolousness and I with my stodginess. But put us together and we make a rather interesting couple, and I like to imagine that God generally finds our marriage an entertaining adventure story.

Of course, the ultimate and greatest of all adventures still lies ahead of us: death. In some respect it will be an adventure together. One of us is likely to watch the other die—and the other to be watched. But primarily it will be an individual adventure for both of us. For the most part dying is something that must be done alone. And what a going into the unknown it will be! Speak of bungee jumping! There will not be any cord that we know of attached to us when we leap into that abyss.

Nor do we know whether there will be anything on the other side—anything at all. And if there is, we have no idea how we will get there. There'll be no Caledonian MacBrayne ferry for that trip. Should we survive the crossing, what will we find? We don't know. We don't have a reservation at a hotel, starred or otherwise, awaiting us. I am terrified. Strangely, however, there is the tiniest part of me that is almost looking forward to the adventure of it all. Mind you, I'm in no hurry for it. I don't begin to be that tired yet.

CHAPTER XV

CONSIDERATION
SUNDAY, JUNE 14

Although we had not come for stones, they proved to be the prime pay-off in our adventure to the Outer Hebrides. Strange though it might seem for an isle in the North Atlantic, on the edge of the Arctic Circle, Lewis had clearly been one of the capitals of megalithic civilization. The climate is what makes this seem strange. The storm of yesterday is titularly past. The gale is over. Today is merely cold and unrelievedly gray with frequent showers drifting across the bogs, and we suspect it is a rather typical day for these parts toward the end of the twentieth century. But climates can change, and there is conclusive evidence that six thousand years ago Lewis was a much warmer and sunnier isle, rich with vegetation.

Our first site on this Sabbath day was the Garynahine stone circle. It was not an easy find, reachable only by a combination of good map reading, good luck, and good exercise. Unmarked and invisible from the road, it required that we navigate a substantial bog, hurdle a fence, and climb a long hill. But it was worth the trek. Garynahine may be the smallest circle in the British Isles, a mere five yards in diameter and formed by a mere five stones. But lovely stones they were, however, lichen covered, rough hewn, eight-foot-high ancient slabs silhouetted against a bleak and endless rolling moor.

Our next destination was even tinier and more romantic. The Baraglom stones—there are but three of them—stand in the nook of an island cliff. A most unusual spot for megaliths, and one of the most striking, we looked through the stones across a sweet strait to the rugged shores of the main island. Also eight feet tall, one had been sculpted by the wind and rain into a unique swirling pattern.

Continuing to dodge the showers, we drove on to Callanish, which is actually three sites: two relatively minor ones—the southern and northern Callanish small circles—and a very major one, all within a half mile of each other. We took them in that order.

The southern Callanish small circle consists of approximately a dozen standing stones, roughly six feet tall. Still others have fallen to the ground. As best as I could guess, the monument had originally been two concentric stone circles: an inner one perhaps eight yards in diameter, and an outer one ten yards.

The northern Callanish small circle contains just five stones but was more impressive. They formed a semicircle ten yards in diameter. Whether there had initially been more of them to form a full circle I do not know. What I do know, on the basis of aesthetics alone, was that at least three of the five had either been quarried or selected for their different, striking shapes. The tallest was particularly dramatic as it rose eleven feet into a dramatically sharp point.

But the real drama lay ahead, and we could see it in the distance: a close grouping of roughly forty megaliths standing on a plateau silhouetted against the gray sky hundreds of yards off. That far away we still could sense this was the stuff of which legends are made. The site has various names, none of which is adequate. One is the "great" Circle of Callanish, to distinguish it from the small circles we'd just visited, but, as we were soon to see, it is much more than a circle. Another name is simply "the Standing Stones of Callanish," but this fails to distinguish them from the much lesser adjacent sites. In any case, the most recent legend, from obviously post-Christian times, is that the megaliths were sinners who had been turned to stone for such heinous crimes as playing on the Sabbath. Peering up at them across the bogs on this gray Sunday, the legend somehow did not seem all that unbelievable.

We drove up to the site and parked at a nondescript little lot. No more was needed. During our hour there we shared the monument with no more than eight other people. This is remarkable given the fact that it is one of the four greatest megalithic sites in the world, perhaps even on a par with Stonehenge. During an hour on any given day, Stonehenge probably averages more than a thousand visitors encircling the perimeter of its "look from a distance but do not touch" fence. Of course Stonehenge is both very famous and centrally located while Callanish is neither.

We'd never even heard of it until two days ago when we were embarking for the end of the habitable world. Now, freely strolling among the stones and occasionally touching them in solitude, we are cognizant of the virtue of the isolation of the Outer Hebrides.

And of the compelling need to give the site a deserving name. Its situation is utterly undistinguished. Although slightly elevated on the plateau, there is no view to speak of, no scenery to frame it. The surrounding countryside is relatively flat and dull. The stones themselves are uncapturable in their entirety either by photograph or painting: There are too many of them. Yet it is they in their entirety, their pattern as a whole, that makes the site so unique. The best I can do is to name this strange monument the Great Configuration of Callanish.

Any grouping of stones is a configuration. Other than tombs and dolmens, the most common megalithic configurations are stone circles. They come in all shapes and sizes and settings, and we thrill to their variety. But Callanish, as I have said, is much more than a circle, and it is its complex configuration, found nowhere else in the world, that makes it so extraordinary.

More than any other megalithic configuration, Callanish has an obvious "key" or focus. This is a single, particularly striking menhir. Three things make it so striking. One is its height. It is the tallest stone in the configuration, rising fourteen feet into the sky. Another is its shape: Menhirs are often quarried or selected for their flatness, but this was the flattest one we'd ever seen. Furthermore, its top, rather than being rounded or pointed or irregular, as is usually the case, was also flat and sharply angled. Although the most regular of megaliths, it had irregularities to strangely enhance its severe beauty; its base broadened out as if to strengthen its roots in the earth, and a third of the way up on one side it had a bulge like that of a knee or elbow. I will refer to this very special stone as "the monolith." Strangely, it is embedded in the consciousness of tens of millions of people who have never heard of Callanish, much less been to the Outer Hebrides. The famous movie *2001* essentially begins with the image of a single, mystical megalith. In size and shape it is so similar that my first reaction at the sight of the monolith on Callanish was one of *recognition*. The most obvious explanation is that the artistic producer of the movie had either been to Callanish or seen photos of it. The less obvious explanation is that the shape—the essence—of this monolith is an ancient, universal archetype somehow contained in the human collective unconscious.

And this is still not the most dramatic thing about the monolith. Its most striking feature is its position in the configuration as a whole. It stands inside a ten-yard-wide circle of a dozen only slightly shorter twelve-foot-high menhirs. Radiating out from the circle are five rows of lesser standing stones, although none of them is a slouch: short, single rows toward the south, west, and east, and a much longer double row toward the north. At its northern end this double row begins with relatively small stones that gradually rise from five feet in height to ten as they approach the circle. In other words, all the stones build up toward the center. It is not possible to decently describe such configuration in words. A picture is worth a thousand words, they say. As already noted, however, it is not possible to decently capture the site by photo or art. So a diagram is very much in order (as opposed to a map, which signifies some degree of cartographical, scientific accuracy).

It shows how the monolith is the real center of the whole configuration. But it is a wonderfully off-center focus, standing fot in the middle of the circle but to one side. At its foot, occupying the middle, is a rectangular single grave or crypt (marked by dots in the diagram). The southern and one of the two northern stone rows, however, are not aligned with the center of the circle; they are aligned with the monolith.

Why did people construct this great monument of standing stones five thousand years ago? We can surmise that the long double stone row was likely a processional avenue. Beyond that we don't know, although we can hazard a few very good guesses as to what the creation was not.

It was not the creation of archaeologists. Callanish is one of those monuments that has been excavated but not restored. It was excavated in the nineteenth century by peat diggers. A dozen or more centuries of falling leaves had buried the stones six feet deep in decayed compressed vegetation—the precursor of coal that is to this day the primary fuel of the Hebrides.

The peat preserved the monument so intact that when archaeologists finally came along the only change they had to make was to erect a single fallen stone in one of the northern rows. Beyond that, there has been no tinkering. The configuration stands as it was constructed.

Why such a configuration? One seemingly obvious explanation is that it was a grave of some chief so great that all the stones were erected to magnify it. According to this theory the monolith would have been the gravestone, and all the other stones an elaborate peripheral decoration. But there are problems with this theory. If the monolith was a gravestone, then Callanish was a monument that centered not on a grave but its stone. Next, there is no evidence that menhirs were ever used as gravestones in megalithic times. The gravestone appears to have been a post-Christian invention. Next, the megalithic people, it will be remembered, practiced communal entombment rather than individual burial. It will also be remembered that the communal burial cairn inside the Temple Wood circle in the Kilmartin Valley is believed to have been constructed a thousand years after the stone circle. So it is with Callanish. The best guess of archaeologists is that long after the Great Configuration of Callanish had outlived its purpose someone came along who thought it would be a neat place to bury a single relative.

Then what was the original purpose of the configuration? The most prevalent theory is that its stones were precisely configured to make complex sightings of the planets, sun, moon, and stars so as to accurately celebrate solstices or predict eclipses. This is also the most prevalent theory to explain all the other great megalithic sites, Stonehenge included. It is so prevalent because it is the most written theory. There is even a whole school of such theory, to which its subscribers have given the impressive label "archaeoastronomy." I personally don't buy any of it. Astronomy is a scientific discipline. Archaeology is a scientific discipline. Archaeoastronomy is *not* a scientific discipline; it is currently a New Age fad.

It is said that nature abhors a vacuum. On the level of psychology this can be translated to mean that the human mind abhors a vacuum of knowledge, and when we are confronted with a striking unknown, like Stonehenge or Callanish, we humans have a profound tendency to rush headlong in with explanations for which there is no significant evidence—even to the point of making up evidence to justify our explanations. Although it does not always succeed in doing so, true science is all about combating this tendency of ours. The scientific method is our best strategy against jumping to hasty conclusions. We scientists also love to rush in wherever there is great mystery, but we try to do so with great caution.

Not so most New Agers. While "Old Agers" tend to go to the other extreme of discounting everything they can't explain by simply ignoring the Callanishes and Stonehenges of the world, New Agers dive into them without even a bathing suit in a naked innocence that is often more pathetic than charming. Megalithic monuments are among their most favored targets. The New Age Movement is predisposed to seek out anciently vague, prehistoric, non-Western "wisdom" cultures. And the motion of heavenly bodies is additionally attractive because astrology is one of those ever so ancient "wisdoms" that can be used to explain anything, no matter how fallaciously. Mind you, the vociferous writings drawing the connection between megaliths and early astronomy purport to be scientific. Certainly they are as unreadable as the most abstruse scientific monographs—and filled with all manner of numerical calculations. It is possible I do not understand all their arcane verbiage and numbers, but to date I am of the opinion that "archaeoastronomy" is "pseudoscience," and am less comfortable with it than I am with the reality that we simply haven't a clue as to why the creators of Callanish configured it as they did.

Jumping from the ethereal mystery of megaliths to the very earthly mystery of feelings and individual human differences, Lily loves Lewis. While I am thrilled by its stones, the isle profoundly depresses me. As far as I am concerned it is not only the end of the world geographically and climatologically but also scenically and sociologically. Except in a corner of Stornoway, we saw no trees. There aren't any bushes to speak of either. The northern and largest part of the island lacks the dramatic rocks of Harris. The grass is green but not the emerald green of Ireland. It is more of a gray-green until it merges into the vast brown peat bogs that comprise the center of the isle.

Peat would seem to be the number one industry of Lewis. It is either being dug everywhere or has been, leaving little scars across the land. How much of it is exported I do not know, but it is certainly consumed locally, for the air is full of its fumes. Reluctantly, I will admit to finding the smell of burning peat a rather pleasant one, but that is the extent of my homage to the land. The only other discernible industry, as in the rest of Scotland, is sheep, but after a while the animals lose their charm. Indeed, long before we hit the Outer Hebrides, Lily had already come to call them "field maggots."

Despite this apparent lack of industry, we are surprised, as we were yesterday in Harris, by the number of houses and a population density far greater than that of the Inner Hebrides or, for that matter, much of the mainland. For no discernible reason, there are quite a few people here. The mystery of what they do to support themselves may possibly be cloaked by the fact that this day is the Sabbath, and they are perhaps all holed up in their houses in Presbyterian prayer.

These houses rim the isle in profusion, away from the deserted central peat bogs, near the coast yet strangely not on the coast. The people seem to have no interest in views. Or beauty. They are not pretty houses. Without exception, they are modest functional little brown boxes that mostly congregate in conformist rows, somewhat like queues. There is a tendency throughout Britain to build houses in rows. It cannot be a tendency of Roman origin since the Scots, not the English, seem to have perfected it. The acme of such exciting urban planning is on Lewis.

So, despite the phenomenal stones, I find it a dreary place on a dreary day. Lily begs to differ, claiming the isle to be the high point of our trip. She can offer nothing to substantiate this subjective assessment, which is all the more bizarre given the fact that she is suffering. She desperately needs to go to the bathroom.

Urinating in the countryside is no problem for me, whether I'm in Connecticut or Scotland. Indeed, it is almost a hobby, and Lily has been known to compare me to a male dog wont to stake out his territory in such a manner. This I deny. While it may be an instinct to let go whenever I feel like it, there is nothing territorial about my motivation. It is a male thing, I suppose, in that I am sexually advantaged in this respect. I'll even admit that my gift for outspokenness is likely involved in my behavior. Beyond assuring that I will not be arrested for indecent exposure, however, I see no reason not to let it all "hang out" when I am in pain. Although I'd never use the stones like hydrants, I am physically comfortable now precisely because I did relieve myself on the periphery of both Garynahine and Baraglom.

Nearing Callanish, Lily had announced that she would soon need to go. Although one of the four greatest megalithic sites of Christendom, it had proved not to be the site of any tourist toilet. Leaving it over roads across the endless deserted bogs, I suggested that she could relieve herself anywhere. "There's not even a bush in sight," she objected.

"There's also not a person in sight," I countered. "In fact, I doubt there's one within five miles. Except me, and I promise I won't look."

But there was no way she was going to squat in the open and no point to my pushing the issue. We were on our way to the Carlaway Broch, one of those pre-Christian, Celtic, round fortresses like the ones we'd seen at Glenelg on our route to Skye. The guidebooks, which tend to slight megaliths, portrayed it as the isle's greatest tourist attraction. "I hope and pray there'll be a bathroom at the Broch," was all I could say in my helplessness.

When we reached it we drove into a parking lot far more developed than the little, natural space at Callanish, and indeed there was a bathroom there. To one side of the lot was a low building that contained not one but *four* bathrooms: one each for men and women and one each for handicapped men and women. All four were locked. They were not locked from the inside because they were in use; they were padlocked from the outside because the authorities clearly did not want them to be used.

Perhaps because of her bladder or because she was just tired, Lily did not care to climb the muddy, rocky path to the broch, perched on the bleak hillside. I raced up and down it, scrambling past the surprising number of visitors so as to waste no time. My priority was to get back on the road in the hope of *somehow* finding an unlocked bathroom for Lily *somewhere*. I was furious. Until now I had been deeply impressed by the thoughtful hospitality with which Great Britain treats tourists. Providing well-marked public toilets is an act of real consideration on the part of the British. Providing them and then locking them, in this instance, however, struck me as an act of sadism.

Fuming at the gross inconsideration, I was soon back in the car and we were speeding across more bogs toward Clach an Trushal. Empathy is an essential ingredient of consideration. It is possible I was in as much pain as Lily. I hate useless suffering, and one of the reasons I relieve myself with such abandon out of doors is that I see no point in doing otherwise. She was in physical pain, but I was profoundly irritable and agitated imagining her discomfort, almost to the point of feeling my own bladder musculature stretching unbearably. By now I was in a literally as well as figuratively *pissy* mood.

About fifteen miles away from the Carlaway Broch we passed a medium-sized brown church—plain to the point of being ugly—out in the middle of nowhere. Its windows were bare. It had no lawn, no decoration, and one couldn't have discerned its back from its front save that there was a wall in front with an entrance between two little outhouse like structures. "Stop!" Lily screeched as we sped past. "There may be bathrooms in front of that church!"

I couldn't imagine this being the case, but I spun the car around and pulled back to park as close as we could get to this strange entranceway. Lo and behold, Lily was correct. At each side there was a tiny, roofed, and doored toilet stall, and both doors were unlocked. Hallelujah!

Afterward I prowled the perimeter of the church. The windows were too high for me to peer into and the door to the building itself was locked. The place was clearly deserted. Had it been filled with parishioners that morning, I wondered? It felt as if it hadn't been used for decades, yet its toilets were certainly functional. I searched in vain for a sign of some sort. There was none. No name. There was no way to identify whether it was a Presbyterian church or a Baptist one or Roman Catholic, and I was frustrated how to write to thank it for its unusual ministry of hospitality. Where would I address a letter of gratitude: The Church, with two bathrooms out in front, Somewhere in the middle, Isle of Lewis, Scotland? No, that would hardly do. Yet this church embodied what a Christian church ought to be about, and I hope that someday a member of its congregation might read these pages and know that its anonymous grace did not go unnoticed.

So it was that in the course of less than an hour we were offered an example of extraordinary consideration—civility—side by side with an extraordinary example of incivility or lack of consideration. One might think I could take these things in stride. Indeed, this trip was enabled by the fact that I'd just completed the major drafts of a book about civility and, typical by the time I've mostly put a work of nonfiction to bed, I'm bored by the topic. Still, it is not often that within a few minutes, time one is experientially confronted by the essential paradox of human nature: that we humans possess the capacity to behave with unparalleled viciousness and unparalleled charity. It is not that humanity falls somewhere in between the demons and the angels; it is that we are both demons and angels. Thus I find myself passionate once again on the subject of consideration.

Lily's and my marriage has survived for all manner of reasons. It is a profoundly overdetermined phenomenon. But I think most fundamental of the reasons is that, each in our own way, we are deeply considerate people.

In the beginning it was rather primitive. It had more to do with self-image than anything else. We wanted to think of ourselves as good people, so we tried to be good. Being good meant being considerate, and we knew the great rule of goodness or consideration: Do unto others as you would have done unto you. So we tried very hard to treat each other the way we wanted to be treated. Only it didn't work out very well.

Consideration, of course, comes from the verb "to consider," which can simply be defined as "to think." Considerate people think about others: They treat each other thoughtfully. This is something that narcissists cannot do. The primary reason Lily and I have unlisted phone numbers and other elaborate cloaking devices is to protect us from the narcissists of the world. Before we developed them a decade ago, it was becoming increasingly common for the phone to ring at 2:00 A.M. When we answered, it would be a stranger wanting to discuss some fine point with me about what I'd written. "But it's two o'clock in the morning," we'd protest. "Well, it's only eleven out here in California," the voice at the other end of the line would explain, "and besides the rates are cheaper now."

Narcissists come in two strengths: mild and foursquare. The foursquare ones, like midnight callers, do not stop to think of other people at all. Lily and I had long outgrown such gross inconsideration by the time we wed. We wouldn't have dreamed of phoning one another—or anyone else—between eight in the evening and eight in the morning, their time, unless it was an emergency. We entered marriage as the milder type of narcissists, exquisitely polite but not yet wise.

While we mild narcissists think of each other, we don't think very well, because we assume that everyone is just like us or else misguided. Had this day occurred twenty-five years ago, practicing the Golden Rule, wanting to treat Lily just like me, I would have excoriated her with kindness. Endlessly I would have insisted, "Oh, sure, honey, you can go to the bathroom in the field. I'll make certain that no one's in sight. I'll stand guard for you. No, it doesn't look undignified. Just relax and be human. Here. Here's some Kleenex. There's no need to be shy. Come on now, don't let your hang-ups get in your way. I can do it so I know you can. There's no need to be silly about it" . . . and on . . . and on.

But I am a wee bit smarter now. It has gradually dawned on me not only that urinating with cleanliness is not quite the same simple matter for women as for men, but also that Lily, in ways that I am not, is a deeply private, even secretive person. She is *different* from me. Not just biologically. That's the least of it. She has a different personality, and does not operate according to all the same rules as I.

Lily has also become more clever. Twenty-five years ago, trying to considerately lift my spirits, she might well have said, "Come on, Scotty, you really do like Lewis. It's so windswept! Doesn't the starkness appeal to you? Look at that pile of peat over there. It's so fascinating to see the way people live in other cultures. And isn't it quaint the way they build their houses in rows? Surely, you *must* love it here." Today, thank God, she doesn't insist that I love Lewis. She largely leaves me be as I do her because we have slowly grown sufficiently out of our narcissism to recognize, and usually respect, the *otherness* of each other.

So the Golden Rule is just the beginning. The advanced course teaches: Do unto others as you would have them do unto you if you were in their particular, unique, and different shoes. It is not easy learning. After almost six decades of living, Lily and I are still learning it and sometimes feel like beginners. But more than anything else, this growing out of narcissism is what life is all about. And we've been fortunate not only to have the college of our marriage but also the graduate school of FCE. The only rigorously scientific study of FCE's work to date reports that no more than three quarters of the participants in its public workshops experience a strong sense of community, but virtually all of them express an increased awareness of interpersonal differences.

This scientific confirmation is heartening, because one of the characteristics of a genuine community, as opposed to a clique or cult, is not merely the appreciation but the actual celebration of interpersonal differences. For instance, Lily's and my differences create the spice of our marriage. But it goes deeper than that. Our differences create the *wisdom* of our marriage. The expression "two heads are better than one" would be meaningless if both heads were exactly the same. Because Lily's and my heads are so different, when we put them together—as we do in child raising, money management, the planning of vacations, and the like—the outcome is invariably wiser than if either of us had acted alone. The process is called "collaboration": laboring together with wits as well as brawn.

It is through our management work with FCE that we have also taken an advanced course in collaboration. Sometimes it seems as if we can't lift a finger anymore without checking it out first with at least a half dozen others who are likely to see it quite differently. Yes, it can be tedious; the alternative, however, is a kind of group craziness that these days is called "dysfunctionalism." No, it is not all that easy, and one of the things we have learned from our experience over the past few years in management is that a great many people simply have no idea what is meant by collaboration. One of the tasks ahead of FCE may be to almost simplistically teach basic collaborative skills—the rules for what should be routine consideration in organizational settings.

Right now Lily and I are collaborating in trying to find Clach an Trushal, reputedly the single largest megalith in Scotland. Collaboration is required, for the task is not easy. It is in one of the more habitated areas. On the map, the streets are designated in English; on Lewis, however, the signs are in Gaelic. Occasionally there is a vague correspondence between the two languages, but for the most part, to our foreign eyes, written Gaelic might as well be Czechoslovakian. To some extent I understand the issues of national-istic self-esteem that are involved, and on some other day might find the phenomenon quaint. But I am still in a pissy mood, and such moods tend to be tinged with a hint of paranoia. It is obvious that Lewis does not cater to tourists—why should it?—but by now I am beginning to wonder if their street signing is not but one piece of a well-organized plot to actively discourage visitors. To discourage us.

Eventually, however, we succeed. Although open to the public, the stone is essentially in the front yard—or backyard; it is impossible to tell which—of one of Lewis's typically nondescript little brown houses. It is a hoary monster of a stone, a good twenty feet high and leaning slightly, like the Tower of Pisa. While sour as ever on Lewis, I cannot fault its stones and must acknowledge I would have traveled all the way for this single one, just to stand at the base of Clach an Trushal.

Evening is approaching as we drive the undulating bogs, dodging sheep as always, back to Stornoway. We have seen all the megaliths of Lewis, and I am ready to call it a day. But on the other side of the city is a sizable landmass, the Peninsula of Eye. There is no reason to believe that Eye won't be as dreary as the rest of Lewis. The guidebook, however, notes its major attraction to be Dun Bayble, and Lily announces she wants to see it. "Why?" I ask. "It's only a stupid cairn."

"Because I want to," she replies not with reason but pure intent, the kind of intent that brooks little interference under ordinary circumstances. I decide that these circumstances are indeed ordinary.

So off we go to Eye, even though she knows full well that a cairn is but a pile of rocks. Occasionally, cairns will cover a tomb, but in Scotland that is very far from the norm. For some unfathomable reason the Scots are enamored of making rock piles. Sometimes they throw in a little cement and add a little plaque so as to call it a monument to this obscure person or that obscure event. Mostly, however, the little piles are uncemented, dotting virtually every hilltop. The Scots are also wont to dump rocks in the middle of ponds, and when they have created a cairn that is surrounded by water they call it a dun. We've already seen a large number of them. Why Lily wants to see another, I have no idea. But I am obedient.

And when we find it I still have no idea why it should have a name, much less be noted in our guidebook. I must admit it is a bit larger than most duns, rising almost four feet out of the water and being almost ten yards in diameter. I must also admit that it is a unique dun in that it is connected to the shore by a narrow ten-yard-long causeway of loose stone, presumably so as to allow visitors to walk out to it and maybe even add another rock to the pile. Silently I pray that Lily will not choose to be such a visitor and likely break her ankle. Surprisingly, my prayers are answered. "Aren't you glad we came?" she asks.

"I wouldn't have missed it for the world," I answer.

"It really is beautiful, isn't it?" Lily exclaims rhetorically.

"I'll always remember it in my mind's eye," I respond. "I may even write about it someday."

We are teasing, of course. For all I know, the reason Lily wanted to see Dun Bayble in the first place was purely to tease me. She's so straight-faced I couldn't tell. I, too, am rather good at being straight-faced. Indeed, we find we must warn new acquaintances they may have difficulty discerning whether we're being serious or not. It is no accident that April Fool's Day is a high holiday at our house.

Thus we do not deal with our differences solely by respecting them. Sometimes we tease the hell out of each other over them. It is a great deal of fun, but only because we've learned enough consideration over the years to know when and how to tease—and when and how *not* to tease. Still, we are not perfect at this business of dealing with differences. We are two extremely strong-willed people. By virtue of consideration, we can actually use our differences to operate in sync. Usually our different but combined wills collaborate like great waves crashing rhythmically on the shore with enormous power, whether it be in teasing or more serious endeavors. But there are times when we get out of sync. Most commonly they occur in the evening at the end of a long day. Then, suddenly, as in a riptide, the waves turn on each other in a gigantically ineffective clashing. Such rageful moments seldom last long. Yet another aspect of the art of consideration is knowing when to separate, to be alone, and when to go to bed and sleep it off.

Although it has been a long day and we are in different moods, we're still in sync when we finally get back to the hotel and plot tomorrow's activities. We have reservations on the early afternoon ferry back to the mainland. It is a four-hour crossing, which means we'd have a rushed and late drive to our night's lodging. I have no desire to stay on Lewis any longer than necessary, and Lily acknowledges there isn't anything left to see. With wild abandon we decide on an unscheduled alteration to our itinerary. We shall attempt, without reservations, to board the 6:00 A.M. ferry. So we'd best get to bed.

The beds had been made while we were gone, but the glasses hadn't been changed or the ashtrays emptied. This is strange behavior for the lowliest of Best Westerns, much less a British hotel designated by three stars, and I fall asleep pondering the mystery. Could it be yet another ploy in the immense plot of the Isle of Lewis against tourists? Possibly. There is, however, another explanation. This day was a Sunday, and I had heard that the Scotish Protestants revere the Sabbath. Might it be that they don't clean house on Sundays? That they don't do anything except stay home and pray? And they believe no one else should behave differently, which would be reason to lock their public toilets for the day?

This would also explain why we'd seen no one but a few tourists about. We'd spied not a soul tending sheep or digging peat. Although a good explanation, it left me feeling even more uncomfortable than with my paranoid notion of a plot. The reason to remember the Sabbath and keep it holy is to remember to take time out to think. There is no point in thoughtless worship. The locking of public toilets is not an act of worship. It is an act of thoughtlessness, of inconsideration and incivility. I believe that the practice of Christianity should have something to do with consideration. If this explanation for the locking of toilets is correct, then it would seem that in remembering the Sabbath the good Christians of Lewis had forgotten their Lord's teaching that man was not made for the Sabbath, but the Sabbath for man.

Then how to explain the fact that we found healing hospitality this Sunday at the unlocked toilets of a church? Possibly it was an oversight; they had simply forgotten to lock them. But I would prefer to think that it was a remembrance, and that there is to this day at least one anonymous little Christian congregation who chooses to remember how Jesus, in defiance of custom and with thoughtful deliberateness, stopped to heal a man on a Sabbath once upon a time long ago.

CHAPTER XVI

SPACE
MONDAY JUNE 15

As an emotionally more secure individual would have assumed, we had no trouble getting on the ferry without a reservation. We ensconced ourselves in one of its lounges with a variegated assortment of humanity: young backpackers sleeping, middle-aged Scotsmen playing cards and already drinking at six in the morning (the Sabbath is over!), and German tourists conversing. It is crowded, but that is because no one cares to go outside. Although the sun has been up for fours, the clouds are so thick it feels like night. There is not much to see anyway. The harbor of Stornoway is not dramatic like that of Tarbert. Besides, it is cold and windy. So, we are inside for most of the four-hour crossing of and wide body of water between the Outer Hebrides and the northern mainland that is called, typical of the Scots' way with names, "the Minch."

We emerge the last hour for several reasons. One is that the sun is itself beginning to emerge, and doing so with high drama, here and there shooting a laserlike shaft of light through the gloom to glisten a patch of whitecaps. Soon the clouds part even more and we can see the highlands. From here they are brown and barren. Our harbor destination, Ullapol, however, is way inland, up the fjord of Loch Broom, and the closer we get to it the more verdant the mountainsides become.

Ullapol is a charming little town, but soon we are driving out of it, heading farther up the loch, through rich fields and a valley ever more beautiful by the mile. God, I'm glad to be back on the mainland again! At the end of the loch we climb a gentle pass over the moors and soon come down into an even greener land and the town of Strathpeffer.

Strathpeffer is a surprise. The guidebook refers to it as a Victorian spa. So it is, with neighboring mineral baths and golf courses and complete with a gigantic gazebo in the town center. There was something strangely un-Scottish about it. We felt we'd been transported to upstate New York, where the valleys are dotted with similarly quaint Victorian villages and watering holes. However disconcerting, it was a pleasant place to stop, and we had a major reason for doing so.

The reason was, of course, stones. Or rather a well-known single stone. What we knew in advance from our best guidebook was that it was called the Eagle Stone because of a carved eagle on its face. What we didn't know was that we were about to embark on yet one more unexpected twist in our journey, a quite different turn in our adventure with stones.

We found the stone in a pretty hillside meadow

down a short path at the edge of town. It had the flattened shape of a typical menhir but was no more than three and a half feet tall. One of its broad faces was bare. Into the bottom of the other there was carved a bird that did indeed look for all the world like an eagle, although there was a faintly primitive quality to it. What the guidebook hadn't warned us about was that above the eagle there was another carving. It looked like a horse-shoe with circular and triangular markings inside it.

What to make of it? At this point we didn't know enough to even speculate. The guidebook identified it as a Pictish stone. Presumably this meant it had been carved by Picts. We knew that around the time the Romans invaded Britain in the first century A.D. the Celtic peoples of Scotland had evolved into two major groupings: the Scots in the west and the Picts in the east. The Romans had given the Picts their name because their fierce warriors painted pictures on themselves. Apparently they also liked to carve pictures in stones. By A.D. 900 the Picts had been absorbed by the Scots, leading us to suspect that the Eagle Stone had been carved between perhaps A.D.. 200 and 800. Beyond that we knew nothing. In the days ahead we were to learn a great deal more in some respects, and in other respects we would encounter only mystery.

One mystery already haunts us. Although its shape is right, the Eagle Stone is not large enough to be considered a megalith. But one corner of the horseshoe carving is missing at its top. The guidebook indicates the stone to have been relocated at least several times, and certainly somewhat modern hands had embedded it in cement at its current site. Clearly it was once a larger stone. But how much larger? We do not know, nor do we know when, where, or how it was shortened or why. Could it have been a menhir of the megalithic people three thousand years before the Picts came along to carve on it? It is a question to which the answer has been irretrievably lost. But the mystery would continue to haunt us, for it bears on other stones as well.

On the way from Strathpeffer to Inverness we stopped to view two obviously normal, uncarved menhirs standing eight feet tall in fields on opposite sides of the main road. Almost jaded by the plethora of stones on Lewis, we decided not to invade the fields to touch them, but they were handsome in the distance. It was somehow comfortable to gaze on their B.C. mystery uncomplicated by additional A.D. mystery.

Our ultimate destination was Culloden House, a famed *five*-star, twenty-room hotel in a seventeenth-century mansion. A historic spot, it had served as Bonnie Prince Charlie's headquarters before he was crushed by the British in 1746 at the battle of Culloden Moor, the last pitched battle on British soil. The mansion is located in Culloden, a suburb of Inverness, the northernmost major city of Scotland. There seemed no way to get to it except by driving through the city center.

Inverness is a beautiful city stretched out along both sides of a great canal connecting Loch Ness and Moray Firth, a city of many church steeples and apparent gentility. It is also a confusing city— or, to be more precise, the way from its center to Culloden is confusing. Indeed, we're not sure there is a way. Our way, at least, seemed blocked at every turn, and we must have crossed the same central bridge a half dozen times before we finally stumbled into a suburb. The suburb was not Culloden, however. We're not sure what it was; we couldn't find it on any map. Despite our having stocked up on the most elaborate maps, the plain fact of the matter is that we were utterly lost—lost in space.

Mention the word *space,* and most people instantly think of outer space. The famous TV program "Star Trek" begins with that dramatic exclamation: "Space, the final frontier!"

While I am in awe of the stars and galaxies on a clear night, the exploration of the heavens has never struck me as the ultimate adventure. When I was still practicing psychotherapy I used to tell my patients that they were hiring me as a "guide through inner space." There, I believe, is where the real adventure must be. And to succeed at "deep" psychotherapy, the patient must be every bit as much an explorer as any astronaut, driven by curiosity about his own thinking processes, his dreams and his genes, his memories and blind spots, his feelings and follies. Indeed, I think there is much more riding on the "conquest" of inner space than there is on the conquest of the celestial realms; the key to the preservation of civilization may reside in our coming to regard the explora- tion of our unconscious minds as "the final frontier." And I am a "Trekie" precisely because the real subject of "Star Trek" is not so much intergalactic travel as the inner journey of the travelers.

More recently, through our work with FCE, Lily's and my focus has come to be on a still less recognized kind of space: group space. It is even more a frontier, a realm of extraordinary mystery about which we know almost nothing. Is there such a thing as a group unconscious, for instance? Or, for that matter, can there be group consciousness as distinct from the consciousness of the group's individual members? How might one influence a collective consciousness for better or for worse—particularly for the better? The future of civilization will probably depend not only upon the conquest of individual inner space but also upon the answer to these related questions about group space.

Right now, however, Lily's and my immediate survival would seem to depend upon our capacity to conquer—at least successfully navigate— geographical space. Today we had covered a not insignificant piece of the earth's surface, steaming across the North Atlantic Minch and driving through valleys and over moors from the west coast to the east coast of mainland Scotland. We had covered this macrospace without a glitch, but here we were at sea, so to speak, in the microspace of Inverness and its suburbs. Are there different rules for managing microspace as opposed to macrospace?

Of course. Consider the weather. We love to poke fun at the mistaken predictions of meteorologists, but they do pretty well in the big scheme of things. They themselves admit, however, that they have much more trouble dealing with what they call "microweather." This is a matter of some consequence for sailors. It is possible, for instance, for a particular bay to be socked in by fog while another bay ten miles up the coast is glistening in the sunlight, and meteorologists will be largely at a loss to explain the difference much less predict it in advance.

"Micro" and "macro" are prefixes of relativity. The city of Inverness is microspace relative to the macrospace of Scotland, but it is macrospace relative to the space of one of its inhabitants, who I shall call Martin MacMac. And Martin himself is macrospace compared to a tiny collection of cells in his colon. But if I look at those cells under a *micro*scope, the spatial configuration of just a few of them can tell me whether they're malignant or not and allow me to make a reasonably accurate prediction of roughly how long Martin has to live.

The point is simply that there are almost innumerable levels of space, and every level has its own importance. The spatial configuration of cells at a microscopic level in Martin MacMac's colon is of great import to Martin and his family. It is the larger spatial configuration of the stones at Callanish that makes it such a unique monument. Moreover, the central monolith of Callanish is so remarkable not merely by virtue of its size but also its shape—both of which are spatial manifestations. It was the shape, the spatial configuration, of the lines etched in its granite face that made today's Eagle Stone distinctive and gave it its name.

In any case, the art of reading a city map is not quite the same as reading one of the countryside, and the spatial configuration of the Inverness suburbs lacks any discernible coherency. Lily is in an overdetermined panic. She is tired. Although she loves puzzles, there is a difference between solving a maze puzzle in a book and actually *being* in a maze. While much the better map reader, she lacks my acute sense of direction. In the role of primary navigator she feels she has somehow let me down. Everything is crowding in on her, and the circuits are on overload.

Surprised, I do my best to talk her down. What's surprising to me isn't that she should be in a panic but that I'm not. Usually I'm the one to panic over being lost, and it's always been that way. Since forever.

One of my earliest memories is of terror at being lost. "We're going to be lost, we're going to be lost," I would shriek at the age of four whenever I was in the car and my parents were driving into territory I hadn't seen before. And shortly, "We are lost. I know we are. You're making it up when you say we aren't. We are. I know we're lost." It was intense, irrational, and repetitive. It was, in other words, a phobia.

The psychoanalyst in me has no idea of what originally produced this phobia. I cannot remember anything my parents did that might have caused it. I can, however, remember them exacerbating it. Although they were, for the most part, excellent parents when I was young, they did have a certain streak of sadism. This manifested itself in a kind of teasing that occasionally crossed over the line into unwitting cruelty. On a visit with them to New York City's Chinatown when I was six years old, they ducked into an alley behind me so that they might have the fun of seeing if they could precipitate a panic in me. They succeeded. Tending to possess this same little sadistic streak, I have teased Lily by suggesting the *real* reason I might have married her—a Chinese woman who still speaks good Cantonese and fair Mandarin—is that I could wander with her into the Chinatowns of the world without having to worry about getting lost.

Typical of childhood phobias, mine *seemed* to superficially evaporate. The only time I was ever seriously lost—geographically—was one summer day in my eleventh year. A boyhood companion and I, out hunting with our rifles, came to the end of a trail in a vast stretch of woods and stupidly decided to go farther. Much farther. By late afternoon, when it dawned on us that we were dramatically lost, my friend began to panic. I would soon have followed suit had we not shortly stumbled upon a little brook. It occurred to me that water flows downhill, and brooks tend to flow into streams, and streams into rivers or lakes where there's likely to be habitation. So it was really rather simple. All we had to do was keep following the brook, and sooner or later we would be "un-lost." Although not necessarily infallible, it proved a workable principle in this case. We did reach the Housatonic River and civilization by sundown, in time to phone my parents before they had phoned the police.

Although I may, to some extent, have outgrown panic about being geographically lost, I suspect my childhood phobia translated itself into an adult terror of being spiritually lost. Might not my thirst for meaning be rooted in this terror, in an unwillingness to simply be at sea on the journey of life? Is my intense goal-directedness the result of an equally intense anxiety at the prospect of ever being directionless? Is it an accident that I grew up to become a professional "guide through inner space," knowledgeable about the psychological equivalents of such rules as "if you follow a stream downhill you're likely to find a larger stream"? And isn't it remarkable that a child with a phobia of being lost should eventually become somewhat famous by writing, among other things, about life maps?

There is a principle in certain quarters that God can even use our sins. Might it be possible She also isn't above using our neuroses?

I like to think that God has used me, but I don't like to be too serious about it. Toward the conclusion of some of its workshops, FCE employs a teaching tool it calls the "Masks Exercise." Participants are asked to draw their masks—pictures of their personas or the faces they present to the public that may be ever so different from what they feel about themselves inside. Whenever I have participated in the exercise I have stamped the forehead of my mask with the word FOUND in large letters—as in the lines of the hymn "Amazing Grace": "I once was lost, but now am found, Was blind, but now I see." While on the outside I appear to others as one who has firmly found his way, on the inside I am constantly wary that I will lose it again around the next bend.

At the spiritual level of inner space this wariness is not such a bad thing; there are pitfalls to be watched out for on the journey. On the level of geographical space, however, I tend to overdo it. My ancient fear of being lost almost unconsciously dictates a surprising amount of my behavior. Why is it then that on this afternoon I am relatively calm while Lily is figuratively "spaced out"? It is because, as always, I have been unconsciously checking out the sun. It is no accident that I have the better sense of direction. I have been practicing that sense since childhood, honing it, continually orienting myself in space lest I become lost. Thus I am now less disoriented than Lily. Having charted at the edge of my awareness the course of the sun over northern Scotland, hour by hour, I know where I am in relation to it.

As far as Lily is concerned, we are simply lost in the suburbs of Inverness. I, however, have the advantage of knowing we are specifically lost in a *southern* suburb. I am acutely conscious of which direction is north, and that we must strenuously avoid going in it lest we end up crossing that same damn bridge for the seventh time. So we continue to plow well south before we turn west, and then well to the west before we dare turn north again, and, voilà, we eventually found ourselves in Culloden.

Only we were still lost. We knew we were on the right road, but where was Culloden House? We drove by a palatial driveway—so palatial we assumed it to be the entrance to a grand museum of some sort. Nearby we turned down a side street and saw in the distance the back of a palace— probably the same museum. It wasn't until we had made several more passes that we decided to check out the museum on the off-chance it might possibly be our hotel. More likely, someone there could give us directions *to* our hotel.

So we turned down the drive, drove past a dovecote and then through great gates along a circular road until we parked in front of the palace between a Jaguar and a BMW. We combed our hair before daring to walk in the front door. Inside we learned to our amazement that we were expected, and we were led to a large airy bedroom on the ground floor that looked out over a vast expanse of lawn.

We unpacked a bit tentatively, as if we still were not quite sure we belonged there. But both Lily and I have a way of quickly becoming accustomed to elegance. We had been on the go since four-thirty in the morning and traveled far in space. With a huge sigh of relief we threw ourselves down on the beds and were almost instantly asleep for our first nap of the trip.

Lily was awoken by a helicopter landing on the back lawn to disgorge a guest. I slept through the commotion to later awaken to the sound of bagpipes. An elderly kilted gentleman was marching the lawn, piping away. It is nice to emerge from sleep in such fashion, and I consider it a fine custom to pipe one's guests to dinner. A fine dinner it was, too, beginning with cocktails and menus in the living room as we had come to expect of classy British restaurants. It concluded with our sole experience of miscommunication resulting from the Scottish brogue. At the end of the meal the same elderly kilted gentleman asked whether we'd care for some coffee or tea. I declined but Lily expressed interest in the tea. "Regular or hair-ball?" the man inquired.

"Hair-ball?" Lily repeated, aghast.

"Yes, Madam, hair-ball tea," the man insisted.

"I think he means herbal tea, dear," I suggested.

Lily chose the regular.

As cat lovers, we'd had an unfortunate amount of experience with hair-balls. Never had we considered putting them to use, much less as a product to be reingested. The thought was so repellent as to be morbidly humorous, and we giggled ourselves to sleep over it. Although our first night in a literal palace, we'd already come to feel quite at home. And not the least bit lost.

CHAPTER XVII

TIME
TUESDAY, JUNE 16

Our palatial digs relaxed us. We slept late and had a leisurely breakfast. I carefully prepared a fax and hung around to assure its transmission. It was already eleven by the time we finally hit the road. Because we'd be returning to Culloden House in the evening, we felt under no pressure. It was a mistake.

We ambled along the gentle shores of Moray Firth, stopping here and there. First we visited a seventeenth-century doocot. We didn't know what a doocot was, but the map indicated it to be a famous monument. We found it perched on a little hilltop and realized that "doocot" is simply the Scottish word for a dovecote or building that housed doves. I thought it a rather pretty structure—more so than the one at the entrance to our hotel—and a charming spot. Lily vociferously wondered why I'd dragged us off the road and wasted the time just to look at an unused pigeon coop. I countered that it was a damn sight more interesting than Dun Bayble, the pile of rocks in the pond on Lewis she'd dragged me to see. Naturally it was a standoff.

Our next stop was in the wooded entrance to Brodie Castle to check out the Rodney Stone, our first Pictish cross slab. The Picts carved many different kinds of figures on many different kinds of stones. Seven feet high, three feet wide, six inches in breadth, and perfectly rectangular, this was clearly not a menhir; it was, as named, a stone slab. Protected from the elements by a small roof, an elaborate, curlicued, Celtic cross was carved on one side and a number of strange-looking mythical beasts on the other. The cross was obviously Christian. But what about the beasts? Were they pre-Christian? Yes and no. The Picts carved some of these creatures, and other more abstract symbols, before they were Christianized by St. Columba and his men in the sixth century. The Eagle Stone we'd seen yesterday was perhaps such a pre-Christian "symbol stone." But it was after their Christianization that the Picts became most prolific in their carving. The Rodney Stone is a typical example of their predominant seventh- and eighth-century product: cross slabs simultaneously carved with their new symbol, the cross, on one side, and their more ancient, traditional, and obscure symbols on the other.

This particular Pictish cross slab was identified as the Rodney Stone because it had been discovered in the mid-eighteenth century by one Rodney, the local ratcatcher and gravedigger. He'd unearthed it in the course of business while laboring in a nearby churchyard. The location of the find and Rodney's profession led us to wonder if the slab itself had once served as a gravestone. That is one of the theories in use to explain the two hundred or so cross slabs that have been discovered since Rodney's days. More are being unearthed all the time. Another theory is that they were some other type of memorial monument—commemorating a battle, for instance. Or a marriage. Still another theory is that they served as boundary markers. But these are all, of course, just theories. We don't know. Perhaps the function of the cross slabs was overdetermined, which is to say they may have served more than one function.

In any case, our next stop down the coast was another cross slab, Sueno's stone. This was not just another stone. It is far and away the largest Pict cross slab known. A good twenty feet tall, one side, naturally, was devoted to the carving of a giant and ornate cross. The other was devoted primarily to carved human foot or horse soldiers rather than stylized animals. We would see other soldier/cross slabs, and there is reason to believe their military faces, as opposed to their religious ones, celebrate particular battles in which the Picts had been notably victorious. We never learned why this one was called Sueno's stone. Had there been an information plaque it would probably have told us, but the site was being actively reconstructed by a small swarm of workmen. Indeed, the stone itself had recently been enclosed in a gigantic glass case. We had mixed feelings about this. It was obvious that the carvings had been seriously eroded, and it is entirely proper that drastic measures should be taken to protect such a national treasure from the ravages of time. On the other hand, something very powerful is lost by putting a work of art under glass or, as in the case of Stonehenge, by roping it off. Barriers are needed. Even Lily and I need barriers between each other. But it is sadly *final* when the barriers are permanently impermeable. Sueno's stone was not the turn-on it would otherwise have been.

We are bouncing back and forth this day not only between the centuries but the millennia. Our next pilgrimage down the coast is to Findhorn, an old, lovely, and delightful coastal village. The reason for our detour there is to visit a late-twentieth-century New Age commune on its outskirts that has adopted its name. Like the Isle of Iona, we'd heard exciting reports about it, ranging from mystical cabbages that had reached a miraculous size to its unique, spiritual vibrations that had similarly affected people's souls. And like Iona it was a bust, only more so. For us it was a vast disappointment.

Ten to twenty years ago something very special may have been occurring there, but the Spirit has a way of moving on. Most of the commune, as far as we could see just by dropping in on a June day in 1992, consisted of a widely spaced but otherwise unkempt and rather pathetic-appearing trailer park. The only building of consequence was the so-called Visitors Center fifty yards beyond the trailers. On it a great deal of attention had obviously been lavished, but the product was even more out of sync with Scotland than Strathpeffer had been. Built of swirling polished redwood, it was artfully inlaid with stained glass—only the art was that of Big Sur on the California coast and not that of the coast of Moray Firth. We eagerly entered, seeking both information and bathrooms. The latter we found thankfully unlocked, albeit with some difficulty since the place was almost totally dark. Only a little light filtered through the stained glass windows into the main room. As for information, despite the name of the building, there was none. It was not only dark but deserted. The main room was hung with photographs of groups of smiling people in the bygone days of the sixties and seventies, and while we could make them out slightly in the gloom they were not a particularly effective means of communication. Nor was a tape recorder, located God knows where, playing over and over a woman's saccharine voice saying, by way of introduction, "Now I'm going to take you on a Guided Meditation . . ." Echoing through the deserted, darkened hall, this ghostly mechanical presence was downright eerie.

We did not linger. The environs of the commune we found equally disconcerting. Between it and the village was a street of B&B (bed and breakfast) cottages advertising "peace and healing." On the other side, there was a large RAF base, clearly advertising something else. Its advertisement was the more effective because we were stalled for ten minutes on departing Findhorn by vigorously flashing red lights giving precedence to the landing of a squadron of jet fighter planes.

Lily and I would not have made this detour of pilgrimage were we not ourselves New Agers of a sort. FCE, in which we are so deeply invested, is in certain respects a New Age organization,

challenging the old paradigms of human relations. We put our money on "peace and healing"
rather than what that RAF base stands for. When
we poke fun at the New Age movement it is
precisely for the same reasons we poke fun at
the Christian church: we are deeply saddened,
horrified even, by the ways that both so glaringly
fail to live up to their potential and manage to
pervert almost all they have going for them.

Waiting at the foot of the runway for the
fighters to land and the flashing lights to stop, it
dawned on us that we drastically needed to revise
our leisurely pace. It is already clear we will not
be able to visit the city of Aberdeen. That is not
crushing. We aren't "city people." But we are
also beginning to realize that we won't be able
to see all of its environs either, and that is tragic
because they are rich in stones. I, the great
schedule-maker, have made a serious miscalculation, and am feeling deservedly mortified.

So we race inland through some of Scotland's
most beautiful countryside where a leisurely pace
would have been more appropriate. Nonetheless,
we do take our time at the Loanhead of Daviot
stone circle. From a well-marked parking lot we
strolled up a pleasant wooded path hand in hand,
enjoying the singing of the birds, and emerged
to where the monument sits in a peaceful hilltop
meadow. Since the New Age commune at
Findhorn, we have retreated five thousand years.
Or advanced. We are glad to be back with our
megalithic friends.

There are two circles on the site. One, marked
only by a circumference of gravel, is called a

"cremation circle" because several dozen burned bodies had been unearthed within it. The other circle, twice as large, may also have served as a tomb of sorts. Its center is filled with small rocks—a low-lying cairn. The reason to visit it, however, is the outer circle, twelve yards in diameter, of a dozen thick standing stones up to eight feet in height. What makes the site particularly remarkable is that wedged in between two of the taller ones is a slightly lower, huge boulder. Archaeologists refer to such boulders as recumbent stones. We have seen our first "recumbent stone circle."

Although unheralded in our guidebook, Lily has spotted a marking on the survey map of the locale that suggests there may be more stones just two miles off through the fields. But how to get to them? Fortunately, we find a friendly farmer who confirms that there are some megaliths on another hilltop and precisely described the right tractor path we could take to get to them. What we found when we reached the place was a circular copse of tall trees. At one edge of the copse were two massive eight-foot-high menhirs with, once again, a gigantic five-foot-high boulder between them. That was it, except for the detail that the menhirs served as anchoring posts for strands of barbed wire that encircled the rest of the copse. We could reasonably guess that centuries ago the copse was the site of a full circle—and perhaps a burial cairn through which the trees had grown—but farmers had removed the other menhirs. So likely what we are looking at was the remains of a second recumbent stone circle very close to the first. Why, we wondered, had the megalithic people of this area built their circles with a recumbent stone while in most other areas it was an unneeded feature? Who knows?

But this is not a time for deep questions; it is a time for planning. Specifically it is four o'clock. We must be back at Culloden House by eight at the latest or else miss out on a palatial dinner for which we'd made reservations. It's a two-hour drive back, which means we've got two hours at the most for more stones. It's not nearly enough. Had we the energy, we could prowl around the environs of Aberdeen looking at stones until midnight and still not cover them all. So we pick a stone relatively nearby that is quite famous, and regretfully choose to pass all the others by. Regretfully? It's a euphemism for such pain. We hate, hate, hate to give up opportunities when they're so close.

Anyway, our target is the Maiden Stane, and when we reached it we found it had many virtues. One was that it stands right by the roadside and did not require a time-consuming hunt or walk. It is a ten-foot-high Pict cross slab, typical in that it has a Celtic cross on one side and carved Pictish symbols on the other. It chief virtue, however, is its atypicality. Most other cross slabs are rigorously rectangular. This had a narrowed bottom, an irregularly rounded top, and a great gash in one side. It was this irregular spatial configuration far more than its carving that made the stone (or "stane" in Scottish dialect) a thing of beauty. Why this unusual irregularity? The other cross slabs are obviously and precisely quarried. Could this have been unquarried? Probably not, but the possibility exists. Possibly it was a natural stone that the Picts used to carve upon. Might it even have been standing before they did so? In other words, might it have been a mighty menhir three thousand years before it became a cross slab? The question of yesterday had returned to haunt us.

Regardless, it is the stone's unusual shape that gave rise to legend, and legend that gave it its name. As legend has it, there was a maiden who was accosted by a handsome and charming stranger. They got to flirting, and he boasted he could build a locally needed road in no time. Not in the time it would take her to bake a loaf of bread, she parried. With a smile he asked whether he could have her if he proved her wrong. Thinking it no harm—the feat was so impossible—she agreed to the wager. When the road was built before her bread was done, she realized the stranger was the devil in disguise and attempted to flee him. He caught up with her and grabbed her by the shoulder. She wrenched away, praying that she be turned to stone rather than become the devil's woman. Her prayer was granted, and the only piece of her the devil got was that gash in the stone where he had grabbed her shoulder.

I do not believe that the devil is chasing us on this evening, but surely we are in the grips of the demon Time. Or is it an angel? I do not know which. Probably both. Today we are particularly conscious of its grip, but the angel/demon is ever lurking in the background, clutching at us in a myriad of ways. It has always been thus.

My life is run by the clock. Departure times. Flight connections. Lecture schedules. Phone appointments and conference calls. Book deadlines. Occasionally I feel like an automaton. Actually, I am lucky to have more flexibility than many executives. Lily, as primary homemaker with her gift of flowing, has still more, but often she, too, is in executive mode managing meetings, coordinating events, and juggling priorities. Any effective person in society is run by the clock because society runs by the clock. I've heard of other cultures where time is handled differently, where appointments may or may not be kept and punctuality is not a business norm. I find it hard to imagine how such societies could work very well—at least on an economic level—and my informants tell me they don't. Some of us compulsive types may pay it more homage than we should, but after fire and the wheel I think the clock should be looked upon as civilization's greatest invention—probably ahead of the printing press, certainly ahead of computers, and even ahead of air-conditioning.

I've been fortunate to have a varied career with a number of different professional identities: psychiatrist and psychotherapist, author, lecturer, community organizer, management consultant, and, may God have mercy on me, evangelist. Yet all these roles can be subsumed under one: efficiency expert. In each of them I've been trying to teach people, one way or another, how to live their individual and corporate lives more efficiently. An essential part of the teaching is that true efficiency is effectiveness; it is not how many little things you can cram into a day but how many big things you can cram into a lifetime. Much of the art of it is knowing when and how to take time off for vacations, for thinking, for prayer, and, most frightening of all, for doing absolutely nothing. So I am into time management. But it is a paradoxical profession because in the long run we cannot manage time; it manages us. Even if we had planned the day better, there would still have been more for us to see in the great Aberdeen peninsula than we could possibly have crammed in, and on this late afternoon, time is slipping away from us.

There is fierce poignancy in the reality that time is mightier than we. A. E. Housman was writing about time management when he penned the verses:

> Loveliest of trees, the cherry now
> Is hung with bloom along the bough
> And stands about the woodland ride
> Wearing white for Eastertide.
> Now, of my threescore years and ten,
> Twenty will not come again,
> And take from seventy springs a score,
> It only leaves me fifty more.
> And since to look at things in bloom
> Fifty springs are little room,
> About the woodlands I will go
> To see the cherry hung with snow.

This is good time management, but in another forty years there'll only be ten left and it still won't be enough. And then the cherry watcher will plaintively lament with another poet, Ralph Hodgson:

> *Time, you old gypsy man,*
> *Will you not stay,*
> *Put up your caravan*
> *Just for one day*

The poignancy may be brutal. These days it is women who talk the most about it as they understandably hope to cram both motherhood and a business career into their lifetimes. Usually they start with business, but as they approach forty they are haunted by what they have come to starkly identify as the biological clock. The problem is, in part, one of options. A psychiatrist once suggested that we old fogies tend to resent young people for what he termed *the omnipotentiality of adolescence*. And the fact that all options are still open to them is a factor contributing to the frequent smugness of youth. I hardly envy them, however, since the downside of their omnipotentiality is a lack of definition. It is nerveracking to not have much of an identity. As they become older they make the choices by which they largely define themselves. They become lawyers or dentists or homemakers. They develop identities.

But each choice of an option is usually foreclosure of another. Choose to go to medical school and it is not likely you will ever go to law school. Choose the track of hopefully becoming a corporation CEO and you will very likely choose not to fulfill your potential for motherhood. Lily and I have been extraordinarily lucky in the number of options we have been able to fulfill, but they're hardly endless anymore. Indeed, as our energy inexorably diminishes with our aging, they are becoming fewer and fewer. Eventually—and it's not all that far off—there will be but one left: death. Will it be the final foreclosure or a new beginning? God knows. We shall see . . . maybe.

One of the many strange phenomena about time has been called "synchronicity." It refers to a tendency for related events to occur together although they have separate and seemingly unrelated, independent causes. Yesterday our natural focus was on space, in which we had gotten ourselves lost. Today's obvious theme is time. Is this contiguity an accident? We certainly didn't plan the trip that way. Accident or minor miracle, the fact of the matter is that the concepts of space and time are so closely related as to be essentially inseparable.

We measure time by space and space by time. Indeed, time can best be defined as a change of space. It is the changing spatial relationship of the sun and earth that determines whether it is morning, midday, evening, or night. Watch the sun rise or set over the horizon and you are watching time. The earliest chronometer, the sundial, was a primitive instrument to demonstrate the passage of time by displaying the changing spatial configuration of the sun's shadow. The clock, which eventually could be worn on one's wrist, was a vast improvement; it was not only far less cumbersome and more accurate but also served its function at night and on cloudy days. But it still works by spatial configuration. We can tell time by the way its hands move through space.

Conversely, we often measure space by time. It is valuable to know that Lily and I are a hundred miles away from Culloden House. But are the roads wide or narrow, straight or curving? It is a more valuable measurement to say that we are a two-hour drive away from our destination. Just as it was to describe our ocean journey of yesterday as a four-hour crossing of the Minch. So it is also with outer space. The most common measure of distance in use by astrophysicists is light-years—the *time* in years it takes light to travel from a distant star to earth or from one galaxy to another.

It is the ultimately inseparable relationship between space and time that led Einstein and other twentieth-century physicists to the general theory of relativity. I am not enough of a scientist to explain this theory, but an example of it is most meaningful to me. One of those modern physicists, Werner Heisenberg, pointed out that it is impossible to measure the velocity of a very tiny particle without changing its direction in space, or impossible to measure the direction of such a particle without altering its speed—that is, distorting its timing. This phenomenon has come to be known as the Heisenberg effect or the uncertainty principle. Uncertainty is its essence.

What it means—and this is profound—is that there are limits to scientific investigation. The phenomenon has its reflection in my own scientific discipline of psychology. Up to a point—a certain limit—we psychologists can study a person's behavior without him knowing we are doing so. Beyond that point, however, he becomes aware that he is being studied, and this awareness will inevitably alter his behavior. We cannot be certain how he would behave were we not studying him.

We have tended to look to science for salvation. It now is beginning to come as a shock to us in this lingering Age of Reason to learn what scientists have been saying for three generations: There is only so far that they can go. The limits have hardly all begun to be reached, but one thing is becoming painfully clear: As long as we keep our sanity, the universe will never be certain for us. We are inevitably consigned to live with at least some degree of uncertainty.

The relativity, and uncertainty, of time is nowhere more clear than in our consciousness of it. As any child knows, when she is amused time goes quickly, and when she is bored it goes slowly. We may attempt to define time as something objective, but our experience of it is subjective—subject to whom I am at any particular moment. We adults would like to brush off this subjective relativity of time by ascribing it merely to mood, but the matter is not so simple. As I have recounted, in my thirties and early forties I "experimented" with marijuana—experimentation being a euphemism for regular recreational usage. But I also used it for more than recreation. As an introspective psychiatrist I was fascinated by what the drug did to my mind, and I believe I learned much more from it than a younger, less introspective person would have. One of marijuana's more dramatic effects is its alteration of time sense. Typically, a new user will exclaim, "Wow, I just looked at my watch, thinking an hour had passed, and it's only been five minutes." Space perception is, of course, changed as well. Opposite from the effect of alcohol, a driver under the influence of marijuana is likely to drive way under rather than over the speed limit. He will sense the roadside to be whipping past as if the distance between telephone poles had suddenly become much shorter.

I used the term *alteration of time sense* rather than *distortion*. When investigating pleasurable psychoactive drugs, we tend to look at the ways they impair performance while disregarding ways in which they might enhance it. Under the influence of marijuana people behave differently, but is the difference for better or for worse? The answer is some ways one and some ways the other. Because marijuana shifts us away from our "normal" time sense, we assume the shift to be a distortion. But is it? Maybe it is a shift toward reality. As soon as we ponder things in this manner, we come to conclude we don't know what real time is. Conventional time, yes, but real time? The reality of time is relative. I am put in mind of the old Zen Buddhist conundrum: "Last night I dreamt I was a butterfly . . . or am I a butterfly today dreaming that I am a man?"

Some theologians go even further than psychologists or physicists in conceptualizing the variable reality of time. They have suggested that there are at least two utterly different kinds of time: *chronos* and *kairos*. By chronos they mean time as we ordinarily think of it, with changing spatial configurations and distances—fleeting time, with birth and death, beginnings and endings. It is human time. By kairos, however, they mean God's time. They are understandably vague about the rules of this kind of time beyond suggesting that none of our human rules may apply. In God's time perhaps it is possible for a being to be in more than one place at once. Perhaps in kairos birth and death are mere illusions. Perhaps there are no beginnings and endings. Or perhaps all beginnings are endings and all endings are beginnings. The rational scientist in me would be quick to dismiss such a notion as utterly fanciful were it not for very occasional hints of distant reports to suggest that something like kairos may exist, that there may be a level of reality where the clock would appear fanciful and we would laugh over the fact we ever thought we were ruled by it.

But we do not have to be so speculative to realize that the reality of time is, among other ways, relative to human consciousness, and our consciousness is relative to our "state of mind." And that our state of mind, in turn, can be dramatically altered by many factors. It is not only boredom or excitement, agony or ecstasy, and drugs that can produce "altered states of consciousness." Our time of life or age does so without us even thinking about it. Tell a four-year-old that he can get a cowboy outfit in another year, and you might almost as well be talking of eternity. In fact, you are speaking of a period of time that represents a quarter of his existence up until that point. For a seventy-year-old man, a year represents less than two percent of his life on earth. We are talking of a twentyfold difference in perspective. Time tends to move slowly when more than ninety percent of our life is ahead of us, and it seems to move very rapidly when there's not much of it left.

Aging is so poignant not merely because our mortality is looming but also because we seem to be declining in power and beauty. Gerard Manley Hopkins captured the wrenching quality of it when he wrote:

How to keep—is there any any, is there none such,
    nowhere known some, bow or brooch or braid or
    brace, lace, latch or catch or key to keep
Back beauty, keep it, beauty, beauty, beauty . . . from
    vanishing away?
Oh, is there no frowning of these wrinkles, ranked
    wrinkles deep,
Down? no waving-off of these most mournful
    messengers, still messengers, sad and stealing
    messengers of gray?
No, there's none, there's none—oh, no, there's none!
Nor can you long be, what you now are, called fair—
Do what you may do, do what you may,
And wisdom is early to despair.
But, as always with time, appearances can be deceiving

and the reality filled with paradox. Most elderly
do simply look withered. Yet in a minority something
strange and wondrous occurs. They develop a
light, an indefinable light so powerful it outshines
all their wrinkles to give them a beauty before
which that of a young girl pales. Is this so surprising
when the same sort of thing happens even with
the inanimate? Three hundred years will either rot
a refectory table or else give its wood a precious
glow that we call the patina of age. It strikes us that
the same sort of thing has happened to certain
megaliths over the millennia. They are particularly
beautiful not only because of their shape and
size—their space—but also because of their lichens
and weathering. And perhaps something beyond
cause. Somehow these great ones almost shriek to
us of their magnificent age.

Lily and I are at that in-between point of late middle
age. We are not quite elderly, and it is still too
early to tell whether we will be fortunate enough to
develop the wonderful glow, the human patina
of age. But we are also becoming distinctly tired.
We've already crammed much more than most
into our lifetimes, and there are evenings when I feel
older than the moon. God willing, we shall
continue for a while. Occasionally, I even wonder
whether the glow may occur only in those
enlightened ones who have miraculously managed
to go beyond their endurance yet still live on a
bit for our edification.

At this moment on a Tuesday evening we are not
beyond our physical endurance but have run out
of the day's allotted time. We begin to race back

north and west, and shortly in our racing we round a bend just outside the village of Bellabeg and there, right off the road, tucked away in a tiny valley, is the grandest surprise of our trip. It is a henge. But not just any henge. It is *huge*. At least a hundred yards in diameter, it fills the valley floor with its ten-foot-high rim, deep ditch, and thirty-foot-high center.

We are flabbergasted. In the Lake District of England we'd deliberately traveled to see King Arthur's Round Table, designated as a major National Trust site on all the maps and featured in the guidebooks. Now, by pure accident, we have stumbled upon a henge three times as wide, ten times as deep, and a hundred times more impressive. Yet it is unmarked on the map and unmentioned in the guidebook. Why such neglect?

The neglect is not total. Hidden in the grass at the roadside is a rusted little marker indicating the spot to be protected under the Ancient Monuments Act (the predecessor of the National Trust) and someone has seen that the grass has been kept mowed. Likely the caretaker is aided in this regard by sheep. Certainly by rabbits. At this evening hour the whole henge is swarming with hundreds of rabbits hopping and grazing away in the soft light. The spot is pregnant with gentle mystery. Looming over the mystery of why it is so relatively ignored is, of course, the greater mystery of why it had been constructed in the first place. We know the henges were built by the megalithic people. Next to the stones themselves, henges were their most distinctive calling card, etched in the earth to announce their civilization five thousand years ago. But as to what end or purpose they were laboriously dug with only antlers for tools, we have no idea.

Lily and I desperately desired to cross the fence to climb the henge and stroll its mystery. Unlike the rabbits whom we envied, however, we had not the time. Our own dinner lay well ahead of us. Forcing ourselves away, we left the treasure untrod and continued our race across the rolling land. Everything seems to roll today: gently rolling fields, rich rolling forests, and grandly rolling moors and mountains—like God's own henges, so to speak.

We arrived back at Culloden House in time— barely. We'd missed out on the bagpiper and leisurely cocktails. But suited and tied we were in the living room, menus in hand, by eight. It was another elegant dinner, although we passed up on their hair-ball tea. Afterward I wrote up the notes on this full day, and it was midnight before I was done. Although the sun had long set, it was still light enough in the room for me to read what I'd written at that hour. Lily was softly snoring. I wondered how Muslims survived in northern Scotland during Ramadan, the monthlong period when they are required to fast throughout the daylight hours—daylight being precisely defined as the time when a person with unimpaired eyesight can still discern a white thread. They'd have no hardship at all when Ramadan fell in winter, but they'd go insane when it fell in June or early July. There were two possibilities, I imagined. One was that they'd be given a dispensation of some sort. The other was that perhaps there are no Muslims in northern Scotland.

With such idle imagining I went to sleep only to unexplainably awaken a mere hour later. Although not enough to read by, and probably not enough in which to see a white thread, it was still light. I could see the trees three hundred yards in back of our palace and beyond them the silhouette of mountains ten miles in the distance. This is not because there is a moon to bathe the scene in the whiteness of moonlight. (There is none.) This is a *blue* light the likes of which I have never seen before. Furthermore, it does not bathe the scene so much as diffuse it. Although strange, it is not eerie; rather, it is a friendly sort of light, almost warm. I can make out some rabbits munching on the lawn and birds are chirping as if it were already dawn. Which it isn't really. This light is different from dawn. It is far more beautiful.

So time, which I'd been begrudging all day, gently picked me up out of sleep to witness a marvel: the spatial configuration of sun and earth four days from the summer solstice just south of the Arctic Circle. We already realize that we want to come back to Scotland. Over a week ago we missed out on much of Loch Lomond because of poor weather. Today we missed out on much we wanted to see around Aberdeen because of poor scheduling. Will there be time left in our lives for us to come back here together? It is probable. If so, I hope that it will also be in late June. Although I did not miss out on the light, it is something that I would very much like to see again just once more before we die.

CHAPTER XVIII

ART
WEDNESDAY. JUNE 17

I remain annoyed at myself for not having scheduled things better& We are reductant to pack, to load the car and depart our palace. We are travel weary. It would have been smart had I scheduled us a rest day at Culloden House—a day to loll around in elegance doing nothing, maybe spending most of it in bed. It would also have been smart on behalf of my back, which has been hurting more each day.

We are not weary of the trip; just weary. Indeed, the trip has been such fun we are reluctant to see it end. As for my back, it is clear it will soon give out. But that seems a small price to pay for all this fun. My prayer is only that it will hold up until we are done. "If I can just make it to Edinburgh," I keep saying to Lily. But Edinburgh is several days off. Tonight we have an assignation in Dundee and, reluctant or not, we must be moving on.

Our only mandatory stop on the way is just a few miles down the road in the southern suburbs of Inverness: the famed Clava Cairns. We find them easily. They are three stone circles about twenty yards apart from one another. Each is fifteen yards in diameter and each contains within it a cremation cairn. A few things are notable. For some unknown reason the southwest stone of each circle is the largest. The cairns themselves, each twelve yards in diameter, are piled higher than usual with small rocks and bordered by minor megaliths. Finally, unlike the other such sites we'd visited, archaeologists are of the opinion that the stone circles and the burial cairns were built at the same time.

The site is not only excavated but well restored, and this is a problem for us. We prefer our spots to have a touch of wildness to them. This one reminds us of a neatly manicured highway rest stop; we wonder where the picnic tables are. Very probably the restoration is accurate, but we are left wondering whether our megalithic ancestors were such prissy people or whether the place has been inadvertently tamed by modern hands. It was not a turn-on.

So we do not linger long, and in no time we are on the great motorway headed south. I soon turn the wheel over to Lily. One reason is my aching back. Another is that I want to take over the navigating. By the superhighway it is no great distance from Inverness to Dundee, so we have four hours to spare. I have decided to use it by guiding Lily to a mystery place, a destination of which she is unaware. She doesn't know whether to be pleased or angry. On the one hand, she is pleased I have cooked up a little adventure for her. On the other, she is the one accustomed to navigating and to keeping secrets. Can she trust me to be in such control? Bravely, she decides to do so.

Our mystery destination is the hamlet of Fortingall. The night before last I'd read about it to her from the guidebook, and she had seemed interested in its three hallmarks. It is apparently the only real village left in Scotland that still has thatched roofs. Its churchyard is the site of supposedly the oldest tree in all Europe: a three-thousand-year-old yew. Finally, it prides itself on being the legendary birthplace of Pontius Pilate. All of these distinctions may be apocryphal, but the last seems particularly questionable. There was some commerce between Britain and the Roman Empire before the birth of Christ, but the likelihood of a Scottish country lad ending up as a provincial governor in the Middle East struck us as remote. And unprovable.

It was another failed pilgrimage. The few thatched roofs were nowhere near as exciting as those that abound in the southwest of England. The yew tree was not impressively large, and the tiny village had no museum or information center to provide documentation about old Pontius. Nonetheless, the point of pilgrimage is not so much the destination as the journey, and the scenery along the route was gorgeous.

On our way back to the superhighway we searched for three separate stones in vain. All were behind houses with signs: No Trespassing or Private Property, Keep Out, or Beware of Dog. Such signs are not that common in Britain, and we can assume that the homeowners' privacy had previously been violated by other stone searchers. We did not begrudge them their need for protection, but it made us all the more grateful for those friendly farmers who had not only allowed us on their property but actually directed us to their megaliths.

But why our strange, incessant addiction that propels us to prowl people's backyards? Returning to this question we must also return to the old question of why the megalithic people were themselves, in a sense, addicted to stones. I have pooh-poohed the usual explanations of forums and gravestones and astral observatories. Theorists in this Age of Reason have, I believe, overlooked the obvious. And the reason for their oversight is that the stones are, on a certain level, unreasonable.

One obvious thing overlooked is that the stones were art. When people look at Pictish carvings of horsemen and crosses and animals and symbols, they know they are looking at art. Even when they inspect the simple rings carved into stone by the megalithic people they suspect they are viewing art, no matter how primitive. Yet when they see the unadorned menhirs or dolmens or stone circles they fail to reach the obvious conclusion that when the megalithic people erected these monuments they were, among other things, creating art.

Art is too large to submit to any single adequate definition. There are many such things: love, beauty, light, goodness, community, prayer—all of which have something to do with God. But one of the characteristics of art is its unreasonableness. Other human creations have an obvious reason: They are necessary; they serve a clear function; they are useful. No one would ponder the purpose of a fork or spoon, a knife or an axe, a house or an office building. But as soon as you carve something into the handle of that fork or the blade of that knife or the molding of that building, you are doing something that is not strictly utilitarian. You are engaging in the strange practice of adornment and have entered the not entirely reasonable realm of art.

I hardly mean to imply that adornment is without motive. Of course there are reasons for art, but its reasons are subtle and complex, highly relative and extremely subjective. For instance, even though I am a psychiatrist, I have no more understanding of why men—and, increasingly these days, women—should want to get themselves tattooed than I do of why the Picts painted themselves. For that matter, I don't even comprehend why women like to use makeup. I have yet to meet one who didn't look better without it—to my eyes. But I am aware that at least some men see it quite differently. I also suspect that the predominant motive of most women using makeup is more obscure than the simple desire to be sexually attractive. As an efficiency expert regarding the extraordinary amount of time, energy, and money such women expend on their makeup and clothes, I would have to conclude this practice of self-adornment the most wasteful activity on earth unless . . . unless I regard it as art. For many women, makeup is a kind of creative play whereby they make an art form of themselves.

I still might consider such art frivolous were it not for a thought-provoking novel of many years ago entitled *You Shall Know Them* by Vercors. Through the fictional discovery of a "missing link"-type creature—between ape and human— the book's plot provokes a legal dilemma and formal debate in the House of Lords on the definition of "human." Eventually the conclusion is reached that the most salient distinguishing feature between humans and the other creatures is our unique propensity for self-adornment. The thesis is debatable. Nonetheless, whatever the reasons, the other creatures do seem blessed or cursed with a lifestyle that is distinctly utilitarian in comparison to our own. Whether we are painting on ourselves or on canvas—or carving on stones, writing poetry, or making music— we are doing something human. Art may be the essence of our humanity.

Art implies consciousness: not only the consciousness of self, implied by the practice of self-adornment, but also the consciousness of beauty external to ourselves. As already noted, however, consciousness is relative; beauty is too large to be defined and very much in the eye of the beholder. The most beautiful poem and most beautiful novel I have ever read came to my attention as a member of two editorial selection boards. In each case the submission was rejected with me being outvoted four to one. The other editors could discern no virtue whatsoever in these creations so magnificent to my eyes.

Eventually, authors come to be slightly inured to the exquisite subjectivity of editors and critics. For my own part, I can guarantee in advance that any new book of mine will receive at least one rave review and one that will disparage the work as excrement, and it will be hard to imagine that the reviewers read the same volume.

Add to the subjectivity of the individual critic the immense social pressure of ephemeral fashion, and you get relativity squared. The only thing in art sadder than the uninspired plethora of fashionable works is those excellent ones that fail to get published or otherwise catch on simply because they are not on this year's stylistic bill of fare. Some great art is forever lost this way. But some survives—like Shakespeare or Beethoven, Michelangelo or Rembrandt—precisely because it is so timeless as to transcend fashion. And that is why there are still a few stones left and a few people as weird as us to continue to search them out. They are great art.

It is not surprising that art is so relative, since space and time are relative and art has so much to do with both. We're accustomed to think about space in regard to the visual arts. Shape, a fundamental aspect of space, is critical in sculpture and painting. I am therefore astounded that no one, to my knowledge, has previously written about megaliths in terms of art. Even the most ordinary ones were obviously selected for their height, width, and breadth. But these are primitive dimensions of space. Is it an accident, do you suppose, that the focal stones of the more complex megalithic configurations—such as the "heel stone" at Stonehenge, Long Meg, or the central monolith at Callanish—are stones of not only great size but also strange, unique, compelling, and, yes, beautiful shapes?

In the visual arts we speak not only of shape but of the relationship of shapes to each other and perspective. This crucial factor is called "composition." In speaking of The Great Configuration at Callanish I was talking about it as a composition. Its stones did not just happen to fall into that configuration. The monument was planned, composed. Even the simplest stone circle is a composition.

A part of composition is the relationship between "figure and ground," between the focal object and its surroundings. We were so turned on by the dolmen at Long House Farm not only because of the composition of the stones themselves—resembling an altar—but also because of their setting on a hillside overlooking a magnificent bay. Was that setting an accident? Even the most rigorous scientist, immune to aesthetics, would have to agree that the builders made a choice to lug boulders to that particular spot and not some other. Probably the choice was overdetermined, but it struck us as a deliberately artful one.

We also speak of a piece of music as a composition and call its author a "composer." Knowing of FCE's use of silence and the critical concept of "emptiness," a famous opera singer once commented to me, "You know, more than half of Beethoven is silence." Indeed, it is the empty space between the notes that makes music music; otherwise it would just be noise.

In the art of writing, space also plays its role. A sentence more than four lines long is almost unreadable. A book in which every sentence is exactly two lines long would probably also be unreadable. The good writer instinctively knows—or learns—how to orchestrate her sentences so as to produce a kind of variety likely to keep her reader's attention. And it is not just sentence length: A comma represents a tiny rest stop; a semicolon a small one; a colon a still larger one; and a period screeches "Halt." Even more dramatic is the end and beginning of paragraphs, signified by the actual indentation of space on the printed page. Although its effect is "cute" at best, it is not surprising that a few modern poets have attempted to space their lines on a page into a visual sculpture of their subject matter.

Space and time being relative to each other, the spatial mechanics of literary or musical compositions are virtually inseparable from their temporal dynamics. Is the length of a sentence a measure of its size in space or the time it takes to read it? We are speaking of rhythm. Whether we label it a spatial or a temporal phenomenon, it is essential to music. It is less essential to writing. One can convey a message in words without rhythm. Should the message be lengthy and complex, however, one is unlikely to convey it well unless she has something of the ear of a poet, which is not utterly dissimilar to that of a musician. There is even rhythm in the visual arts. Great sculptors and painters, for instance, have the ability to depict motion in their work. How is this done? How does one somehow capture motion in a static piece of marble or on the flat space of a canvas?

This almost unanswerable question introduces another dimension in the relationship between time and art. Whatever inborn talent or genius an artist might possess, such as for depicting motion, her work is likely to be painstaking and time-consuming. The creation of art takes time.

It used to irritate me no end when I was working in an organization when something needed to be written and another executive would say, "Hey, Scotty, you do it—you're a good writer." The assumption was that because I was a professional writer I could brush the piece off in no time. The fact is that in many ways writing does not come easily to me. I am a slow writer. A part of my gift is simply that I am more patient than others when it comes to words. But only words. When I watch our son draw or paint I am in awe of *his* patience and pertinacity, and I am certain that if I watched a musician at work I would be in similar awe. One of the reasons that megalithic monuments can inspire awe in us is our sense of wonder at the sheer time that must have been taken in their construction. In regard to the greatest of them, archaeologists speak in terms of "millions of man-hours."

But why? Making the point that art is essentially human still doesn't explain the why of it. Why those millions of megalithic man-hours? Why should artists in every age lavish such care and extraordinary amounts of time on their creations when there's likely to be precious little money in it for them? What is the payoff for making something beautiful? It's overdetermined, of course. But a few years back I happened to stumble upon a reason that I suspect is more profound than all the others.

With a single exception, I have written my first drafts in longhand on yellow pads. Lily doesn't read them or the final ones; she's usually heard it all before. The exception began when my back went out while we were on vacation in 1988, leaving me flat in bed, unable to even read, with no sources of amusement other than prayer and a Dictaphone. The strange idea came to me to write a novel. Because I couldn't sit up to use my yellow pad, I started dictating it. By the time my back improved I'd gotten the hang of it and decided to continue with the draft in that mode.

Shortly thereafter Lily and I were leading a workshop in the Canadian Rockies. I was still dictating in my spare time. Stuck with me in the same hotel room, she was forced to listen as she tried to concentrate on more important matters. Possibly motivated by resentment over this punishment, she commented at dinner one night that I was a driven person. "It's probably because your father was such a driven man," she suggested, "driven himself and driving his children."

I agreed that I was "driven" in certain respects. "But it's not just my father," I added. "You're right that he's part of it, only there's something else involved. I'm not sure what."

The next day we had off. I dictated in the morning and we went sightseeing for the afternoon. Over cocktails in our room when we returned Lily said, "I was listening to what you were dictating this morning, and I thought it was good."

"What?" I queried in surprise.

"I thought it was good," she repeated.

Well, talk about driven! I dove across the bed for my Dictaphone and was dictating in a minute. Within another minute I stopped, laughing at the ridiculousness of my behavior. Unable to ignore it, I began to ponder why Lily's positive literary judgment had just been such a driving force for me.

It was then that I had one of those moments of inspiration that do occasionally bless artists or theologians. Almost as fast as I had dived for my Dictaphone, I was across the room again, rummaging in the bedside table for its Gideon Bible, opening it to Genesis 1, the account of creation, to read how God separated the land from the sea; and how as soon as He saw it was *good* He went right to work again creating plants. When He saw that they, too, were *good*, He continued on to make the sun and moon. They also looked *good*. By now He was in a frenzy of creation. He moved on to do the fish and birds, and when they were *good*, He tried His hand at the land animals. And they turned out to be *good*. Finally, He created humans, and after six days of this orgy, He sat back and rested, very pleased with Himself because He saw that all of it was *good*.

The message was clear: The assessment of goodness is the most compelling ingredient of the creative process. The obvious implication of the story is that if God had seen that what He had created was not good, He would have stopped right there and then. Conversely, it was precisely because His early efforts at creation looked good to Him that He kept going, spurred to ever-greater feats of artistic finesse. Is it any different for humans, whom He created in His own image? I think not. We may indeed create for many different motives: money, power, prestige, lust, service. But when all these motives are wasted and gone—as they can be—we will continue to create as long as we know that what we are still able to create is good.

This similarity between us and God poses a question: When we humans indulge ourselves in creating art, are we attempting to be God or, at least, play at being God. The answer is "Yes." But so what? It is what is intended. It does require a hubris of sorts, which is why artists invariably demonstrate at least a certain kind of narcissism. Consider yourself to be utterly unworthy of making any public statement whatsoever, and it is unlikely that you have all it takes to be an artist. When I mentor artists, including those who practice perhaps the most subtle art of all, the art of leadership, it is usually a part of my role to judiciously and realistically nurture their self-confidence. Perhaps art is so essentially human because it is godly. In any case, I like to imagine that when the megalithic people finished erecting their very first menhir—or dolmen or stone circle—they stood back in great pleasure at what they had created and exclaimed, "It is gooood!"

Still, too much narcissism is a poison in all human endeavor, and art is not one jot excluded. I wrote of how foursquare narcissists cannot or will not think of others, which means they cannot or will not love. They can create in a fashion, but they cannot create well since love is the second most compelling ingredient in the creative process, hardly separable from the first. The subjective judgment "it is good" needs to be tested by the objective effect of your art upon at least a few other human beings. Granted that taste is ephemeral, if you create a work that is not deeply appealing to a single other person in your lifetime, it is probably not because your opus is timeless; likely, it is because you have not loved enough, and your sole assessment that your work is "good" is something that is only and forever, like Narcissus' fatal attraction to himself, in your head.

In any case, when I write I do my best, within constraints, to bear my reader in mind, and the successful artists I know do likewise. Frankly, it is a bit erotic. I am ever mindful of my beloved. I want to clothe my words in semicolons and perfume my phrases with metaphor in such a manner as to make the product as exciting and appealing to her as possible. I want my taste to taste good to her lips, and I am not so arrogant as to refuse to submit to a modicum of self-alter-ation at my own hands or those of editors in this aim. The constraints involved relate to issues of seduction and manipulation. It is not my intent to distort the truth; it is to take the unvarnished truth and varnish it—not to diminish or distort it but enhance it by highlighting its inherent sweetness and palatability.

Many equate Eros with creativity. To the strict Freudian, artistic endeavor is nothing more than sublimated sexual activity. While I don't buy this view in its totality, I think there is something to it. Certainly the basic biological function of sex is pro*creation*, a rather important matter since it ensures the propagation of the species. In this respect, sex is very serious business. Indeed we may not take it seriously enough, as the pope is unpleasantly wont to remind us. On the other hand, sex also happens to be the most delightful and liberating form of play in town.

This same paradox is reflected in one of the great paradoxes of art: Art, too, is both serious and playful. I spoke of our practice of adorning ourselves with makeup as creative play. So it is with the making of mud pies, the art of writing, and all other art. Serious art is not easy. As someone once put it: "There's nothing much to writing. You simply sit down in front of a typewriter and slice open a vein." I couldn't endure the painful concentration required unless I was not also having a bit of fun in the process. Adorning my subject as best I can for my beloved reader, I get some real enjoyment in the process out of "playing with words."

One other characteristic of great art is its freshness. Whenever a new artist of stature emerges from the crowd it is because she has something new to say or says it in a new way. A fresh vision, a new sound, a unique voice, a groundbreaking style has appeared on the scene. We wake up to the fact that the best artists are also leaders, way out in front of the pack. Of course this year's new style is likely to become next year's new fad and the following year's formula, and in a decade or two we may look back on what once seemed so fresh and find it stale, flat, and empty. The miracle of that greatest art which is timeless is that it magically manages to preserve its freshness. In part, this is a matter of unadulterated genius: No one has ever managed to do it better over the years. In fact, no one will ever do it as well; the mold, as they say, has been broken.

I suspect the problem we had with the Clava Cairns this morning was not just the fault of its restorers. Its stones were not only unusually neat and even but also dull. Not one of them had a distinctive shape or memorable texture. Why the dullness of this site in comparison to others? A possible explanation is simply that it was not an original; it was a copy. Perhaps by the time it was created its builders had settled for a formula. They had lost their creativity. They added nothing of their own imagination because they had fallen into cookbook megalithicism. I don't know, but at least I have the theory.

Cookbooks are very useful, and it is not diffi-cult to understand why people tend to go with formulas. What is infinitely more mysterious is the origin of originality. Where does a fresh vision come from? A startlingly different imagination? What creates a creative genius?

The mystery of it was very clear for me a few years ago when I took a week-long course at Harvard on "The Fundamentals of Music." In the closing session I raised my hand for the first time. "This course has been entirely about the science of harmony," I said. "I've gotten a great deal out of it, but I'm struck by the fact that there's been virtually no mention of melody. I wonder if this may reflect the possibility that musicologists do not have a science of melody. Is that an accurate conjecture?"

"What do you mean by a science of melody?" the professor, a wonderfully gracious lady, queried.

"A set of rules for what makes a good melody," I replied. "We've been presented with lots of rules for what creates good harmony, and I have reasons now to discern between good harmony and poor harmony. But I have no rules to distinguish between good and bad melody."

"There's no such thing as good or bad melody," the professor retorted, naturally a bit defensive. "Melody just is. It's completely relative. What Americans might think is good melody, Indians might think an atrocity."

"I partly agree with you," I persisted. "The appreciation of melody is, to some extent, relative, as you pointed out. Still, within a culture, there are few melodies that really catch on while most don't. Why? Are there any rules to discern why one melody is so catchy when others aren't?"

The gracious lady bowed to my ignorance. "Since you've agreed with me that melody is in some respects relative," she said, "I must agree with you that there is not yet any science of melody."

But why not? Why wouldn't there by now be a science of melody? The answer, I believe, was provided almost three hundred years ago by Johann Sebastian Bach, a composer I myself find rather short on melody, when he explained, "God writes my music." The same can be said of all great art. Artists are no more religious than other people. When they are secular-minded, they have a notable lack of desire to discuss the issue of where their art comes from. They suddenly turn prosaic, saying, "So and so taught me this technique" and "So and so taught me that one," as if the matter of inspiration, an influx of the Spirit, was irrelevant. When they are religious-minded, they will simply agree with Bach, but they'll be quiet about it, because talking about such things in society can get one into trouble.

So we are back with the mystery of gifts. Pondering the origin of originality, the creation of creativity, the source of great talent and inspiration and the nature of genius, about all we can do at the end of the matter is shrug our shoulders and change the subject by lamely proposing, "I guess it's a gift." It would seem that all great and timeless art, like an outstanding melody, is more likely to come from the realm of kairos than from the land of chronos.

Which doesn't really explain anything, of course, in this Age of Reason. Nonetheless, let me take one more little step into these murky, mystical waters. Lily described me as "driven," and I certainly was, in relation to writing my novel as well as my other works. The religious word for such drivenness is "calling." On the average, it takes me at least two years to write a book from start to finish. That is a long time for an impatient man. I have to laugh when people ask me what strategy I had in mind for writing this book or that. I'm not patient enough to spend two years actualizing a strategy. In each case I've been able to keep my nose to the grindstone only because I felt "called" to write that particular work. I'm not suggesting that I'm a great artist or a godly man. I'm only suggesting that I didn't have all that much choice about it. And that many authors or creators have found themselves in the same sort of not unpleasant predicament of operating "under orders."

Going to Dundee on this afternoon, however, was purely a matter of rational choice. The city sits between Inverness to the north and Edinburgh to the south, and had seemed to me the right mathematical spot to stop for another day's exploration. Beyond that, our knowledge of Dundee was limited to its marmalade—a drawing card that could hardly be considered to constitute a calling.

Like our other rational choice of Cardiff, it didn't seem so reasonable when we finally arrived at our hotel after negotiating an almost endless maze of circuses—the sometimes efficient and sometimes terrifying circular road junctions through which Britain plots its traffic. The Swallow Hotel is partly an old castle but mostly an adjoining drab modern motel. Despite its stars, we were assigned another small and airless room with a fine view of the parking lot. Quite a comedown from Culloden House! But at least we are out of the circuses and actually glad for the relief from fine dining as we sit in our room munching store-bought cheeses and meat pies. We also know we are assured of elegance when we reach Edinburgh, where we shall be staying at the Caledonia—or Caley, as it is affectionately nicknamed—one of Britain's greatest old establishments.

Still, I am slightly depressed. I am very much aware that the trip is winding down and, as usual, I am mourning its end before the fact. It is amusing that many think me a workaholic. If only they knew how much I love vacations! And the work ahead of me will be mostly rewriting, which is seldom as uplifting as the first draft of a new project. But it is necessary. At least half the art of writing is that of rewriting. The polishing can be tedious and seem interminable at times. Nonetheless, there is pleasure at its conclusion when I can sit back and conclude, "Yes, it was good from its conception, but now it finally looks just right."

I'd rather be searching for stones, however. Typically, I fall asleep wondering about them. The megalithic people were artists. Were they called to their art? Pondering the extraordinary communal time devoted to their projects, I think it must have been so. How did the calling come? Did God actually speak, clearly instructing them, "I want you to raise great stones out of the earth and erect them for my glory?" Possibly. But more probably, as for other artists, it was almost a quiet sort of thing. A day came when, for no apparent reasons, the idea was simply there to raise stones, as if it had been inseminated into their minds while they'd been sleeping. Then they would have thought about this new idea, vaguely calculating its costs. But soon they would have stopped worrying about the cost, because the more they played with the idea the more right it felt to them. Finally, it felt so right that it felt wrong not to do it, and that was the point at which they went to work.

CHAPTER XIX

INTEGRATION
THURSDAY, JUNE 18

A surprisingly satisfactory day began with a surprisingly good breakfast. The Swallow's restaurant sits in the old castle part of the hotel but has been modernized with many windows looking out upon a pleasant garden. The kippers were excellent with toast and Dundee marmalade. The only flaw was learning from the waitress that the marmalade firm is now operated not out of Dundee but some city in England, and for all we know the product itself is currently being made in Taiwan or Thailand. Another great WASP icon falls by the wayside! Whether we like it or not, it's a changing world.

Our first stop was a plain little house in the plain little village of Meigle, but what an important stop! The building is a museum and houses the best collection of carved Pict stones in the world along with a small gold mine of booklets about them. The curator, a pleasant elderly lady, did not thrust herself upon us but glowed with delight at the opportunity to answer our questions. She told us that the Pictish symbols (other than the cross) and stylized mythical creatures were believed to represent a language of sorts, although scholars to date had been unable to crack the code. We do not know the meaning of the messages. She positively beamed when I asked her whether the Picts had ever used any of the prehistoric, megalithic menhirs to carve upon. It was quite probable, she responded, since several of their symbol stones also have cup marks in them—such marks, together with rings, being the most common form of megalithic art other than the stones themselves. It was a pleasure to encounter a curator who both knew and loved her job.

Next we stopped at the tiny ruined church in Eassie. The reason was the Eassie stone, a rather typical Pict cross slab under glass inside the roofless church. Actually we became more interested in the less ancient stones outside. All manner of them, fallen and standing, simple and ornate, ranging from around 1500 to 1972, occupied the little graveyard, and we wondered whether our custom of gravestones might have evolved from the Pict cross slabs or even from the three- to four-thousand-year-old menhirs the early British

Christians would have observed dotting the countryside.

From Eassie we went to the Stones of Aberlemno. There are four of them. One, yet another typical cross slab, stands unprotected in the graveyard of the church of Aberlemno. By now these slabs were beginning to bore us, and we could have skipped it. But not the other three. About fifty yards apart from each other, they line the roadside a half a mile away from the church. The stone wall of the adjacent fields had been built around them so that each stone has its own niche.

The middle stone appears to be of soft, brown sandstone. It stands five feet with an uneven, strange shape. Two faint circles are carved on it. The stone looks extremely weathered. Its carved circles seem more sophisticated than megalithic rings yet more primitive than Pictish symbols. The outer stone closest to the church is a typical ten-foot-high cross slab, also of a soft, brown stone but relatively unweathered. The other outer stone is of gray granite, standing five feet high at an angle. The face closest to the road is clearly etched with abstract Pict symbols. The other face contains no cross and is bare (save for cup marks at its bottom that we didn't even notice but later read about). Together, these three Stones of Aberlemno comprised one of the highlights of our trip.

Why? It wasn't the first time we'd seen three or more standing stones together—many of them far more massive. One reason is the mystery of the site. No one knows what to make of the middle stone, which appears to be the oldest of the three. Some think it may even be a hoax. A possibility, however, at least in our imagination, is that it was a menhir upon which postmegalithic but pre-Pictic people had carved. The possibility doesn't seem all that unreasonable since such people were around for at least two thousand years. As for the cross slab, it was clearly a product of the eighth or ninth century A.D. But what about the symbol stone? Why no cross on its other face? Might it have been carved by the Picts prior to their Christianization? Quite probably, but no one knows for sure. In fact, no one knows how the three such different stones ended up adjoining each other along the same roadside. Most likely at least one and probably two had been moved there. But when and why? We don't know. No one does.

However they happened, the three Stones of Aberlemno constitute a unique multicultural, multitemporal monument, quite possibly representing the work of human hands in 3000 B.C., 200 B.C., 400, and A.D. 800, all brought together by still later mysterious human hands to comprise an outdoor museum of history. That is why it was so exciting for us.

It was not the only time we've been thrilled by a multicultural, multitemporal monument. The Plaza des Tres Culturas in Mexico City consists of an ultramodern Mexican high-rise housing development surrounding a small square containing a sixteenth-century Spanish colonial church and excavated still earlier Aztec ruins. It is an impressive site.

Even more impressive is the great mosque at Cordoba in southern Spain. Construction of this huge, almost plain but elegantly simple mosque was begun in A.D. 785 by Abdar Rahman shortly after the Moors had conquered Spain. Long after Cordoba was recaptured by Spanish Catholics, Emperor Charles V ordered that a great new cathedral be constructed on the site of the mosque. The Christian stone masons frantically went to work, and had already completed the chancel when the emperor finally arrived for a visit. Although he had no one but himself to blame, the moment he saw what was left of the mosque he was horrified. "My God," he exclaimed, "you have been destroying one of the most beautiful buildings in the world." So he ordered the masons to stop, with the result that today out of the very middle of a one-story, magnificently spread out and austere mosque there rises the six-story-high, dramatically baroque Gothic chancel of an uncompleted Catholic cathedral. It is the most extraordinary architectural juxtaposition and study in contrast that we know.

But why? Why are we so thrilled by such cross-cultural, cross-temporal juxtapositions? And why are we so fascinated by the esoteric question of whether or not the Picts used prehistoric menhirs to carve upon? Cordoba provides a clue. The mosque itself had been constructed on the site of an earlier Christian church, and that church on top of a still earlier Roman temple. This is not a surprising sequence in archaeology. It was a normal practice. Throughout history it has been the norm for a conquering religion to build its temples on top of the temple ruins of the conquered one. Why? Again, it is overdetermined behavior. One reason is the opportunity for the new religion to demonstrate its power over the old one—on the spot, literally. Yet there is also a strangely opposite motive. Whenever a spot has been used for religious purposes, no matter what religion, it becomes hallowed ground after a century or two. What better place to erect a temple than on already hallowed ground? The efficiency expert in me can only appreciate such behavior.

Finally, there resides in the breasts of at least some human beings a desire for integration. I suspect Charles V was such a person. Upon seeing its beauty, he wanted to preserve the mosque. Why didn't he then destroy the cathedral portion? Perhaps because to do so would have offended his fellow Christians. But I like to think it was because the church, although incomplete, was also beautiful in its own right and very different way. So he preserved the beauty of both through an extraordinary integration and example of what these past few years has come to be called "win/win decision making."

The reason, then, we are so excited by the three Stones of Aberlemno is because they are an integration, and we have a passion for integration. For racial and cultural integration. For religious integration. For the integration of ideas. And perhaps, above all, for the integration of the past with the present—and with the future.

Given this passion, it is not surprising that what fame has happened to come my way has come primarily because I am an integrator. I am most known for the integration of science in general, and the science of psychology in particular, with theology. But while these are my specialties, life is not a specialty, and I am driven to integrate everything that is properly interrelated. I am an evangelist of integration.

The noun "integrity" comes from the verb "to integrate." We psychiatrists have a verb for the opposite of integrate: to compartmentalize. It means to take things that are properly related and stick them in separate, airtight compartments in our minds where they don't have to rub up against each other and cause us any stress or pain, friction, or tension. An example would be that of the man who goes to church on Sunday morning, devoutly believing that he loves God and God's creation, and then on Monday has no trouble with his company's policy of dumping toxic wastes in the local stream. This is, of course, because he has put his religion in one compartment and his business in another. He is what we have come to call "a Sunday-morning Christian." It is a very comfortable way to operate, but integrity it is not.

The word *diabolic* is derived from the Greek *diaballein*, meaning "to throw apart" or cast apart or fragment. Like everything else, compartmentalization has a place, a circumscribed usefulness. When unconstrained, as in the millions of Sunday-morning Christians, however, it is indeed diabolic. Compartmentalization is not the root of all evil; it is, however, the principal psychological mechanism of evil. Deprive an evil man of his capacity to compartmentalize, and he will be like a general without an army. Or, better yet, he will undergo a conversion to goodness—a conversion to integrity.

Compartmentalization is painless; integrity never is. Integrity requires that we fully experience the tensions of competing demands and conflicting ideas. Three hundred years ago, as the Age of Reason began to hit its stride, the intellectual leaders of Europe and Great Britain unconsciously developed an unwritten social contract to deal with the tensions among science, religion, and government. It was a contract of compartmentalization, dividing up the turf among the three. Government was not to interfere with religion; there would be separation of church and state. Nor with science or vice versa. Science would henceforth be apolitical and, supposedly, "value free." It would also be secular. Isaac Newton at the time became president of the Royal Society of London for Improving Natural Knowledge. What was meant by *natural* knowledge? Science, which was defined as secular and totally distinct from *supernatural* knowledge or theology, which henceforth would be the province of the Church and a separate realm of thought.

As noted, compartmentalization can have its place. All manner of good initially came from this unwritten social contract of compartmentalization. We stopped burning witches, for instance. Democracy was established without anarchy.

The Church focused its energy away from politics to tending souls. And science thrived, leading to an industrial, technological revolution beyond our wildest dreams. The problem is that the contract no longer works. Its compartmentalization has gotten out of hand. Indeed, it is increasingly diabolic, leaving us, at the end of the twentieth century, with secular, valueless public education, family breakdown, an impotent and privatized religion, and an often inhumane technology that seems to be running wild.

I have consistently poked fun at reason. This is because we are living in the Age of Reason, and are so embedded in it as to be blind. Were we still embedded in the Age of Faith, I suspect it would be blind faith, and that I would be teasing it with equal vigor (assuming I could avoid the Inquisition). I am, in fact, a great advocate of reason. I am only against unrestrained, unimaginative, and narrow-minded reason.

In this Age when we think we should know *the* reason for everything and that there is only one reason—a time when the concept of overdetermination is foreign to our minds—we are cursed by either/or thinking. Either stone circles were used as astral observatories or as marketplaces. Education should either be secular or religious. Riots are caused either by a breakdown in family values or by oppressive racism. One must be either a Democrat or a Republican, a conservative or a liberal.

I don't know who originally coined the term, but a few of us theologians are increasingly exalting "the Holy Conjunction." The Holy Conjunction is the word *and*. Instead of an either/or style of mentation, we are pushing for both/and thinking. We are not trying to get rid of reason but promote "Reason plus." Reason *and* mystery. Reason *and* emotion. Reason *and* intuition. Reason *and* revelation. Reason *and* wisdom. Reason *and* love.

So we are envisioning a world where a business can make a profit and be ethical. Where a government can promote political order and social justice. Where medicine can be practiced with technological proficiency and compassion. Where children can be taught science and religion. Our vision is one of integration. By integration we do not mean squashing two or more things together into a colorless, unisexed blob. When we talk of integrating science and faith we are not speaking of returning to an age of primitive faith, where science is discounted, any more than we are arguing for the status quo where a limited science is idolized while faith is relegated to an hour on Sunday. The Holy Conjunction is the conjunction of integrity. Way back when our trip began I wondered what, if anything, might lie beyond the Age of Reason. I don't know. But I hope it will be the Age of Integration. In that age science and religion will work hand in hand, and both will be more sophisticated as a result.

Before we can arrive at the Age of Integration, however, we must become more sophisticated in our thinking. Specifically, we must come to learn how to think paradoxically.

Paradox is a word that has popped up repeatedly during this trip. That is no accident. It is the word we use when reason and the Holy Conjunction become integrated. Tongue in cheek, I ascribed my fascination with paradox to my birth date of May 22, making me a baby Gemini who can always see two sides at once (being naturally two-faced). For all I know that might be the reason for my "gift" of paradox, but the gift was nurtured by my twenty-year flirtation with Zen Buddhism. Naturally, my favorite lightbulb joke is: How many Zen Buddhists does it take to change a lightbulb? The answer: Two: one to change the bulb *and* one to not change it.

We may laugh at this business of paradox, but it is very real. Lily and I are able to be traveling on this day in Scotland only because other people are *not* traveling, most notably Gail and Susan, who are back in Connecticut taking care of our complex affairs and sending us the very occasional fax. Remember the professor who was asked by one of his students, "Sir, it is said you believe at the core of all truth is paradox. Is that correct?" "Well," the professor answered, "yes and no." Without my twenty years of meandering around Zen I don't think there is any way I could have been prepared to swallow the literally god-awful paradoxes that lie at the core of Christian doctrine (the paradox of grace and works being but one of many).

Several years ago I had the opportunity to offer a set of ten recommendations to the state commissioners of education who had gathered to wrestle with the complex issue of the teaching of values in public schools. One of my recommendations was that Zen Buddhism should be taught in the fifth grade. I was not speaking tongue in cheek. It is around the age of ten that children are first able to deal with paradox, and it is a critical moment for imprinting which should not be lost. I doubt, however, that the commissioners took me seriously.

It is not going to be easy for people to learn how to think paradoxically in this Age of Reason. Indeed, translating directly from its Greek root, paradox literally means "contrary to reason." Paradox is not actually unreasonable. It seems that way because we tend to think in words—and particularly in nouns. Nouns are categories, and language compartmentalizes. "Cat" is a category for furry land animals with whiskers. "Fish" is a category for water creatures with scales. Consequently, a creature that falls in the cat category cannot fall in the fish category—unless it is a "catfish," but then we really know that a catfish belongs to the fish compartment. Life and death are opposite compartments. Even verbs are categorical. "To find" is the opposite of "to lose." What then are we to do with someone who teaches, "Whosoever will save his life shall lose it; and whosoever shall lose his life will find it?"

Five years ago a reporter quoted me (correctly) when he wrote in the *Los Angeles Times*, "And if that isn't arrogant enough, Peck says, 'Perhaps the greatest political problem in this country is how 5 percent of us who comprehend paradox can communicate with the 95 percent who don't.'" My arrogance aside, why would I have

437

called this a political problem? Isn't it merely an intellectual problem?

The question itself bespeaks of our tendency to fragment, to compartmentalize. It places our intellectual activity in one compartment and our political activity in another. And, indeed, one of the many things that deeply concerns me about my nation is the extent to which this separation has actually been effected. Two hundred years ago our political leaders—Washington, Jefferson, Hamilton, the Adamses—were also intellectual leaders. They were not professional politicians. But by now, with only an occasional exception, politics has become a profession, a specialized career track, and has largely lost it roots in our intellectual life. This worries me. It appears you can divorce government from science and religion and the intellect in the short run, but whether they *should* be divorced is another matter. It seems as dangerous to me to separate our political from our intellectual life as it does to separate our business lives from our religious ones.

Be that as it may, society is faced, as it always has been, with only two *viable* choices: reformation and revolution. I see these choices as inherently intellectual and spiritual, but certainly they are political in practice. I further see the difference between them as a matter of integration. Reformation attempts to integrate the past with the future, whereas revolution attempts to move into the future by making a radical break with the past. The Protestant Reformation may have seemed a revolutionary rebellion to the Catholic church at the time, but in retrospect it is properly named. It did not throw out Christianity. To the contrary, it preserved the essence of Christian doctrine while making room for much greater latitude of practice, including the latitude for purification of abuses of practice. It integrated the future with the past. The Russian Revolution, on the other hand, threw out the past in its entirety: the czars, the whole political structure, the economic system, and even the religion. In comparison, the American Revolution should be thought of more as a colonial rebellion coupled with an imaginative, thoughtful political reformation that largely preserved the most basic British political, economic, religious, and intellectual traditions.

Although we ourselves shall pass away in the not too distant future, as parents and grandparents and citizens, Lily and I have a considerable investment in continuity. Hence this distinction between reformation and revolution has emotional in addition to intellectual meaning for us. We are profoundly predisposed toward reformation. We energetically hope that the best of the past will be integrated into the future. This is not so much because we are attached to the past as we are to the future. We can easily countenance the discarding of rituals that have been beloved to us for many decades and originated before we were born. We rejoice that our children may do it differently. Change is the name of the game. It's just that the track record of reformation is pretty good while that of revolution is rather poor. As with the Russian Revolution, revolutions tend to be unsuccessful and very bloody. We do not like to think of our progeny suffering horribly much less being utterly wiped out in a grand but failed and violent social experiment.

Meanwhile we work as best we can at reformation in our own lives. I have long spoken of my need for extensive "prayer times"—averaging two hours a day in total. During those times I am seldom down on my knees or reading the Bible. Mostly I am just thinking, and this thinking is the work of integration. What new activities might I take on to meet the needs of the future? I am pondering, and what old activities of the past should I relinquish to do so? I do ask myself revolutionary questions. Should I give all my money away? Should I totally stop lecturing? But the answers are virtually always ones of paradoxical balance and reform. I am likely to reach such conclusions as: "It's time to increase our charitable donations twenty-five percent; let me check it out with Lily"; or "It's time to cut back our donations"; or "I think I should decrease the number of my speaking engagements from forty to thirty in 1994 . . . or maybe even or twenty but raise my rates"; or "I believe the time has come where I ought to trash that old lecture on the arms race and develop a new one on balancing the budget."

I feel justified referring to these contemplative periods as prayer times because during them I am also trying to integrate God into the picture. "Hey, God," I am asking, "how does my life look to your eyes? Am I doing the best I can? Do you really want me to keep lecturing? Do you think I ought to take more time off? Devote more to the family? Is there anything new that you're calling me to, Lord?"

Together, Lily and I spend considerable time asking the same sorts of questions as we contemplate our intertwined lives and preserve the integrity of our marriage. The planning of this trip was an example. It is not a revolutionary journey for us. We have traveled much before. But it does represent a distinct change—a reformation, if you will—in our pattern of traveling. We had deliberately decided together that it was time for a more relaxed pace, to generally spend two nights in a hotel instead of one, to take three weeks instead of two, to cover less territory in greater depth.

And together with others in FCE we spend much similar, prayerful time in meetings. One way or another the focus is always integrity. Is this proposed action or change integral to our mission, in consonance with our vision, philosophy, and espoused values? The mission of FCE is to teach the rules of true community, which are the rules for authentic communication within and between groups. The two go hand in hand, and FCE must walk its talk. I've already commented how FCE has made every organizational mistake in the book but has somehow survived, I believe, because it has made these mistakes with integrity. They've been honest mistakes.

Authentic communication is not the norm in group settings: church, business, politics. Inauthenticity and the fudging of integrity are what's normal. Some therefore see FCE as a revolutionary organization in that we are attempting to radically alter the way people behave with each other in certain settings. But only in certain settings. We're not out to abolish rank or propriety, for instance; simply to teach people how to set such things aside when they're getting in the way. And not one of our teachings is new. They've been practiced by the Desert Fathers and ancient Sufi masters, by the early Quakers and, most recently, by Alcoholics Anonymous. They are not the norm simply because they are difficult, and seem revolutionary only because we are so accustomed to copping out in our organizational lives.

In a similar vein, I sometimes ponder whether FCE is a New Age organization. The paradoxical answer is, "yes and no." For instance, one of our stated values is "openness to new ideas"— a cherished value of the New Age Movement. Another stated value, however, is "valid data"— a distinctly "Old Age" guideline. It is accurate, I believe, to see FCE as an organization that is attempting to integrate the old age and the new age. Our task is reformation, not revolution.

But integrity, as I have pointed out, is never painless. Consequently, reformation is not an easy matter. Although far less likely to succeed, revolution often seems less complex and more exciting, even seductive. We have at FCE a distinct "marketing problem." Despite endless discussion of the matter, after eight years we've not yet been able, with integrity, to make our product of social reformation seem sexy.

Almost a decade ago I had the opportunity to

grapple with others over much the same issue in a very different setting. A consortium of "Christian" businesspeople gathered together about a dozen religious leaders for a three-day think tank to discuss "The Future of the Christian Church in the United States." For some reason they considered me a religious leader, and I was happy to rise to the bait. By the time we were halfway through we reached consensus that the Church had become hollow, even blasphemous, by virtue of the fact that it had lost touch with its own Christian theology. It had lost its integrity. We further agreed that genuine Christian theology was highly unpalatable to the vast majority of modern American churchgoers. The issue then became very focused in a clear question: How do you market a product to people who don't want it? Because the superficials had been stripped away to reveal the clarity of the issue, the energy became as high as I've ever seen at a meeting. We decided to creatively brainstorm possible answers. I was feeling extremely hopeful, and I believe the others were, too.

And it was exactly at that point that the meeting was totally derailed. Within an hour the energy had utterly evaporated, and the next morning we disbanded early with nothing having been accomplished. I had no idea at the time what happened. Nor did any of the other ever-so-educated and well-meaning theologians. Only in retrospect did I realize that the meeting had been single-handedly derailed by a man who was not a "religious leader" but one of the sponsoring businesspeople who had not previously spoken. He was brilliant. A more effective preacher than any of us, he not only had the gift of gab but a superb sense of humor. He told us one riotously funny (but irrelevant) story after another. He had sidetracked us through mere joking, and the rest of us were all unaware of what was happening.

Given the intensity of the dilemma posed by the question on the table, I doubt that we religious leaders would have come up with a satisfactory solution, no matter how critical the issue and genuine our motivation. What makes me sad, however, is that we never had the chance. One of the weaknesses of the New Age Movement is that it grossly underestimates the power of evil. The reason I tell this story is to make clear a most unpleasant factor in the equation. It is not solely a matter that reformation is difficult, that we will attempt to avoid the pain and paradoxical complexity of it all and that we inherently resist change. The fact of the matter is that there are also certain people of great persuasive power, like the man I described, who will brilliantly attempt to destroy reformation and integrity whenever it effectively starts to raise its pretty head. And we will never understand their motives.

But do not be discouraged. Yes, you will be beaten from time to time, but do not be seriously discouraged. A few dichotomies in life are clear. There is but one alternative to the combination of courage and integrity: despair. It is easy to despair. So many signs of decay and destruction surround us. Yet there are other signs, often subtle ones, that we take for granted. It is sad that most of the great stones have been destroyed. Consider, however, the strange fact that three stones representing four thousand years of history were not only preserved but mysteriously brought together to stand yet another thousand years later at the side of a country road in Scotland. Most people do care.

Our hearts uplifted by the Stones of Aberlemno, we proceeded on to the city of Brechin. While much larger than St. Davids in Wales, it is more of a town than a city save it has a sixteenth-century cathedral. The most remarkable thing about the cathedral is that it was constructed adjacent to a previously freestanding eleventh-century round tower—another example of integration. We'd seen round towers a dozen years before when we'd visited Ireland. There they had been built in the ninth century by Irish monks to protect themselves from Viking marauders. Although erected a millennium later, they are much smaller in diameter and simpler in construction than the brochs, and do not appear as if they'd been effective fortresses. Why they'd been imported to Scotland we do not know. It was not, however, a large importation, since there is only one other such tower in Scotland today (and none, as far as we know, in England or Wales). Regardless of their effectiveness, the round towers are quite tall and have a pleasant symmetry to them. The one at Brechin is actually a more impressive architectural structure than its relatively modern cathedral annex.

From the round tower we departed Brechin by

445

tiny lanes deep into the countryside to visit the Brown and White Caterthuns. These are two equal-sized and -shaped hilltops a mile apart. Straddling a gentle valley they served as Celtic fortifications slightly before the time of Christ. Crowned solely by multiple eroded circumferential earthworks, the Brown Caterthun is so named because these works are obscured by brown heather. It is believed to have been replaced by the White Caterthun that is topped by a huge circular rim of small white stones—obviously the better fortification and obviously white in the distance.

Huffing and puffing, we together climbed the Brown Caterthun. Except for a fine view, it was not a climactic experience. Lily rested while I alone climbed the White Caterthun. It also would not have been a climactic experience except that, as I stood on its peak two RAF fighter jets roared past me on each side of the Caterthun. It was the first time off a tarmac I'd ever been eye level with one of these awesome thunderbolts of death hurtling through the air at full throttle. It was sobering.

From the Caterthuns we ambled back to our nest at the Swallow Hotel. On the way we passed a few modest menhirs standing in the middle of fields of crops. The crops did not deserve trampling, and though they were to be our final megaliths, we left both crops and stones untouched.

It had been a sunny, gentle day, but the fighter jets had left me uneasy. So many monuments in Great Britain are monuments to war: the brochs, the caterthuns, the round towers, the castles—all constructed for defense. Even the cathedrals are filled with the mementos of battle: knights carved on sarcophagi in their full armor, plaques to slain soldiers, regimental banners. And where there was defense there was offense. The jet fighters were not defensive weapons even if their ultimate purpose might be to defend freedom. I have no reason to believe that the British are more warlike than other people—or that any modern society on earth is less militant than another. Was there ever a truly "peaceable kingdom"? Probably not. There are suggestions that the megalithic people had a communal society, and we have no evidence that they waged war. Still, they were human, and the most likely assumption is simply that their weapons have been lost in time.

Nonetheless, that is an assumption. It remains conceivable that before the advent of metal the megalithic people did somehow possess a deeply shared integrity that made them wondrously peaceful for a hundred generations. Their only surviving monuments are their enduring stones—menhirs, tombs, rows, and circles—and their henges in addition to one strange, man-made hill in southern England. We do not *know* the reasons for these monuments save the tombs. It is clear, however, what they were not used for. They plainly served no discernible military function.

CHAPTER XX

DESPAIR
FRIDAY. JUNE 19

It is less than two hours from Dundee to Edinburgh. There were many things we could have done to string the journey out—some more hill forts, for instance. But we imagined they would probably be like the Caterthuns of yesterday and not, therefore, exalting. Or we could have visited a few of the famed and ancient golf courses that my father so loved to play when he was in his still vigorous late seventies. It would have been a kind of posthumous homage to him two years after his death. But we continue to pay him homage in other ways, and there's not too much point in visiting golf courses unless you're up to playing the infernal things yourself. And we were not up to it. Lily is not passionate about golf, and while I am, my back was not feeling passionate. Besides, our travel-weariness had not yet been catered to.

So we sped ahead. Had there been some megaliths around in their extraordinary variety, that would have been an entirely different matter. But there weren't. The thread had run out. For this trip at least.

Consequently, by two o'clock in the afternoon we were already ensconced in our room at the

Caley in Edinburgh. Although Joan, at our request, had ordered us one of its cheaper rooms (without a view) the place dramatically lived up to its reputation. The doormen and concierge took charge of our faithful rental car, promising to personally remand it to Avis as if it were silly of us to even consider some other means of disposal. On its outside, fronting a park at the foot of the castle, the building is a massive master-piece of urban Victorian architecture—as faceted, complex, and thoroughly *solid* as the British Empire itself at the time of its construction. Inside all is muted, genteel, dignified. There is a characteristic, unmistakable *feel* to the great hotels of the world, and the Caley is one of them.

Other than perhaps the Caley itself, Edinburgh has one land-mark above all others: its castle. The castle is literally as well as figuratively above all else, standing upon a gigantic, several-hundred-feet-high outcropping of rock in the very center of the city, dramatically dominating it and its suburbs and holding sway even over the hills beyond. It is a very large castle. As far as we know, it was never conquered. It is the most impregnable fortress we'd ever seen.

Although the weather was predicted to be good again on the morrow, it seemed we ought to take advantage of this clear and sunny afternoon. So off we went to the castle, appreciating its impregnability all the more as we climbed the steps built into the side of the cliff, stopping for breath at each little landing, until we finally arrived at its grand entrance where for $6 apiece we purchased tickets that permitted us to climb a cobblestone road still higher among the many gray buildings and battlements. The views alone were worth the admission price. In addition, we saw a few other sights that mildly interested us: a hall full of swords and other military cutlery, a chapel where one could worship in the midst of war, a cannon of record-breaking size for its day, and the usual dungeons. We could have learned more had we hired a guide, but there wasn't much more that we wanted to learn, and we happen to have a congenital aversion to guides in any case. We generally prefer to explore on our own.

Besides, we had the input of a good friend who'd been to Edinburgh a few months before and *had* hired a guide. "When the tour was essentially over," he recounted, "the guide pretty much summed it all up, saying, 'I've been telling ye about this battle and that, and ye may ha'e been wondering who we've been fighting all these centuries. Who were our enemies? They were the same people who are still to this day our enemies: the bloody English!' "

Amusing? Yes, but only because it is black humor. Our friend, Bill, a corporate lawyer in a past life and a community builder in this one, told us the story precisely because he knew that we would appreciate the pathos of it—the pathetic sickness of warfare in general and repetitive warfare in particular.

Our minds flash back to the jet fighter planes that roared yesterday through the valleys on either side of the White Caterthun—and to those that roared overhead while we drove that valley on our first day in Wales and others that swept through other valleys I haven't boringly bothered to recount during this trip. The RAF is clearly practicing its mountain valley flying. Why? Despite their antipathy, the Scots, English, and Welsh have not actually been at war for over three hundred years. Could they be practicing to do their work in the valleys of Northern Ireland? Or Eire? Or is their concern for lands farther away from home? For the mountain valleys of Yugoslavia, perhaps, where subtle intercultural hatreds would seem no more deeply rooted than those between the Scotch and English but the people—currently, at least—more willing to kill? Or might they be preparing to go back to Iraq? Or maybe into the valleys of beautiful Sri Lanka, where Buddhists and Hindus have begun to slaughter one another? Or India, where Hindus and Muslims have long been at it? Or Afghanistan, where Muslims are at it with one another? Or South Africa, where the violence seems to escalate in response to the very smell of freedom?

What in God's name is wrong with us?

From childhood on when I exercised my calling to peacemaking, I assumed I was doing something noble. Had not Jesus said that we peacemakers were blessed? He also said that we'd be blessed if we were persecuted for righteousness's sake, so I was prepared to be persecuted. I was prepared to be hated. To be vilified. To be scorned. What I was not prepared for was to be blandly, politely, and consistently ignored.

It has taken me forty years. I am prepared now. For a long while I wondered if my words and deeds were not eloquent enough. I assumed that I would not be ignored if I could just do it better. But there are compatriots in this business of peacemaking who are braver and more eloquent than I, and over the decades I have watched them being placidly ignored with the same stunning efficacy. I continue to push, but I have finally wised-up. These days I expect us to be ignored. Still, it hurts as much as it ever did. Of course I would like to be loved. Far more, however, I would like to see peace loved. Only it isn't. As some have pointed out, the opposite of love may not be hate; it may be apathy. Hate, at least, is energetic.

But why? Why this oppressive apathy? I have never met a man who said he didn't want peace. Or a woman. Or heard a politician or a commentator. What's going on here? Are they all liars?

Yes and no. First, it must be said that there are evil people in the world. I mentioned one in yesterday's account, a man who derailed a meeting the moment there was a possibility it might have a constructive outcome. I would question the sanity of my analysis of that situation had I not had similar experiences before and since. The reality is that there are men and women who do not want peace, who like to see failure, who enjoy watching death and the destruction of humans and human endeavor. But there are few of them. They are in a very tiny minority, and they tend to hide themselves and their sadism under a sophisticated veneer of lies. The vast majority, however, are quite genuine in their desire for peace. Why then their apathy? It is because their desire for peace, of which they are conscious, is more or less equally counterbalanced by their strong, albeit usually subconscious desire for war.

The two finest books I know on the subject of war were written and published in the United States within the last thirty-five years. *Report from Iron Mountain* brilliantly addresses the multiple, large-scale, social reasons why governments are actually motivated to avoid too much peace. War provides them with opportunities to manipulate their economies, enhance societal cohesion, stimulate technological development, and achieve political control. *The Warriors* compellingly addresses the multiple, psychological reasons why individuals are equally drawn to war: excitement, comradeship, relief of sexual and aggressive inhibitions, desires for power, even aesthetic delight and spiritual transcendence. Its lengthiest chapter is entitled "The Enduring Appeals of Battle." Enduring is a key word. Such motives have endured from the beginning of human history through the time of the Men of Harlech until the present day.

Given the reality that there are occasionally evil governments as well as individuals, it would be naive to think that there are never valid geopolitical reasons for a nation to go to war. The far more common naïveté, however, is to think that war or peace are solely dictated by geopolitical concerns. What both books make clear on their different levels is that war is a profoundly overdetermined phenomenon.

This is not to mean there is no possibility of

human reformation in the direction of greater peacefulness. To the contrary, the two books I mentioned are so important because they provide the kind of enlightenment that is a prerequisite for reformation. Since almost all people at least profess peace, however, one would think such enlightening books would be popular and widely read. The fact is that they are both usually out of print and almost unobtainable. I am sick at heart and could easily despair.

In recent years, looking at my society, I believe I have reasons even greater than war for despair. The Civil Rights Movement at least partially succeeded, yet we have descended into a social psychology of entitlement. Our inner cities have become war zones. A permanent underclass seems to have developed. Crime escalates unabated. The fastest-growing profession is that of private security guards. Women, recently liberated to work outside the home, now have to do so for economic survival. The few rich become richer while the poor grow ever poorer. And when I speak about the criminality of our unbalanced federal budget I encounter exactly the same kind of apathy I used to find when I spoke about the arms race. Communism has gone down the tubes, but there are days when it looks like democracy will shortly follow suit.

So why don't Lily and I just say, "Screw it. Screw society. Since we can't beat 'em, let's join 'em in looking out solely for ourselves?" There are moments when this is tempting, and they are all the more frequent these days. For the fact of the matter is that we ourselves aren't doing too well either. Our energy is fading rapidly. I quoted Gerard Manley Hopkins as concluding that there's no way to keep beauty from vanishing away and that "wisdom is early to despair." That's old hat for us. Our physical beauty isn't vanishing; it has already vanished, and we're well into the second, even gloomier part of his poem, which proceeds to advise:

> Be beginning; since, no, nothing can be done
> To keep at bay
> Age and age's evils—hoar hair,
> Ruck and wrinkle, drooping, dying, death's worst,
>   winding sheets,
> tombs and worms, and tumbling to decay;
> So be beginning, be beginning to despair.
> Oh, there's none—no, no, no, there's none:
> Be beginning to despair, to despair,
> Despair, despair, despair, despair.

But that's not all. Obvious physical dying and the prospect of death may be the least of it. The death of dreams probably preoccupies us the more. The dream of a close family life has been eroded as our children have either kept their distance or totally shut us out. There are no new ideas anymore to inflame us. It seems that most of the books we read we've read before. We've outgrown all our mentors and have no heroes left. Many people have let us down, and those who struggle with us still are, like ourselves, incurably imperfect. Both of us thoroughly empathize with Alexander Pushkin, when he wrote, generations ago:

I have outlasted all desire,
My dreams and I have grown apart;
My grief alone is left entire,
The gleanings of an empty heart.
The storms of ruthless dispensation
Have struck my flowery garland numb—
I live in lonely desolationAnd wonder when my
    end will come.

So why don't we despair, except very briefly and occasionally? The answer, naturally, is over-determined.

A part of it may be temperament, which has been defined as the biological part of the personality. I sometimes think I have been blessed with a relatively sunny disposition. But even if that's so, it's a small part. More clear than my sunny disposition is Lily's biologically gloomy one, yet we've both somehow managed thus far to come out on the other side of despair.

The biggest piece of the puzzle, I believe, was provided by the great psychologist Erik Erikson, who delineated better than anyone else the stages of psychospiritual development. His genius in this regard was to phrase these stages in terms of "crises" or critical decision points in the human life cycle. Writing of childhood crises, he imaginatively echoed Freud. Moving into adulthood, however, he broke entirely new ground, and nowhere was he more brilliant than when he described the final crisis of old age as "Integrity vs. Despair." It is not simply artifice that yesterday's chapter was on integration and today's on despair. As our journey moves us into old age,

these issues gradually and naturally sift themselves out and rise to the surface toward the end.

Lily and I are faced, therefore, at this point in
our lives, with a choice between integrity and
despair. A major factor preventing us from slipping into despair has been our past decade of
experience with community building. Perhaps
the most common group dynamic in a community-building workshop is the conflict between
light and darkness. Realizing after a while that
genuine community requires the "confession of
brokenness," certain members of the group will
begin to speak of their suffering: the abuse they
received as children, their lost dreams, their
terrors and illnesses, their failures at business and
at marriage and child rearing. After a period of
this other members of the group will protest in
rebellion. "Why do we have to talk about all this
sad stuff? I happen to be very happy in my life,
and I think we need to restrict ourselves to the
positive and uplifting." This rebellion is both
healthy and unhealthy. It is unhealthy because it
is motivated in part by pain avoidance and a lack
of compassion. The rebels often simply do not
want to bear the pain of truly hearing and
digesting the pain of their fellow human beings.
Their protest is healthy, however, insofar as it
challenges an incipient group norm that community building should be a kind of "suffering
sweepstakes" in which everyone must be in active
agony in order to join.

At this point an either/or struggle is engaged
between those who claim they have every right
to their suffering and those who claim every right

to their contentment. Usually this important struggle takes no more than an hour. It is resolved when each side agrees that the other is, in part, correct. It is not healthy, they realize, to view the world through rose-colored glasses, nor is it healthy to look at everything with gray-tinted lenses. It is a both/and resolution. Everyone realizes he or she—or the group—needs spectacles of both cheerfulness and gloom for integrity. Shortly after this resolution the group usually reaches community and then, hardly realizing it, the sad will be speaking of their joy and the happy of their grief.

Community building is not a specifically Christian process. But G. K. Chesterton touched upon the dynamic a century or so ago when he explained, "The purpose of Christianity is to comfort the afflicted *and* afflict the comfortable."

A major reason, then, that Lily and I do not much despair is that our dedication to integrity compels us to also look on the bright side of things. In the midst of decay there *are* the signs of new life. That humanity is enamored with war is an atrocity, but after almost fifty years of impotence the United Nations does seem to be coming alive. Although nothing has been done yet to combat it, deficit spending is for the first time a matter of more or less genuine public debate. It may be superficial and only at the level of the upper middle class, but at least there blacks and whites have become more integrated. Some of my books may not be as widely read as I would like, yet they remain on the backlist and do not fall out of print. The work of FCE has not received the attention it deserves, but there are enough organizations and committed individuals in an otherwise apathetic world to keep that work going. And while our children keep their distance from us, it is probably necessary for their sakes that they do so, and we rejoice at how well they have managed to independently establish themselves in this demanding life.

Although it may lead us to truths that are paradoxical, it seems to me that reason dictates we should regard the whole picture. It is perfectly reasonable to look at both the dark and the light sides of things. Unremitting despair, as well as continual elation, are, in fact, unreasonable. So it is old-fashioned reason more than anything else that keeps us from falling for long into the slough of despondency.

But faith also keeps us going. My faith is overtly Christian. Lily, with her gift for secrecy, is much less open about it; she is what I have come to call a closet Christian. In either case our faith did not come easily to us. As a child I was lukewarmly exposed to Christianity. Lily was exposed to it with a vengeance. Neither of us bought it at the time. Only after we had passed the midpoint of our lives did it begin to make sense to us, and then it was not a straw that we grasped in desperation. Rather it was an understanding that we were reluctantly dragged to by years of accumulated experience.

Some of that experience had to do with evil. Not with the so-called natural evil of fire and earthquake, plague and famine, death and accident. For some reason we have been spared much of this. Our lives have been remarkably free of tragedy. But we have taken note of human evil, including that of the demonic, and have been forced to consider alternative viewpoints or theologies in its regard.

The most common is the theology of denial. It can take many forms, but they all have in common the belief that there is no such thing as human evil. Its most ancient form is the theology of Hinduism and Buddhism (far predating that of Christianity) where both good and evil are simply regarded as illusionary concepts of an "unawakened" human mind. Its most modern form is in New Age theology, where goodness is celebrated but belief in human evil is decried as "negativity." In it the three monkeys—see no evil, hear no evil, speak no evil—are exalted to guruhood. To even think evil is to create it, many New Agers hold, and if we can simply "affirm" everyone in their innate goodness there will immediately be an end to all human strife.

More sophisticated and subtle is the prevailing "theology" of psychotherapy, which holds that there is goodness and badness in all of us, but the badness is not evil; it is wholly explainable "psychopathology" resulting from defenses we have erected to deal with past traumatic experiences. Although it takes a great deal of time and effort, such badness or psychopathology can be cured through psychotherapy, and most of it could be prevented by sweeping social programs that would minimize childhood and other trauma. Many liberal Christians and Jews and

Muslims concur with this theology, particularly when they are allowed to equate psychopathology with sin and past trauma with "original sin."

It is no accident that this theology of the denial of evil is the most common. Having many forms, it allows for a great deal of theological latitude in outlook. People of all religious persuasions can embrace it, as well as agnostics and atheists. It is a hopeful theology. In each of its forms it provides us a way out of the dilemma of evil through enlightenment, the power of positive thinking, or the combined exercise of psycho-therapy, psychobiology, and humane social action. Finally, it is immensely appealing by virtue of its reasonableness—and this is what has been most seductive about it for me. There are great many reasons to believe in it. Good and evil more often than not are mere narcissistic, hypothetical constructs of the mind and often illogical names for various things in our life that we happen to like or dislike at the time. How many times have I looked back on something I'd thought was evil and recognized it to be "a blessing in disguise"? Or, even more discon-certingly, have I striven for some result I'd thought was good only to see it backfire in the larger scheme of things? We do indeed, as New Agers hold, frequently create evil by our condem-nation and quickness to rush to judgment in doing so. People *are* more likely to respond posi-tively to affirmation than condemnation. And psychotherapy does heal people who want to be healed. And drugs do control destructiveness in people who are willing to take them in order to stop being destructive. And social programs like Head Start of FCE do work and do prevent illness from developing in society.

There is but one problem with this theology, and that is that it doesn't take into account a few rather aberrant human phenomena. It doesn't quite integrate the whole picture. It doesn't adequately define those few people who like to destroy goodness not out of explainable psychopathology or biological compulsion but because of their pure choice to destroy—people who not only don't want psychotherapy but can eat psychotherapists for breakfast whenever they are of a mind. It does not account for that even smaller number who are possessed by demons, in whom the demonic will stupidly reveal itself upon rare occasion. When this happens, all who are present will know the reality of evil because they have seen the quantum leap between it and ordinary, explainable human sin. And it doesn't tell us when to stop affirming the Hitlers of the world (and their many followers) but instead combat them with every means at our disposal, including weapons of death, lest all humanity in the world be destroyed.

But at least it is not a theology of despair.

Of the three others, two are theologies of despair. Since it is so seemingly difficult for the human mind to embrace paradox, including the paradox of human evil, one of them naturally is the opposite of the denial of evil: It is the denial of human goodness. Seldom is it stated out loud, even by militant atheists. It holds that we humans are, in essence, evil, and that human goodness is, in fact, an illusion. In its view, altruistic behavior is the manifestation of sickness and self-delusion. Reality is that we "are evil from the day of our conception." It is purely a dog eat dog world, and anyone who doesn't act accordingly is stupidly naive and deserves the fruits of his blindness. The problem with this theology, like that of the denial of evil, is that it fails to take into account all the facts. The fact is that the ordinary human is quite courageous in his or her own way, and that there are a surprising number of human beings whose altruistic behavior is not explainable in terms of psychological defense systems. The mystery of human goodness is even greater than that of human evil, and the problem of a theology of evil is that most of us behave far better than it would predict.

Another theology recognizes the reality of both good and evil, suggesting that they are in equal balance. The world is ruled by the two great gods of Darkness and Light, of Destruction and Creation, and all history is the working out of the ongoing, neverending struggle between them. This theology of dualism flowered in the Persian religion of Zoroastrianism and was adopted by many early Christians. Eventually, within Christianity it became known as the heresy of Manichaeanism, and was vigorously suppressed. I have labeled it a theology of despair because it offers no possibility for real evolution or improvement or progress; the darkness of the world may take different forms at different times, but it will always be as strong as it is today. The Truth and the Lie are coequal for eternity. Moreover, I have seen this theology lead to frank mathematical nihilism. Since the "positivity" and "negativity" of the world are equal, put them together and it is like adding plus one to minus one—you end up with zero. The result is nothing, nada, zip, ha ha; there is no meaning, so anything goes.

Neither of these theologies are entirely unreasonable. It is not difficult—particularly looking at the institutional corruption prevailing in government, church, and business—to conclude that evil is more real than goodness. Indeed, St. Paul referred to the devil as being "the ruler of this world," and many Christians since have simply given up on this lifetime. Nor is it difficult to think of the combat between good and evil as going nowhere. Nothing seems to happen. The Scots and English have always been enemies and it is easy to despair of it ever being any different.

Finally, there is a most *unreasonable* theology. While it, too, acknowledges the reality of both good and evil, it does not consider them coequal. Not only does it hold the God of Light to be more powerful than Satan, the Prince of Darkness, it makes the outrageous claim that human evil has been defeated. This is the Christian theology of redemption. Specifically, it posits that the devil was forever defeated the moment Christ was killed on the cross. Through that act of dying for us, Jesus redeemed humanity for eternity. The victory was complete. The war is over. Oh, yes, there are still a number of evil people around, and the forces of goodness are still engaged in battle with them, but it is in the nature of a simple mop-up operation. Evil people are like those

Japanese soldiers hiding out for years in the jungles of the Philippines because they could not believe that Japan had lost the war. Mind you, the combat can still be bloody. Good people are still getting killed, and there are days when we are so caught up in the struggle that the war seems as hot as ever. But that's just an illusion. The ultimate victory has been won.

Unreasonable though it is, this has come to be my *wary* faith. I am wary about it mostly because, like any doctrine, it can be misused. It *is* misused. Millions of Christians smugly sit around believing that they don't have to do anything because they've been redeemed, and they thereby contribute to that public apathy that is so poisonous.

With that very large caveat, I ascribe to this strange theology in part because it explains something that none of the others can account for. They do not explain why the world should gradually be getting better when there are in fact some evil folks yet wandering about. Many would find it highly arguable that the world is getting better, even by fits and starts. Be that as it may, the broader the historical perspective I take, the more hopeful little pieces of data I find. All this started, for instance, when I spoke of how close I can come to despair over humanity's propensity for war. Many, regarding our modern technology of mass destruction, believe war has actually become worse. Nonetheless, these days it is an illegal exception to kill or torture prisoners of war. A thousand years ago it was a common but unsanctioned practice. Two thousand years ago it was a ritual norm to disembowel them.

I also ascribe to this unreasonable theology precisely because of its unreasonableness. Moses, Buddha, Lao-Tse, Muhammad, were all reasonable men, wise and sensible. Jesus, too, was wise, but he was also *weird*. I do not know how to explain him in purely human terms. It is, of course, a tenet of Christian doctrine that Jesus was paradoxically both human and divine—and not fifty percent one and fifty percent the other, but somehow "fully human *and* fully divine." As a scientist in the Age of Reason, I doubt that I would take much stock in this divinity business if I could explain him away otherwise. But I can't. Parts of the Gospels are PR. Most of them, however, reek of authenticity. No one could have made up the man described in them. Something very unreasonable happened in the area of Palestine almost two thousand years ago—so unreasonable as to compel me to suspect that God really did "come down to live and die as one of us." And that this was redemptive if for no other reason than the fact that ever since there have been a substantial number of reasonable people who can't quite get Jesus—and what he said and stood for—out of their craw. Indeed, it is all so unreasonable that it is clear to me that such people are never going to die out in the world. The Christian church, as we knew it, may fade, but we're stuck with its namesake.

Here I've been speaking of faith as an explanation. Earlier I spoke of it as a gift. It finally needs to be looked upon as a choice. As William Ralph Inge put it, "Faith is the choice of the nobler alternative."

We have a choice of faith—or theology. As a psychotherapist I have had the wondrous opportunity of witnessing a few people make a deliberate choice to switch their allegiance from a theology of despair to one of hope. I have sadly also had the experience of seeing people choose to cling to a theology of despair not because it was the more realistic but because it was the more comfortable. But why? Why would someone choose to despair? How can despair be comfortable?

There are two sets of reasons. One I have some very personal familiarity with. It will be recalled that I went through a two-year period of indolent depression as I approached the age of fifty—when I was going through the Dark Night of the Senses and dealing with midlife issues. In the midst of that period I was accosted by "a spirit of Mirth" that I tried for a while to resist. The primary reason for my resistance was simply that I'd become accustomed to gloom. Wear dark glasses for a year, and if you take them off the normal light will hurt your eyes. Quite likely you will want to put your sunglasses right back on. It will be the darkness that seems normal, comfortable, like an old shoe, utterly reasonable and even friendly. Patients who respond to antidepressants will frequently stop taking their pills as soon as the medication starts to work. Their depression has become their friend.

Depression may be looked upon as the

emotional side of despair. Cynicism is its intellectual side. It is possible to have one without the other. Many depressed people are not cynics and many cynics are not depressed. Cynics who despair of any human spiritual progress and lack faith in anything other than narrow self-interest are often at least as vigorous as the rest of us and usually very pleased with themselves. Although likely to become miserable in the final days of their old age, until that time they are prone to think of themselves as happy. They do not, however, look very deeply at their supposed happiness.

Cynicism is even more common than depression and far more deadly to society. It is so common and so deadly because it is self-justifying. In the cynic's own mind anything is expectable if not justifiable: ruthless competition, greed, stinginess and miserliness, manipulation, dishonesty when you can get away with it, war, and even torture. And, above all else, apathy. Why invest yourself in the betterment of society when you know it will be a fruitless endeavor? Why invest yourself in charity or altruism when you believe these to be illusions? Invest yourself only in the stock market; otherwise, keep your cool and stay detached. Fortunately, I have not been able to pull off such a lifestyle. I have within me a distinct streak of self-centeredness, but somehow I have also been gifted by a counterbalancing streak of compassion that will not allow me to be a cynic.

Consequently, my books are comedy as opposed to tragedy. Most simply defined, comedy is that which has a happy ending and tragedy that with an unhappy one. If all authors were busily engaged in writing comedy, I am sure I would want to try my hand at tragedy in the interest of reality. There is a great deal of tragedy around, and I do not believe it should be overlooked. Given the fact that plenty of tragedy is published, however, I see no point in adding to the misery of the world. My nonfiction is, I believe, an integration of realism and hope. As for my one novel, by its conclusion three of its major characters have come to no good, but at least five others have grown for the better.

I have not been surprised that these books have received some bad reviews. The only thing that has astonished me has been the vitriolic intensity of a couple of them. The critics in these cases expressed their cynicism with great vigor. One of these reviews was particularly revealing.

It was a review of *The Different Drum* together with a book by Konrad Lorenz. It began, as best I can remember, by stating, "If there's anything worse than a 'save the world' book, it's two of them published in the same season." Speaking of my volume in particular, the review concluded, "If a book as muddled and pretentious as this can become a best-seller, then the world really does need saving." The most telling part of the piece, however, came in its middle when the critic labeled Lorenz and me as "tourists at the abyss."

It was an intriguing observation that had the ring of truth. But what did the man mean by "abyss"? I have used the word for chasm of death into which one must leap without the certainty that there will be another side to land upon. If that was the abyss he meant, implied was his certainty that there is no other side: There is only death. Death without hope and despair are identical twins. In parts of Calcutta and New York and other cities, the Spirit of Death prowls the streets, and it is indistinguishable from the prevailing utter despair pervading these places. I suspect what the author of the review meant by the abyss was not only the pit of death but also that of evil and despair.

And he was correct—at least about me. I have visited that abyss and peered into it with a mixture of trepidation and curiosity. I have occasionally descended just a few of the many steps into its depths, but mostly I have stayed on top of the edge as a gawking, temporary visitor and, in no way, a permanent resident. I have remained relatively untouched.

I had two reactions to the reviewer's penetrating comment. One was unease about myself. Somebody else once called me a "holy innocent." I am uncertain whether that was an accurate appellation, but I am sure this reviewer would concur I was an innocent—a man not in the know. Was I harmfully ignorant, I wondered, naive to a fault? I still wonder sometimes.

But my predominant reaction was a mixture of sadness, pity, and compassion for the reviewer. He would not have discerned me so accurately as a tourist at the abyss were he not himself a permanent resident. What must it be like to reside at the bottom of the pit of despair and look up to see tourists not living with you but gawking at you from a distance? I could understand the man's fury. Moreover, the book in question was something of a lifeline, a way out of the abyss, a rope ladder of sorts that I had flung down into it. The man had a choice. He either had to take it and start climbing or disdain it. I was reminded of C. S. Lewis's vision of Hell as a place where the gates are wide open. In this view (with which I agree) God does not put souls in Hell; they can walk right out at any time, but they are in it because they choose not to do so. My point here is not to pass judgment on somebody who once criticized me but to be empathetic. Yet it backfires. Watching me unsheath my tourist's camera and sheath it again, the man is bound to find such empathy as something that is all the more infuriating in its seeming condescension.

The choice not to despair is the choice for integrity. More than anything, I suspect, it is a choice not to give into fear.

There are many people who are not frankly evil but are almost compulsive unconscious liars. They don't speak in paradox; just out of both sides of their mouths. They are Christians one minute, crooks the next.

I believe they lie for the same reason as little children: They are afraid to admit responsibility for their choices and behavior. The compartmentalized, unintegrated, Sunday-morning Christian is afraid to stand up for his theology. He is comfortable with his company's policy of dumping toxic wastes in the local stream because he is so uncomfortable, so fearful, of losing his job. Or, if he is the policymaker himself, so fearful of losing profits. Or so fearful of losing anything.

I could not live my life at such a level of sheer terror. When I watch these men and women they seem to me to be constantly squirming, moving this way to cover up that and then wriggling sideways to cover up the cover-up. Were I in their shoes I would long ago not only have had high blood pressure but apoplexy.

Yet physically these people appear to be at least as healthy as I. This used to puzzle me until I realized I might have just as much fear as they, only I choose not to give into it. Perhaps giving into fear is less stressful than fighting against it. Certainly fighting against fear is what we mean by courage. Courage is not the absence of fear but the capacity to go ahead in the very direction of which you're afraid. And the persistent exercise of courage may wear us down.

As I've made clear, I'm for the most part a physical coward. But when, where, and why did I choose to fight against my fear and not lie? I don't know. I can't remember. Until this very day I'm conscious of temptations to lie, but I can't remember when I first began resisting them.

In one of my lectures I define salvation as "an ongoing process of becoming increasingly conscious." I emphasize it as an ongoing process because I see peril in our traditional vision of it as a onetime thing. Recently a woman in my audience, who was probably the better theologian, rebutted me. "I disagree," she said. "Salvation is a single moment—in your terms the moment one decides for consciousness. The ongoing exercise of that decision is the *process* of sanctification." If she is correct, then that time I can't remember when I first—by grace—resisted the temptation to lie was my salvation, and ever since I've been on a journey of sanctification.

I don't feel particularly sanctified, much less complacent. I am very uneasy about the health of the human race. Some despairing days it does seem to me that out of our deceitful greed and petty tribal pride we're consigning civilization to oblivion. Nonetheless, the reality is that there are people around in increasing numbers who have transcended traditional local culture . . . people by the hundreds of thousands fighting against their fear and developing honesty into a habit . . . people who come to community building and learn how to appreciate—yea, celebrate—their differences. So there are other days when I think it quite possible that the Scots will not always be hating "the bloody English." Particularly those days when I stop to remember that the human race, unreasonably but continually, seems to receive a good bit of outside help.

CHAPTER XXI

CONCLUSION(S)
SATURDAY, JUNE 20

I'd been hoping my back would hold up until we got to Edinburgh, and so it did. This morning it gave out while I was doing my exercises. Number six in my ritual of nine is sit-ups, where I reach for my toes or beyond. Now that our rental car had been handed in and the driving was done, I'd thought it was time things should start to improve. I also thought I'd help them along by doing the exercises with extra vigor. On the third sit-up I really stretched to grab the soles of my feet, and something snapped. It was to be my last sit-up for some weeks.

The problem would prove not to be serious. There was no leg pain. Whatever I'd done, it hadn't for the moment affected any of the nerve roots. But I had plenty of muscle spasms in the back itself. Fortunately, I also had plenty of codeine and Percodan for just such an emergency.

Codeine and Percodan, like all the other major pain relievers, are morphine derivatives. Past a certain point, pain becomes a vicious cycle and begins to feed upon itself. Enough tissue irritation and you get painful muscle spasms, spasms that still further increase the irritation to cause more pain and spasm. The major pain killers interrupt this cycle. Without them there have been many occasions when I think I would have gone mad. Pain itself can be a gift, serving as a signal that something is wrong. But as with any blessing, too much of it becomes a curse. Intractable physical pain is a curse indeed. There is nothing redemptive about it, and morphine properly needs to be looked upon as one of God's greatest gifts to humanity.

Thanks to this gift, I was eventually able to hobble with Lily along a few of Edinburgh's streets. The city was not doing well. Although not as depressed as Glasgow, every third building seemed to have a FOR RENT sign. We hope that things will soon be better for the cities of this beautiful land.

We visited the one museum that had a megalithic people. Then we took a taxi to the Museum of Childhood. There we had a touching moment when Lily spied a nineteenth-century infant feeding bottle, and recalled it was the kind she'd been fed with during the mid-1930s in Singapore. After this brief foray, we taxied back to the Caley for long naps and to rest my back.

We dinner in the Caley's Pompadour Room. From the name we had expected it to be large and ornate. In actuality it was surprisingly small and the decor elegantly simple. Through its huge windows we could view the castle in the evening's light. The other guests were genteel. The service was artful and the food superb, with all the time needed to savor it well. Admittedly, I was mellowed out on Percodan, but Lily agreed it was the pleasantest experience of fine dining we'd ever had—and probably ever would have in our years ahead. There was something magical about it coming as such a fitting conclusion to a magical trip.

There were some other conclusions as well on this concluding day.

Facing a six-hour train ride to London the next day and an eight-hour flight to New York on the one following, along with assorted drives, loading and unloading of luggage, and customs, I was worried how well we'd handle it with my pain. I was not cursing my back; I was cursing myself. I'd known my back was on the verge of going out, and had I given it the rest it needed it would probably have healed itself. I could clearly remember at the beginning of my third sit-up that morning, thinking that the first two had been inadequate, saying to myself, "Come on, Scotty, you can reach farther than that," as if I could make my back well by true grit. Instead, I hurt it the more by my determination. It was not the first time I had hurt myself through such self-will, and I was forced to conclude that determination in excess can be harmful.

It was not a new conclusion. Nine years before I was quite accustomed to lecturing all day long in one city and getting on a plane that evening to lecture all the next day in another. That was when I contracted pneumonia. Treating myself, I continued working, certain my little antibiotics would take care of it. Only, as I've recounted, I damn near died. I had a slow and thoughtful

476

recovery during which I concluded seriously for the first time in my life that I needed to set some limits on myself and my determination. I was no longer a total iron man.

Even then it was not a new conclusion. For over two years I'd been leading groups into "community." Several times I'd had the experience that my leadership was failing. I'd redouble my efforts, and redouble them again. Finally I had to accept defeat. There was nothing more I could do and, certain there was no way the group could ever achieve my goal, I hopelessly gave up. Each time that happened the group did in fact come into community within the hour. It dawned on me this timing might not be accidental. Indeed, I would soon be teaching it as a principle, instructing new leaders that at certain times it would be necessary for them to surrender their leadership to God in order for their work to succeed. But it is not an easy instruction.

Such surrender of determination often feels like dying—particularly when one is strong-willed, as a good leader must be. I've identified a strong will as one of the greatest blessings that can be bestowed upon a human but also noted how too much of any blessing can become a curse. Some lessons need to be relearned over and over again, and I am particularly forgetful of those that pertain to my will. How many more times, I wonder, shall I need to conclude yet once again that I have been self-destructively slow to surrender?

★   ★   ★

On this day our wills are torn. We do want to return to the United States. Although my lecturing is no longer a turn-on for me, it is highly profitable. There is more writing to which I feel called. Our work together with FCE is occasionally a burden, but on the whole, it is the single most exciting endeavor we could imagine being engaged in. We want to see our friends who work with us. We want to see our children and catch up on our infant grandchild. Our sprawling house, nestled in the New England wooded hills, is a place of grace and beauty.

A bit travel worn, we are not, however, homesick, and we must acknowledge that there is also a substantial part of us that does *not* want to return home, a part that would like to stay in Scotland for a while yet. We'd like to see Loch Lomond in the sunshine and more of the area around Aberdeen. We wonder what's to the north of Inverness. Above all, we'd like to keep wandering along the tiny lanes in search of more stones.

Three conclusions are obvious.

One is that, God willing, we shall return to Scotland.

A second, God willing, is that we shall hunt for more stones, not only in Scotland but elsewhere. The addict, always terrified that he will run out, is quick to pick up on potential new sources of supply. Develop a new passion and it will not take you long to learn more ways for its fulfillment. We are not scholars, yet in this brief time—by reading books, speaking with other fanatics, and keeping our ears open to rumors—we know there are many more stones to find. The Ring of Brodgar and other monuments in the Orkneys and Shetlands, islands of Scotland to the east and even more northern and barren than the Outer Hebrides. Brittany, the northwestern part of France, where it is reputed that there are menhirs dwarfing any to be found in Great Britain. As well as a little place called Carnac, where the megalithic people erected thousands of stones in strange rows within an area of a few square miles. We also hear mention of stones in Portugal and the Pyrenees. Even in Poland. And a whole village in England itself, Avebury, that resides within a monumental stone circle. Clearly, our passion has not been exhausted.

A third conclusion is that, God willing, we shall take more long and leisurely vacation trips abroad. Previously we had traipsed out of the United States once every two years on the average. This is not to be sneezed at. Relatively speaking, we are well-traveled people. But before now these trips were a bit rushed, always with an eye on budget and business, covering the maximum amount of territory in the shortest reasonable time. Had we done that this trip there would have been no space for us to stumble on the mystery of the stones. Sooner or later we shall probably run out of stones, but if we make more leisurely journeys what other new mysteries and passions might we discover?

This conclusion is perfectly practical, but only because we now have the money to make it so. Time is money and money is time, they say. Since it looks like the money will continue to come in for a while at least, what this means, among other things, is that we do not *have* to work so hard. This trip has been enormous fun and, given that our children are grown, the truth is that we can continue to have such fun.

So we are being nudged toward yet a more radical conclusion: retirement. A few years ago it would have been unthinkable. Not only were our children financially dependent upon us but so was FCE. Neither is now the case. Oh, they both could still use some monetary help, but it is no longer a life-or-death matter. In addition, my father left us a modest inheritance above and beyond what he gave us in earlier years. We are actually sitting rather pretty. So why not retire? And why should retirement be such a radical conclusion?

Back in the chapter on aging, I mentioned that one of the problems of growing old is the lack of empathy we are likely to receive from the youthful as we grow decrepit. Nowhere is this lack more obvious than in relation to the issue of retirement. The young cannot understand why it is a big deal. The issue of death has much more reality for them. They know they can be killed crossing the street. They know of people in their thirties who have died from AIDS, and even from heart attacks or cancer. Death already lurks at the edge of their consciousness. But what thirty-five-year-old still beginning the climb up the corporate ladder gives the slightest thought to retirement— beyond following the accountant's advice, if they're lucky, to stash a few tax-deferred dollars into some vague thing called a pension plan? Death may be just around the corner, but retirement's decades away, out of sight and mind.

Yet no issue can be so fraught with significance.

Old Merlin comes back to mind. It will be recalled that in the huge body of Arthurian legend there are four different major versions of his last years. One is that he fell into dotage and in thrall to a seductive, wicked young woman who sapped him of whatever wits and energy he had left. Another holds that he left society somewhat in the lurch by running off with a young woman, but she was a good person and they had a ball together for his remaining time. A third version has it that he retired ever so responsibly after first assuring that the realm was in the best shape and no longer needed his services. A woman apparently had nothing to do with the matter. The final version is that Merlin never did retire; he worked until the very end and gave hints that he would return from the grave if he was truly needed again.

What an extraordinarily rich body of myth, come to think of it! Not one, not two, not three, but four different and competing versions of a man's disengagement from "the affairs of men"! Why? Why this richness were not this issue of retirement one of the biggest deals in the human life cycle? But what's the issue at stake?

It is the issue of power. And power is addictive. It is the powerful we most look up to in our society: the wealthy, the famous, the "shakers and movers," the magnates of industry. Since power confers status, nothing can be more enhancing of self-esteem. No matter how badly

481

things might be going for me at any given moment, as long as I still have power I can continue to console myself by thinking: "But look at how *potent* I am, how important and needed and effective."

While many get hooked on power for its own sake, the issue can be even deeper than that of self-enhancement. There is also the power to serve. For instance, each year I receive hundreds of unsolicited manuscripts requesting my assistance one way or another in getting them published. Because it is unpleasant to reject requests, and because almost all of them are outside my areas of interest or seriously lacking in quality, it is a chore to wade through them—even though my wading is superficial and our staff must write the actual rejection letters. It is tempting to prepare a simple form letter: "We are sorry but Dr. Peck no longer reviews manuscripts of any kind." But I haven't done this yet. The reason is that one manuscript out of a hundred is surprisingly worthy, and with relatively minor effort I am able to be of major assistance to its author in finding an agent or publisher. There is little glory in this, but it is deeply satisfying to me, because I have been able to be of some service.

So it is that in a certain version of the myth, Merlin turns his back not only on the trappings of power but also the call to service. Indeed, this is why he may come across as a stupid or self-centered bad guy: He has rejected the needs of society; he has let people down.

Since power in all its varieties can be so

alluring, it is no wonder that most people cling to it for all it is worth and as long as they can— usually until it is finally wrested away from them by a palace coup, a changing of the guard, a disgrace, a debilitating illness, death, or that relatively recent invention of society, "mandatory retirement." But mandatory retirement is not truly retirement. Merlin's issue and mine is *voluntary* retirement—that is, the relinquishment of power by choice at a time when we can still hold onto it and before we are compelled by external circumstance to hand over the reins. That's what's at stake here.

But why not retire? There are many reasons, all psychological. For one, Lily is just coming into her own as far as the wielding of power is concerned. She has for many years, to a considerable extent, managed me and the children and our home. Now she is managing people outside the home—more and more of them—and she is starting to develop a taste for it. As well she should, because she is very good at it. Despite the terrible burdens of power, she's not yet tired of it. And she's needed. At the moment, the consideration of retirement does not mean our retirement. It primarily means my own. There may be some subtle problems to my retiring at the same time as she is expanding her sphere of influence. But such problems are hardly insoluble. Besides, they are the kind of grist for the mill of our marriage that keeps its wheels turning in interesting ways.

A greater problem is my own ambivalence about power. I love it and hate it. The reasons may not be the usual ones, but they are simple. Power demands exertion, particularly at those moments when the exercise of power is the most critical. I am tired. I do not feel up to much exertion anymore. And if I have to exert myself these days I'd rather do it on my own schedule than that of the externally dictated moment of history. Yet I would still like to be able to be responsive to history. I've had enough visible power to no longer need any more for self-glorification, but if people really *need* me, how can I not respond? T. S. Eliot, that wonderful mentor I never met, once described middle age as "when they keep asking you to do more and more, and you're not yet decrepit enough to turn them down." I do still want to be of service. Indeed, upon occasion I will seek out a hidden way or two to serve. But most of the time when I am asked to serve I do not think that I am really needed; I suspect a younger more energetic person is around who could do it better—someone who enjoys all the meetings more than I. But am I yet ready to declare myself totally decrepit? Maybe yes and maybe no.

What I would like, you see, is some sort of semiretirement. I'm feeling ready to gradually phase out. But that's not so easily done. It requires exquisite balance. I'm not sure I want to be totally phased out, but I'm also no longer eager to stay in the saddle, and in between the two there's a sort of fence-straddling that itself takes a good deal of energy to maintain.

Be that as it may, since we probably have enough money, a decision to retire still might not seem so radical. But then there is my father's ghost to contend with. A famous lawyer, he worked full-time until his firm's mandatory retirement age of seventy-five. As with the other senior partners, however, they gave him an office for life, and he went to it almost daily, continuing to stay busy serving in this way or that for another nine years. In his mid-eighties, when he became physically unable to make it to the office anymore he slipped into a severe depression that shortly killed him. So it went for my primary male role model; he died in the saddle as best he could. What am I doing thinking about throwing in the towel at least twenty years earlier than he?

But I am not my father. I have some of the same moles and mannerisms, the same strong will and determination. Otherwise, we are so different that he went to his death puzzled by me. I am a contemplative. He was not. There were all manner of things he didn't like to think about: little things like death, aging, illness, philosophy, religion, psychology, and the meaning of life. He also had better physical health and more stamina than I—perhaps because he avoided such issues. I, however, enjoy thinking about them. It is easy for me to just sit and meditate. Indeed, I want more time to do just that. He found it most diffi-cult to "do nothing," which is quite understandable, since there were so many matters he preferred not to ponder. Whatever the nature and timing of my retirement might be, another conclusion is inescapable: I do not have to do it like my dad.

The full gamut of Merlin myth does not seem

available for me to choose from. I have never been so messianic as to consider myself up to returning from the grave, and now that my energy is declining, the thought of working until I drop is purely repelling. Given my already declining libido and Lily's relatively good health, my contentment with our marriage and my still remaining street smarts, running after some wicked young lady also does not seem to be much of an option. But there is this in-between ground with its issues of responsible as opposed to irresponsible retirement—the conflict between enjoyment and social obligation.

My writing is no problem. I will continue to write as long as I feel called to do so. Lecturing is another matter. It drains me. I learn little from it anymore. Yet some still seem to benefit from hearing me, often from some small chance remark I happen to make in a question-and-answer period—particularly people in the out of the way places: Scranton, Duluth, Salinas, Amarillo, Gulfport, Fresno. Shall I talk to them no more? FCE is also a problem. Already I have announced my intention to resign from its board of directors in a year or so. It will be healthy for the organization for me to step aside at the top, but workers will continue to be needed. I would love to still advise, of course. Everyone loves to give advice. What is needed, however, is not advice about fund-raising but people to do it. People to get out and market its services. People to organize workshops. There are enough generals to succeed me. There will never be enough foot soldiers, and I do not know when I should call it quits.

No, it is unclear how far and fast I will retire. The details need to be worked out in prayer. Nonetheless, on a certain level during our trip, the conclusion has been reached: The time to start working on those details is *now*.

I have also reached some conclusions about the stones.

Helpless to solve the mystery of the megaliths, the French canon Father Mahé, in 1825, cried out at them in frustration, "Speak to me! Why won't you speak?" Commenting on this lament almost ninety years later another French priest, Father Millon, remarked, "Although the stones are silent, scholars have been loquacious on their behalf." Although the stones are silent, scholars have been loquacious on their behalf." He was referring to the plethora of theories that had even by then already been offered to explain them on the basis of no real evidence.

It would be stupid for me to throw my hat into the ring eighty years later were it not for the simple fact that I am not a scholar. I make use of the work of scholars, but I have never made a pretense of being one myself. This deficiency may give me an advantage. I am reminded of the late Buckminster Fuller, who ascribed his intellectual success to the handicap of being extremely near-sighted as a young child. Since his condition went unrecognized for some years, he became accustomed to understanding the world through its large patterns simply because he couldn't see the details. I, too, tend to be a "big picture" thinker, and sometimes may be able to see the woods for trees because my deficiency as a scholar prevents me from becoming lost in the details.

For instance, I have already presented one conclusion about the stones that seems to have been missed despite its obviousness: They were often art. Writers about them were so busy speculating on their reasons, their possible utilitarian purposes, that they failed to notice their beauty. Mind you, I do not think that they are all beautiful. In some instances I very much doubt that in erecting them the megalithic people were functioning as artists. Nonetheless, in many cases they were so concerned with shape and composition it seems to me an inescapable conclusion that they were artistically motivated.

I do not mean to imply that the creation of art was their sole motive. Indeed, I am virtually certain their monuments were often overdetermined; they served multiple functions just as today architects may design a complex of buildings not only to house people but also to provide them with beauty, efficiency, and space for serenity.

I don't know any more than the scholars what the multiple utilitarian purposes of the great stones might have been. I'm not saying they weren't designed for the observation of heavenly bodies in order to mark the solstices or predict eclipses, as has so often been proposed. That might have been one of the reasons for some of the megalithic monuments. The primary purpose of others was certainly the housing of the dead—

singly or communally, below ground or above. I suppose still others were primarily used as meeting places, markets, temples, or even theaters. But as with that unreasonable human activity we call art, I have a way of looking beyond the purely rational to consider reasons that are not strictly utilitarian or merely materialistic. So I have a further mixture of conclusions and conjectures that scholars have strangely overlooked.

Scholars have not ignored the extraordinary amount of physical labor that went into most megalithic monuments: the quarrying of some of the great stones, their transport, digging foundations, raising them into those foundations, and then capping some with lintels. They have spoken of thousands and millions of man-hours. They have commented how communal and complexly organized this labor must have been. They have even surmised that a significant number of people would have been injured or killed in such dangerous construction work. What they have ignored is the element of emotion. The underlying motive of the megalithic builders, more radical than their utilitarian intent, must have been passion. Only great passion could have inspired them to such monumental effort.

Passion for what? A ridiculously simple conjecture would be a passion for stones. It strikes me as quite possible that the megalithic people loved great stones. They grooved on them. They adored them.

What causes intense passion? Many things. Sex, survival, art. I would suggest, however, that there is one human passion often more powerful than any of the others. It is the most common inspiration for art. It inspires some to renounce sex. It even leads some to choose suffering and death over health and life in times of peace. I am referring, of course, to religious passion. To passion for God. To worship.

What I am suggesting—this is still conjecture, not a firm conclusion—is that the megalithic people worshiped the great stones. This may seem silly, but the fact of the matter is that since the dawn of history people have been worshiping almost everything under the sun, including the sun itself: certain trees, rivers, mountains, caves, animals, and leaders. Why not certain stones?

I must acknowledge a personal idiosyncrasy in seriously considering this conjecture. It is not so eccentric, however, that others haven't shared it. Almost as she gathers golf balls, Lily tends to gather small stones—not for their mineral value but for their peculiar shapes, colors, and textures. Carl Jung, during his old age, had a large stone in his garden to which he attributed some mystical significance. I have pondered my relative fascination with megaliths in comparison to my relative disinterest in medieval cathedrals. It is overdetermined. The stones are more mysterious, for instance. But there's more. Although the cathedrals were constructed as acts of worship as well as places for worship and monuments to God, the stones in them were mere utilitarian building blocks without significance in and of themselves. So it is with some megalithic monuments. This is why I was not much turned on by the tombs;

the megaliths in them were used for something else. They did not feel sacred to me. Yet other megaliths, like those dolmens that may not have been burial chambers and the menhirs that stand alone or in circles, struck me quite differently. Whether or not they were sacred in the eyes of their erectors five thousand years ago, they were sacred for me. And Lily. They somehow seemed to embody the holy.

Although I suspect the megalithic people worshiped certain stones, I doubt that they worshiped only stones. If they worshiped stones at all, I am certain they also worshiped *through* them. One reason for my certainty is that such would be typical of much human religious behavior. I am referring to icons. Icons are objects, usually works of art, that are symbols of God. They are different from idols. One bows down before an idol, such as golden calf (or money), because he believes the object *is* God. An Eastern Orthodox Christian, however, may bow down before a painting of Jesus or Mary or even a saint not because she believes the image, the icon, is a God but because it is such a powerful representation of God for her that she believes it deserving of veneration—so powerful, indeed, that it has captured *something* of God within it. If the megalithic people worshiped stones, I believe they did so in this fashion. They would have thought that something of God was within the stone but also known that God was much greater than the stone itself.

As I've said, the supposition that the megalithic people worshiped certain stones as icons is

491

conjecture and not a conclusion. I think we can definitively conclude, however, that certain stones and monuments were used by them for worship. In other words, their greater monuments, such as Stonehenge or Callanish or Long Meg and Her Daughters, were temples. This doesn't mean that these monuments had no secondary purpose, such as the practice of astronomy. Remember the effort they took to construct and the particular power of religious passion. A passion for astronomy alone would not have been a sufficient motive. Whatever the other reasons for their construction, the great megalithic monuments were primarily created to be places of worship.

What kind of worship? Who or what was their God—or gods? Recognizing its potential for passion, scholars have speculated vigorously about megalithic religion. Given the fact that they have so little evidence to go on, their speculations vary widely. Nonetheless, these speculations have one feature in common: None of them postulate a megalithic belief in an abstract monotheism. In other words, the scholars assumed that in their religion the megalithic people must have thought very differently from Jews, Christians, and Muslims.

The most common speculation is that the megalithic people worshiped the sun or the moon or both. This is one of the reasons for popularity of the observatory theory of Stonehenge, Callanish, and other monuments. It both acknowledges the power of religious passion and the power of scientific observation. It also happens to cater to the New Age religious passion for astrology and antipathy to Western religion. In addition, it makes good sense because we know that many cultures, ranging from the Egyptians of 2000 B.C. to the European Celts of A.D. 300, worshiped the sun and moon. As well they might have. The provider of all light to earth and center of our rotation, the sun can indeed be considered the Giver of Life. And the moon to this day has a mysterious power to incite human beings to romance and other more or less transcendent notions.

Speaking of romance, a second major school holds that megalithic religion centered around sex and fertility. This, too, is not unrealistic speculation. Cultural anthropology again provides us with well-studied examples of such spiritual centers in many "primitive" cultures. I've not been so impressed by it, but Lily, as well as others—men and women alike—have perceived a certain phallic quality to many menhirs. The only piece of sculpture known to be megalithic is a modest-sized doll with what appears to be immodestly sized breasts and hips. It is assumed to be a fertility idol. Furthermore, fertility does have a great deal to do with our passion for survival, and sexual passion has at least a covert, unconscious relation to religious passion. Within the context of this school, the great megalithic monuments were locations for strange fertility rituals—possibly even orgies. It is fun to fantasize about.

A third school is somewhat less exciting but contains all of the most scientifically dedicated archaeologists. It posits that megalithic religion was focused on ancestor worship. Once again this is realistic. Other primitive and not-so-primitive cultures have had the same focus. Moreover, the only thing we know with absolute scientific certainty based upon massive evidence is that the megalithic people spent a considerable portion of their extraordinary effort entombing at least some of their dead in a whole variety of imaginative, if not gruesome, ways.

Since each of these schools is quite reasonable, I see no reason not to declare all of them to be winners. I have no trouble imagining that the megalithic people worshiped their ancestors *and* the sun and moon *and* fertility gods and goddesses—*and* certain stones to boot. If this sounds like they worshiped almost everything, it would not have been out of line with a great deal of religious tradition. The most common variety of so-called primitive religion, and perhaps the most common religion still extant today, is animism. Animists believe that there are all kinds of active little gods lurking in rocks and caves, birds and beasts, in the waters and in the forests. In other words, they believe that the whole world is animate—alive—with divinity. Although it can give rise to enslaving superstition, animism may not be that far from the mark. Certainly it expresses a vision of the world that frequently seems more interesting than our own mechanistic and materialistic vision in this Age of Reason.

But my imagination about the megalithic people extends still further. I noted that scholars have never suggested they might have believed in a kind of abstract monotheism. Why not? I suspect two assumptions underlie this vacuum of suggestion. One is the assumption that the megalithic people, living as they did five thousand years ago, were primitives. The other is that primitive people are incapable of abstract thought. Both assumptions are questionable.

For instance, when Europeans first encountered Native Americans they assumed them to be primitives. "Savages" they called them. These so-called savages clearly had an animistic sort of religion. They worshiped buffaloes and hawks and thunder, among other things. It did not seem to the Europeans that these things were icons. They assumed that when the Indians worshiped a hawk they were solely worshiping the bird and incapable of abstracting to anything beyond it. Part of what accounts for the recent flourishing of interest in Native American religions, however, is the white man's dawning realization that at least some Indians had a very acute awareness of an aliveness beyond that which could be just seen or heard—of a God who was somehow the ground of all being.

So "primitives" may be capable of abstract thought. Besides, it is questionable how primitive the megalithic people were. Prehistoric does not mean stupid. Without any technology beyond tools of stone and bone they erected monuments of a sophistication that would not be seen again in those parts for three thousand years.

Who first got the idea to erect a giant stone in the ground and why? She or he was a leader, of course. Anyone who gets a new idea and persuades others to help execute it must be a leader by every definition. Did such leadership originate with God? Was that person "called," so to speak, as I suppose all great artists are? We don't know. We who hardly begin to comprehend our own minds will never know what went on in the mind of a prehistoric person. But we can imagine. In my own, purely speculative, imagination, I wonder if his or her thoughts didn't go somewhat like this:

Stones.
God.
Glory.

> *Stones . . .*
> *God . . .*
> *Glory . . .*
> *Oh, God,*
> *You are the stones:*
> *Complex,*
> *Many faceted,*
> *In the pebble and the boulder,*
> *Ageless and everywhere.*
> *You surround us.*
> *You raise us out of the ground.*
> *You feed us.*
> *You are our children and our ancestors.*
> *Without You there is but death.*
> *How can we give back to You?*
> *Let us make You a gift,*
> *Praise You to Yourself.*
> *Stones.*
> *We return them to You.*
> *Circles and rows,*

Alone and together,
We make You monuments and temples,
Altars and menhirs.
We lift them up
Out of the earth,
Stand them as signals
For the generations,
Signals of remembrance,
Signals of praise.
We break our backs for You
In adoration
And gladness.
Amen.

RELATED READING

Buechner, Frederick. *The Magnificent Defeat.* New York: Seabury Press, 1966.

Bunyan, John. *The Pilgrim's Progress.* New York: Penguin Books, 1987.

Burl, Aubrey. *Prehistoric Avebury.* New Haven: Yale University Press, 1979.

Castleden, Rodney. *The Stonehenge People*: *An Exploration in Neolithic Britain, 4700–2000* B.C. London & New York: Routledge and Kegan Paul, 1987.

Chaucer, Geoffrey. *The Canterbury Tales.* (Trans. David Wright.) Oxford: Oxford University Press, 1985.

Dean, Christopher. *A Study of Merlin in English Literature from the Middle Ages to the Present Day.* New York: Edwin Mellen Press (Box 450, Lewiston, NY 14092), 1992.

Delaney, Frank. *The Celts.* Boston: Little, Brown & Co., 1986.

Eliot, T. S. *The Complete Poems and Plays,*

1909—1950. New York: Harcourt Brace and Company, 1952.

Gray, J. Glenn. *The Warriors: Reflections on Men in Battle*. New York: Harcourt Brace and Company, 1959.

Kendall, Alan. *Medieval Pilgrims*. New York: G. P. Putnam's Sons, 1970.

Lewin, Leonard C. *Report from Iron Mountain*. Cutchogue, N.Y.: Lightyear Press, Inc. (P.O. Box 168), reprinted 1993.

Lewis, C. S. *Pilgrim's Regress*. New York: Sheed & Ward, 1944.

McMann, Jean. *Riddles of the Stone Age: Rock Carvings of Ancient Europe*. London and New York: Thames & Hudson, 1980.

Martin, Malachi. *The New Castle*. New York: Dell Publishing, 1974.

————. *Hostage to the Devil*. New York: Bantam Books, 1977.

Mohen, Jean-Pierre. *The World of Megaliths*. London: Cassell Publishers, 1989.

Roberts, Jack; Dick Gunther; and Stan Gortikov. *Who Needs Midlife at Your Age: A Survival Guide for Men*. New York: Avon Books, 1983.

Service, Alastair, and Jean Bradbery. *Megaliths and Their Mysteries*: *A Guide to the Standing Stones of Europe*. New York: Macmillan, 1979.

Shah, Idries. *Reflections*. New York: Penguin Books, 1972.

Sherman, Cecil W. *George Fox and the Quakers*. Richmond, Ind.: Friends United Press, 1991.

Untermeyer, Louis, ed. *Modern American Poetry and Modern British Poetry*: *A Critical Anthology*. New York: Harcourt Brace and Company, 1936.

Vercors. *You Shall Know Them*. (Trans. Rita Barisse.) Boston: Little, Brown & Co., 1953.

All who wish to explore FCE's services
or support its mission
are welcomed to write or call
The Foundation for Community Encouragement
P.O. Box 449
Ridgefield, CT 06877
Phone: 203/431-9484
FAX: 203/431-9349

ABOUT THE AUTHOR

M. Scott Peck, M.D., is a psychiatrist, lecturer, management consultant, best-selling author, and a founder of the Foundation for Community Encouragement. He lives in northwestern Connecticut.